Robert B. Lees
Grantham
12 March 1976
1839

Studies in Church History

II

THE MATERIALS SOURCES AND METHODS
OF ECCLESIASTICAL HISTORY

CHURCH SOCIETY AND POLITICS

PAPERS READ AT
THE THIRTEENTH SUMMER MEETING AND
THE FOURTEENTH WINTER MEETING
OF THE
ECCLESIASTICAL HISTORY SOCIETY

EDITED BY
DEREK BAKER

PUBLISHED FOR
THE ECCLESIASTICAL HISTORY SOCIETY
BY
BASIL BLACKWELL · OXFORD
1975

Studies in Church History 12

Church Society and Politics

This volume of some 360 pages will be available in
September 1975 at a retail price of about £12,
(excluding postage) and may be obtained from your
bookseller or from B.H. Blackwell, Broad Street,
Oxford, England.

Order Form

To :- Messrs. -------------------------------------

Please supply me with   copies of <u>Studies in
Church History</u> 12 (<u>Church, Society and Politics</u>)
published by Basil Blackwell, Oxford (1975) at a
price of about £12, (excluding postage) and in-
voice me accordingly.

-------------------- (signature) -------------(date)

Address for despatch

   (Name)   ----------------------------------⎫
   (Address) ----------------------------------⎬ Block
               ----------------------------------⎪ capitals
               ----------------------------------⎭ please

Contents

THE MATERIALS SOURCES AND METHODS of ECCLESIASTICAL HISTORY

PAPERS READ AT
THE TWELFTH SUMMER MEETING AND
THE THIRTEENTH WINTER MEETING
OF THE
ECCLESIASTICAL HISTORY SOCIETY

EDITED BY
DEREK BAKER

PUBLISHED FOR
THE ECCLESIASTICAL HISTORY SOCIETY
BY
BASIL BLACKWELL · OXFORD
1975

1839

ISBN 0 631 16930 x

Printed in Great Britain at the
Stanbrook Abbey Press
Worcester

PREFACE

This eleventh volume of *Studies in Church History*, on the theme 'The Materials Sources and Methods of Ecclesiastical History', contains a selection from the papers delivered at the twelfth summer meeting of the Ecclesiastical History Society, held at Bristol in July 1973, and the thirteenth winter meeting, held at London in January 1974, under the presidency of professor R. M. T. Hill.

It is the second volume of the series to be produced by the Ecclesiastical History Society itself, in association with Basil Blackwell.

The Society wishes to acknowledge the generous financial help given by the British Academy towards the production costs of this volume.

Derek Baker

CONTENTS

CONTENTS

CONTRIBUTORS

DEREK BAKER, lecturer in history, university of Edinburgh

BRENDA M. BOLTON, senior lecturer in history, polytechnic of north London

MARTIN BRECHT, professor, director of the Evangelisches Stift, Tübingen

W. D. J. CARGILL THOMPSON, lecturer in ecclesiastical history, King's College, London

MARY CHENEY, fellow of Lucy Cavendish College, Cambridge

CLAIRE CROSS, senior lecturer in history, university of York

ROBERT W. DUNNING, editor, Victoria County History of Somerset

W. H. C. FREND, professor of ecclesiastical history, university of Glasgow

SHERIDAN GILLEY, lecturer in ecclesiastical history, university of St Andrews

DIANA GREENWAY, institute of historical research, London

ROY M. HAINES, professor of history, Dalhousie university, Canada

MARGARET HARVEY, part-time lecturer in history and tutor, university of Durham

ROSALIND M. T. HILL, professor of history, university of London

DAVID J. KEEP, senior lecturer in religious studies, Rolle College, Exmouth

R. A. MARKUS, professor of medieval history, university of Nottingham.

JANET L. NELSON, lecturer in history, King's College, London

DOROTHY M. OWEN, university library, Cambridge

W. B. PATTERSON, associate professor of history, Davidson College North Carolina

ROSAMOND PIERCE, Clare Hall, Cambridge

MICHAEL RICHTER, university of Marburg

KEITH ROBBINS, professor of history, Bangor

SIR STEVEN RUNCIMAN

PATRICK SCOTT, lecturer in English literature, university of Edinburgh

ix

CONTRIBUTORS

MICHAEL WILKS, professor of medieval history, Birkbeck College, London

DIANA WOOD, lecturer in medieval history, university of East Anglia

NIGEL YATES, assistant archivist, Carmarthenshire county record office

INTRODUCTION

When John Selden declared that 'to know what was generally believed in all ages, the way is to consult the liturgies, not any private man's writings' it was not his aim to deny the value of individual witness and evidence, but rather to emphasise the greater importance for establishing and elucidating what was generally believed in an age or society of the modes of belief and convention, the forms of observance and practice, and of the classes of documents which embody them. It is a view which is shared by many of the contributors to this volume, devoted to the discussion of the materials, sources and methods of ecclesiastical history. It emerges in the discussion of 'Frankish' penitentials and early medieval *ordines*, in the presentation of the recusant view of history, in the investigation of nineteenth-century parochial sources. It can be seen in the picture of 'cultural imperialism' presented by the examination of nineteenth-century religious periodicals, in the attitudes towards truth and evidence on the part of writers and historians evinced in the studies of Welsh historiography, the writings of John Strype, the sources for the history of the humiliati, and of a twelfth-century English manuscript. It even appears in the description of the sermons of pope Clement VI as beautiful, and therefore true! For all his emphasis, however, Selden would have been the last to claim that liturgies were history. He would have agreed with the author of the paper on medieval *fasti* that sources and records of this sort were 'the raw material out of which history is fashioned', and required a long and laborious digestive process. This is stressed in the particular studies of a twelfth-century council, of university letters, of a fourteenth-century episcopal register, of the records of the unestablished churches in the early modern period, and, more generally, in the presidential address. 'Great men are atypical – it is in studying the activities of ordinary people that we can see most clearly into the history of a past age', and professor Robbins is in essential agreement when he suggests that 'arguably the best theologians had the least impact on the mass of churchgoers'. Both professors Hill and Robbins recognise, and their view is re-inforced by professors Frend and Brecht at opposite ends of the chronological scale, that this concern with the ordinary, with the mass of people, and of evidence, demands a greater pooling of resources, and a wider acceptance of teamwork. It is also evident in the contributions of these writers, and of other authors included here, that the scope of ecclesiastical history is much wider than it latterly was, even if some of the extension is simply a matter of semantics – 'Religion and Society' is scarcely a larger subject than 'Church and Society', though it may, as professor Robbins indicates, be a more popular one. Papers on the contribution of archeology to the history of christian Nubia, the socio-linguistic approach to medieval language and communication, the social and super-social culture of nineteenth-century catholicism, indicate some of the fields and techniques which are germane to the modern study of ecclesiastical history, and which help to undermine those 'institutions and illusions' which, in professor Robbins's view, so complicate the task of the modern ecclesiastical historian: it is, at the very least, refreshing to find it suggested that the concern with secularisation, which has so obsessed continental scholars in recent years, is 'facile'. Yet if there is much that is new – in material, attitude and technique – to which the modern ecclesiastical historian should be receptive, there is a core of old wisdom which he should cherish. No facility in sociological typology or cultural analysis can replace that humane, critical faculty, so admirably exemplified in professor Wilks's discussion of his 'misleading manuscripts', nor should it diminish the pleasurable appreciation of those 'uncovenanted blessings', to which professor Hill referred: Martha should gather her flowers, and Dr Dunning's reverend Henry Price is too good to miss.

ERRATA

The title and running heads of the article beginning p. 1 should read: 'Church history and the early church historians'.
The title of the article beginning p. 163 should read: '*Maximus sermocinator verbi Dei:* the sermon literature of pope Clement VI'.

CHURCH HISTORY AND EARLY CHURCH HISTORIANS

by R. A. MARKUS

FROM the beginning the christian group took an interest in its own past. Ecclesiastical history is a specialised form of this corporate self-awareness. The fourth and fifth centuries were the period in the christian church's history when this form of self-awareness crystallised. The father of church history[1], Eusebius, was the fountainhead of a tradition of historiography which came to dominate the work of his successors. His *Ecclesiastical History*[2] straddles the constantinian revolution. Eusebius began working on it before the end of the last persecution, that under Diocletian and his colleagues; by the time he came to add the last touches to his final edition, twenty or more years later, the social conditions of the church's existence had come to differ profoundly from those which obtained at the time he began writing. The age of the martyrs and of a persecuted church in a hostile empire were becoming a heroic age recollected in tranquillity. The following century was to take the church very much further along the road away from the situation of the church that Eusebius had been writing about. It was also during that century or so that the tradition of ecclesiastical historiography became set in the moulds first impressed on it by Eusebius; and the traditional mould survived unbroken until at least the end of the sixth century. Did the christian church of the fourth, fifth and sixth centuries live with a self-awareness distorted by an image projected from its own heroic age and increasingly inapplicable to it in its new situation? Was there a conflict between the tasks of the church historian and the norms of his genre as they were hardening into a firm mould? Were Eusebius's followers conscious of any tension rooted in such conflicting claims? Did their received traditions so constrict their horizon that sectors of the church's life beyond the normal

[1] F. C. Baur, *Comparatur Eusebius Caesariensis, historiae ecclesiasticae parens, cum parente historiarum, Herodoto Halicarnassensi* (Tübingen 1834).
[2] Here and throughout I have followed Edouard Schwartz's conclusions on the composition and editions of the work. See his article 'Eusebios' in *PW* VI/1, pp 1370–1439, at 1395–1407.

I

scope of the genre were ignored? How far – if at all – did the consciousness of any new needs modify the historiographical traditions they inherited from Eusebius? It is questions of this kind I want to consider.

Eusebius had set out to record, as he tells us himself, the notable events of the 'ecclesiastical history' since the time of Christ.[3] His use of the phrase in his opening sentence almost suggests an already crystallised meaning behind it. Whatever this may be, we have his own statement two paragraphs later[4] that he was a pioneer in the field. Certainly what we know of Hegesippus, or of the chronographical enquiries of Sextus Julius Africanus and Hippolytus on which Eusebius drew, gives us no grounds for doubting Eusebius's originality. His claim to the title 'father of Church history' is secure, even though the creative work in the field of christian chronography had been done well before his time[5]. The identifying features of ecclesiastical history are those which it received from Eusebius. Three among them require our attention: (i) chronological scope, (ii) literary form, and (iii) the themes dealt with. I take these in ascending order of importance, and begin with (i), chronological scope.

Classical historiography had a very strong tendency to be, or to become, contemporary history. Church history, in comparison, attended more to the past. Eusebius's original programme had been to bring his *Ecclesiastical History* down to the year 311, to Galerius's edict which marked the end of the 'great persecution'. It was only in later editions that the last books were added; and apart from a handful of intrusive documents which the archivist in him could not resist including, they contain little more than his ecstatic celebration of the 'bright and glorious day that dawned over the world with its unclouded brilliance and illuminated the churches of Christ with heavenly light'[6] with the advent of the first christian emperor. Eusebius's tenth book is in effect the messianic 'new song unto the Lord'[7] in which his public was invited to join. It is little wonder that Rufinus, when he came to translate the work into latin, should have found it lacking information – *perparum habet in rebus gestis* – and decided to omit it from his translation.[8]

---

[3] *HE* I.1.1.
[4] *Ibid* I.1.3.
[5] Generally, see A. D. von den Brincken, *Studien zur lateinischen Weltchronistik bis in das Zeitalter Ottos von Freising* (Düsseldorf 1957).
[6] *HE* X.1.8.
[7] *Ibid* X.1.3.
[8] Rufinus, *HE*, *Praefatio*.

Eusebius's *Ecclesiastical History* was not intended, least of all in its original conception, to be contemporary history.[9] A long perspective in the past of the christian church came to belong to the stuff of ecclesiastical history.

The contrast between late roman secular and ecclesiastical history is not, however, absolute in this respect. Ecclesiastical historians often ended their work very close to their own times, and secular historians – Ammianus Marcellinus notably – often went far back in time. The contrast between the two traditions is much sharper when we consider them in relation to the second of my headings, literary form.

The ample use made by Eusebius of documents and their frequent inclusion *in extenso* in his *Ecclesiastical History*, and his avoidance of invented speeches mark his work off sharply from the classical tradition of history writing. This is all the more remarkable in view of the practice followed by St Luke in the *Acts of the Apostles*: a work in almost every way much closer to classical historiographical conventions than Eusebius's.[10] In avoiding *Acts* as his model, Eusebius seems to be deliberately turning his back not only on classical, but on christian historiographical precedents. To a historian within the classical tradition his work would have ranked as *hyle syngraphēs* rather than *syngraphē*:[11] more like an archivist's collection of material than a historical narrative. Eusebius's disparagement of oral tradition[12] betrays the cast of his mind.

This gulf between the two styles survived as long as the classical tradition of history writing continued alongside the newer tradition of church history. At the end of the sixth century Evagrius wrote for a public which would have had expectations very different from those held by readers of Procopius or Agathias. Yet all three, though laymen, were christians. To read the work of Procopius or Agathias is to enter a different universe of historiographical discourse: for all that appearances suggest, one might be reading the work of pagan historians. Their christianity is obliterated, as Alan and Averil Cameron have so

---

[9] Though much can in fact be obtained from the later additions and recensions; see R. Laqueur, *Eusebios als Historiker seiner Zeit, Arbeiten zur Kirchengeschichte*, 11 (Berlin 1929).

[10] See W. van den Boer, 'Some remarks on the beginnings of Christian historiography', *Studia patristica* 4, *Texte und Untersuchungen* 79 (Berlin 1961) pp 348–62.

[11] The old distinction made by Olympiodorus in reference to his own work is reported by Photios, *Bibl[iotheca]* 80, ed W. Henry, I (Paris 1959) p 166; Müller, *FHG* IV p 58.

[12] *HE* VI.33.4; but too much must not be inferred from this.

3

ably shown in a series of studies,[13] by the grip of classical conventions on their work. It is hard to imagine Procopius writing an ecclesiastical history, though the intriguing suggestion has been made that he had this in mind.[14] Procopius and Agathias belong to the world of Thucydides, Dexippus and, nearer to their own time, Ammianus Marcellinus; Evagrius stands in the line of Eusebius, Socrates and Sozomen. The dividing line runs not between pagan and christian, but between secular and ecclesiastic history.[15] The conventions of classical historiographical traditions pressed only lightly on ecclesiastical historians. Their pressure may be seen in the cult of elegance by Sozomen, probably a relic of his early literary studies at Gaza. This is what made him curtail the documentation which, he tells us,[16] he had at first intended to include in his *Ecclesiastical History*. A similar concern, perhaps, led Evagrius to relegate his documentation to a separate companion volume.[17] If such quirks of style and presentation are really to be seen as the result of a tension between the demands of the new genre and the classical moulds of historiography in the consciousness of these writers, it was a tension which showed only in the form, not the substance.

[13] See their 'Christianity and tradition in the historiography of the late Empire', *Classical quarterly*, ns 14 (London 1964) pp 316–28; Averil Cameron, 'The "scepticism" of Procopius', *Historia* 15 (Wiesbaden 1966) pp 466–82 and *Agathias* (Oxford 1970) caps 6–9.

[14] The suggestion has been made by [A. Momigliano], 'L'età del trapasso [fra storiografia antica e storiografia medievale, 300–550 D.C.'], *Settimane di studio del Centro Italiano di Studi sull' alto Medioevo* 17 (Spoleto 1970) pp 89–118, =*Rivista storica italiana* 81 (Rome 1969) pp 286–303 p 113, on the basis of (i) *BG* IV (VIII) 25.13, (ii) *Anecdota* 11.33 and (iii) *Anecdota* 1.14. The reference in (i) is to 'things that Christians fight about among themselves', ἥπερ μοι ἐν λόγοις τοῖς ὑπὲρ τούτων γεγράψεται; in(ii) and (iii) Procopius promises to deal with matters ἐν τοῖς ὄπισθεν . . . λόγοις: in the first case matters concerned with Justinian's treatment of heretics, in the second matters to do with the fate of pope Silverius. These are among Procopius's unredeemed promises. To infer from them an unfulfilled intention of writing an ecclesiastical history seems highly hazardous.

[15] Despite G. Downey, 'The perspective of the early church historians', *Greek, Roman and Byzantine studies* 6 (Durham, N. Carolina 1965) pp 57–70: 'The Christian historian was not merely a Christian historian. He was a representative and protagonist of a new kind of history to which a certain section of his society would be hostile' (p 58). The failure to distinguish a 'christian history' in general from ecclesiastical history in particular vitiates Downey's conclusions, *ibid* pp 69–70. See also H. Zimmermann, 'Ecclesia als Objekt der Historiographie', *Österreichische Akademie der Wissenschaften, Philosophisch-historische Klasse, Sitzungsberichte* 234/5 (Vienna 1960).

[16] *HE* I.1.

[17] *HE* VI.24.

The third and most important of my identifying 'notes' of ecclesiastical history is its characteristic range of themes. In his preface Eusebius gave a list of the themes he intended to deal with in his *Ecclesiastical History*. He was going to give an account of (i) the bishops of the most illustrious sees, (ii) the heralds, oral or literary, of the Word of God in each generation, (iii) heretics, (iv) the fate of the Jews, (v) pagan attacks on the Word of God and (vi) the sufferings of the faithful witnesses to the Word. A final phrase points to the end of the persecution in 311 with which the work was to conclude. With the addition of only one item, the development of the New Testament canon, the list is in fact an adequate and fairly complete inventory of what is to be found in the work. It scarcely arouses surprise; its items have become the central themes of ecclesiastical history, and not only among Eusebius's continuators and imitators in antiquity. Yet questions need to be asked: why this selection? is there any unifying notion of ecclesiastical history embodied in their choice? Edouard Schwartz once noted the 'motley collection of subjects which no inner link seems to hold together'[18] in Eusebius's programme. Certainly, Eusebius's conception of his subject matter was no very sophisticated one and is only dimly discernible in his itemised list of themes. Following Eusebius's own exposition, I have enumerated six of these. They fall fairly readily into two groups, with an overlapping margin between them. The first two headings, episcopal succession in the major churches and the sequence of christian writers, teachers and preachers, along with the unlisted item of the scriptural canon, all have to do with the internal life of the church. They are bound up with what, in Eusebius's eyes, gave the church its enduring identity as the church. Then comes heresy: a shadowy land to which we shall need to return. The three remaining items, Jews, pagan attacks and martyrdoms, all have to do with the church's relation to what lies outside it. So we have two groups of themes: one concerned with the church's self-identity, the other with its external relationships; and, between them, heresy, a region of doubt and obscurity.

A part of Eusebius's intention was to show that despite the claims made by heretics, heresy lay outside the church and belonged to its hostile environment. The situation of the christian community in the secular society of the roman empire served Eusebius as the paradigm

---

[18] 'Uber Kirchengeschichte' (1908), *Gesammelte Schriften* I (Berlin 1938) pp 110–30 at p 117. Schwartz, however, also detected a certain latent unity of conception in the *EH*.

of his notion of the church in relation to a separate, alien and all too clearly non-ecclesiastical world beyond it. Even though in the divine plan church and empire may have been destined for harmonious concord, the historian of the pre-constantinian church had no problem about discerning the boundaries of his subject so far as it marched with the secular world.

The crucial area was the shifting internal frontier between heresy and orthodoxy. The boundary here was less easily identified than was the church as a distinct institution, group or sub-culture within secular society. Much of Eusebius's work is in fact concerned with establishing the claims of the true *ecclesia* against *ecclesia*-like groups of various kinds. This is the reason not only for his interest in heresies and heretics, but in the first group of his main themes: the threads which define the identity and continuity of the true church. In this connection the antique tradition of philosophical doxography gave him a very serviceable precedent; it may even have awakened him to the importance of the *diadochai* in the principal communities. The true church, like the true school, is defined by lineal succession and a continuity of teaching which Eusebius, like most of his contemporaries, allowed to merge into identity. The gross simplification of the problem of heresy involved in this model has a long history before Eusebius; but the prestige of his *Ecclesiastical History* assuredly helped to establish it until challenged in the seventeenth century. Hegesippus, Eusebius and many others saw the crisis of identity that the church underwent especially in the second century in terms of a dilution of the original pure doctrine of the gospel by false teachers who came to corrupt the virgin church later. Origen perhaps alone came within sight of appreciating that the problem of heresy was much more complex; that far from 'orthodoxy' being primary and 'heresy' derivative, they both arise from previously undifferentiated traditions in more or less peaceful co-existence in the church. Eusebius transmitted to his followers the view he had learnt from Hegesippus: that orthodoxy was simply continuity with the apostolic church, heresy discontinuity. This became the unquestioned assumption of the ecclesiastical historians for whom his work served as a pattern. The arian Philostorgius in the fifth century made heretic and orthodox change places in his account: he was no exception otherwise.

Eusebius had seen the church clearly marked off from the secular world and he tried to see it marked off, almost as clearly, from the heterodox groups on its fringes. These two concerns set him the central themes of his work and came to define its subject, the 'Church', with sufficient exactitude. The doctrinal controversies of the fourth and fifth centuries provided ample scope and ample material to his successors for continuing an interest in heresy and its conflict with orthodoxy. The historiographical form created by Eusebius lent itself only too readily to the indulging of such interests in the period between Nicaea and Chalcedon and beyond.

The second assumption, however, which determined Eusebius's choice of themes ceased to hold long before the age of Theodosius II, the golden age of ecclesiastical historiography: the assumption that the church had a clearly recognisable identity within boundaries which marked it off sharply from the secular world. This assumption, which Eusebius had been able to make almost without thought when he began working, was destroyed before he completed his last recension. He seems to have been aware that the advent of Constantine really did mark the end of ecclesiastical history as he conceived it. In the constantinian empire Eusebius saw the duality of *ecclesia* and *basileia* overcome. The previously distinct realities of the church and empire were beginning to coalesce in a christian *politeia*.[19] As the fourth century wore on, the 'new people' whose history Eusebius had been writing[20] was rapidly becoming identifiable with the peoples of the roman empire and its fringes. If Eusebius's *Ecclesiastical History* is, in a sense, the history of a nation – and it is beyond doubt that Eusebius did see it as such and could therefore model himself on Josephus as a historian of the jewish nation – that nation was now becoming identifiable with *Romania*.

The vanishing of a clear line of demarcation between the church and secular society in the roman world is the major problem that confronted church historians after Eusebius. While the conditions of the church were changing dramatically, the conventions of the new historiographical form were becoming fixed in a way more rigid than those of literary forms of much greater antiquity. We have recently been reminded[21] of the 'formidable power of tradition' in late roman historiography; Ammianus Marcellinus, continuing the work of Tacitus, the writers of the *Historia Augusta* continuing Suetonius's imperial biographies, and Zosimus, whose *Historia nova* is in the

---

[19] On the meaning of this see F. E. Cranz, 'Kingdom and polity in Eusebius of Caesarea', *Harvard Theological Review* 45 (Boston, Mass 1952) pp 47–66 and H. Berkhof, *Die Theologie des Eusebios von Caesarea* (Amsterdam 1939) pp 53–9.
[20] See for example *HE* I.4.2; X.4.19.
[21] 'L'età del trapasso', p 94.

opinion of its latest editor[22] little more than a *contaminatio* of his sources, all testify to the ubiquitous force of literary traditions. The tradition which came to dominate the writing of church history was infinitely tighter than the traditions at work in secular history writing. For one thing, it was a single stream deriving from a single source. It is significant that none of Eusebius's successors[23] thought it worth their while to offer a new account of the period covered by Eusebius. They seem agreed in canonising Eusebius's as the definitive account of pre-constantinian church history.

But there was a further reason for the monolithic solidity of the tradition: ecclesiastical historians saw themselves almost as members of a kind of diachronic syndicate responsible for the instalments which would add up to make a single, cumulative 'ecclesiastical history'. This is what made Ferdinand Christian Baur, in his *Die Epochen der kirchlichen Geschichtsschreibung* (1852) speak of Eusebius's followers as 'so to speak, only one'; 'in none of these historians', wrote Baur, 'is there the least internal distinction in historical perspective; their relation to one another is merely one of aggregation or of chronological order.'[24] Baur's judgement may need some revision; but it will serve as an initial reminder of the coherence of the tradition we are considering. By the end of the fourth century there were historians whose aim was merely to continue the work of Eusebius beyond the point he had reached. Such were Gelasius of Caesarea, whose lost work appears to underly much of the two books which Rufinus added to his 'translation' of Eusebius,[25] and, of course, Rufinus himself. The work saint Jerome had in mind when he mentioned a 'history on a larger scale' which he was thinking of writing[26] might have fallen into the same mould, had he written it. Socrates, Sozomen, Theodoret and Philostorgius, all writing in the time of Theodosius II, considered themselves as continuators of Eusebius; and Evagrius at the end of the sixth century as a continuator

[22] F. Paschoud, *Zosime: Histoire nouvelle* I (Paris 1971) pp lxi–lxiii and lxviii.

[23] Except apparently Jerome in the work he intended to, but never did, write–*Vita Malchi* 1.

[24] F. C. Baur, quoted from the English translation ed P. C. Hodgson, *Ferdinand Christian Baur on the writing of Church history* (New York 1968) pp 67 and 69.

[25] On Rufinus and Gelasius of Caesarea see most recently F. Winkelmann, 'Untersuchngen zur Kirchengeschichte des Gelasios von Kaisareia', *Sitzungsberichte der deutschen Akademie der Wissenschaften, Klasse für Sprachen, Literatur und Kunst*, 1965, no 3 (Berlin 1966) where previous views are discussed. See also the same, 'Charakter und Bedeutung der Kirchengeschichte des Gelasios von Kaisareia', *Byzantinische Forschungen* 1(Amsterdam 1966) pp 346–85.

[26] *Vita Malchi* 1: *latiorem historiam* from the beginnings to these bad times under the christian emperors.

of their continuations. Even more impressive an indication of the coherence of the form can be found in the numerous compilations:
Theodore *lector* in the sixth century announced his programme thus:
'to put together those who have set forth the ecclesiastical histories
and to synthesise them into a single orderly account';[27] and a little later
Cassiodorus, in his preface to the *Historia Tripartita* compiled by his
monk Epiphanius wrote in almost identical terms.[28] Gelasius of Cyzicus
in the fifth century compiled a work from the ecclesiastical histories of
Eusebius, Socrates, Sozomen, Theodoret, Rufinus and Gelasius of
Caesarea to which he referred as his 'Ecclesiastical History'[29] as well as
by its more modest and more realistic title, *Syntagma*. The distinction
between compilations such as his – and Rufinus's at the beginning of
the century – and independent works of ecclesiastical history could be
a very fine one. Scissors and paste were the classical method of ecclesiastical historiography. Their successful use was made possible by a
singular unity of purpose, of method and of underlying conception
shared among its practitioners.

In the course of little more than a century an impressively consistent
form of historiography had come into being. What is even more
striking is that the new genre appears to have established itself not only
among its writers, but in wider circles. This is the implication of the
well-known self-defence inserted by Socrates in his preface to the
fifth book of his *Ecclesiastical History*. There is no reason for not taking
it at its face value. He is answering critics who have objected to the
inclusion of secular matters in the already published parts of his work.
There clearly was a reading public, presumably not confined to pious
emperors and court officials such as Lausus, readers who snatched each
instalment eagerly from the press and were quite fastidious about what
they got; and they did not like their favourite form of literature diluted
with foreign matter. Socrates's self-defence rests on two grounds: first,
on that fundamental tenet of theodosian ideology,[30] that disorder in

---

[27] συναγαγεῖν τῶν ἐκκλησιαστικῶν ἱστοριῶν τοὺς ἐκθέντας καὶ μίαν τινὰ ἐξ
αὐτῶν ἁρμόσασθαι σύνταξιν . *Theodoros Anagnostes Kirchengeschichte* , ed G. C.
Hansen, *GCS* (1971) p 1. On τοὺς ἐκθέντας see J. Bidez, 'La tradition
manuscrite de Sozomène et la Tripartite de Théodore le lecteur', *TU* 32.2
(Leipzig 1908) p 46, apparatus to line 7 of text.
[28] *de tribus auctoribus unam facere dictionem CSEL* 71 p 1.
[29] See the subscriptions to books I and II, the titles to books II and III, and other
passages: *Gelasios Kirchengeschichte*, ed G. Loeschke and M. Heinemann, *GCS* 28
(1918) pp 25, 26, 137, 138, 139, 140, 155.
[30] See, for instance, Theodosius writing to the council of Ephesus: 'The stability
of the commonwealth is dependent on the devotion whereby God is

the church is reflected 'by a sort of vital sympathy' in the state and disorders of the state in the church; and, second, that christian emperors have in fact a large part in the affairs of the church, summoning councils and the like. The second of Socrates's pleas need not detain us. It is a very natural and fairly obvious extension into the post-constantinian era of the interest Eusebius had already canonised in the relations between emperors and the church. Even on the narrowest view of the subject matter the inclusion of emperors who 'exert a powerful influence on the church'[31] in an ecclesiastical history would seem to raise no problems. But Socrates felt it necessary to justify his having done so; moreover, to add, for good measure, a much more far-reaching pretext for dealing with secular matters in general.

His practice, however, appears to call for very little apology. It is true that he does include some fairly solid blocks of secular history at several points. The biography of Julian,[32] with the attention given, for instance, to Julian's reforms of the imperial household, seem at first sight remote from the concerns of the ecclesiastical historian; but Socrates goes out of his way to point to the link between these reforms and the image of the philosopher-king which the emperor wished to project. Only the most captious of his critics could have objected to the inclusion of a character-sketch of the apostate emperor. A chapter[33] about the Goths and their entry into the empire, again, scarcely strains the bounds of relevance. The early chapters of book IV, concerning the civil troubles under Valens and a similar chapter about the usurper Magnentius[34] come closest to apparently needless inclusion of non-ecclesiastical subjects: both are given the justification invoked by Socrates in his general apologia, the appeal to the pre-ordained harmony between ecclesiastical and civil disturbances.[35] A modern critic could find more reason to complain of Socrates including too little secular material than his contemporaries had for objecting to too much. Yet the little there was was more – much more – than could be found

---

worshipped, and there is a close link and relationship between the two. They are connected, and each gains from increase of the other. True religion flourishes in blamelessness of life, and the commonwealth, being compounded of both, benefits from both,' Mansi 4 col 1112. Whether Socrates had Theodosius's letter before him or not, his views express the principles which animated Theodosius II in 431.

[31] *HE* V.1.
[32] *Ibid* III.1.
[33] *Ibid* IV.34.
[34] *Ibid* II.25.
[35] *Ibid* II.25; IV.4.

in the pages of Eusebius; and it was enough to raise eyebrows among the readers of ecclesiastical histories. And that Socrates himself was uneasy about it is suggested not only by his apologia, but, even more strongly, by what he says about the work of his contemporary, Philip of Side: but to him we shall need to return when we have considered Socrates's other contemporary, Sozomen.

Sozomen's *Ecclesiastical History* was written very soon after Socrates's, and drew heavily on this. The greatest part of it, though written in a more self-consciously cultivated style, falls into a similar mould. In his first seven books Sozomen shows an even greater reserve towards including non-ecclesiastical topics, despite the greater width of his canvas, than does Socrates. The brief allusions to civil wars under Constantius[36] and the chapter devoted to Julian[37] are just about all that could come under the heading of secular history, and it could all be justified, without special pleading, as sketching in the necessary context of the main narrative.[38] In his preface Sozomen makes a point of saying that 'what is called monachism' is not foreign to ecclesiastical history: like Socrates and like the readers of ecclesiastical histories, Sozomen was evidently sensitive to questions about what the genre demanded, and for the greater part of his work he tried to keep closely to his brief. But in the last two books (the last two of those we have) his resolve seems to have broken down progressively. Book VIII opens with the death of Theodosius I (395); an account of the coup d'état against Rufinus opens the sluices. From here on until the end of the work there are large blocks[39] of material on secular matters, in great part actually taken from the lost work of the pagan historian Olympiodorus. Almost the whole of book IX is devoted to the troubles in Italy under Stilicho and Alaric. The narrative is punctuated with apologies for these digressions into secular history: the murder of Rufinus brought an increase in piety;[40] whereas conflicts in the church of Constantinople, it appears, brought invasions by Huns and Goths;[41] for dissensions in the church bring troubles in the state. It is God's design, proved by the history of the times, to show that the piety of princes is rewarded with safety and prosperity, and that 'without piety armies, great

---

[36] *Ibid* IV.4, 7.
[37] *Ibid* V.1.
[38] *Ibid* IV.7, for instance, leads straight into the (related) troubles of Athanasius in ch 8.
[39] For instance *ibid* VIII.4 and 25; IX.1–14.
[40] *Ibid* VIII.1.
[41] *Ibid* VIII.25.

authority and political power are useless.'[42] God has rewarded Honorius's devotion with securing the stability of imperial power, and a profound peace, we are assured, reigned after him; wars and civil conflicts have ceased, and God has set the seal upon his favour by permitting the discovery of many holy relics.[43] This must have been comforting doctrine for Theodosius II to read, and it may, as comforting words sometimes do, have carried some conviction. But it cannot disguise the fact that in his last two books Sozomen has allowed the line which marked ecclesiastical history off from secular to become obliterated. The last book, especially, except for a single chapter about the discovery of the relics of the prophet Zechariah and of Stephen the martyr,[44] is a straight and, happily, full secular history, such as one would expect to find, and indeed does find, in the work of a writer like Zosimus; not in an ecclesiastical history. The same phenomenon can be observed in what we know of the last two books of Philostorgius's *Ecclesiastical History*: only one short paragraph among the surviving fragments[45] deals with church affairs.

Unlike classical history writing, ecclesiastical history was not intended to be contemporary history. Sozomen, as we have already noted, was more under the power of traditional tastes than most of his fellow-practioners of the craft. It may be that the closer he came to his own day, the harder he found it to keep to conventions so much at variance with his rhetorical education. His interests simply burst through the limits set for ecclesiastical history by its eusebian mould, and he found himself writing history of the kind than Eunapius before him and Zosimus a little after him were writing. The only difference was in the religious position of the writer: an unconcealed, and indeed often aggressively christian stance is disclosed in many of Sozomen's didactic passages. His reflections on the pre-established harmony between princely piety and public welfare have their exact, if pagan counterparts in Zosimus's moralising remarks. In almost every way the final parts of Sozomen's and Philostorgius's *Ecclesiastical Histories* belong with Zosimus's *Historia Nova* rather than with Eusebius and the tradition inaugurated by his work.

Another of Sozomen's contemporaries, Theodoret, tried to keep the eusebian tradition alive unpolluted by matters foreign to it. Even the

[42] *Ibid* IX.1.
[43] *Ibid* IX.16.
[44] *Ibid* IX.17.
[45] *Ibid* XII.11.

theme of monasticism, which Sozomen decided to include, though, as we have seen, with an *apologia*, was relegated by Theodoret where it belonged: to a *Philotheos Historia*, a 'religious history' separate from his supremely narrow *Ecclesiastical History*. Photius, assuredly a connoisseur both of ecclesiastical and of secular history, found Theodoret's style the one best suited to the subject matter of ecclesiastical history.[46] Instinctively, perhaps, he could appreciate the specific characteristics of the genre and see them most starkly displayed in the narrowest of the mid-fifth century writers.

It was in fact at the moment that ecclesiastical historiography was reaching its zenith that it was also coming to face a crucial choice. It could, following Theodoret's direction, exclude ruthlessly all that was foreign to its conventions at the cost of artificial exclusions and constrictions. Alternatively, it could go further along the way that Socrates, Sozomen and Philostorgius had set out on: including much that was traditionally alien to ecclesiastical history to allow the distinction between it and secular history to become blurred.

The trail for this course had been blazed not long before Socrates and Sozomen by Philip of Side. His *Christianikē Historia* has not survived, though Photius had at least a part of it in his library.[47] Socrates tells us[48] that it consisted of thirty-six books, each in several volumes—twenty-four, according to Photius—totalling almost a thousand, with the table of contents taking up a whole volume. By both accounts it was a rag-bag of a work, containing, in addition to a world-history beginning with the creation to AD 430 a great heap of geographical and scientific erudition and 'other matters of little moment' as Socrates says. It is unfortunate that from the scraps of information about the work its real purpose can only be guessed at;[49] it seems more likely to have been intended to be a universal history with vast digressions than a christian encyclopaedia containing historical alongside other information. Socrates is emphatic that it was a 'christian', not an 'ecclesiastical' history, and it certainly appears to have differed from his work not only by its lack of clarity, conciseness and workmanlike presentation, but, perhaps even more, by whatever conception underlay its mammoth bulk.

This was something very different both from ecclesiastical and from secular history of the kind that was to be written by christian authors

---

[46] *Bibl* 31.   [47] *Ibid* 35.   [48] *HE* VII.27.
[49] On it see E. Honigmann, 'Patristic studies XII: Philippus of Side and his "Christian history"', *Studi e testi* 173 (Rome 1953).

such as Procopius and Agathias in the sixth century. Philip's loose baggy monster seems to have had no immediate progeny, though it may be that some much later medieval treatises should be placed in the same genre. But if it had no future, it was not entirely without a past. Though there is no record of anything of this kind being done on a scale approaching his, Philip's work seems in fact to be the old chronicle writ very large. A generation before Philip Sulpicius Severus had written an elegant and concise little work which began with the creation and ended with the year AD 400. With the older chronographical works of Julius Africanus, Hippolytus and Eusebius (just translated by Jerome) Sulpicius Severus shared his starting point, a marked interest in chronological problems and, though in practice only to a very modest extent, a professed intention to bring diverse information drawn from the *mundiales historici*[50] and the *scriptores saecularium litterarum* into the framework of the *sacra* or *divina historia* derived from the scriptures. What distinguished it from the older chronicles – with which its shared it title[51] – was its extended narrative form. It is best seen as a synthesis of the chronicle with history of the short summary type which the fourth century epitomes were making familiar among a new kind of reading public.[52] It made use of the chronicle framework and packed into it material to edify both the learned and the simple.[53] Only the scale and the amount of the material packed in seem to have distinguished Sulpicius Severus's from Philip of Side's work a generation later. Both were in principle as foreign to ecclesiastical as to secular history.[54]

It was not until the age of Theodosius II that the genre of ecclesiastical history really began to show the strains imposed on it by the

[50] See for instance *Chronicon* I.1.4 and II.14.6–8.
[51] Gennadius, *De scriptoribus ecclesiasticis*, PL 58 (1862) col 1072.
[52] See S. Prete, *I Chronica di Sulpicio Severo: saggio storicocritico* (Rome 1955) p 119. On historical epitomes in the fourth century see A. Momigliano, 'Pagan and Christian historiography [in the fourth century A.D.', *The conflict between paganism and Christianity in the fourth century*], ed A. Momigliano (Oxford 1963) pp 79–99 at pp 85–6. On the value of epitomes to christians in a hurry with little time to waste 'much labour for the sake of a few facts', see Augustine, *De doctrina christiana* II.39.59.
[53] *Chronicon* I.1.4.
[54] Only the narrowness of focus and the slightness of Sulpicius Severus's interest, in practice, in secular history allow a *rapprochement* with the last two books of Rufinus's *HE*, almost exactly contemporary. See also Paulinus of Nola, ep 28.5. The scope and genres differ despite this limited convergence. A further form to be distinguished from all those here discussed is Orosius's *Historiarum adversus paganos libri septem*: a work of historical apologetics rather than any kind of history.

change undergone by its subject matter in post-constantinian times. The eusebian tradition could only be preserved in its purity at the cost of rigid adherence to a narrow range of topics. The topics canonised by Eusebius as the component threads of ecclesiastical history were few. They did not embrace themes as central as the development of christian worship, and he had touched on many social aspects of christian community living and even on forms of organisation only incidentally. There was much that the eusebian tradition left out; but it had made some kind of sense for a period when the church was a more less sharply distinct group in society. Monasticism was the only major additional theme which only a purist like Theodoret refused to admit into the canon. Even with this addition, however, and with re-interpreting the role of emperors in the church, the conventions were breaking down with the vanishing of a line to mark off the church in the midst of secular society. Since Eusebius the church had come to fill the whole horizon. Understood in a wide and ancient sense, the 'Church' could now be taken to include the whole roman world. If 'ecclesiastical history' were defined by its object, the church, it would in effect have become merged with roman history, or with history *tout court*. But of course ecclesiastical history was not defined by its object but by the conventions of its writing. Socrates, Sozomen and Philostorgius were conscious of tensions between the range of their interests and the constraining conventions, but they adhered to their genre with some tenacity.

To be sure, there was a way in which the tension could be eased. This was through finding some new way of marking off the church as a distinct group in society. A constricted, clericalised conception of the church had long been developing, but it is striking that the principle destined for so long a life in canon law that *in sacerdotibus ecclesia constat* was first stated in imperial legislation in the year 430.[55] The lines which marked out the christian people in the world had melted away, but new lines had come to mark out a clerical élite among them. To the extent that a historian identified the church with this élite, perhaps instinctively, the constraining conventions of ecclesiastical history could be eased or disguised. The standard sort of ecclesiastical history could continue to be written provided that it was confined, more or

---

[55] Sirmond, *Appendix Codicis Theodosiani* cap 20 in Haenel, *Corpus legum* 1183, p 241. On some its medieval echoes(see K. F. Morrison, *The Two Kingdoms* (Princeton, N.J. 1964) p 39 and Y. M. J. Congar, *L'ecclésiologie du haut Moyen Age* (Paris 1968) p 98 n 173.

less, to the history of the clerical élite. Accounts of doctrinal controversies and councils, of disputed elections and schisms, of the persons and works of churchmen continued to be the stock in trade of ecclesiastical history, at the cost of excluding more and more of the church's life. Church history could only survive as a distinct tradition in virtue of a tacit assumption that the church, or what mattered in the church, was its clergy. If the convention was to survive the subject matter would have to shrink to the dimensions of its mould.

The alternatives of discarding the conventions to allow for the expanded subject matter, or keeping the conventions at the cost of mutilating its increased range rarely presented themselves in their starkest form. Only perhaps Philip of Side discarded the old genre entirely; only Theodoret seems to have adhered to it with utter determination. More generally the tension engendered the kind of uncertainty we have observed in the work of Socrates, Sozomen and Philostorgius. In some manner they were aware that the original conception of the church behind the historiographical tradition they inherited was losing applicability. This, surely, is the reason for that 'dispersion of themes and lack of linearity' on which professor Momigliano has remarked in the work of the late roman historians, of which he saw the inclusion of 'materials foreign to their narrative' by the church historians as the most striking example.[56] In my view it is to this falling apart of traditional form and concept, albeit unformulated concept, that we should attribute this uncertainty of purpose and scope; rather than to see it, as Momigliano is inclined to see it, as reflecting the uncertainty of the historian's position in society.

Despite this loss of clarity, however, ecclesiastical history continued to hold its own amid the great diversification of history writing in the later fifth and sixth centuries. The fixity of its traditional form is best displayed in the compilations by Gelasius of Cyzicus, Theodore the lector and Cassiodorus-Epiphanius; its elasticity and adaptability in the hands of Evagrius at the very end of the sixth century. Its identity remained intact, distinct both from secular history (Procopius, Agathias) and from the newer form of national history (Cassiodorus, Jordanes, Gregory of Tours). In the conflation of genres which can be detected in the early parts of Gregory of Tours's *History of the Franks* the distinct traditions may still be discerned juxtaposed.[57] I am not at all sure how long the eusebian tradition of ecclesiastical historiography

[56] 'L'età del trapasso', p 103.
[57] K. F. Stroheker, *Der senatorische Adel im spätantiken Gallien* (Reutlingen 1948)

survived substantially unaltered, and I am unable to pursue its des-
tinies beyond the end of the sixth century. But I should like to allow
myself to conclude with the guess that one more symptom of Bede's
creative genius may turn out to be his easy mastery of the old convention and his ability to integrate it unobtrusively with the distinct
tradition of national historiography into a personal and infinitely more
coherent synthesis than Gregory of Tour's mechanical juxtaposition.

We have been exploring the pressures of changing circumstances on
a historiographical form whose moulds were setting exceptionally
rapidly and rigidly. Perhaps we should acknowledge a debt of gratitude
to the ecclesiastical historians who carried on their work with a confidence uninhibited by theological or methodological self-criticism.
They secured the survival of a great tradition of historiography which
was, in due course, to serve as a model for modern scholarly history.[58]
But we should also ask whether, and how far, a historiographical convention came to determine a mode of self-awareness; how far, particularly, the traditional form of ecclesiastical history helped to make a
narrow, 'clerical' conception of the *ecclesia* generally acceptable? When
bishop Chromatius of Aquileia asked Rufinus to translate Eusebius into
latin, he did so in the hope that amid the sea of troubles afflicting Italy
in the first years of the fifth century the readers' minds might be so held
by reading about the past that they would become oblivious of the
troubles of the present'.[59] I should not like to try to guess how effective
an anodyne Eusebius was, but I am strongly inclined to believe that
Eusebius and the eusebian tradition of ecclesiastical historiography did
engender oblivion: oblivion not of present ills but of the great divide
between the pre-constantinian and the post-theodosian church. Perhaps
the vogue for church history, especially in the conspicuously pious
court circles was due in no small part to the strong sense of continuity
it fostered. It was not easy for Theodosius II or his palatine officials to
see themselves as the lineal descendants of the church of the martyrs.
The unbroken chain of the ecclesiastical history linking their age with
that of the apostolic church must have helped.[60]

---

p 128 has pointed out that in his initial conspectus of world history Gregory
draws on chronicle material; thereafter, until the end of the fourth century,
ecclesiastical history is the basis of his narrative, and only with the fifth century
does roman secular and finally frankish history come in.

[58] See Momigliano, 'Pagan and Christian historiography', p 92.

[59] Rufinus, *HE*, *Praefatio*.

[60] I wish to thank Dr Margaret Gibson for most helpful criticism of the first
draft of this paper.

17

RECENTLY DISCOVERED MATERIALS FOR WRITING THE HISTORY OF CHRISTIAN NUBIA

by WILLIAM FREND

CHANCE discoveries have been among the 'uncovenanted blessings' that have fallen to the study of new testament times and the early church. The finding of the Isaiah scroll by a shepherd boy in the judaean desert in 1947 led to the greatest discovery in biblical studies of all time, that of the Dead Sea scrolls and the essene monastery of Kharbet Q'mran. Similarly, the recovery of the gnostic library of 48 separate books from a christian cemetery at Nag-Hammadi, not far from Luxor, in 1946, has thrown a wholly unexpected light on the complex of beliefs and attitudes of orthodox christianity's great rival during the second and early third centuries, gnosticism. Recently, professor Morton Smith has made the boldest claims on behalf of a 'secret Gospel of Mark' used apparently in Alexandria in the second century AD. An extract from this gospel he found in the library of the monastery of Mar Saba near Jerusalem, quoted in a letter which may be attributed correctly to Clement of Alexandria circa 190 AD.[1]

Some of the discoveries made since 1960 in the area of the middle Nile once occupied by the christian nubian kingdoms have been equally surprising. In 1960 the egyptian government obtained the help of UNESCO and thence of a number of international teams to salvage as much as possible of the material remains of the successive civilisations that had occupied the stretch of the Nile valley from Aswan to the third cataract. They were destined to be flooded beneath the waters of lake Nasser formed through the building of the high dam of Aswan. The work, however, of the international teams like that of those who researched into the Dead Sea scrolls rested on a long tradition of scholarly endeavour. Long before Faras and its frescoes became famous the salient features of nubian christianity were known and many of the main sites had been surveyed.

[1] H. M. Smith, *The Secret Gospel*, (New York/San Francisco 1973), *Clement of Alexandria and a Secret Gospel of Mark* (Harvard 1973).

The reconstruction of the life and thought of any vanished civilisation depends on the historian's ability to combine literary with other forms of evidence. The progress that has been made towards understanding medieval nubian christianity has depended on there being some literary sources to which the archaeological discoveries could be related. For the conversion of Nubia to christianity, the monophysite historian John of Ephesus (died c 585) has left a near contemporary, if strongly biased, account of the rival missions sent to the court of king Silko of Nobatia, the northern of the three nubian kingdoms, by Justinian and Theodora in 542.[2] Probably christianity had already begun to penetrate Nobatia. There was a bishopric at Philae on the frontier with Egypt, and Theodora's mission may have owed something of its success to the help of Theodore, the bishop there, who was an ardent supporter of the monophysite cause.[3] The victory of Silko over the still heathen Blemmys commemorated on an inscription from Kalabscha around this date confirmed the Nubians in their choice of faith.[4]

John of Ephesus gives some impression of conditions in Nubia during the sixth century. His information about nubian history is supplemented by incidents incorporated in the account of the coptic-monophysite patriarchate at Alexandria, compiled in the tenth century by Severus of Asmounin under the title of the *History of the Patriarchs of Alexandria*.[5] Though some of the details of the intervention of the Nubians in egyptian affairs during the mid-eighth century for the benefit of the coptic patriarch Michael may be legendary, Severus left the impression of a nubian kingdom governed by powerful monarchs

---

[2] John of Ephesus, *HE*, ed E. W. Brooks, *CSCO, SS*, 3 (1924) III, iv, pp 6–8, 45–53.

[3] See L. P. Kirwan, 'Prelude to Nubian Christianity', *Mélanges offerts à K. Michalowski* (Warsaw 1966) p 126, and [W. Y.] Adams, ['Post-Pharaonic Nubia in the light of Archaeology'], 2, *J[ournal of] E[gyptian] A[rchaeology,]* 51 (Cairo 1966) p 172. Theodore's influence is demonstrated by a coptic text in the temple of Dendur in which the priest, Abraham, states that he set up a cross there which he received from Theodore. Abraham stresses that he did this on the orders of the nubian king Eirpanome. The date is either 22 January 559 or 574.

[4] Silko attributed his victory to 'God' (θεός) while the defeated Blemmys had to swear on their idols (εἴδωλα) to keep the peace. For the inscription see *CIG* 3, 5072 and J. B. Bury, *History of the Later Roman Empire* (London 1923) 2, p 330, note 1. Silko cooperated with the byzantine general Narses, and the date could be as early as 539, when the byzantine treaty with the nubians was abrogated. This had left open the temple at Philae for annual celebrations by the pagan nubians.

[5] Published in *PO* 1, 5 and 10.

based on Dongola.[6] These were well capable of defending themselves against the muslim armies of Egypt and had a number of lesser kings subordinate to them. One of these rulers, king Mercurios, is now known to have been the founder of the cathedral at Faras in 707. In 836 the *History* tells of an embassy sent by king Zacharias and headed by his son Georgios to the caliph of Baghdad, which resulted in a commercial treaty between Egypt and Nubia.[7] This was an important event in nubian history for it demonstrated that Nubia counted throughout the muslim world: both rulers connected with the embassy are recorded also among the inscriptions found at Faras. It may be significant that the great period of nubian prosperity typified by the complex of churches and official buildings at Faras and the finely decorated christian pottery of the classical period of nubian art dates from this era.[8]

The later periods of nubian history are only sparsely recorded in the arab chronicles. Events, however, like the raid by Saladin's brother, Shams ed Doula on Q'Asr Ibrim in 1173, and the last known offensive operations by the Nubians against muslim Egypt, consisting of the attack on the Red Sea port of Aidhab in 1272 by king David[9], have been preserved. A generation later, however, a Fung muslim dynasty was established in the kingdom of Makuria at Old Dongola and a tablet commemorated the conversion of the church (in fact the royal palace) into a mosque.[10] It was assumed that after the death in 1323 of Kudanbes, the last known christian nubian king of Dongola, christianity declined rapidly in favour of islam.[11]

Literary evidence provided just enough outline of nubian history to make sense of the archaeological remains which confronted the antiquities services of Sudan and Egypt after the formation of the anglo-egyptian condominium in 1899. Thence to 1960 knowledge of christian

[6] *History of the Patriarchs*, ed B. T. Evetts, 1, cap xviii, *PO*, 1, p 144.
[7] *Ibid* 1, cap xx, *PO*, 10, pp 505-7. See G. Vantini, 'Le Roi Kirki (Georgios) de Nubie a Bagdad: un ou deux voyages?', in K[*unst und*] G[*eschichte*] N[*ubiens in christlicher Zeit*], ed E. H. Dinkler (Recklinghausen 1970) pp 41-9. The journey is authenticated also in the contemporary chronicle of Dionysius of Tell Mahre: *Chronique de Michel le Syrien*, ed J. B. Chabot (Paris 1903) 3, pp 90-4. The wealth and magnificence of the nubian embassy was a matter of wonder.
[8] Abu Saleh, [*Churches and Monasteries in Egypt and some neighbouring countries*], ed and trans A. J. Butler and B. T. Evetts (Oxford 1895) p 295.
[9] Mufazzal ibn Abil-Fazail, *Histoire des sultans mamelouks*, ed E. Blochet, *PO* 10, p 375.
[10] See Adams 3, *JEA* 52 (1966) p 152. The information that the 'church' was the royal palace I owe to professor K. Michalowski.
[11] Thus, P. L. Shinnie, *Medieval Nubia* (Khartoum 1954) p 7.

nubia accumulated steadily through thorough surveys of sites and the excavation of selected areas. One major discovery was the extraordinary tenacity of the byzantine legacy, even though direct contacts between nubian kingdoms and Constantinople must have been limited to occasional trading contacts and embassies. Griffith's publication in 1913, for instance, of the first nubian documents to be discovered, revealed that the nubian language was written in greek characters but included some coptic and nubian letters to represent non-greek sounds.[12] In addition, eleventh and twelfth century inscriptions cut in comparatively good greek were found, and on some of these there were traces of byzantine commendatory prayers for the dead.[13] The *Euchologion Mega* was being used in nubian liturgy between 1000 and 1200 though it was not used in coptic Egypt. These discoveries confirmed statements by arab chroniclers that the Nubians, though 'jacobite' christians used greek as well as nubian in their liturgy.[14] Evidence also came to light of an episcopal organisation and of monasticism, though the latter was not as pronounced as in Egypt. The nubian court ceremonial and organisation was also conducted on byzantine lines as shown by the use of medieval byzantine titles, such as *Eparchos*, *Primicerios* and *Protodomesticos* in nubian texts.[15] Nubia had clearly been a cultural outpost of Byzantium which retained even more links with this aspect of its origins than other areas of byzantine mission such as Ethiopia and Armenia. By the outbreak of the second world war enough was known about Nubia for the archaeologist Ugo Monneret de Villard to collate into a comprehensive outline a history of christian Nubia from the seventh to the fourteenth century in his *Storia della Nubia Cristiana*, published in 1938.

Thus, when a large part of Nubia was threatened with destruction enough possible lines of research existed to challenge the skill of international scholarship. By far the most important site proved to be Faras,

---

[12] F. Ll. Griffith, 'Nubian Texts of the Christian period', in *AKPAW*, Phil. Hist. Klasse 8 (Berlin 1913) and in a British Academy lecture, 'Christian Documents from Nubia', *PBA* 14, (1928) especially p 14.

[13] H. Junker, 'Die christliche Grabsteine Nubiens', *Zeitschrift für agyptische Sprache*, 60 (1925) pp 111–48, and J. F. Oates 'A Christian Inscription in Greek from Armenna in Nubia', *JEA* 49 (1963) pp 161 et seq, and his conclusion that in the eleventh and twelfth centuries 'Greek was alive and widespread' in Nubia, p 171.

[14] Thus, Abu Saleh, p 272.

[15] See U. Monneret de Villard, *Storia della Nubia Cristiana* (Rome 1938) cap 20, and the writer's 'Nubia as an outpost of Byzantine cultural influence' *Byzantino-Slavica*, 18 (Prague 1968) pp 319–27.

just over the sudanese border on the west bank of the Nile. Its significance had long been realised by the Sudan antiquities department, and two large churches had already been uncovered, one of which had contained painted frescoes.[16] It was, however, the polish team led by professor Kazimierz Michalowski which discovered the cathedral below the great mound that dominated the site. Thanks to him the magnificent frescoes that covered the walls layer upon layer were salvaged and identified, and now, intimately studied, provide the means for a further and more detailed understanding than before of the religious history of medieval Nubia.[17]

First, there is the sheer magnitude of the find. Some 400 inscriptions and 169 frescoes, including palimpsests were uncovered.[18] The completion of the cathedral by bishop Paulos in 707 in the reign of king Mercurios was recorded on two fine inscriptions in greek and coptic.[19] Mercurios was already known from the *History of the Patriarchs*, and by the monophysite writer John the Deacon as king of Dongola, whom the Nubians knew as 'the new Constantine' in true byzantine style.[20] Under him the two kingdoms of Nobatia in the north and Makurrah round Dongola had united, and the Faras inscription provided further proof of his achievement and authority.

The inscriptions also proved that the cathedral had been the seat of the metropolitan at least until the twelfth century. In a niche in one of the walls was found thirty-one lines of inscription written in black ink listing twenty-seven bishops who ruled between 827 and 1169, recording the length of their episcopate in years, together with the month and day of their death. It was drawn up in greek probably originally near the end of the tenth century and then added to, and there were some entries in coptic and nubian.[21] This in itself was a discovery of the greatest importance, because it enabled an accurate chronological framework to be established without which archaeology can only deal

---

[16] F. Ll. Griffith, *Liverpool Annals of Archaeology and Anthropology*, 13 (1926) pp 66–93, recording discoveries made in four years' work, 1910–13.

[17] See [K.] Michalowski, *Faras: [Die Kathedrale aus den Wüstensand]* (Zürich 1967) a commendably rapid and fascinating publication of six season's work.

[18] I am accepting this more conservative estimate communciated to me by W. Y. Adams. For a higher figure of 'about 500 inscriptions , see [S. Jakobielski 'La Liste des Eveques de Pachoras'] *Travaux [du Centre d'archeologie meditérranéene de l'Academie polonaise des Sciences]*, 3 (Warsaw 1966) p 152.

[19] [S.] Jakobielski ['Some new data to the History of Christian Nubia as found in Faras' Inscriptions',] *Klio*, 51 (Berlin/Wiesbaden) p 500.

[20] *History of the Patriarchs*, part i, cap xviii, *PO* I, p 144.

[21] *Travaux* 3, pp 153–70, at p 154.

with approximations. At Faras, however, ecclesiastics used elaborate methods of dating, including the 'era of Diocletian' (AD 284), 'from the beginning of the world', the 'cycle of Alexandria' and 'the Ethiopian era' ('from the birth of Christ'): on the tombstones of some of the bishops of Pachoras there would be a combination of two or more eras.[22] In addition, some of the *acta* of the bishops were included on inscriptions. For instance, bishop Cyros, the fifteenth bishop of Faras, who ruled for thirty-five years, from 866–902, made considerable alterations in the cathedral and was the first bishop to be described as 'metropolitan bishop'.[23] The nubian church was shown, like its coptic neighbour, to have been monastic oriented, some bishops being described as 'abbot', and two as 'archimandrite'. Promotion from monastery to bishopric seems to have been in the ordinary course of affairs.

In addition, the frescoes commemorated some of the rulers of Nobatia and occasionally members of their families, high court officials and senior monks. All these were represented as being protected either by Christ or the Virgin or a saint, usually Michael.[24] Information derived from inscriptions associated with the frescoes established the dates of the rulers Georgios I, who as a prince had gone to Baghdad on an embassy, and who died in 920 after a reign of fifty-six years, and Georgios II (969–1002). The prominence given to the queen-mother among certain groups of royal personages suggested that a leading place was reserved to the latter in the nubian court.[25]

Furthermore, the careful uncovering of the frescoes enabled clearly defined periods of nubian religious art to be established. In the eighth and ninth centuries a style in which much use was made of violet and mauve colouring predominated, to give way to a 'white' period for the next country, a 'red yellow' style for the magnificent fresco of the youths in the fiery furnace (eleventh century) and more elaborate and garish colouring in the twelfth century. In this period the paintings have a wide-staring ethiopian look superseding the byzantine style of earlier centuries.[26]

The Faras excavations provide one of the foundations on which the

---

[22] Jakobielski, p 502.

[23] *Travaux* 3, p 159.

[24] See the fine illustrations in Michalowski, *Faras*, plates 71–90, and B. Rostkowska 'Iconographie des personnages historiques sur les peintures de Faras', *Travaux* 6 (1972) pp 196–205.

[25] See P. L. and M. Shinnie 'New Light on Medieval Nubia', *Journal of African History*, 6 (Cambridge 1965) p 270.

[26] See Michalowski, *Faras*, pp 72 *et seq.*

story of nubian christianity will be based. Already, detailed examination of the style of the paintings has raised the question whether Nubia remained true to its monophysite origins throughout its long history. Not only the existence of byzantine liturgical sequences, but the representation of the Christ as a suckling child has suggested to some critics that there were intervals, particularly in the eleventh century, when the court accepted the chalcedonian formula that acknowledged Christ in two natures, Godhead and manhood, inseparably united.[27] So far, however, the alleged chalcedonianisms have all been found in monophysite environments, and the lack of physical evidence, such as the deliberate covering up of prominent monophysite bishops and rulers, argues against any such change.[28] Modifications in ritual and vestments there may have been, but not in the basic religious outlook accepted at the period of the conversion to christianity.

The British excavations under the auspices of the Egypt exploration society at Q'Asr Ibrim on the east bank of the Nile some fifty-five miles north of Faras, complement the discoveries from Faras. Q'Asr Ibrim was a fortress strategically placed on a high cliff overlooking the Nile. It was the seat of a bishopric and of a local ruler, probably an eparch, though in the final christian period he was known as 'Ourou Dotawo'–(king of Lower Do) in contrast to the king of Do-n-houl (= Dongola).[29] Throughout the christian era the site was dominated by a finely built stone church dedicated, we are told by the chronicler Abu Salih, to the Virgin.[30] Q'Asr Ibrim produced no frescoes. Instead it provided the excavators with a wealth of manuscript material preserved thanks to the extreme dryness of the climate. The most remarkable of these were found in January, 1964, by professor J. M. Plumley, attached to the thighs of a bishop who had been crudely buried or

---

[27] See Adams pp 172 *et seq* arguing on the basis of the melkite patriarch, Eutychius, *c* 890, *Annales* asserting that all Nubia was originally orthodox but transferred its allegiance to monophysitism in *c* 719 after the suppression of the melkite patriarchate in Alexandria, *PG* 111 (1863) col 1122D. Supported by Michalowski, *Faras* pp 91–3, but criticised, to my mind effectively by M. Krauze, 'Zur Kirche und Theologiegeschichte Nubiens', *KGN* pp 71–86, and [P. van] Moorsel, ['Die stillende Gottesmutter und die Monophysiten',] *KGN* pp 81–91.

[28] Moorsel.

[29] See, T. Save Soderbergh, *Late Nubian Sites, Churches and Settlements; the Scandanavian joint expedition to Sudanese Nubia* (Stockholm 1973) p 17.

[30] Abu Saleh, p 291. The fullest account to date is that by the present writer, in the *Abhandlungen des vii Internationalen Kongresses für christliche Archäologie* (Trier 1965, publ Rome 1968) pp 531–8. Also J. M. Plumley, *JEA* 50 (1964) pp 3–5.

rather deposited beneath the arch of the west crypt of the church.[31] They consisted of two paper scrolls, one in Bohairic coptic (the only Bohairic document found as yet on a nubian site), and the other, in arabic. When unrolled in the museum of antiquities at Cairo, they proved to be the consecration deeds of the dead man, giving his name as Timotheos and his see as the joint see of Pachoras (Faras) and Tilybe (Ibrim). Most important, however, was the fact that his consecration was performed by the patriarch Gabriel IV in Old Cairo, and Gabriel was in office between 1372–80. The mention too, of 'the most pious bishops who have come with him to carry out his enthronement in the church in which the bishops of the see [used to be enthroned]' shows that an organised episcopate existed in the northern kingdom of Nobatia as late as the last quarter of the fourteenth century, or fifty years later than had previously been thought.

The continued survival of nubian Christianity into the european later middle ages was indicated by another discovery. Excavating on another part of the site, the present writer found a large sealed pot which had been hidden amidst the rubble of a house and protected from destruction by a large beam that had lain across it.[32] Inside were nine leather scrolls written in the nubian language. They were of christian date, as shown by a latin type cross in the top left-hand corner of the scroll. The hand-writing in black ink was on the soft inner side of what had been probably pieces of leather garments made from gazelle skin, and it was clear and bold. It was immediately possible to distinguish a royal name 'Joel', and further research by professor Plumley has established that his kingdom was known as Dotawo, and that there was a bishop Merkcos of Ibrim, and also other officials.[33] The date, however, worked out from a combination of greek symbols and modern nubian words and related to the era of the martyrs (AD 284) appears to be AD 1464.[34] Until confirmatory evidence is discovered this must be treated with reserve. Though the scroll in question was the last to be inserted before the jar was sealed, and the leather was still supple when discovered, so late a date for an organised christian kingdom would appear to go beyond other evidence for

[31] Publication is expected in 1974, with commentary by professor Plumley, as an Egypt Exploration Society monograph.
[32] To be published by J. M. Plumley and the writer.
[33] See J. M. Plumley, 'The Christian period at Q'Asr Ibrim. Some notes on the MSS finds', *Acts of the Warsaw Colloquium on Nubian studies* (1972) ed E. H. Dinkler (Bonn forthcoming).
[34] *Ibid*

organised christianity even in more remote areas of Nubia below the second cataract where its survival could be presumed.[35] There were also economic movements which led to major shifts in patterns of trade away from Nile traffic to trans-desert routes that favoured the dominance of the desert nomads against settled agriculturists such as were the christian Nubians.[36] Nubia had flourished partly because it had a monopoly of the transit trade between the Mediterranean and Africa south of the Sahara. This was steadily eroded by the desert tribes who had been converted to islam. Already by the mid-fourteenth century neither Nubians nor the Mamelouk armies from Egypt could contain this threat. It is surprising too, that while the coptic and ethiopian churches were known about in Europe and were represented at the re-union council of Florence-Ferrara 1439–45, nothing was heard of nubian Christianity at this time. It would seem unwise, therefore, for the moment, to push the survivial of christian Nobatia much beyond the first decades of the fifteenth century.

The scrolls were historical documents, and they have been supplemented by the discovery of some remarkable texts written in nubian or arabic on paper which appear to be letters to the bishop or eparch of Ibrim. A series of arabic texts studied by Mr Ahmed al Bushra at Cambridge date to *c* 1150–70.[37] They concern relations between the eparch and fatimid palace official who owned ships in the port of Aidhab on the Red Sea, and seems to have acted as agent for the nubian rulers by sending them goods, and selling slaves on their behalf. Their existence confirms the existence of friendly relations between Nubia and fatimid Egypt at this time. Another group of four letters, however, written a short time later, foreshadow changes towards a more aggressive policy by the Egyptians, including a demand for tribute.[38] This may well have been an issue that led to the war between the Nubians and the new ayyubid dynasty, which came into power in Egypt in 1171, that resulted in the temporary capture of Q'Asr Ibrim in 1173. Perhaps the loss or deposit of these letters may have been connected with this event.

Apart from the wealth of secular texts, there were scattered in a

---

[35] Adams believes that christianity 'probably lasted until the end of the fifteenth century on Kulubnarti island, 130 km south of Wadi Halfa', *KGN* p 150, but the churches both there and in other fortified christian sites in the same area seem to date to the fourteenth century at the latest.
[36] Thus Adams, 2, p 175.
[37] Cited by J. M. Plumley, *The Christian Period at Q'Asr Ibrim*, (forthcoming).
[38] *Ibid*

layer just above the floor of the cathedral, and hidden in tombs or under stones outside, what can only have been the remains of the cathedral library. As had been noted elsewhere,[39] these texts consisted of fragments written on vellum, parchment and paper in greek, nubian and coptic. They were often torn or charred, and some had been obviously salvaged and hidden. So far as preliminary research allows one to say, they were liturgical and homiletic pieces, and fragments of the new testament, acts of martyrs, eucharistic sequences and prayers. As at Faras, it seems that while coptic was retained as the principal language for biblical reading and patristic work, the liturgy and more popular works, such as the extracts found of acts of martyrs were in greek or nubian.

Faras and Ibrim have proved to be outstandingly important sites, but the accurate assessment of the discoveries made there depend on the study of material from a large number of other nubian sites that have been investigated in recent years. Some, like the church of Abdallah Nirqi near Abu Simbel, excavated in 1963-4 by the dutch expedition, produced frescoes rivalling those of Faras and earlier than most of the latter.[40] Apart from the leather scrolls from Q'Asr Ibrim the most important evidence for the declining years of christian Nubia has come from the desolate area in the northern Sudan, known as Batn el Hajar, where rudely constructed churches under the shadow of fortifications point to a final period of insecurity as the threat from the bedouin tribes from the west gradually increased.[41] Indeed, as with christian north Africa, the nomads seem to have proved more deadly enemies to christianity in the middle Nile valley than the hostility of muslim rulers.[42] This is obviously an important field for future research.

The discoveries which have been made in recent years on nubian sites have opened up new fields of study, particularly monophysite

[39] See the writer's 'Coptic, Greek and Nubian at Q'Asr Ibrim', *Byzantino-Slavica*, 32, 2 (1972) pp 224-9.
[40] Hans D. Schneider, 'Abdallah Nirqi—description and chronology of the central church', *KGN* pp 87-103.
[41] Thus E. H. Dinkler, 'Die deutsche Ausgrabungen auf den Inseln Sunnarti, Tangur und in Kulb' *ibid* pp 259-72. For the possible survival, however, of christianity in the southern kingdom of Alwah, (around Soba near Khartoum) see P. L. Shinnie, *Excavations at Soba*, Sudan Antiquities Service, *Occasional Papers*, 3 (Khartoum 1955) pp 12-13 (cites references).
[42] Thus Adams, 3 *JEA* 52 (1966) pp 150-1, for North Africa, see the writer's 'North Africa and Europe in the Early Middle Ages' *TRHS*, fifth Series, 5 (1955) pp 61-81.

christianity. The nubian kingdoms stood midway between the Copts and the Ethiopians and were influenced by both while developing their own distinctive christian culture. It is now possible to see the eight hundred years of nubian christianity in terms of a succession of changes from period to period, and to study these in some depth. Stefan Jakobielski's work on the *History of the Bishopric of Faras*, will be a basic study of the history and administration of northern Nubia.[43] Between the tenth and twelfth centuries, when Nubia was a very prosperous area, something of the detail of its relations with its neighbours can be worked out, as well as possible developments in its religious life. Its religious art and liturgy can also be related to that of other kingdoms in the byzantine east. Old nubian as the language of a christian kingdom awaits further research and a project of a *Fontes Rerum Nubicarum* planned by the Heidelberg and Warsaw academies of science is under way.

There is, however, always need for care in handling the archaeological evidence. For instance, at Q'Asr Ibrim the discovery of the bishop's body under the arch of the west crypt has been taken sometimes as an indication of the use of the church down to the end of the fourteenth century, and that, in consequence, the scattered remains of the library found in light silt above the floor of the church must therefore be even later, perhaps early fifteenth century. A moment's thought, however, suggests the fragility of this reconstruction.[44] The bishop's body had been deposited where it lay: it had hardly been buried: only a thin covering of dirt obscured it when it was discovered lying askew and hunched up as though placed by bearers who had no time to dig a grave. It would hardly be credible in the heat of the nubian summer for services to have been conducted with the stench of a corpse emanating from the crypt only a few feet away. The deposit of the body with the scrolls attached to it is more likely to mark one of the grimmer scenes in the final era of christianity in that part of Nubia. The arch of the crypt already half filled with rubbish in the abandoned cathedral, would provide a suitable resting place for a bishop who may himself, have come to an untimely end.[45]

The nubian discoveries illustrate the variety of sources that contribute towards building up a picture of a hitherto little known christian society. They also illustrate the variety of skills required to derive the

---

[43] Published as *Faras*, 3 (Warsaw 1972).
[44] I owe this suggestion to professor W. Y. Adams, March 1973, though professor Plumley has since raised objections of some weight to it (July 1974).
[45] When found, one of his feet was missing.

greatest amount of information from them. In investigations spanning as much as a thousand years of history, and including material connected with the organisation, language, and liturgy of a church as well as its place in society, team work is all important. In this the polish academy of sciences under professor Michalowski have shown what can be done, and their example has been followed elsewhere on the continent. In Britain we have been slower to learn.

In this field as in many others there has been a tendency to adhere to methods of excavation and the organisation of research that have served well in the past but are now out-dated. With all the difficulties taken into account, publication of the results has been too slow and too meagre. Attitudes towards collaborative scholarship also have been over-cautious. A nubian institute on the lines of its polish counterpart would not be possible to-day owing to financial and other stringencies. If however, the rich material to hand from Q'Asr Ibrim is to be studied and nubian research in the United Kingdom linked with that proceeding apace on the continent, fresh attitudes are essential. In particular a greater combination of disciplines and institutions will have to be brought into play than hitherto.

THE 'FRANKISH' PENITENTIALS

by ROSAMOND PIERCE

THE penitentials in use in the frankish lands in the eighth and ninth centuries were designed as handbooks to aid the priest in the administration of private or secret penance, being at their most simple, tabulations of various misdemeanours associated with particular vices stipulating the penances to be performed.

In the early centuries of the christian church however, penance seems to have been performed in public, involving both confession and an act of contrition before the assembled congregation.[1] It was, moreover, then undergone only in cases of severe crimes, usually one of three capital sins of homicide, perjury and adultery. The ritual of penance is described fully by Basil the Great, from whom we also learn that the physical act of the laying on of hands by the bishop was the outward sign of reconciliation.[2] This severe form of penance was gradually mitigated and its rarity lessened as it became associated with the increasingly more common practice of death-bed confession and penance, as well as with the lenten period of fasting and contrition, both of which practices are particularly evident in the church in Gaul in the fifth and sixth centuries.[3] Both the bishop and, in the case of the absence of the bishop, the priest, were now empowered to reconcile the penitent.

For a time in the carolingian period there is evidence that a different, more frequent and wholly private penitential system was in use. The

---

[1] For the early history of penance the following are valuable: B. Poschmann, *Die Abendländische Kirchenbusse im Ausgang des Christlichen Altertums* (Munich 1928) and *Die Abendländische Kirchenbusse im Frühen Mittelalter* (Breslau 1930); O.D. Watkins, *A History of Penance*, 2 vols (London 1920); R.C. Mortimer, *The Origins of Private Penance in the Western Church* (Oxford 1939); E. Amann 'Pénitence-Sacrement,' in *DTC* (1909) XII, cols 783 *et seq.*

[2] Basil, *Epistola ad Amphilochium*, ep 227, *The Letters of Basil of Caesarea* (London 1934) III p 241.

[3] See for example the sermons of Caesarius of Arles, *sermones* 62–8 and 143, ed G. Morin, *Sancti Caesarii Arelatensis Sermones, CSEL* 103 (1953) pp 263 *et seq* and p 588, and H. G. H. Beck, 'The Pastoral Care of Souls in Southeast France in the Sixth Century' *Analecta Gregoriana*, 51 (Rome 1950).

penitential books were so popular in the first decade of the ninth century that a number of capitularies list them among the requisite handbooks for the priest in the exercise of his pastoral functions.[4] The episcopal statutes that can be dated to this same decade also advise the parish priest to ensure he possesses a *paenitentiale*.[5] At the same time however, Theodulph of Orleans was one of the first to object to the penitentials on the grounds that penances should be performed according to the canons of the fathers rather than to human caprice.[6]

Theodulph's view was by 813 widely held among the frankish clergy, for the reform councils of that year condemned the penitential books in no uncertain terms, and these, incidentally, summarise the prevailing attitudes towards the administration of penance at the time.

> In many places the doing of penance according to the ancient institution of the canons has lapsed from use and neither is the ancient custom of reconciliation observed . . . let help be sought from the lord emperor that if anyone sins publicly he may be punished by public penance and be excommunicated and reconciled in accordance with his deserts and according to the order of the canons . . . Moreover, the measure of penance to those who confess their sins ought to be imposed . . . either by the institution of the ancient canons or by the authority of the holy scriptures, or by ecclesiastical custom . . . the booklets which they call penitentials being repudiated and utterly cast out, of which the errors are certain, the authors not.[7]

The synod of Paris was even more emphatic in its condemnation, urging the bishops to seek out these erroneous booklets and consign them to the flames, lest through them unskilled priests deceive men.[8]

The main objection to the penitentials appears to have been to their illegitimate and undoubtedly foreign origin, for the penitentials were

---

[4] *Interrogationis examinationis*, cap 3, and *Quae a presbiteri discenda sint*, cap 7, *MGH Cap* I, pp 234–5.

[5] For example, Haito of Basle, *Statuta* cap 6, *MGH Cap* I, p 365 *et seq*, Gerbald of Liege, *Statuta* cap 8, *MGH Cap* I, pp 243, and the statutes contained in the 'Freising' manuscript cap 32, ed Emil Seckel, 'Studien zu Benedictus Levita, II' *Neues Archiv*, 27 (Hanover/Leipzig 1904) pp 386–93.

[6] Theodulph of Orleans, *Statuta Secundum*, section III, ed Carlo de Clercq, *La Legislation Religieuse Franque depuis Clovis à Charlemagne* (Paris/Louvain 1935) pp 378–80. Although the authenticity of the latter part of this *Statuta* is in doubt, it is reasonably certain that this particular section is by Theodulph.

[7] *Concilium Cabillonensis* (813) caps 23–5, 28, *MGH Conc* II, i pp 278–81, and compare *Concilium Mettensis* (813) cap 53, *ibid* p 272, *Concilium Arelatensis* (813) cap 26, *ibid* p. 253 and *Concilium Rhemensis* (813) cap 16, *ibid* p 225.

[8] *Concilium Parisiensis* (829) cap 32, *MGH Conc* II, ii p 633.

an irish import. Indeed their rejection could be another instance of the xenophobic tendencies of the Franks.[9] At first there was some attempt to replace the *libelli poenitentiali* by a work of the same type. Such a work was produced by bishop Halitgar of Cambrai at the request of Ebbo of Rheims in about 830. Halitgar included his penitential, which he claims to have taken *ex scrinio Romanae ecclesiae*, as the sixth book of his *De Vitiis et Virtutibus et de Ordine Paenitentium Libri Quinque*.[10] Although this claim to roman origins was more likely to have been an attempt to give a more authoritative veneer to his collection rather than to be a statement of fact, Halitgar's work represents in fact the last overt attempt on the part of the frankish church to provide on an official basis for the practice of private penance according to the methods implied in the penitentials, and can be seen as a transitional work between the anonymous collections of penitential canons we are about to discuss and the more formal works on ecclesiastical discipline such as Hrabanus Maurus's *De Institutione Clericorum* and Regino of Prum's *De Disciplina Ecclesiastica*.

In due course, as part of the wish to reassert the authority of older conciliar decisions on ecclesiastical and secular discipline, the practice of public penance as it had been observed in the early christian centuries was prescribed once more, although a distinction was preserved between public and private penance, as we observed for example in the canons from the reform councils of 813.[11] Hrabanus Maurus, writing in about 840, also distinguished between public penance for crimes committed publicly and the private penance to be undergone for private sins.[12] Provision for an enhancement of the bishop's powers as well as the now standard practice of public penance can be seen in Hincmar's statement; *quod presbiteri curari debeant ut publici peccatores poenitentiam accipiant et episcopo referre quomodo illam agant*, made in his episcopal statutes issued in 852.[13] A further objection to the penitentials therefore must have been the enhanced spiritual powers with

---

[9] On some instances of the antipathy felt towards the Irish see Bernhard Bischoff, 'Theodulph und der Ire Cadac-Andreas' *Mittelalterlicher Studien*, 2 (Stuttgart 1967).

[10] Halitgar of Cambrai, *De Vitiis et Virtutibus et de Ordine Paenitentium Libri Quinque*, PL 105, (1851) cols 664 *et seq*.

[11] see n 7 above.

[12] Hrabanus Maurus, *De videndo Deum, de puritate cordis et modo poenitentiae; De quaestionibus canonum poenitentialium, and* in particular see the prefatory letter, addressed to Otgar, of the *Poenitentium Liber*, cap I, PL 112 (1852) cols 1262–1431, particularly col 1400.

[13] Hincmar of Rheims, *Statuta* (852) cap 4, *Mansi*, 15, col 491.

33

which they endowed the ordinary priest, rather than preserving it as a bishop's prerogative to pronounce absolution as it had been in the gallo-roman church. A further refinement is added, again by Hincmar, in his discussion of the adultery of count Stephen of Auvergne in 860. Hincmar concluded that Stephen for his own sake should make private confession and do secret penance, but for the welfare of the souls of all the people he should be made an example of, and perform public penance as well.[14] This public ritual of penance was as it had been observed in the time of Caesarius of Arles, and private penance, in accord with the wishes of the reformers, was based on the more ancient canons of the church contained in such collections as the *Statuta ecclesia antiqua*, the *collectio Hispana* and the *Dionysio-Hadriana*, as well as in the innumerable canonical collections of the carolingian period itself.

The penitentials, therefore, were an ephemeral and ultimately despised intrusion into the frankish church. A detailed description of the many different manuscripts and recensions cannot be attempted here, but some suggestions can be put forward about the material and the problems it presents. As well as being a further example of the generally unsophisticated theological writing of the eighth and ninth centuries, the penitential books themselves were part of the development in the sixth and seventh centuries towards more frequent and private penance, and are closely linked with the habit of spiritual examination common among monks and ascetics. Side by side with the development of penitential practice was the appearance of theories of morality and treatises on the vices and virtues, the most influential of which were John Cassian's tabulation of the eight principal vices, *superbia, luxuria, avaritia, ira, invidia, tristitia* and *accedia*,[15] and the battle between the vices and virtues described by Gregory the Great.[16] These moral treatises seem to have influenced the structure of the penitentials.

The earliest penitential books were designed to serve monastic communities, and it is now generally agreed that they originated in the British Isles, possibly among the British in Wales in the sixth century, while we owe the oldest and most complete books and the fullest development of the penitential system to the Irish.[17] The most influen-

---

[14] Hincmar, ep 136, *MGH Epp* VIII.

[15] John Cassian, *De Coenobiorum Institutione*, bk V, *De Spiritu Gastrimargiae*, cap 1, *PL* 49 (1846) cols 202–3.

[16] Gregory the Great, *Moralium Libri sive Expositio in Librum Beati Job*, bk XXXI, cap xlv, *PL* 76 (1849) col 621.

[17] The irish penitentials have now been edited and translated with an excellent introduction by [Ludwig] Bieler, [*The Irish Penitentials*,] *Scriptores Latini Hiberniae*, 5 (Dublin 1963).

tial among the Irish documents are the sixth century work ascribed to
Vinnian, and the seventh century compilation of Cummean the Long.
The Irish missionaries introduced their system to the Anglo-Saxons,
the penitential of Theodore being the most important.[18] Both Irish and
Anglo-Saxons imported the system and the books to the continent
where the late sixth century work of Colombanus was written. The
later 'frankish', collections are almost wholly dependent on irish and
anglo-saxon sources. Indeed, all these manuscripts of penitentials written
and used on the continent are in insular script or in continental hands
revealing insular symptoms.[19] The manuscript evidence is our sole
witness to the popularity and dissemination of these handbooks throughout the eighth century, for they are only referred to in other sources in
the ninth century.

In their printed form, the editions of the 'frankish' penitentials made
by Wasserschleben[20] and by Schmitz[21] are virtually our sole source for
the material and are still indispensible.[22] Schmitz's work however,
despite the many more manuscripts he was able to examine, is a little
marred by his determination to attribute roman origins to the canons
and his inconsistent dating, but more significantly by his misleading
entitulation of different manuscript collections as if each were a new
individual penitential, rather than a further variant collection of penitential canons. Unfortunately, later work on the subject has preserved
these distinctions, so that although valuable investigations of the
sources of canons,[23] their relation to secular law[24] and the development

---

[18] *The Penitential of Theodore*, A. W. Haddan and W. Stubbs, *Councils and Eccle-siastical Documents relating to Great Britain and Ireland* (London 1871) III, pp 173–205, and P. W. Finsterwalder, *Die Canones Theodori Cantuariensis und ihre Ueberlieferungs Formen* (Weimar 1929).

[19] See Bieler, introduction, and [John T.] McNeill and [Helena] Gamer, [*Mediaeval Handbooks of Penance,*] *Records of Civilisation, Sources and Studies*, 29 (Columbia, New York 1938) p 64.

[20] F. W. H. Wasserschleben, *Die Bussordnungen der Abendländischen Kirche* (Halle 1851).

[21] [H. J.] Schmitz, *Die Bussbucher [und das Kanonische Bussverfahren nach Hand-schriften Quellen]* (Düsseldorf 1898) and *Die Bussbucher und die Bussdisciplin der Kirche* (Mainz 18–83).

[22] A selection and translation of many of the collections of penitential canons dealt with by Wasserschleben and Schmitz was made by McNeill and Gamer.

[23] See in particular P. Fournier, 'Etudes sur les penitentiels' *Revue d'Histoire et de Littérature Religieuses*, 6 (Paris 1901) pp 289–317; 7 (1902) pp 59–70; 8 (1903) pp 528–53; 9 (1904) pp 97–103; and W. von Hormann, 'Bussbucher Studien' *ZSR, KA* (1911–14).

[24] For example, T. Oakley, *English Penitential Discipline and Anglo-Saxon Law in Their Joint Influence* (New York 1923).

of the commutation system[25] have been made, the fundamental confusion remains. It would seem that were the established nomenclature abandoned along with the urge to postulate an archetypal manuscript or an author-compiler for a particular collection, some sense could perhaps be made of the welter of manuscripts extant, for their distribution and provenance alone can tell us a great deal about the practice of penance in a particular area, and, further, provide us with more valuable evidence of the extent of irish influence on and contribution to the development of medieval european society.

The structure of the 'frankish' collections suggests some lines of procedure for dealing with this material for they can be roughly divided into two groups according to their principal sources.

The first group includes the collection known as the Pseudo-Cummean or *Excarpsus Cummeani*, which was probably the form in which the irish penitentials attained their greatest popularity in Europe[26] being as it was a composite production drawn from the penitentials of Cummean, the *Bigotianum*, Theodore, Gildas and Colombanus, as well as a few early conciliar decrees such as those of the council of Ancyra concerning incest. The collections known as the *Rheims*, *Vindobonensis*, *Vigilanus* and *Dacheriana* penitentials, the *Canones Gregorii* and the twenty-six untitled manuscripts containing variants, omissions and additions can be included in the Pseudo-Cummean group.[27] Most of these texts begin with the opening words from the prologue of Cummean, *Diversitas culparum diversitatem facit poenitentiarum . . .*, and some also include the sermon on the twelve remissions of sins attributed to Caesarius of Arles. Often both a heavier and a lighter penalty from different sources for the same sin are enjoined. For example a canon from the *Excarpsus-Cummeani* reads, *qui dimiserit uxorem suam alteri coniungens se, VII annos peniteat cum tribulatione vel XV levius peniteat*.[28]

The second group of manuscripts is more obviously organised on what Schmitz defined as a 'tripartite' basis, each being divided into three sections dependent on Cummean, Theodore and canons from gallo-roman and african councils respectively. In this group can be included those collections referred to as the Martene, Merseburg,

---

[25] C. Vogel, 'Composition legale et commutations dans le système de la penitence tarifée', *Revue du Droit Canonique*, 8 (Strasbourg 1958) pp 289–318; 9 (1959) pp 1–39 and 341–59.

[26] Pseudo-Cummean, ed Schmitz, *Die Bussbucher*, and see J. F. Kenney, *The Sources for the Early History of Ireland* (New York 1929) p 243.

[27] For a handlist of these manuscripts see McNeill and Gamer, pp 432–50.

[28] Pseudo-Cummean, ed Schmitz, *Die Bussbucher* cap V, xxx.

Valicellanum Primum and Valicellanum Secundum, S. Hubert, Bobbio, Fleury, Paris, Burgundy, Tripartite Saint Gall, the Thirty-five chapters and the so-called 'roman' penitential of Halitgar of Cambrai. Again there are many variations within these collections, and it is difficult to determine to what extent the variation in organisation and inclusion of canons concerning particular offences is due merely to the vagaries of a particular scribe rather than to a conscious intention to produce a wholly new book. Some idea of a scribe's methods can be seen in the tripartite Saint Gall penitential, where the first chapter deals with the subject of homicide, then halfway through the second chapter on marriage and related topics there is suddenly a subheading, *interum de homicidiis*, and two canons follow which are important ones appearing in most collections, as if the scribe had suddenly realised that he had forgotten to include these canons and hastily put them in.

The carolingian genius could be said to be the synthesis they made of the diverse elements of their intellectual, religious and social heritage, and certainly their cheerful plagiarism is particularly evident in the penitential literature. Their innovation to the genre was the incorporation of canons from earlier church councils, and this in itself could point to a later date of compilation than the Pseudo-Cummean group, for the preoccupation with older canons and decrees belongs to the ecclesiastical climate of the ninth century, reflecting the Carolingian's characteristic predilection for the sanction of patristic or pseudo-patristic authority which achieved its most audacious expression in the eponymously termed Pseudo-Isidorean decretals.[29] Dating and placing of the penitential collections would however have to be far more precise than at present for a development to be traced. Although no 'primary' text is proposed, there was undoubtedly a common pool of disciplinary canons, as well as the definitive irish and anglo-saxon collections upon which the different compilers could draw. Further work on these collections may be able to establish one text or group of texts which suggest a pattern of dissemination, and deducing from the tendency towards the more frequent recurrence of lighter penalties

---

[29] Much could and still needs to be said about the relation between the penitential collections, the *Canones Hibernenses* and the Pseudo-Isidorean decretals. Many important comments can be found in P. Fournier and G. le Bras, *Histoire des Collections Canoniques en Occident, depuis les Fausses Decretales jusqu'au decret de Gratian* (Paris 1931), Emil Seckel's series of articles on Benedictus Levita in *Neues Archiv* (Hanover/Leipzig 1899-1932), and now more recently, H. Fuhrmann, *Einfluss und Verbreitung der Pseudoisidorschen Dekretalsammlung* (Munich 1972).

in (possibly) later texts, provide a more precise picture both of the development of penitential discipline and of the social conditions of the time.

It would appear therefore that the most that can be said decisively about the 'frankish' penitentials at this stage is that they were the compilations of various individual scribes designed for practical use by the priest for his flock, in order to fill a real need for some authoritative corpus of ecclesiastical discipline and a guide to social behaviour in a small community, at a time when there was little written secular law and no cohesive and strong government, and when the frankish church as a missionary church had to struggle hard to combat the disruptive and the pagan elements in the society which it had set out to make christian.

The tendency of the *libelli poenitentiali* to reduce the performance of penance to a mere external mechanical act no doubt made the reformers among the frankish clergy anxious to reassert the spiritual sincerity of confession and repentance. The desire for deeper spirituality and self-awareness was met by other theological writings of the period, while the need for outward disciplinary legislation was also met from other sources, not only by the secular law codes and collections of canon law, but also in the capitularies and conciliar decrees, synodal legislation and episcopal statutes of the frankish church. Quite simply, the penitentials became old-fashioned. For a church anxious to establish a general and uniform system of ecclesiastical organisation and discipline over the whole kingdom, with one eye cast backward to the practices of the early christian church, and towards the Rome of its own day, the penitential books in their variety and multiplicity, external signs of particularism and dispersed authority as they were, were rapidly superseded. Lacking the weight of recognised sanctions, their life was short. Indeed it seems to be a feature of new laws that on being introduced they require the sanction of an older and earlier authority to ensure their success.[30]

Due, therefore, to the determined and ultimately successful effort on the part of the frankish clergy to be rid of the penitentials, these booklets are a negative source for the history of the carolingian church, in the sense that their chief significance is that the clergy found them so antipathetic to their purposes and ideals. Yet their fate as well as their content are worthy of attention, for as moral guides and handbooks

[30] R. Sprandel, 'Über das Problem neuen Rechts im früheren Mittelalter', *ZSR, KA*, 48 (1962) pp 117–37, has some interesting things to say in this respect.

with a limited circulation and of dubious reputation, handbooks designed for the use of priests of rudimentary education, whose principal means for the moral training of his *fideles* remained the sermon and the parish school, the 'frankish' penitentials were an important and necessary stage in the development of medieval church and society.

RITUAL AND REALITY IN THE EARLY
MEDIEVAL *ORDINES*

by JANET L. NELSON

T O know what was generally believed in all ages, the way is to consult the liturgies, not any private man's writings.' John Selden's maxim, which surely owed much to his own pioneering work as a liturgist, shows a shrewd appreciation of the significance of the medieval *ordines* for the consecration of kings.[1] Thanks to the more recent efforts of Waitz, Eichmann, Schramm[2] and others, this material now forms part of the medievalist's stock in trade; and much has been written on the evidence which the *ordines* provide concerning the nature of kingship, and the interaction of church and state, in the middle ages.[3] The usefulness of the *ordines* to the historian might therefore seem to need no further demonstration or qualification. But there is another

I am grateful to professor Walter Ullmann for first showing me the importance of the *ordines*, to professor Dorothy Whitlock for her generous help on several points relating to tenth-century England, and to John Gillingham for his always stimulating criticism.

[1] The quotation is from Selden's *Table-Talk* (London 1689) under 'Liturgy'. His great work on liturgy, *Titles of Honor*, was first published in 1614. I have used the third edition of 1672.

[2] G. Waitz, 'Die Formeln der deutschen Königs-und der Römischen Kaiser-Krönung vom zehnten bis zum zwölften Jahrhundert', in *Abhandlungen der Königlichen Gesellschaft der Wissenschaften zu Göttingen*, 18 (1873); [E.] Eichmann, 'Königs—und Bischofsweihe', in *Sitzungsberichte der bayrischen Akademie der Wissenschaften. Phil. Hist. Klasse*, Abh. 6 (Munich 1928), and many other articles; P. E. Schramm, *A History of the English Coronation* (Oxford 1937), *Der König von Frankreich* (2 ed Weimar 1960), *Herrschaftszeichen und Staatssymbolik* (3 vols Stuttgart 1954-6), various articles on the west frankish, anglo-saxon, and german *ordines*, originally published during the 1930s, now conveniently reprinted in vols II and III of his collected papers, *K[aiser,] K[önige und] P[äpste]* (Stuttgart 1968). The imperial *ordines* have been edited by R. Elze, *Ordines Coronationis Imperialis, MGH Fontes Iuris Germanici Antiqui*, 9 (Hanover 1960). But only royal *ordines* will come under consideration below.

[3] See, for example, R. W. Southern, *The Making of the Middle Ages* (London 1953) pp 97 *et seq*; W. Ullmann, *P[rinciples of] G[overnment and] P[olitics in the Middle Ages]* (London 1961) pp 129 *et seq*; *The Carolingian Renaissance and the Idea of Kingship* (London 1969) pp 101 *et seq*; B. Tierney, *The Crisis of Church and State* (Englewood Cliffs 1964) pp 25 *et seq*; J. M. Wallace-Hadrill, *Early Germanic Kingship in England and on the Continent* (Oxford 1971) pp 133 *et seq*.

side to the coin. The value of the early medieval *ordines* can be, not perhaps overestimated, but misconstrued. 'The liturgies' may indeed tell us 'what was generally believed'—but we must first be sure that we know how they were perceived and understood by their participants, as well as by their designers. They need to be correlated with other sources, and as often as possible with 'private writings' too, before the full picture becomes intelligible.

Amongst the various materials for early medieval king-makings, such as laws, charters, chronicles, and sometimes literature or hagiography, the *ordines* occupy a singular position. As liturgical texts, they belong to a type of historical record not normally used by general historians: thus their limitations, and the special problems of interpretation which they present, have not always been clearly recognised. If we are to 'consult' them with profit, we should consult liturgical scholarship also. With this in mind, I want briefly to consider certain aspects of the *ordines* which seem to bear on their value as historical material. I shall select most of my illustrations from the anglo-saxon *ordines*, because these texts are most easily available, and probably most familiar, in this country.[4]

The *ordines*, by their very nature, are far from providing complete or accurate records of specific actual king makings. They are incomplete because they cover only the intra-ecclesiastical part of the process of installation. Sometimes, fortunately, some other source survives to fill in details of the ritual procedures outside the church. Perhaps the best-known example is Widukind's account of Otto I's inauguration in 936.[5] But for some tenth-century anglo-saxon cases comparable information can be pieced together. We can be fairly sure, for instance, in the light of a charter apparently issued by king Eadred just after his consecration in 946, that the liturgical rite was then preceded by a formal election in which magnates from all over the realm took part.[6]

---

[4] Thanks especially to the publications of the *H[enry] B[radshaw] S[ociety]*. For the anglo-saxon *ordines* discussed below, the relevant editions are those of *The Lanalet Pontifical*, by G. H. Doble HBS 74 (for 1937); *The Benedictional of Archbishop Robert*, by H. Wilson, HBS 24 (for 1903); *Three Coronation Orders*, by J. Wickham Legg, HBS 19 (for 1900); *The Claudius Pontificals*, by D. H. Turner, HBS 97 (for 1964, publ 1971). Other editions will be cited below. As yet, unfortunately, there is no complete edition of the english *ordines*.

[5] Widukind, *Rerum Gestarum Saxonicarum Libri Tres*, ed H. E. Lohmann, rev P. Hirsch (Hanover 1935) pp 64 *et seq*.

[6] W. G. Birch, *Cartularium Saxonicum*, 3 vols (London 1885–93) no 815. This charter, dated 946, is translated with an excellent commentary by D. Whitelock, *English Historical Documents*, I (London 1955) pp 508 *et seq*. The presence

Again, two pieces of hagiography, the *Vita Dunstani* for 956, and the *Vita Oswaldi* for 973, show that the feast which followed the consecration had major significance in the series of legitimating acts.[7] Yet the *ordo* used in mid tenth-century England says nothing of the prior election outside the church, and mentions the feast only in the laconic concluding line: *Post pergant ad mensam*.[8] The *ordo* used in 973 opens with the king leaving the *conventus seniorum*, but does not elucidate the significance of this meeting, which I take to have involved a formal election by the Witan; and it says nothing at all about the feast.[9]

Many of the earliest *ordines* are scarcely more than lists of prayers. The king's consecration in the early tenth-century *Leofric Missal*, for example, which may well represent the earliest *ordo* to be used for a west saxon king, consists of seven prayers linked by rubrics which in most cases are no more explicit than *Benedictio* or *Alia*.[10] This layout represents an early phase in the development of such major rites as royal consecration or episcopal ordination. Only the broad structure was fixed, the details being left to the clerics who stage-managed each individual occasion. In the case of the bishop's rite, a letter written by Hincmar of Rheims provides details of an actual performance, and we can see how the bare bones of the texts in a ninth-century pontifical

---

of northumbrian magnates and welsh princes at Eadred's inauguration may be inferred from the witness-list.

[7] *Vita Dunstani* (Auctore 'B') ed W. Stubbs in *Memorials of St Dunstan RS* (1874) p 32; *Vita Oswaldi* ed J. Raine in *Historians of the Church of York*, RS (1879) I, pp 437 *et seq*, this passage reprinted in Schramm, *KKP*, II, pp 241 *et seq*. On the significance of the feast, see K. Hauck, 'Rituelle Speisegemeinschaft im 10. und 11. Jht.', in *Studium Generale*, III (Heidelberg 1950) pp 611 *et seq*.

[8] See P. L. Ward, 'An early version [of the Anglo-Saxon coronation ceremony]', in *EHR*, 57 (1942) pp 345 *et seq*, at p 358. I hope to show elsewhere that this *ordo* represents mid-tenth-century usage. For the priority of this *ordo* over that of 973, see Ward, 'The coronation ceremony in medieval England', in *Speculum*, 14 (1939) pp 160 *et seq*, at pp 169 *et seq*. Compare the earlier view of J. A. Robinson, 'The coronation order in the tenth century', in *JTS*, 19 (1917) pp 56 *et seq*.

[9] The text is most conveniently consulted in Schramm, *KKP*, II, pp 233 *et seq*, at p 239, showing manuscript variants. See also the text of BM Cotton Claudius Aiii, in Turner's edition, pp 89 and 94. For the association of this *ordo* with 973, see Schramm, *KKP*, II, pp 180 *et seq*; and the more convincing arguments of C. A. Bouman, *S[acring and] C[rowning]* (Groningen 1957) p 18 and n 1. Some of the objections raised by H. C. Richardson and G. Sayles, *The Governance of Medieval England* (Edinburgh 1963) pp 397 *et seq* have been answered by E. John, *Orbis Britanniae* (Leicester 1966) pp 276 *et seq*.

[10] Ed F. E. Warren (Oxford 1883) pp 230 *et seq*, the *ordo* reprinted in Schramm, *KKP*, II, pp 223 *et seq*. See also Bouman, *SC*, pp 167 *et seq*.

would be fleshed out in liturgical practice.¹¹ As for the 'Leofric' *ordo*, fortunately later manuscripts give fuller rubrical directions which seem to represent the way the rite was originally performed.¹² In the later middle ages, the *ordines* have increasingly detailed rubrics, prescribing, for example, the king's behaviour during the period preceding his consecration, the procession from palace to church, and the concluding feast.¹³ But no *ordo* before the thirteenth century gives anything like an account of the ritual procedures as a whole.

In view of these severe limitations, the early medieval *ordines* might seem far less useful as historical sources than the later elaborate and explicit texts. But a further important consideration partly redresses the balance: it was in the early middle ages, particularly in the ninth and tenth centuries, that the first royal *ordines*, which decisively shaped all their successors, were actually composed. For this period alone, therefore, they are contemporary witnesses in the strict sense. The conservatism of scribes, and the universal, timeless and normative character of liturgy in general, ensured that an *ordo* would go on being copied out and used at times and places often far removed from those of its original composition.¹⁴ Indeed only quite rarely is it possible to date precisely the genesis of a prayer-text, or even a complete *ordo*. The clergy designing a rite for a specific royal consecration usually preferred to follow the main lines of a received indigenous tradition. But sometimes, as for instance when the practice of royal consecration itself was being introduced in a given realm, an imported *ordo* might

---

¹¹ Hincmar's letter to Adventius of Metz has been edited and well-discussed by M. Andrieu, 'Le sacre épiscopal d'après Hincmar de Reims', in *RHE*, 48 (1953) pp 22 *et seq*. The best general introduction to this subject is to be found in Bouman, *SC*, part II, esp pp 70 *et seq*.
¹² See Schramm, *KKP*, II, pp 223 *et seq*. I have argued for a ninth-century dating for the whole *ordo* in my unpublished Cambridge dissertation, *Rituals of Royal Inauguration in Early Medieval Europe* (Cambridge 1967) cap 5.
¹³ See, for example, the *ordo* of Burgundy, ed E. Eichmann, 'Die sogenannte römische Königskrönungsformel', in *Historisches Jahrbuch*, 45 *Jahrbuch*, 45 (Cologne 1925) pp 518 *et seq*. I cannot agree with L. Böhm, 'Rechtsformen und Rechtstitel der burgundischen Konigserhebungen im 9.Jht.', in *Historisches Jahrbuch*, 80 (1961) pp 27 *et seq*, that the text of this *ordo* as it survives in manuscripts of the thirteenth and fourteenth centuries represents ninth-century practice. Two later medieval english *ordines* may be found in the fourteenth-century *Liber Regalis*, ed L. G. Wickham Legg, *English Coronation Records* (Westminster 1901) pp 81 *et seq*, and in the fifteenth-century *Liber Regie Capelle*, ed W. Ullmann (*HBS*, 92 for 1959, publ 1961) pp 74 *et seq* and introduction, pp 22 *et seq*.
¹⁴ See A. Baumstark, *Comparative Liturgy*, rev B. Botte, new ed and trans F. L. Cross (Oxford 1958); and Bouman, *SC*, pp 55 *et seq*, 79 *et seq*.

be used; or partial revisions might be made in a traditional text. In such a case, the *ordo* clearly would not reveal 'what was generally believed' in quite the same sense as it would in its original context of time and place.

The point is illustrated by an *ordo* which survives in more than a dozen french pontificals copied during the central and later middle ages, including the splendid *Coronation Book* of Charles V (1365). Here, in the anointing prayer itself, is a reference to the 'sceptres of the Saxons, Mercians and Northumbrians.'[15] John Selden was moved to indignation: 'The negligence or forgetfulness that left these names in were almost incredible if we saw it not'.[16] Perhaps he asked himself in what conceivable sense these words in a fourteenth-century French liturgy revealed anything of 'what was generally believed' in fourteenth-century France! What they do reveal is, first that they were added to the anointing prayer originally in England, in the mid tenth century (though not a single anglo-saxon manuscript has survived to witness this), and second, that for the french scribes who copied them, and for the archbishops of Rheims who pronounced them, contemporary political relevance mattered not a straw. For the mention of the Saxons, Mercians and Northumbrians had nothing to do with french dynastic claims to the realms of the english king:[17] the names appear already in french manuscripts of the eleventh and twelfth centuries, and I doubt whether even then their original meaning was understood in France. Nevertheless they are not without meaning. Long after the topical reference to anglo-saxon hegemonial rulership had been forgotten, the solemn copying out of these time honoured words in french manuscripts signified the profound respect of the later middle ages for ritual tradition, precisely observed. The medium itself had become the message.

Similar questions of meaning are raised by the formal similarities which by the close of the tenth century had come to exist between royal and episcopal consecration-rites.[18] It may seem tempting to

[15] The manuscripts are listed by Ward, 'An early version', pp 347 *et seq*, with the 'SMN' variant at p 352 (and n 6). The *Coronation Book* of Charles V has been edited by E. S. Dewick (*HBS*, 16 for 1899), with the variant at p 27.

[16] *Titles of Honor* Bk I, c 8, p 177. Selden quite rightly saw that the names must have been 'without question taken out of some Saxon ceremonial'.

[17] As used to be surmised: see the note by Dewick in his edition, p 80. These names seem to have reappeared at french royal consecrations for as long as the ancien régime lasted.

[18] See Eichmann, 'Königs-und Bischofsweihe'.

regard these as expressions of an ideology which drew constant parallels between the offices of king and bishop and in which kingship was delineated, in terms of a hierocratic doctrine, as the church's executive arm. While not wishing to deny that such significance may perhaps be discerned in some cases, I suggest that many of these parallels manifest 'laws' of liturgical development which governed the elaboration of major rites. For instance, the practice of beginning rites of personal consecration with the prostration of the initiate before the altar affected monastic profession and, later, the wedding service, as well as royal and episcopal consecrations.[19] Not surprisingly, status-changing rites were felt to have a common character in as much as they were the means by which an individual assumed a new social personality. As the preliminary to such a transformation prostration was surely more than 'a gesture of deepest humility and contrition'[20] or 'a supplication;'[21] it symbolised the annihilation of the initiate's former personality in preparation for 'rebirth' into a new status. If, therefore, we find prostration specified before the consecrations of both king and bishop in the tenth century, this might be attributed to a trend in liturgical technique rather than to some ideologically motivated direct borrowing from the episcopal to the royal rite. Other kinds of elaboration can also be referred to the exigencies of actual performance, and as C. A. Bouman observed, 'the *horror vacui* has always been an active factor in the development of the liturgy.'[22]

As a final example of the difficulty of interpreting the texts of the *ordines*, the prayer, *Sta et retine* is worth considering. It seems to have been composed in west Francia early in the tenth century as part of a complete series of seven prayers. Ever since it was brilliantly identified by Carl Erdmann, this 'Seven-Forms' *ordo* has been regarded as unusually rich in political ideas.[23] *Sta et retine*, in particular, refers to the

---

[19] See E. H. Kantorowicz, *Laudes Regiae* (Berkeley 1946) p 36, n 89, and p 90, n 84; Bouman, *SC*, pp 147 *et seq*; K. Ritzer, *Formen, Riten und religiöses Brauchtum der Eheschliessung in den christlichen Kirchen des ersten Jahrtausends* (Münster 1962) p 258. The similarities between status changing rites were first pointed out by A. van Gennep, *The Rites of Passage*, trans M. Vizedom and G. L. Caffee (Chicago 1960).

[20] Kantorowicz, *Laudes Regiae*, p. 91

[21] Bouman, *SC*, p 148.

[22] *Ibid* p 147.

[23] C. Erdmann, *Forschungen zur politischen Ideenwelt des Frühmittelaters* (Berlin) 1951 pp 56 *et seq*, and his edition of the *ordo*, pp 87 *et seq*. See also Schramm's interpretation: 'die Auffassung des Königtums in die Otto I hineingewachsen ist' (—still believing the *ordo* to be a German composition of *c* 960) in his article of

king as *mediator cleri et plebis* in an explicit analogy with Christ's function as *mediator Dei et hominum*, but at the same time, the ritually-superior status of the clergy is emphasised: . . . *quanto clerum sacris altaribus propinquiorem prospicis, tanto ei potiorem in locis congruis honorem impendere memineris.* It seems to me misleading, however, to interpret this prayer solely by reference to its *verbal* content, as an exposition of 'pure' ideology, hincmarian, ottonian, theocratic or what you will. This, after all, is a prayer with a precise ritual function: it is, as Bouman recognised, the sole surviving text specifically designed for the enthronement of the king. Now enthronement may well have been the central act in royal inaugurations before these came under ecclesiastical influence;[24] and it seems likely that, even as late as the tenth century, lay *principes* as well as the officiating bishops continued to take part in this ritual, as they undoubtedly did in the acclamations which followed.[25] In the *ordo* used in tenth-century England, *Sta et retine* appears at the enthronement, immediately after which the king exercises his newly assumed powers in the issue of a three point 'programme' of good government aimed at the welfare of 'the church and the whole Christian people.' Appropriately, therefore, the next and final act of the liturgical drama is the people's three-fold shout, *vivat rex*, in recognition of the new king.[26] The significance assigned to the prayer *Sta et retine* must be compatible with this ritual corollary. From the standpoint of the lay subjects who witnessed it, the enthronement clearly signified the king's installation as holder of an office defined by tradition, in the interests of the 'christian people', and with duties more in evidence than rights and powers. We need constantly to recall that the consecration-rite involved more than the merely verbal component which we can read on the manuscript or printed page: it was replete with audio-visual, and even olfactory,[27] aids, by means of which communication extended to the illiterate lay participants.

1935, now reprinted in *KKP*, III, pp 81 *et seq*. Compare the views of Kantorowicz, [*The*] *K[ing's]* *T[wo]* *B[odies]* (Princeton 1957) p 88; Ullmann, *PGP*, pp 130, 142 *et seq*, and 'Der Souveränitätsgedanke in den mittelalterlichen Krönungsordines', in *Festschrift P. E. Schramm* (Wiesbaden 1964) pp 81 *et seq*; Bouman, SC, pp 137 *et seq*.

[24] See R. Schmidt, 'Zur Geschichte des fränkischen Königsthrons', in *Frühmittelalterliche Studien*, II (Berlin 1968) pp 45 *et seq*.

[25] This is the arrangement envisaged in the 'Leofric', and related, *ordines*. See above p 43 n 10.

[26] For the text, see Ward, 'An early version', p 357.

[27] For the aromatic ingredients in chrism, see P. Hofmeister, *Die heiligen Öle in der morgen-und abendlandischen Kirche* (Würzburg 1948) pp 25 *et seq*.

Once the church performed such essential symbolic acts as investiture and enthronement, the whole king making ritual assumed a strongly clerical colouring. But to view this as a kind of hierocratic take over bid, to term it a 'clericalisation' of kingship,[28] is to risk misrepresenting early medieval reality. In support of a rather different view. I should like to relate the process of *Liturgiesierung*[29] to the general problem of the *ordines'* significance in terms of political ideas.

The clerical performance of the intra-ecclesiastical rites of king making, in particular of the anointing patterned after the biblical *unctio in regem*,[30] certainly resulted from a differentiation of roles within christian society. The clergy were now believed to be uniquely qualified to operate with the symbols that bridged the gulf between the material world of time and flux and the celestial world of the unseen, unchanging, eternal. The practical manifestation of this belief was that the laity confided, and the clergy willingly assumed, specialist ritual functions. The anglo-saxon evidence, at least, suggests no conflict of interests here. The aspect of tenth-century king makings which seems to be of paramount importance is the expression, and presumably the reinforcement, of solidarity between officiants and witnesses, between ruler and ruled. The clearest indication of this is the presence within the *ordo* of a royal commitment to certain recognised norms of right government. We have already noticed the three point 'programme' of one tenth-century rite. In the *ordo* of 973, the formulation shifts from that of a three part command issued by the newly enthroned king, to that of a three fold promise made by the king as the preliminary, and condition, of his consecration.[31] The constitutional implications of this change have been stressed often enough.[32] But perhaps just as

---

[28] Kantorowicz, *KTB*, p 89. Compare the penetrating comments of R. Nineham, 'The so-called Anonymous of York', in *JEH* 14 (1963) pp 31 *et seq* at p 41 *et seq*.

[29] This term was used by O. Treitinger, *Die Oströmische Kaiser-und Reichsidee nach ihrer Gestaltung im höfischen Zeremoniell* (Jena 1938) pp 233 *et seq*, with reference to developments in Byzantium. It is hard to think of an elegant english translation.

[30] See J. De Pange, *Le Roi très chrétien* (Paris 1949); Kantorowicz, *Laudes Regiae*, pp 56 *et seq*; A. R. Johnson, *Sacral Kingship in Ancient Israel* (Cardiff 1955) pp 12 *et seq*.

[31] For the text, see Schramm, *KKP*, II, p 235.

[32] See Schramm, *History of the English Coronation*, pp 179 *et seq*; M. David, 'Le serment du sacre du IXe au XVe siècle. Contribution a l'étude des limites juridiques de la souveraineté', in *Revue du Moyen Age Latin*, 6 (Lyons 1950), p 144 *et seq*. F. Kern, *Gottesg nadentum und Widerstandsrecht im früheren Mittelalter*, rev R. Buchner (2 ed Münster 1954), anhang 14, pp 304 *et seq*, tried (in my view unsuccessfully) to obliterate the distinction between precept and promise. See also Bouman, *SC*, pp 144 *et seq*.

striking as the difference of form is the identity of content between the earlier *mandatum* and the later *promissio*. If the king is the subject of both acts, the recipient of both is also identical: the *populus christianus*.

But the full significance of the introduction of a fully fledged oath in the later tenth century is not apparent in the *ordines* texts themselves. Other evidence fortunately survives. The king was given a copy of the oath in anglo-saxon from which, presumably, he read out its provisions so that all the 'christian folk' present – to whom after all the commitment was given – could understand.[33] This text was then laid on the altar before which the consecration was performed. The manuscript evidence shows that the vernacular oath was linked with an address, also in anglo-saxon,[34] to the new king, exhorting him to keep his promises:

> The christian king who keeps these engagements
> earns for himself wordly honour, and the eternal
> God also is merciful to him. . . . But if he violate
> that which was promised to God, then shall it
> forthwith right soon grow worse among his people . . .

The king is reminded of his responsibility for 'the flock of which thou hast been made the shepherd in this life'. It is he who, on judgement day, will have to 'give account how thou heldest that which Christ afore purchased with his own blood'. The king's obligations are then spelt out in far more detailed and specific terms than in the *ordo* itself:

> The duty of a hallowed king is that he judge no man
> unrighteously, and that he defend and protect widows
> and orphans and strangers, that he forbid thefts . . .
> feed the needy with alms, and have old and wise men
> for counsellors, and set righteous men for stewards . . .

That an address of this type was a feature of late saxon consecrations is supported by the *Anglo-Saxon Chronicle*, MSS C and E, in its account of Edward the Confessor's inauguration in 1043:

[33] For the text, see Schramm, KKP, II pp 243 *et seq*, with references to other editions. This oath is explicitly linked with Dunstan. It was given 'at Kingston', and could relate to 975 (Edward) or 978 (Aethelred).

[34] BM Cotton Cleopatra B xiii is dated to the third quarter of the eleventh century. BM Cotton Vitellius A vii, of the first half of the eleventh century, was damaged in the fire of 1731, but a copy of it survives: Oxford Bodleian, Junius 60. In both manuscripts the address followed the oath. I quote below from the translation by Stubbs, *Memorials of St Dunstan*, pp 356 *et seq*. Professor D. Whitelock kindly drew my attention to this text.

Archbishop Eadsige consecrated him and gave him
good instructions before all the people,
and admonished him well for his own sake and for
the sake of all the people.[35]

Here the archbishop fulfils a representative function: he administers the
oath, admonishes the king, and performs the consecration, but he acts
on behalf of the whole people. They are the recipients of the oath, the
beneficiaries of its terms, the witnesses to the consecration. However
passive they might appear, their participation is vital. In their name
divine sanctions are invoked to constrain the king; and the ritual process of election, consecration and installation reaffirms the collective
interests of king, church and 'christian folk', claiming divine authorisation for the political society thus constituted.[36]

One last point can be made concerning the interpretation of the
early medieval *ordines*: they are better approached as patterns of symbols expressing the continuity and integration of society through the
kingship, than as juristic texts in which conflicting hierocratic or theocratic claims are clearly spelled out. Later, it is true, lawyers and polemicists could, and did, interpret the *ordines* in this latter sense. Much was
made, on the papalist side, of the superiority of those who blessed over
those who received blessing. On the royalist side, the norman Anonymous, finding in an ancient but still current regal benediction (probably
of merovingian origin) the prayer, *Benedic domine hunc presulem principem*, exploited the apparent conflation of episcopal and royal functions
to argue that if the king was *presul, et summus presul est, quia super alios
presules principatum habet*.[37] The frankish and anglo-saxon clerics who
continued to copy and use this prayer-text in the tenth century, when
presul had long since come to be used exclusively of episcopal office,

[35] *The Anglo-Saxon Chronicle: a Revised Translation*, ed D. Whitelock with
D. C. Douglas and S. I. Tucker (London 1961) p 107.

[36] Compare O. Gierke, *Political Theories of the Middle Age*, trans F. W. Maitland
(Cambridge 1900) p 34: 'Lordship was never merely a right; primarily it was
a duty; it was divine, but for that very reason an all the more onerous calling;
it was a public office.' M. Douglas, *Natural Symbols* (London 1970) pp 55 *et seq*
recalling Durkheim's premise 'that society and God can be equated', suggests
a correlation between the development of ritual as 'a system of control as well
as a system of communication' and the value placed on 'effective social coherence' within a given society. See also *ibid* pp 73 *et seq*, where professor
Douglas outlines the social conditions in which ritual is likely to be emphasised.

[37] All the treatises of the Anonymous, including the *De consecratione pontificum et
regum et de regimine eorum in ecclesia sancta*, are now edited by K. Pellens (Wiesbaden 1966). The quotation is from p 160 of his edition; *ibid* pp 166 *et seq*, is the

were slow to react against what should by then have appeared a sole-cism: not until 973 was the wording altered to ... *hunc praeelectum principem*, with a neat double reference to divine and human pre-selection. We must conclude that the *ordines* of the tenth century were neither conceived nor understood in precise legalistic terms, even by clerical specialists. E. H. Kantorowicz contrasted the political ideas of the early middle ages, 'still hedged in by a general framework of liturgical language and theological thought', with the law-centred kingship of the succeeding period: there was an 'evolutionary change'– 'from liturgy to legal science'.[38] Pursuing the implications of this subtle contrast, we might observe that where the lawyer deals in conflicts, operating with logic through nice verbal distinctions, the liturgist deals in communications, operating with faith through a symbolic code. In view of these differences, he who consults the early medieval *ordines* should be wary of imposing on the age of liturgy the preoccupations of an age of law.

---

royal *ordo* quoted in extenso. The Anonymous was using an earlier version of the anglo-saxon ordo of 973: see Nineham, 'The so-called Anonymous of York', pp 34 *et seq*. The prayer *Benedic domine hos presules principes* appears in the *Sacramentary* of Angoulême of *c* 800, ed P. Cagin, *Le sacramentair gélasien d'Angoulême* (Angoulême 1919) fol 168ᵛ. I believe that its content shows it to be a late Merovingian composition: see my unpublished dissertation, pp 44 *et seq*. For the later role of this prayer (referring now only to a single ruler) as part of 'the stock of "regal texts"', see Bouman, *SC*, pp 75 *et seq*. In some tenth-century manuscripts, its *incipit* is recast to read, *Benedic domine hunc principem*, or *hunc regem*, compare Bouman, SC, pp 174 and 180, but *presul* remains in the 'Leofric' *ordo*, ed Warren, p 251, in the *ordo* of the Benedictional of Archbishop Robert, ed Wilson, p 146, and in the *ordo* of the Sacramentary of Ratold of Corbie, ed Ward, 'An early version ', p 357. Compare above p 43 n 10.

[38] Kantorowicz, *KTB*, pp 87 *et seq*.

ECCLESIASTICAL CHRONOLOGY:
FASTI 1066–1300

by DIANA GREENWAY

JOHN LE NEVE is alive and well and is living in the university of London. Indeed, letters are still addressed to him: he received one quite recently from his present publisher, the Athlone Press. It was in 1716 that this petulant, not to say paranoid, cleric confounded his enemies and his creditors by publishing his *Fasti Ecclesiae Anglicanae*.[1] The volume represented years of tiresome research, and it could be argued that Le Neve made a better job with the materials at his disposal than did his nineteenth-century reviser and continuator, T. Duffus Hardy, whose edition appeared in three volumes in 1854.[2]

The latest enterprise to bear Le Neve's name was begun at the Institute of Historical Research in 1955: among the many scholars who had a hand in setting up the scheme none has been more active than professor C. N. L. Brooke, whose generosity with notes, references, advice and encouragement has been a constant inspiration. This new edition has a scope wider in some respects and narrower in others than both earlier editions: we include the priors of monastic cathedrals, but exclude the chapters of non-cathedral collegiate churches and the officers of the ancient universities.[3] We also exclude Sodor and Man, which has fallen to the Scots.[4] The broad intention, however, remains the same throughout the three editions: *Fasti* are chronological lists and not biographical dictionaries. The nature of the work is chronology

---

[1] John Le Neve, *Fasti Ecclesiae Anglicanae: or, an Essay towards deducing a Regular Succession of all the Principal Dignitaries in each Cathedral, Collegiate Church or Chapel (now in being) in those parts of Great Britain called England and Wales* (London 1716).

[2] John Le Neve, *Fasti Ecclesiae Anglicanae*, corrected and continued to the present day by T. Duffus Hardy, 3 vols (Oxford 1854).

[3] [John Le Neve,] *Fasti [Ecclesiae Anglicanae] 1066–1300*, [ed D. E. Greenway], 2 vols (London 1968, 1971) in progress; *ibid 1300–1541*, ed J. M. Horn, B. Jones and H. P. F. King, 12 vols (London 1962–7); *ibid 1541–1857*, ed J. M. Horn, 2 vols (London 1968, 1971) in progress.

[4] *Fasti Ecclesiae Scoticanae Medii Aevi ad annum 1638*, second draft ed D. E. R. Watt (St Andrews 1969).

– the raw material out of which history may be fashioned. The sources and problems encountered in the chronology of the English bishops are well known. In what follows I shall outline briefly the main types of record used to compile *Fasti* of the English cathedral clergy below the rank of bishop.[5]

The primary difficulty that confronts us is so obvious as hardly to require stating: the official records of clergy appointments are in short supply. There are no chapter act books and few bishops' registers before 1300. In the thirteenth century, it is true, the patent and close rolls and the papal registers yield much information on royal and papal appointments, but such appointments were abnormal: royal collations were almost invariably confined to episcopal vacancies, and in all dioceses outnumbered papal provisions before 1300. Surviving original deeds and chapter registers are chiefly concerned with property: there are many documents relating to the foundation of prebends, with some references to episcopal appointments of prebendaries, and a few sporadic records of elections of deans in secular cathedrals and priors in monastic cathedrals. But without bishops' registers official information is scarce. Even the few thirteenth-century registers that survive are not always helpful. At Lincoln, where bishops' rolls run from 1214–15, it is not until 1290, when rolls give way to quires, that episcopal collations to prebends are listed, and the York registers, which begin in 1225, do not regularly record collations to prebends until 1279. In the other secular cathedrals, capitular collations are enregistered: at Exeter between 1257 and 1280, at Wells between 1265 and 1267, at Hereford continuously from 1275 and at Salisbury from 1297. At the monastic cathedral of Worcester, elections of priors and appointments of archdeacons appear in the bishops' registers from 1268. For the bulk of normal appointments in the English cathedrals, however, precise evidence is lacking.

In the absence of a continuous series of official documents of cathedral appointments, we turn to other sources. Clearly if chronological lists of incumbents of offices had been kept at the cathedrals themselves, the task would be greatly simplified. In fact, of the secular cathedrals only one, St Paul's, has such a list: the unique prebendal catalogue, which exists in two versions, one of the later thirteenth century and the other of the early fourteenth century.[6] This list, although it gives no actual

---

[5] For a select bibliography of modern works containing *fasti* covering the period 1066–1300, see *Fasti 1066–1300*, I, pp 100–1.

[6] *BM* Harley MS 6956 fols 91r–6r, and St Paul's Dean & Chapter Library

dates, preserves the sequence of the prebendaries from the foundation of the prebends at the end of the eleventh century. Its central importance for the St Paul's *Fasti* before 1300 is demonstrated by the fact that 82 of the 406 prebendaries named, or 20 per cent, are not known from any other source to have been canons of St Paul's. This is all the more striking because among the eighty-two are many eminent men, whose careers are well known: four bishops of London – Ste-Mère-Eglise (1199–1221), Fauconberg (1221–8), Wengham (1259–62), and Sandwich (1263–73); many dignitaries and canons of other cathedrals; and many royal officials, including chancellors, vice-chancellors, itinerant justices and the like.[7] It seems to follow that without comparable catalogues for the prebends of the other secular cathedrals, the *Fasti* will be incomplete, lacking perhaps 20 per cent of the prebendaries, among whom there may be many prominent royal and ecclesiastical administrators. Among the monastic cathedrals, it is only at Durham that we find any useful medieval lists of priors: the three Durham lists[8] give dates, not always reliable, and their importance is largely overshadowed by the historical productions of the cathedral priory.

Most cathedrals have a history, a chronicle or a series of annals covering at least part of the period between 1066 and 1300. For the monastic cathedrals such material is abundant, notably at Durham.[9] For Worcester there are not only the annals compiled in the cathedral priory, but also some other west-country annals – Tewkesbury, Winchcombe and Evesham – all good sources for the terms of office of the priors and archdeacons of Worcester.[10] The secular cathedrals are perhaps less well endowed with narrative sources, although some important twelfth-century historians were members of secular chapters – Ralph de Diceto of St Paul's, Henry of Huntingdon of Lincoln, Hugh the Chantor of York. There were usually some members of secular chapters

---

WD 2 fols 110/17ʳ–112/19ʳ; see C. N. L. Brooke, 'The Composition of the chapter of St Paul's, 1086–1163', *CHJ* 10 (1951) pp 111–32; [A.] Morey and [C. N. L.] Brooke, *Gilbert Foliot [and his Letters]* (Cambridge 1965) pp 276–88; *Fasti 1066–1300*, I, p. xiv and *passim*.

[7] For example, Simon of Wells (*Fasti 1066–1300*, I, p 33), Robert Losinga (*ibid* p 42), Robert de Esthall (*ibid* p 46), Godfrey de Lucy (*ibid* p 47), Hugh of Wells (*ibid* p 48), Robert Burnell (ibid p 54), William de Greenfield, John Cumin (*ibid* p 55), Jocelin de Bohun, Robert of Salisbury, John de Greenford (*ibid* p 57), and many others.

[8] Durham Dean & Chapter Muniments Cartuarium II fol iᵛ, and Registrum II fol 350ᵛ; and *BM* Cotton MS Vespasian A VI fol 62ᵛ.

[9] See H. S. Offler, *Medieval Historians of Durham* (Durham 1958).

[10] See *Fasti 1066–1300*, II, pp 102–9.

who attracted the attention of chroniclers. High office in government and election to the episcopate were obvious qualifications for contemporary comment; others were a dramatic death – like that of the subdean of Lincoln, murdered in the cathedral by a vicar in 1205,[11] or the drowning of the chancellor of York in 1177,[12] or the death of a canon of St Paul's, who had an apoplectic seizure while watching a game of dice after dinner one autumn evening in 1246.[13] Involvement in violent events was another occasion for appearance in a chronicle – like the kidnapping of a roman canon of St Paul's in the xenophobic events of 1231.[14] To monastic chroniclers, the conversion of a secular canon to the religious life was memorable and is treated thus whenever it occurs.[15]

Historical consciousness in the middle ages was often expressed in, often even confined to, remembrance of the dead. Here is a mystic time-scale where the whole of the christian era is commemorated in a single year. The precise year of death, even the century, is of little interest: only the day and the month of the obit are important. Most cathedrals have obituaries or kalendars with obits: only at Exeter are the years of deaths recorded.[16] Another difficulty in the use of obituaries is that the day and month of commemoration cannot be presumed to be the day and month of death.[17] It was obviously undesirable to have obits coinciding with great saints' days, and distributions to monks or canons had to be arranged at reasonable intervals. Despite these drawbacks, obituaries may provide valuable evidence, sometimes the only evidence available for the identification of some cathedral clergy and their offices: men whose lives are completely obscured from us become known in their deaths.[18]

The groups of records discussed so far provide a considerable amount of information, but the mainstay of the *Fasti* between 1066

---

[11] *Annales de Waverleia, Annales Monastici*, [ed H. R. Luard], RS 36 (1864–9) II p 257.

[12] *Gesta Regis Henrici Secundi Benedicti Abbatis*, ed W. Stubbs, RS 49 (1867) I p 195.

[13] *Matthaei Parisiensis Monachi Sancti Albani Chronica Majora*, ed H. R. Luard, RS 57 (1872–83) IV p 588.

[14] *Ibid*, III pp 210–11.

[15] For example *Annales de Dunstaplia, Annales Monastici*, III p 185.

[16] Exeter Dean & Chapter Library MS 3518.

[17] See, for example, *Fasti 1066–1300*, I, p x, n 1; but compare *HRH* p 9 and n 1.

[18] A large number of canons of Lincoln are known only from their obits, for example: Adam de Ely, Ajax, Alberic, Albinus, Asketil, Ansold, in obituary printed in *Statutes of Lincoln Cathedral*, ed H. Bradshaw and C. Wordsworth, 3 vols (Cambridge 1892–7) II pp ccxxxiv-ccxlii.

and 1300 is the type of evidence that gives a cross-sectional view, a glimpse of the composition of a chapter at one time. Such records fall into two categories: comprehensive lists drawn up for administrative purposes, and lists of witnesses actually present on a particular occasion.

Those comprehensive lists that survive reflect certain practical necessities in secular cathedrals. The need to clarify arrangements for the daily psalter led to the compilation of two remarkable twelfth-century lists of canons found in the psalter of the Great Bible at Lincoln: the list of *c* 1145 names the forty-two prebendaries and their psalms, and the second list, added in *c* 1186, when the number of prebends had risen to fifty-six, names fifty-three canons, three prebends being vacant.[19] Other lists of prebends arose out of that most pressing necessity – taxation. Valuations of the thirteenth century are fairly numerous, but only three of those so far known give the names of contemporary holders of the prebends: for Salisbury a *taxatio* lists the incumbents of all fifty-two prebends in 1226,[20] for Hereford the *taxatio* of pope Nicholas in *c* 1291 names all twenty-eight prebendaries,[21] and for St Paul's a *valor* compiled in *c* 1294 names all thirty prebendaries.[22]

When we consider documents which give lists of witnesses present on a particular occasion, we face not only the familiar problem of assigning dates to undated documents, but also two other difficulties. First, in witness-lists of the early and middle twelfth century, members of cathedral chapters are not always given their titles, so that it is sometimes not possible to distinguish dignitaries and canons from clerks without prebends. At Exeter in *c* 1161 twenty-three witnesses were named in a charter of bishop Bartholomew – two archdeacons, the precentor and twenty others without the title of canon; they perhaps formed the whole chapter (one of the twenty-four prebends probably being vacant) but this cannot be proved.[23]

A more serious difficulty in using witness-lists would arise if, as suggested by Warner and Ellis in 1903, 'witnesses to a charter were not

---

[19] The lists are printed *ibid*, III pp 787–99; in the forthcoming *Fasti 1066–1300*, III (Lincoln) I shall discuss their dates.

[20] *Vetus Registrum Sarisberiense alias dictum Registrum S. Osmundi episcopi*, ed W. H. R. Jones, *RS* (1883–4) II pp 70–5; and see K. Edwards, in *VCH Wiltshire*, III p 160.

[21] *Taxatio Ecclesiastica Angliae et Walliae auctoritate P. Nicholai IV circa AD 1291*, ed T. Astle and others, Record Commission (1802) pp 168–70.

[22] *BM* Harley MS 6956 fols 88ᵛ–9ʳ; and see *Fasti 1066–1300*, I, p 99.

[23] A. Morey, *Bartholomew of Exeter* (Cambridge 1937) app II no 21, and pp 86–7.

always present at its execution, nor even cognisant of it until later'.[24] If it was a common practice 'for a person to be asked by letter to attest a charter which had already been made', it would be unwise, as Stenton wrote in 1922, 'to assume that witnesses to a charter of the late twelfth or thirteenth centuries were all present in the same place at the same time unless there is some definite evidence to that effect'.[25] Without such evidence, *Fasti* based on occurrences of witnesses in charters would be unsound. This appalling possibility has been raised, *sotto voce*, by other historians, most recently by the editors of *Heads of Religious Houses*.[26]

In an article published in 1940, J. C. Russell examined in some detail the attestations of royal and private charters in the reign of John.[27] He showed that for royal charters, there is no evidence to cast doubt upon the idea that witnesses were always present at the attestation.[28] He also gave compelling reasons for believing that the inclusion of absent witnesses – which would have rendered a charter contestable in law – was an exceptional expedient employed within the knightly class, and that letters of invitation to witnesses who had been absent at the 'making' or writing of a charter are to be interpreted as invitations to attend the publication or reading of the charter at an assembly.

Russell's general arguments may be applied to ecclesiastical charters and to those in which cathedral clergy appear as witnesses. First there is an argument of theoretical probability: the early twelfth-century custom of personal presence of witnesses is unlikely to have proceeded to the system described by Bracton – personal attendance required by law – by way of a transition period, covering a few decades either side of 1200, during which time the names of men who had never seen the charters appeared as witnesses. Ecclesiastical practice was no less exacting than that of the English courts of Bracton's time. Indeed, one might say that common, canon and civil law all emphasised the importance of the presence of witnesses. For the authentication of documents the

---

[24] *Facsimiles of Royal and Other Charters in the British Museum*, ed G. F. Warner and H. J. Ellis (London 1903) nos 68–9 and n.

[25] *Transcripts of Charters relating to Gilbertine Houses*, ed F. M. Stenton, LRS 18 (1922) p xxxi.

[26] *HRH*, p 10; also Morey and Brooke, *Gilbert Foliot*, p 201 n 4.

[27] 'Attestations of charters in the reign of John', *Speculum*, 15 (1940) pp 480–98.

[28] In *RR*, II p xxviii, Johnson and Cronne doubted that all witnesses were necessarily present at the attestation of Henry I's charters, but their reason is unconvincing. Compare G. W. S. Barrow's comments on Scottish royal charters, where he finds no evidence to support the view that witnesses were not present; *Regesta Regum Scottorum* (Edinburgh 1960–) I: *The Acts of Malcolm IV, 1153–65*, pp 78–9; and II: *The Acts of William I, 1165–1214*, p 80.

presence of witnesses was prescribed by the civil law, and strict requirements concerning the summoning and suitability of witnesses were adopted by public notaries in the thirteenth century.[29] The practical foundation of this custom lay of course in the need to insure against fraud or dispute. In cathedral chapters this need was no less pressing than elsewhere, and in the area of residence regulations, agreements and elections, it was perhaps more pressing, as witnesses not only attested but also approved. There is no reason to suppose that before the fourth lateran council allowed voting by proxy in elections in certain circumstances,[30] absentees' names had been written as electors and witnesses.

Among documents of importance in constructing the English *Fasti* of the late twelfth and early thirteenth centuries many record the assent of witnesses who were surely present. Sometimes such a document states specifically that the witnesses were present, as does bishop Seffrid II's statute of residence at Chichester in 1197: six dignitaries and twenty-three canons, almost certainly the entire chapter at that time *interfuerunt et assensum suum prebuerunt.*[31] The occasions were rare on which the complete chapter of a secular cathedral was called together, and the occasions on which all the members actually met were rarer still. Two twelfth-century documents from St Paul's illustrate how decisions might be approved over a period of time: in both the constitution of bread and ale of 1150/1[32] and Diceto's statute of residence of *c* 1192,[33] the canons who were present at the meetings when the documents were first approved are listed first, and the canons who were absent but approved when they returned to St Paul's are listed separately. Twenty-one out of thirty prebendaries approved the constitution of 1150/1 – nineteen in the first list, two in the second. Only one of the thirty prebends was not represented in the statute of *c* 1192 – fourteen prebendaries appear in the first list, eighteen in the second; and it seems that before the second list was closed three prebends changed

[29] See C. R. Cheney, *Notaries Public in England in the Thirteen and Fourteenth Centuries* (Oxford 1972) pp 106, 123–5.

[30] *HL* V 2 (1913) p 1353; compare *DDC* V p 242.

[31] *The Acta of the Bishops of Chichester 1075–1207,* ed H. Mayr-Harting, *CYS* 56, no 101 and p 41.

[32] *BM* Harley MS 6956 fols 84^v^–5^r^; this is Matthew Hutton's transcript from St Paul's Liber F fol 35, a volume now lost.

[33] *Radulfi de Diceto Decani Lundoniensis Opera Historica,* ed W. Stubbs, *RS* 88 (1876) II pp lxix–lxxiii; for a witness, William of Ely, omitted by Stubbs, see H. G. Richardson, *EHR* 57 (1942) p 132 n 1. Both documents, of 1150/1 and *c* 1192, are cited in *Fasti 1066–1300* I.

hands.[34] Even if the statute had not stated that the witnesses were gathered on at least two (and probably three) occasions, this would have been apparent: there could be only thirty members of the St Paul's chapter at one time, but the statute has thirty-two witnesses. If documents were often attested over a period of time, we should find traces of this in the order of witnesses: in fact, by the 1180s or 1190s witnesses' names were arranged with careful regard for precedence. As Russell pointed out 'the existence of a consistently high degree of order [in witness-lists] creates a presumption that groups [of witnesses] were probably seen together'.[35]

Witness-clauses of the late twelfth and early thirteenth century bear their own peculiar brand of verisimilitude. If the dean, treasurer and precentor occur in one list, and the dean, chancellor and precentor in another list of the same year or thereabouts, it is reasonable to assume that the treasurer was present on the first occasion and probably not on the second. If it was possible to write in a name without the man's knowledge or consent, then we should not see what we do see – a huge variety of combinations of dignitaries and canons as witnesses. Further we should expect to find as witnesses to important documents important men. In the statutes, agreements and great charters of the English cathedrals we do not find that eminent members of chapters necessarily appear as witnesses. Here the evidence of the prebendal catalogue of St Paul's is significant: this showed that twenty per cent of the prebendaries never appeared in Pauline documents, as witnesses or otherwise, and that a large proportion of this silent twenty per cent consisted of eminent men, pluralists who were administrators in church or state, and whose attestations might have been thought to add weight to transactions.

There are, then, reasonable grounds for thinking that witness-lists of the twelfth and thirteenth centuries are sufficiently reliable to be used in the construction of *Fasti*. In practice, reliance on witness-lists seems to work, so that by the steady accumulation of data ecclesiastical chronology may become ever more precise. John Le Neve, the ghost-writer, still haunts the libraries and archives of the English church, in his never-ending pursuit of chronological truth.

[34] See Morey and Brooke, *Gilbert Foliot*, p 271 n 2.
[35] *Speculum*, 15 (1940) p 481. In a remarkable document of 1147, from Lincoln, sixty-one witnesses appear in four groups, each group being separated from the others by a symbol: the first group consists of twenty-seven canons, the second of five abbots and twelve other ecclesiastics, the third of six knights, and the fourth of eleven men who lived in or near the village of Scarle, with which the charter is concerned: *The Registrum Antiquissimum of the Cathedral Church of Lincoln*, III, ed C. W. Foster, *LRS* 29 (1935) no 921; also printed *EHR* 35 (1920) pp 212–14.

THE COUNCIL OF WESTMINSTER 1175:
NEW LIGHT ON AN OLD SOURCE

by MARY CHENEY

T HE text with which this study is concerned is not the text of the canons of the council of Westminster of 1175. It is the text printed long ago by Wilkins[1] from the single manuscript source, Cotton Claudius A IV folios 191ᵛ–92, where it has the heading *Concilium Ricardi Cantuariensis archiepiscopi*. Wilkins gave it the heading *Canones concilii* . . . and assigned it to 1173, an impossible date, since Richard was not then archbishop. This part of Claudius A IV is a decretal collection, put together from various sources not before, and probably not long after, 1185.[2] Our text, copied as one item in the collection, consists of thirty-seven imperative propositions, all quite short and almost all negative; they all condemn something or forbid something: 'Christians shall not be usurers', 'Lepers shall not in future live among the healthy', and so on. There is little sign of any attempt at arrangement; related topics may appear more or less widely separated.

The rubric proclaims a connection with a council held by archbishop Richard, and the thirty-seven propositions proclaim their connection with the well-known council at which he presided in May 1175, for twenty-two of them, and part of another, have a counterpart among the canons of that council, although the canons are generally much longer, since they are carefully drafted legal enactments, often stating penalties for transgression. But what was the nature of the connection? We can safely assume that the propositions were originally earlier in date than the canons, although the one copy was written ten or twelve years later. If the composer of the propositions had known the canons he could hardly have avoided using their wording so regularly, and he would surely not have pulled one canon to pieces and scattered its three parts among his thirty-seven items.[3] There is therefore general agreement

---

[1] Wilkins I p 474. The canons follow on p 476; they are also printed in *Houedene* ii, 72–7.
[2] [C]. Duggan, [*Twelfth Century Decretal Collections*] (London 1963) p 91.
[3] Propositions 11, 21 and 37 were dealt with together in canon 10.

that the list is some sort of draft, but some fourteen items do not reappear among the canons of the council, and scholars have been wary of trying to define the origin of the list and its precise relationship to the council.[4]

As to its origin, we have a clue in the letter which summoned the bishops of the province of Canterbury to the meeting. One such letter is preserved among the correspondence of Gilbert Foliot.[5] It is probable that the others went out in the same form, for the bishop of London was already acting as dean of the province, through whom the archbishop issued his orders to his suffragans. The archbishop has ordered him, says Gilbert, to summon the bishops to be in London on 11 May, and to bring with them the prelates, secular and monastic, of their dioceses, 'so that matters in need of correction shall be condemned by general agreement, or changed for the better by the grace of God'. In the meantime each bishop was to enquire diligently into the evils afflicting his diocese, so that being brought to notice, they should receive correction or censure. It seems probable that the evils reported by the bishops were listed as they were submitted, perhaps as the bishops arrived, and that somebody – was it Benedict the archbishop's chancellor? – was told to produce a short statement, showing in each case exactly what required correction or censure. This would have produced just such a list as we have in the Claudius manuscript, and this list could then have served as a rather disorderly agenda for the meeting. It would have been considered, formally or informally, before the final series of canons was drafted.

The council was able and willing to proceed to the publication of appropriate provincial canons to cover twenty-two of the propositions in the list, and part of another. These propositions I shall leave aside. It is the others that need consideration, because it is they that have caused scholars to hesitate in defining the nature of the list and its connection with the council. These propositions may have been dropped for a variety of reasons. Some may have been thought superfluous; was there anything to be achieved by more local legislation against usury? Some were, perhaps, thought impossible to enforce; could legislation at Westminster stop the welsh exchanging wives? One proposition ran

---

[4] The list has been discussed in recent times by C. N. L. Brooke, 'Canons of English Church Councils in the early Decretal Collections', *Traditio* 13 (New York 1957) p 472 n 2; Duggan p 92; C. R. Cheney, *Medieval Texts and Studies* (Oxford 1973) p 119 n 1.

[5] A. Morey and C. N. L. Brooke, *The Letters and Charters of Gilbert Foliot* (Cambridge 1967) p 306 no 234.

counter to cistercian privileges about tithe-paying; nothing could be done at the local level on such a matter. A proposal that benefices should not be conferred on persons without a tonsure was perhaps dropped because the council declared that archdeacons should tonsure clerks with too much hair, with or without their consent. On the other hand some propositions, excellent in themselves, met the legal difficulty that a provincial council could not lay down new law. It could only require obedience to existing law, adding penalties if desired. This is why each of the published canons states the authority on which it rests. There is one exception to this rule, a canon entitled *Decretum novum*, and this significantly, deals with patronage and was issued by royal as well as ecclesiastical authority. The vital point here was acceptance by the secular courts. This canonical limitation of the legislative power of a provincial council made it difficult, if not impossible, to deal with new problems which were not adequately or explicitly covered by the old law. This difficulty accounts, at least in part, for the fact that some apparently excellent propositions did not give rise to provincial canons.

But were all the propositions that did not lead to canons simply dropped? We hear nothing, so far as I have observed, in any narrative source or contemporary letters about further action on any of these propositions. But there is, as I hope to demonstrate, other evidence which suggests that quite a few of them were pursued by different means, and led to legislation of a different kind.

The first of the propositions in the Claudius text is one of these. It dealt with one of the big issues of the time, the drive to ensure really effective episcopal control of institutions to parish churches. No one, it declares, shall presume to enter upon a church without presentation by the advocate and institution by the diocesan bishop, or by his officials at his command. The old law did indeed contain ancient general rules to the effect that all churches were subject to the control of the diocesan bishop.[6] But these rules were not couched in the legally precise terms desired by the trained lawyers of the 1170s, and they had not customarily been obeyed in England. It is quite clear that during the preceding century son had followed father, and nephew followed uncle, quietly, almost automatically, and without any sense of guilt, in innumerable parish churches and chapels, without the prior approval or even the knowledge of the diocesan. Often this was done by arrangement with the patron; sometimes the hereditary parson was

[6] *Decretum* C.16 q.7 c.10,11.

MARY CHENEY

also himself the patron. So the vital part of the reform was the absolute necessity for institution by the bishop or by his agent appointed for the purpose.

The first action seems to have been taken by the archbishop. On his own authority he issued a general sentence of excommunication against anyone who obtained a church without episcopal permission. We hear of this from two independent sources. It is mentioned in a commission to English judges-delegate, in which it is called an *interdictum generale* made by the archbishop, 'to the effect that those entering upon churches without the command of the bishop shall be held to be excommunicate'.[7] In this case the affected parson had promptly appealed to the pope, and this, or a similar experience, may have warned the archbishop that his *interdictum* would be thwarted by appeals. He evidently wrote about the problem in general terms to pope Alexander III, and the pope's reply, the decretal *Ex frequentibus querelis* (Jaffé 13817)[8] appears in the *Decretals* of Gregory IX and became part of the law of the catholic church. It is addressed to the archbishop and his suffragans, and I think it is sufficiently interesting to give the text, with slight omissions.

> From the frequent complaints of parsons it has become clear to us that in your land a most evil custom has obtained for a long time ... by which clerks ... receive churches and ecclesiastical benefices without the consent of the diocesan or of his officials who can do this business according to law ... Therefore since you, brother archbishop, wish, as you should, to extirpate so evil a custom from your province, you have, as you tell us by your letter, pronounced sentence of excommunication against clerks who knowingly

---

[7] *Collectio Wigorniensis* 4.50, ed H. Lohmann, *ZSR, KA* 22 (1933) p 119. For particulars of the decretal collections mentioned in this article see *Papal Decretals relating to the diocese of Lincoln in the twelfth century*, ed W. Holtzmann and E. W. Kemp, *LRS* 47 (1954) pp x–xvii.

[8] Decretals will be cited only by Jaffé numbers where these exist. For the convenience of readers these numbers are listed here with references to printed tects.
12412 *Compilatio I* 3.33.14, A[ppendix] C[oncilii] L[ateranensis], Mansi 22, cols 248–454, 15.10.
13794 X 4.8.1, *ACL* 37.2.
13814 *Compilatio I* 2. 20.33, *ACL* 28.14.
13816 X 1.35.6 and 3.39.11, *ACL* 28.8.
13817 X 3.7.3, *ACL* 28.11.
13819 X 5.19.2, *ACL* 16.3.
13823 *Compilatio I* 2. 20.21, *ACL* 10.20.
13976 (not in X or *Comp.* I) *ACL* 20.3 and 4.

occupy benefices obtained in this way ... We therefore [now the pope is addressing the archbishop and suffragans together] declare that sentence lawful and established and confirm it by apostolic authority, and we order each of you to renew that sentence four times a year in your diocese, and to cause it to be observed without contradiction or right of appeal.

A second decretal (Jaffé 13814) with the same address and a very similar incipit, authorised the bishops to force notorious offenders to give up their churches, ignoring any appeal. So proposition number one became law by means of papal decrees. This was a most effective alternative to provincial legislation, whether the object was to overcome the opposition of conservatives, or to remedy the deficiency of the old law, or to remove the right of appeal to the pope, by which disciplinary measures could be thwarted or delayed.

Having seen one of the propositions apparently giving rise to a papal decretal addressed to the archbishop of Canterbury and his suffragans, let us examine the others. The second proposition concerned the cistercians, and was also one which did not lead to a provincial canon. Short as it is, it falls into two parts, one of which has already been mentioned; this part was clumsily phrased and ran counter to papal privileges. It is not surprising that we hear no more about it. But the second part was different. It reads 'They [the white monks] shall not hold churches, contrary to the statutes of their order'. On this matter there is indeed a decretal of pope Alexander III, addressed to the archbishop of Canterbury and his suffragans, although this decretal was not taken into the definitive version of 1234; it is preserved only in three early collections.[9] Omitting the uninformative *arenga*, it runs,

> We have heard that in your country some of these brethren do not hesitate to receive churches and advowsons. We believe this to be contrary to their rule, and since we will not endure that they shall transgress the laudable customs of their elders in this or other ways, we command you not to allow the brethren to acquire parish churches or rights of patronage in future, and you shall compel them to give up any they have previously acquired, without right of appeal.

[9] It is printed in '*Collectio Brugensis*' 19.6, ed E. Friedberg, *Die Canonessammlungen zwischen Gratian und Bernard von Pavia* (Leipzig 1897 reprinted Graz 1958) p 151. The decretal occurs also in *Coll. Bridlington. c.*182 and *Coll. Tanner.* 3.39. Inc. *Quanto magis Deo.*

A papal command also went out on this matter to the cistercians in England (Jaffé 12412). This circulated more widely, and a fragment of the date is preserved; it was issued before October 1175.

Propositions twelve and nineteen concerned the jews. Number 19 forbade jews to impoverish parish churches by occupying their lands or revenues; number 12 forbade jews to receive fealty from christians, or christians to do fealty to jews. A decretal of Alexander III (Jaffé 13976) deals, significantly, with just these two points. In this case the address is lost, but it was clearly sent to all the bishops of an English province. It orders the bishops, 'having consulted our dear son Henry, king of the English', strictly to compel jews to give up any parish churches and revenues which they may hold by purchase or as securities, and to forbid them to acquire such things in future, and also to forbid the faithful to do homage or fealty to jews, and to pronounce sentence of excommunication against offenders, without right of appeal.

Proposition twenty-two was designed to prevent appeals to the pope by men who had left their wives to live with other women. Again a decretal (Jaffé 13823), addressed to the archbishop of Canterbury and his suffragans, deals with the point at issue. 'It has reached our ears,' says the pope, 'that there are persons in your province who leave their wives . . . and live with concubines, and they try to maintain and protect their error by the obstacle of appeal'. And therefore the bishops are ordered, in notorious cases, to compel such persons to take back their wives and put away their concubines, by sentence of excommunication, even though the offenders appeal.

Proposition twenty-eight prohibits clerks from paying pensions secretly from their churches, in order that others may succeed them. Yet again, we find a decretal (Jaffé 13816) of pope Alexander III to the archbishop of Canterbury and his suffragans, dealing with just this problem, carefully distinguishing two aspects of it. 'We have learnt,' says the pope, 'that when parsons of churches die, certain clerks, subject to your jurisdiction, agree to pay higher pensions from those churches, so that they may obtain the living'. The bishops are therefore ordered to remove such offenders, without right of appeal, and to punish them. Also, 'certain clerks in collusion with men of religion' agree to pay pensions from their churches, without the authority of the diocesan bishop, in order that when they die their sons or nephews may be presented to the church by those same religious'. The bishops are ordered to depose anyone who obtained a church by this means, by apostolic authority, without right of appeal.[10]

In the case of proposition twenty-nine, the situation is not quite so simple. This proposition declared that when land was held in pledge for a debt, the profit from the land should contribute to the repayment of the capital. This point is dealt with in a decretal (Jaffé 13819) which stands in the modern edition of the *Decretals* of 1234 with the address to the archbishop of Canterbury and his suffragans. This address needs investigation; it may well be correct, but in many texts the forms are singular, and some give an address to the bishop of Exeter.

A different problem arises with proposition thirty-six, that lepers should not live among the healthy. The archbishop of Canterbury certainly consulted the pope about lepers. The pope's reply (Jaffé 13794) is addressed to him alone, and treats this proposal in passing as a matter of common custom; 'since those who contract leprosy are separated by general custom from the communion of men, and are transferred from towns and villages to solitary places' there is a problem about lepers' marriages, which is the main subject of the decretal. Here the link between proposition and decretal is less certain.

What conclusions can be drawn from this material? It has been shown that there is close correspondence between a proposition in the Claudius manuscript and a decretal of pope Alexander III, addressed to the archbishop of Canterbury and his suffragans, in six, probably seven, possibly eight cases. The correspondence is perhaps most strikingly illustrated in the decretal concerning the jews, in which we find the pope dealing with two unrelated and rather unusual problems in one letter to England, and precisely these two problems are the subject of propositions. I suggest that this correspondence is too close, in too many cases, to be a matter of coincidence, and that these decretals were prompted by reference to the pope following the council of Westminster of May 1175. If this is accepted, a number of further observations, of varying importance, can also be made. All these undated decretals must have been issued after the council, that is, not before about the end of June 1175 at earliest. All were issued as the direct result of the initiative of English prelates, striving to reform the church committed to their care. As regards the thirty-seven propositions, this evidence confirms the view that they had some official status and that we should regard this text as an agenda for the council; a text read or

---

[10] On the significance of these practices see C. R. Cheney, *From Becket to Langton* (Manchester 1956) pp 127–9 .

circulated and discussed during the week between 11 May, for which the prelates were summoned, and 18 May, when the formal session took place. At least one prelate must have taken the text home with him. That text was copied by the compiler of the *Collectio Claudiana*, under the mistaken impression that he had before him a convenient summary of the canons of the council of Westminster, to set beside those of the council of Tours (1163) and the third lateran council (1179). His mistake preserved a document of ephemeral practical use and no legal authority: a type of which very few survive from the early middle ages. For the historian, this document is a source of information about the problems and interests of the bishops of England in the 1170s, about their meeting at Westminster in 1175, about their relations with the pope and about the origin of some papal legislation. These questions are beyond the scope of this article. I hope to return to them, and to some of the unsolved problems connected with this material, on another occasion.

ADDENDUM

In *Bulletin of Medieval Canon Law* ns 3 (1973) pp 52–5, S. Chodorow analyses Paris, Bibl. nationale ms lat 587, fols 133ʳ–4ᵛ. Its readings strengthen the arugument of this article by showing JL 13794, about lepers, with address to the archbishop of Canterbury and his suffragans, but they modify it by attaching the second part of JL 13976 (*ACL* 20.4), about jews, to JL 13810, with address to the archbishop alone.

A SOCIO-LINGUISTIC APPROACH
TO THE LATIN MIDDLE AGES

by MICHAEL RICHTER

There are two lights, a greater and a smaller one, that is to say, the
wiser men and the less wise; the day signifies the wise men, and
the night the uninformed. The greater light illuminates the day,
for the wiser men instruct those who are more able. What is
Augustine if not a sun in the Church? to whom does he speak if
not to the wise? You, however, the priests, knowing less, are the
smaller light, you illuminate the night, for you preside over the
laity who do not know the Scripture and remain in the darkness
of ignorance ... The other section of the clergy who do not
preside over the people of God are the stars, because although
they cannot shine by doctrine, do nevertheless shine by their work
onto the earth, that is, the Church.[1]

These sentences are taken from an anonymous sermon 'On the Priesthood', based on Genesis i, 16-20. The author of the sermon showed the
priests their place in society: even though they did not belong to the
intellectual élite, their profession and knowledge separated them clearly
from the darkness of night in which the laity was imprisoned. In the
course of the twelfth century, this passage from Genesis underwent an
exegetical change and was used, from then onwards, to explain the
political relationship between *regnum* and *sacerdotium*. What did remain
was the notion of a fundamental difference between clergy and laity,
and nowhere was this notion better expressed than in our sermon to the
priests: *quodcunque lumen estis, lumen estis tamen.*[2] In true medieval
fashion, our author equated knowledge with the knowledge of the
Word of God.[3] He also stressed the fundamental difference between

---

[1] *PL* 147 (1879) col 233.
[2] *Ibid.*
[3] Compare Yves M.-J. Congar: 'The Fathers, and our Western Middle Ages
which took this outlook from St Augustine and Cassiodorus, realised with
what resources they had, a unity of wisdom between all knowledge and life
itself, under the souvereignty of the Bible', *Tradition and Traditions*, trans
Michael Naseby and Thomas Rainborough (London 1966) pp 66–7.

light and darkness, between the clergy and the laity. While theology emphasises that ordination makes the clergy by virtue of its office into the mediator between God and man, this was not the main concern of our author. Instead, he voiced the belief, widely shared by the clergy generally, that knowledge as such was the prerogative of the clergy. Such an attitude raises the question of how the clergy was able to achieve monopoly of knowledge, and how it reacted to attempts by the laity to challenge this monopoly. In what follows I propose to enquire into this phenomenon by looking at the linguistic scene in the medieval west.

Our written sources for medieval history are almost exclusively in latin and come from the clergy themselves, and to accept their message uncritically entails the danger of sharing their deceptively calm presentation of what was in fact a complex situation. Sociolinguistics concerns itself with the social function of language, with language in social contact, and it pays more attention to the normative than to the informative aspect of language. In this light, the leading part of the clergy in the medieval west may be outlined provisionally in the following ways: –

a) that christian religion found its most sophisticated interpretation in the west through the latin language, to the extent that latin became the *modus ecclesiasticus* par excellence;[4] and

b) that latin as the *lingua franca*[5] was also used for other than religious purposes, but that in the religious sphere it was given most attention, and that a thorough knowledge of it was intentionally restricted to a limited and controllable section of the community.[6]

Thus, the latin language stood at the cross-road of religious and secular activities, and this double function of one language in preference to others was of crucial importance to the leading position of the clergy.

---

[4] *Modus ecclesiasticus* was contrasted with *sermo vulgaris* in a legal dispute of c 1180; see G. Fransen, 'Tribuneaux ecclésiastiques et la langue vulgaire d' après les *questiones* des canonistes', *Ephemerides Theologiae Lovanienses*, 40 (1964) pp 391–412 at p 394.

[5] For a definition see M. A. K. Halliday, A. McIntosh, P. Strevens, 'The users and uses of language', *The Linguistic Sciences and Language Teaching* (London 1964, repr 1968) p 80: 'One language comes to be adopted as the medium of some activity or activities which the different language communities perform in common. It may be a common language for commerce, learning, administration, religion, or any or all of a variety of purposes: the use determines which members of each language community are the ones to learn it.'

[6] [Jack] Goody, in discussing restricted literacy as a policy, speaks of 'the inhibiting effects of religious literacy that dominated the culture of Western Europe until the advent of the printing press', [*Literacy in Traditional Societies*] (Cambridge 1968) p 15.

A socio-linguistic approach to the latin middle ages

Two preliminary questions may be raised briefly at the outset. First, was latin a *living* language during the middle ages? It seems best to settle for a relative answer and say that, during the eleventh and twelfth centuries, the period under review in this paper, latin was more of a living language than either before or after.[7] Secondly, what is the social function of language as such? Recent investigations of this question which is crucial to our discussion have provided new insights. Thus it has been said that 'a change in the mode of language use involves the whole personality of the individual, the very character of his social relationships, his points of reference, emotional and logical, and his conception of himself.'[8]

Medieval man was conscious of a cultural gulf between those people who knew latin, the *litterati*, and those who did not, the *illitterati/idiotae*,[9] a constellation expressed forcefully in the notion that there was the same difference between literate and illiterate people as there was between man and animal.[10] It is well to remind ourselves of some constituent factors of such a situation. Few people were as fortunate as Wecheleu, the welsh anchorite from Llowes who received the gift of the latin language from God, albeit incompletely, because he could

---

[7] For a review of earlier discussions see Christine Mohrmann, 'Le dualisme de la latinité médiévale', *Revue des Etudes Latines*, 29 (Paris 1951) pp 330–48; see especially p 339: 'Pour les humanistes médiévaux, le latin étant une partie de leur monde a eux, *c'était quelque chose vivant*', again, p 344: 'ce qui est essentiel, c'est *l'instrument vivant*, interprète habile de la pensée médiévale . . . ' (italics mine). This article is reprinted in C. Mohrmann, *Latin Vulgaire, Latin des Chrétiens, Latin Médiéval* (Paris 1955) pp 37–54.

[8] [Basil] Bernstein, ['A Public Language: some sociological implications of a linguistic term', *Class, Codes and Control*] I (London 1971) pp 42–60, at p 54. Professor Bernstein there discusses the effects of change from what he calls 'public' to 'formal' language, thus essentially a change of 'code' of language, but it is assumed here that the adoption of a new language involves similarly fundamental changes. For a recent discussion of the linguistic term 'code' see R. Hasan, 'Code, register and social dialect', *Class, Codes and Control*, II, ed B. Bernstein (London 1973) pp 253–92.

[9] A gulf of some kind was bound to occur. It has been well said that ' "education" implies that a man's outlook is transformed by what he knows', R. S. Peters, *Ethics and Education* (London 1970) p 31. See also the important study by J. Goody and I. Watt, 'The Consequences of Literacy', *Comparative Studies in Society and History*, 5 (London 1962–3) pp 304–45, reprinted also in Goody, pp 27–68.

[10] 'Quantum a beluis homines, tantum distant a laicis litterati', PL 196 (1855) col 1651, which is also quoted by Herbert Grundmann in his excellent article 'Litteratus—Illitteratus', *Archiv für Kulturgeschichte*, 40 (Köln/Graz 1958) pp 1–60, at p 52, n 39, and in [J. W.] Thompson, [*The Literacy of the Laity in the Middle Ages*] (Berkeley, Cal., 1939) p 143.

speak only in infinitives.[11] For most of his contemporaries, the acquisition of latin required a long and difficult process of learning. It is well established that language is best learnt by way of imitation,[12] but imitation almost inevitably effects profound changes in the learner of the new language. Thus, to perceptive contemporaries it appeared that Bernard of Clairvaux 'surpassed all in the elegance of his style and was so saturated in the Holy Scripture that he could fully expound every subject in the words of the prophets and apostles. For he had made their speech his own, and could hardly converse or preach or write a letter except in the language of scripture.'[13] Ironically enough, the same can be observed in a letter of Peter of Blois in which he explained why, as a native french speaker, he found it difficult to converse in english.[14]

In the west, latin was primarily, although not exclusively, the medium used by the church in so far as the church was controlled by the papacy,[15] and the use of a *lingua franca* which was closely related to the language spoken in Italy is itself an indication of the peculiar situa-

[11] Giraldus Cambrensis, 'De rebus a se gestis', *Opera* I, ed J. S. Brewer, *RS* 21 (1861) pp 90 *et seq*, where the anchorite sums up, using finite verb forms: 'Et ab illo die ego sic loqui, et Dominus meus, qui dedit mihi Latinam linguam, non dedit eam mihi per grammaticam aut per casus, sed tantum ut intelligi possum et alios intelligere', *ibid* p 91.

[12] See the comments of John of Salisbury on the teaching methods of Bernard of Chartres: 'Quibus autem indicebantur preexercitamina puerorum in prosis aut poematibus imitandis poetas aut oratores proponebat, et eorum iubebat vestigia imitari, ostendens iuncturas dictionum et elegantes sermonum clausulas', *Metalogicon*, I, cap 24, ed C.C.I. Webb (Oxford 1929) p 56. Also Peter of Blois on his own education: 'Profuit mihi, quod epistolas Hildeberti Cenomanensis episcopi styli elegantia et suavi urbanitate praecipuas firmare et corde tenus reddere adolescentulus compellebar', *Ep* 101, *PL* 207 (1855) col 314.

[13] John of Salisbury, *Historia Pontificalis*, ed Marjorie Chibnall (London 1956) p 26.

[14] Peter of Blois in a letter to ? Peter of Cornwall, prior of Aldgate (1202–12), Erfurt, Allgemeinwissenschaftliche Bibliothek, MS Ampl. fols 71, 209*rb*: 'Hoc enim mihi adhuc ad excusationem superest, quod cum sim Francigena sepe loqui Anglicis me oportet. Et Joseph quidem in Egipto 'linguam quam non noverat audiebat' (Ps lxxx, 6). Ideo quandoque per interpretem loquebatur (compare Gen. xlii, 23). Omnis autem homo expeditius loquitur in lingua consueta quam insolita, quod potes videre in beati Pauli stilo quo utitur in epistola ad Hebreos. Ipse enim dicit: "Malo quinque verba cum sensu loqui quam mille sine sensu" (1 Cor. xiv, 19), ac si dicat "fructuosius mihi est unam scire linguam et ea loqui et intelligi quam scire plures linguas et eis loqui, meumque sensum ab auditoribus non agnosci".' The information, and the transcript of this interesting passage, I owe to the generosity of Herr Rolf Köhn who is working on the manuscripts of Peter of Blois.

[15] Exceptions to this general rule were pre-Norman England and medieval Ireland, both less under the wing of Rome than the rest of Europe. This question requires detailed examination.

tion of the western church headed by the papacy.[16] Most education was provided by institutions affiliated to and supervised by the church,[17] and it is not surprising to find that ethical principles advocated by the church should have permeated education generally. Most people who received formal education to literacy became *clerici* in profession as well as in name, although there always was, and as time progressed increasingly so, a section of the population who were taught to read and write although they did not intend to embark on an ecclesiastical career.[18] This process began with the king who in this respect as in others was acknowledged to be more than a mere layman. The contemporary jingle that *rex illitteratus est quasi asinus coronatus* was widely quoted.[19] An approach of greater subtlety to the need for the king to be educated is shown by John of Salisbury. It is necessary to mention in passing that, according to John's political philosophy, the law of the kingdom should ultimately be derived from God's commandments – the concept of *imago Dei = rex = lex animata*.[20] John emphasised how necessary it was for the king to be literate since he was required to read the law of God daily.[21] But he went further, and thus underlines the change in a person's outlook due to his mastery of the latin language. John said:

[16] This was indicated briefly by W. H. C. Frend, 'Coptic, Greek and Nubian at Q'asr Ibrim', *Byzantinoslavica*, 33 (Prague 1972) pp 224 *et seq.*

[17] For a survey see Philippe Delahaye, 'L'organisation scolaire au XIIe siècle', *Traditio*, 5 (New York 1947) pp 211–68. The most important stages during the period under consideration would appear to have been the roman council of 1079, held by Gregory VII, which ruled 'ut omnes episcopi artes litterarum in suis ecclesiis docere faciant', Mansi 20, col 50, and later the third lateran council held by pope Alexander III, especially c 18: 'per unamquamque ecclesiam cathedralem magistro, qui clericos eiusdem ecclesie et scholares pauperes gratis doceat, competens aliquod beneficium assignetur, quo docentis necessitas sublevetur et discentis via pateat ad doctrinam', Mansi, 22, cols 227–8, which is also in *Decret. Greg. IX*, V, 5,1. See also Pierre Riché, 'Recherches sur l'instruction des laics du IXe au XIIe siècle', *Cahiers de Civilisation Médiévale*, 5 (Poitiers 1962) pp 175–82.

[18] This change of concept is clearly formulated in the early fourteenth century: 'Nec dicas quod debeat exponi "clerici id est literati" more Gallico, sicut quidam exponunt et dicunt quod omnis literatus est clericus', quoted in Wilhelm Wattenbach, *Das Schriftwesen im Mittelalter* (3 ed Leipzig 1896) pp 426–7.

[19] [John of Salisbury], *Policraticus*, IV, cap 6, [ed C.C. I. Webb], 2 vols (London 1909) i, p 254. See also V. H. Galbraith, 'The Literacy of the Medieval English Kings', *Proceedings of the British Academy*, 21 (London 1935) pp 201–38, and Thompson p 126.

[20] *Policraticus*, IV, caps 1–2, i, pp 235–8.

[21] *Policraticus*, IV, cap 6, i, p 254: 'Legenda est ergo omnibus diebus vitae suae. Ex quibus liquido constat, quam necessaria sit principibus peritia litterarum, qui legem Domini cotidie revolvere lectione iubentur.'

legat mens principis in lingua sacerdotis . . . Nam vita et lingua sacerdotum quasi quidam vitae liber est in facie populorum.[22]

While the king was thus obliged, by virtue of his office, to be imbued with some of the educational values offered to the clergy, this happened much less frequently among the aristocracy. Let us look at a case in which it did take place, and see what attitude was taken by a sympathetic cleric to this situation. Take a letter which the abbot Philip of Harvengt wrote to Henry, a layman who had received formal education.[23] In the first place, Philip stated that literacy would put Henry well above his social equals.[24] More than that: so well was Henry educated that he surpassed in his knowledge many members of the clergy.[25] Favourably as Philip regarded Henry's education, he made it nevertheless very clear that the clergy (whatever its educational standard, we may be permitted to add) held the most important place in society.[26] He pointed out that latin was the language which deserved most respect in the west since God's good deeds were praised therein.[27] He conveys the impression that literacy was generally despised by the laity as an unmanly skill, yet acknowledged that this skill would enable Henry to judge the behaviour of knight, prince, and prelate.[28]

So long as literacy was more or less restricted to the clergy, serious anticlericalism was unlikely to arise on a large scale. When it was voiced, some clerics brushed it aside as irrelevant and inappropriate. This impression is certainly given by Geoffrey of Vendôme in a letter to fellow-clerics. He discussed therein the sensitive case of a priest who, when having a mistress, physically attacked and injured her husband because the latter objected to his wife's adultery. Clear as the rights and wrongs of this situation may appear, Geoffrey nevertheless resented any criticism from the laity in this *incerta re*, as he called it: –

[22] *Ibid* p 255.
[23] *PL* 203, (1855) cols 151–6.
[24] *Ibid* ed 151: 'tanto principi adsunt dona charismatum tam preclara, ut in aliis huiusmodi principibus inveniri valeant satis rara'; col 152: 'dignum fuit ut a vulgarium ignorantia, et brutorum hominum stolida caecitate, scientia litteralis educeret, et clara praeditum redderet libertate . . . Multum ergo debes patri tuo cuius tibi cura et diligentia sic providit, ut . . . te . . . vellet quoque super ceteros comites litterarum scientia sublimari.'
[25] *Ibid* col 152: 'tantis, ut aiunt, litteris es imbutus, ut quamplures clericos transcendas in eorum nequaquam numero constitutus.'
[26] See ibid cols 155B, 155D, 156B; see also col 816.
[27] *Ibid* 154B-C.
[28] *Ibid* col 153: 'invenis quid populum, quid militem, quid principem deceat vel prelatum.'

You write to us to say that the priest hates the people for the truth which the people speak of him. I write to you that two things are true: truth creates hatred, and hatred creates lies. It is possible that the priest hates the people because of the truth, and equally that the people lie because they hate the priest. But the people have to be guided, brethren, not followed in accusing the clergy. True is the proverb that says: *praecedere debet qui ducit asellum*. The people are the ass which you must guide, not follow.[29]

In such a milieu, it was all too easy for the educational gulf between clergy and laity to develop into a social chasm. One would like to know how typical of his age Roger Bacon was in saying that: –

> from the beginning of the world the common people (*vulgus*) were separated from the knowledge (*sensus*) of the saints, the philosophers, and all other wise people, and all wise men despised the ways of the common people, nor did they communicate to them the heights of wisdom, for the common people cannot grasp them, they deride and abuse them to their own disadvantage and to the disadvantage of the wise.[30]

The division of society into the informed and the uninformed is described by Roger Bacon as the result of a deliberate choice on the part of the laity. There is, however, no indication that the laity were repeatedly obliged to make the choice themselves. Instead, education was much more commonly regarded by the clergy as a prerogative which was, if not divinely ordained, as some maintained, at least perpetuated by the church. Philip of Hervengt might well emphasise the liberating value of education,[31] but the conservative western church reserved such liberation only for her servants. It has been maintained recently that 'how society selects, distributes, transmits and evaluates educational knowledge it considers to be public, reflects both the dis-

---

[29] *PL* 157(1899) col 180. 'Ducendus est populus, non sequendus', is perhaps a pun on a passage in a letter from Pope Celestine I of AD 429 (*PL* 50, col 437): 'docendus est populus, non sequendus', which was found in all important canon law collections and was finally taken into Gratian's collection; see Dist. LXII, cap 2. A similar view of the priests' exemption from popular criticism is expressed by pope Innocent III, *PL* 214 (1855) cols 697–8.

[30] 'Compendium Studii' cap 3, *Fr Rogeri Bacon Opera Inedita*, ed J. S. Brewer, *RS* 15 (1859) p 416.

[31] *PL* 203 (1855) col 152: 'Unde et litterarum scientiam recte vocant ethnici liberalem, quia eum qui labore et studio sortitur gratiam litteralem, a confuso vulgi consortio et a multitudine liberat publicana, ne pressus et oppressus teneatur compede et hebetudine rusticana.'

tribution of power and the principles of social control'.[32] Similarly, Emile Durkheim argued long ago, when discussing the interaction of education and society, that 'education, far from having as its unique principal object the individual and his interests, is above all the means by which *society perpetually recreates the conditions of its very existence*'.[33]

The conservative nature of the western church can best be seen in her attitude towards the use of the vernacular languages. Although little evidence has been preserved to study popular preaching before the fourteenth century when attitudes began to change, there is good reason to believe that the laity were instructed by the clergy in the vernacular, apparently without great regard to theological subtleties. Thus Peter of Blois wrote: –

> You ask me to send you, in written form, the sermon I gave to the common people; and what I expounded crudely enough for them (for such was their capacity) I should attempt to translate into Latin ... Things can be passed over lightly in the vulgar tongue, whereas the dignity of Latin demands longer treatment.[34]

Peter here expressed an opinion which was generally shared by the clergy, that the complexity of theological arguments increased and should increase with the capacity of the audience.[35] The clergy might have acted in this fashion out of consideration for their audience, yet consideration was but a step removed from condescension. It has been rightly pointed out that latin, as a language foreign to all people in the west, lacked the control of popular usage.[36] As a medium, it was controlled solely by the church, and attempts by the laity to participate more actively in ecclesiastical business in the vernacular were, on the whole, strongly opposed. Thus pope Gregory VII firmly refused the

[32] Bernstein, pp 202–30, at p 202.
[33] Emile Durkheim, *Education and Sociology* (Chicago 1956) p 123 (italics mine). See also further: 'Not only is it society which has raised the human type to the dignity of a model that the educator must attempt to reproduce, but it is society, too, that builds this model, and it builds it according to its needs.' p 122. Lynn Thorndyke claimed that 'in the developed medieval culture elementary and even secondary education was fairly widespread and general', 'Elementary and Secondary Education in the Middle Ages', *Speculum*, 15 (1940) pp 400–8, at p 401, but his paper hardly bears out this claim.
[34] Peter of Blois, *Sermo LXX*, 'Ad populum', PL 207 (1855) cols 750–1.
[35] See, for example, Petrus Cantor, *Verbum Abbreviatum*, cap 65, where he says on the subject of preaching: 'non enim omnibus indifferenter proponere debemus, sed quasi ad quamdam praegustationem maiora maioribus, et minora minoribus offerre', PL 205 (1855) col 198.
[36] R. W. Southern, *The Life of St Anselm by Eadmer* (London 1962) p xxvi.

duke of Bohemia permission for celebrating the divine office in the vernacular. The pope maintained that

> not without reason has it pleased Almightly God that Holy Scripture be a secret in certain places lest, if it were plainly apparent to all men, perchance it would be little esteemed and be subject to disrespect; or it might be falsely understood by those of mediocre learning and lead to error.[37]

This had not always been papal policy. In the celebrated mission to the slavs in the ninth century, pope John VIII explicitly stated to Methodios that

> there is nothing contrary to the faith or to sound doctrine in singing Mass in the said Slavonic language, or in reading the Holy Gospel and the sacred lessons from the New Testament and Old Testament, properly translated and expounded, or in chanting other offices of the hours in the same tongue.[38]

Supporting his approval with reference to the scriptures, he stressed that God should be praised in all languages.[39] Admittedly, such tolerance for the use of the vernacular in the church arose from an exceptional situation, in the west at any rate, which is too well known to require detailed comment here, but the increasing insistence of the western church on the use of latin appears to indicate conscious papal

[37] *Reg. Greg. VII*, vii, 11, pp 473–5, ed Erich Caspar, *MGH Epp sel*, II (1920); see also Margaret Deanesly, *The Lollard Bible* (Cambridge 1920), pp 23–4; Giovanni Miccoli, 'Ecclesiae primitivae forma', *Studi Medievali*, 3 series, I (Rome 1960) pp 470–98, especially at pp 79–81. On the vernacular in worship more generally see Cyril Korolewsky, *Living Languages in Catholic Worship*, trans D. Attwater (London 1957) also Maurice Michaud, 'Langue d'Eglise et droit liturgique', *L'Année Canonique*, 3 (Paris 1954–5) pp 99–128, esp pp 120 *et seq*; for the early period see G. Bardy, *La question des langues dans l'église ancienne* (Paris 1948) and A. G. Martimort, 'La discipline de l'Eglise en matière de langue liturgique. Essai historique', *La Maison-Dieu*, 11 (Paris 1947) pp 39–54.

[38] *PL* 126 (1852) col 906 (Jaffé no 3319); see also A. P. Vlasto, *The Entry of the Slavs into Christendom* (Cambridge 1970) pp 20–79, especially at pp 59–66. Even in the thirteenth century, we find the church occasionally not opposing the use of the vernacular, so in the legislation of the fourth lateran council, c 9: 'Quoniam in plerisque partibus intraeandem civitatem atque dioecesim permixti sunt populi diversarum linguarum, habentes sub una fide varios ritus et mores, districte precipimus ut pontifices huiusmodi civitatum sive dioecesum provideant viros idoneos, qui secundum diversitates rituum et linguarum divina officia illis celebrent et ecclesiastica sacramenta ministrent, instruendo eos verbo pariter et exemplo', Mansi, 22, 998; *Decret. Greg. IX*, I, 31, 14.

[39] *PL* 126 (1852)906: 'neque enim tribus tantum, sed omnibus linguis Dominum laudare auctoritate sacra monemur'.

77

policy of a non-theological nature rather than haphazard evolution and needs itself more investigation. So do the concepts held about the alleged superiority of latin over the vernacular languages. It has been pointed out that Dante was one of the first to claim for the vernacular a status almost equal to the one held by latin.[40] This occurs surprisingly late, at a time, moreover, when the social scene in Europe was undergoing profound changes.

It is true that the appearance of the multitude of languages on earth was associated with man's sinful attempt to build the tower of Babel, but the Lord's blessing had been given to the existence of the vernacular languages in the new covenant and the pentecostal mission of the apostles (Acts ii, 1–11). Henceforth, the vernacular languages could be regarded, in the church, either as a continuation of man's Babel or as a sign of a new beginning.[41] As the treatment of the various heretical movements in the twelfth century shows, the church initially did not take too seriously their concern with the dissemination of the gospel in the vernacular, only to over-react in the second half of the century when her authority was seriously threatened.[42] While in no way wishing to deny that there was substantial theological reason to fight some of the heresies, I have the impression that the linguistic element received more than its fair share of attention. For all its flamboyance, Walter Map's account of the appearance of the waldensians before the third lateran council voiced the then prevalent attitude of the hierarchy towards the use of the vernacular: –

> In every letter of the divine page there flit on the wings of virtue so many sayings, there is heaped up such wealth of wisdom, that any to whom the Lord has given the means can draw from its fulness. Shall then the pearls be cast before swine, the word be given to the ignorant, whom we know to be unfit to take it in,

[40] See H. J. Chaytor, *From Script to Print* (London 1966) p 79, commenting on Dante, *Il Convivio*, I, x, 10.

[41] J. Travers, 'Le mystère des langues dans l'Eglise', *La Maison-Dieu*, 11 (1947) pp 15–38. 'La vrai conclusion, c'est que dans l'Eglise seule les langues sont vraiment réhabilitées, dans l'Eglise seule elles perdent pour les hommes et pour les nations leur charactère nocif', p 25. We must also mention the important study by Arno Borst, *Der Turmbau von Babel. Geschichte der Meinungen über Ursprung und Vielfalt der Sprachen und Völker*, 4 vols in 6 pts (Stuttgart 1957–63).

[42] See Janet L. Nelson, 'Society, theodicy and the origins of heresy: towards a reassessment of the medieval evidence', *SCH*, 9 (1972) pp 65–77; Brenda Bolton, 'Tradition and temerity: papal attitude to deviants, 1159–1216', *ibid*, 79–91.

much less to give out what they have received? Away with such a thought, uproot it![43]

Other ecclesiastics regarded the instruction of heretics in the vernacular as an absurd task, although they were forced to condescend at times.[44] Only a century later did the church take up the challenge to use the vernacular, and then for a very different purpose. When it became clear that the crusades had failed as a military undertaking, some people turned to the idea of conquering the Saracens by converting them to christianity; this was to be done by using their vernacular languages. Suffice it here to point to the rather fantastic plans of a Raimund Lull and a Pierre Dubois at the turn of the thirteenth century.[45]

Within her own confines, the church maintained strict linguistic control. Yet even here the façade began to crack, apparently as a consequence of a development not connected with the use of the vernacular. The rise of satire as a literary genre in twelfth-century Europe has recently been linked with the church's increasing absorption with the technical aspects of government. Those who had received the finest education and who had been instrumental in the reform of the church from the mid-eleventh century onwards, had to yield to the legal technocrats.[46] Their reaction was, on the one hand, to criticise the language used by the papal court,[47] on the other hand to point out

---

[43] Walter Map, *De Nugis Curialium*, I, cap 31, ed T. Wright, *CS*, 50 (1850) p 64; English translation from M. R. James, *Cymmrodorion Record Series*, 9 (London 1923) pp 65 *et seq.*

[44] Roger Howden reports remarks of a cardinal-priest working against the Albigensians in Toulouse: 'quaesivimus ut latinis verbis respondentes suam fidem defenderent, tum quia lingua eorum non erat nobis satis nota, tum quia evangelia et epistolae, quibus tantummodo fidem suam confirmare volebant, latino eloquio noscuntur esse scripta. Cumque id facere non auderent, utpote qui linguam latinam penitus ignorabant, sicut in verbis unius illorum apparuit, qui cum latine vellet loqui vix duo verba iungere potuit, et omnino defecit; necesse fuit nos illis condescendere, et de ecclesiasticis sacramentis propter impertitiam illorum, quamvis satis erat absurdum, vulgarem habere sermonem.' Houedene, ii, p 157.

[45] For Lull see his *Liber de fine*, ed Adam Gottron, *Ramon Lulls Kreuzzugsideen*, *Abhandlungen zur mittleren und neueren Geschichte*, 39 (Berlin 1912), esp pp 66–9, and p 88; for Dubois see *De recuperatione terre sancte*, ed Ch. — V. Langlois, *Collection de textes pour servir à l'étude et à l'enseignement de l'histoire* (Paris 1891) pp 47–51, 59–60, 68, 108 *et seq.*

[46] Colin Morris, *The Discovery of the Individual, 1050–1200* (London 1972) pp 122 *et seq.*

[47] Nigel Wireker: 'Si scribat dominus papa, etiam sine omni conjunctione et adverbio plane et aperte, ita ut nihil sit ambiguum (text: *ambiguus*), nihil contrarium, mandatum tamen eius nihilominus eluditur.' 'Tractatus contra curiales et officiales clericos', *The Anglo-Latin Satirical Poets and Epigrammatists*, 2 vols, ed T. Wright, *RS* 59 (1872) i, p 205.

gleefully how insufficiently educated were these newcomers in church administration. Significantly, such criticism came from the educated class itself, whose members, like Henry, Philip of Hervengt's correspondent, having been educated to know what the ideal standards were, became rather sharp in their reaction. Nigel Wireker could write about William of Longchamp, bishop of Ely and justiciar of England: 'If the bishop is led to the book like the ox to the water, this saying could be applied to you not unfittingly'.[48] We may also mention the case of the priest who offered his bishop what he thought were 200 eggs and who had to give him eventually 200 sheep because by mistake he had offered *oves* when he had intended to offer *ovas*, and the bishop took him at his word.[49] Yet insufficient education was not confined to the lower clergy. We hear of Robert, abbot of Malmesbury, being cross-examined by papal delegates because he had been accused of illiteracy. When asked to explain the phrase *Factus est repente de coelo sonus*, he explained *repente* as follows: *Repente, il se repenti*.[50] One may wonder in how far the purity of teaching could be maintained in a language unfamiliar to the laity and difficult to grasp even for those who were educated.

We have highlighted so far the impact of the latin language on the medieval west within the community of christians rather than in the political sphere. We have seen that latin was a social language in the sense that the familiarity with the language determined a person's social standing in his own country and in society in general.[51] It has become evident that this situation gave a unique place in medieval society to the clergy, not by virtue of its office but by virtue of its education. There were, however, also occasions when opinion could differ over language use, and, objectively speaking, there was no independent authority to which appeal could be made when such ambiguity occurred, especially at the highest level. From what has been said so far, it is hardly surprising that the church assumed this control over language use.

The best-known incident of this kind is perhaps the dispute between pope Adrian IV and the German emperor Frederick I over the significance of the imperial coronation. It occurred over a letter of the pope

[48] *Ibid* p 224: 'Si dicitur episcopus ad librum sicut bos ad aquam, . . . apud te titulus iste tibi non potest opponi'.
[49] Giraldus Cambrensis, 'Gemma Ecclesiastica', ii, 34, *Op* ii, ed J. S. Brewer, *RS* 21 (1862) p 332.
[50] *Ibid* p 346.
[51] Bernhard Bischoff, 'The Teaching of Foreign Languages in the Middle Ages', *Speculum*, 36 (1961) pp 209–24, at p 210.

to the emperor which was delivered in 1157 to the diet at Besançon. The pope's reminder, in that letter, that he had conferred the insignia of the imperial crown on the emperor and that he would not regret giving even greater *beneficia* to him[52] caused a storm of protest in the assembly. The imperial chancellor, Rainald of Dassel, translated the crucial passage in this letter to his audience in a particularly offensive manner by giving *beneficium* the meaning of *feudum*.[53] The extent to which the pope claimed control over the use and interpretation of the latin language can clearly be seen in another letter which he wrote to the emperor in the following year, explaining what he had meant in the disputed passage. We should note both that the pope felt a need to elaborate on his earlier statement in order to make it clearer, and also that he openly admitted to giving his words a special meaning. He wrote: –

> Admittedly, this word *beneficium* is used by some people with a meaning different from the original one. But it ought now to be understood in the sense in which we used it and which it is well known to have carried ever since;

similarly, on the technical term *conferre*, the pope said: –

> Certain persons have tried to twist this word and another, in the phrase 'we have conferred on you the emblem of the imperial crown' ... For by saying 'we have conferred' we simply mean, as stated above, 'we have placed' ...[54]

This incident was more than a quarrel over the interpretation of a few words; it epitomised the long struggle between empire and papacy over their respective places in the world. Thus it was understandable

---

[52] [*Ottonis et*] *Rahewini* [*Gesta Friderici I. Imperatoris*], ed G. Waitz, 3 ed, *MGH in usum scholarum* (Hannover/Leipzig 1912) p 175: 'imperialis insigne coronae libentissime conferens . . . neque tamen penitet nos . . . si maiora beneficia excellentia tua de manu nostra suscepisset'.

[53] The whole incident has been subjected to a very thorough scrutiny by Walter Heinemeyer, '*beneficium—non feudum sed bonum factum*. Der Streit auf dem Reichstag zu Besançon 1157', *Archiv für Diplomatik*, 15 (Köln/Wien 1969) pp 155-236.

[54] *Rahewini* p 196: 'Licet enim hoc nomen, quod est "beneficium", apud quosdam in alia significatione, quam ex inpositione habeat, assumatur, tunc tamen in ea significatione accipiendum fuerat, quam nos ipsi posuimus, et quam ex institutione sua noscitur retinere', and: 'unde quod quidam verbum hoc et illud, scilicet "contulimus tibi insigne imperialis coronae", a sensu suo nisi sunt ad alium retorquere . . . Per hoc enim vocabulum "contulimus" nil aliud intelligimus, nisi quod superius dictum est "imposuimus".'

81

that a mere explanation of words was not sufficient to close this particular episode. It shows that language use could become a problem of international dimensions, and that, in the medieval west, the church was the ultimate authority with regard to the use of the latin language.

As we have shown in this paper, this situation was closely linked with medieval education. It would thus appear to be more than coincidental that Italy, where papal control was particularly felt and resented, should have become the first country to revive secular schools on a large scale, and that Frederick II, the great adversary of the political papacy, should have been the first ruler in medieval Europe to found a purely secular university, outside the control of the church (Naples, 1224).

We have attempted to sketch the social position of the church and the clergy from a single point of view, that of language and language control. We have given some avenues of further study and indicated some effects of the linguistic situation in medieval Europe. There may be others which the linguistic situation might, if not explain, at least show in a different light: is it not possible to account for the relative sterility of theological thought in the post-patristic west compared with the fecundity of the multilingual east by reference to the papacy's conservative and effective language control? Be that as it may, a sociolinguistic approach to the latin middle ages offers a great variety of further fields for research. All written material from the middle ages is a potential source of information when approached with the help of the linguistic social sciences. In the light of what has been said here, that widely used term the 'latin middle ages' should be, to the historian, a challenge rather than a statement of fact.

SCISSORS AND PASTE: CORPUS CHRISTI, CAMBRIDGE, MS 139 AGAIN

by DEREK BAKER

AMONGST the manuscripts bequeathed to Corpus Christi College, Cambridge, by Matthew Parker in 1575 is one of the most important surviving collections of sources for the history of the north of England in the twelfth century. Manuscript 139, as it now is, contains, amongst other items, unique, or almost unique, copies of the so-called *Historia Regum*, which had been ascribed to Symeon of Durham before the end of the twelfth century, its continuation by John of Hexham, and the *History* of Richard of Hexham. It was a prime, and in part a unique, source of Twysden's pioneering edition of 1652,[1] and its value is in no way diminished today. This apart, the manuscript is of great interest as a manuscript, and the problems of its date, provenance and composition are still the subject of debate. The most recent and definitive account of the manuscript was given by Peter Hunter Blair in a fifty-five page article contributed to the volume of essays edited by Nora Chadwick under the title *Celt and Saxon*.[2] His conclusions, which supersede all earlier views, were that the manuscript was compiled in the period *c* 1165–70 at the cistercian house of Sawley in the West Riding of Yorkshire, and the subsequent discovery of an erased Sawley *ex libris*, now visible only in ultra-violet light, and dated by Ker to the late twelfth/early thirteenth century,[3] reinforced his view. Yet there still remain problems and uncertainties, and my

---

[1] R. Twysden, *Historiae Anglicanae Scriptores X* (London 1652).

[2] [P. H.] Blair, ['Some observations on the *Historia Regum* attributed to Symeon of Durham'], *Celt and Saxon* (Cambridge 1963) pp 63–118. See also [H. S.] Offler, 'Hexham and the *Historia Regum*', *Transactions of the Architectural and Archeologised Society of Durham and Northumberland*, ns 2 (1970) pp 51–62. I am grateful to Mr David Dumville for his criticism of this paper, and for a preview of his two valuable forthcoming papers on the 'Nennius' material in MS 139. See [David] Dumville, 'The Corpus Christi *Nennius*', *Bulletin of the Board of Celtic Studies*, 25 (1972–4) pp 369–80, and 'Nennius and the *Historia Brittonum*', *Studia Celtica* 9 (1974).

[3] N. R. Ker, *Medieval Libraries of Great Britain* (London 1964). See below p 98 and n 77.

purpose here is first to sketch in a little of the history of the manuscript in its present form, and secondly, by further examination of particular aspects of its to supplement and qualify Blair's conclusions.

The manuscript is now a volume of 182 folios written in several hands of the later twelfth century, in double columns, generally of thirty-six lines. It was, unfortunately, rebound in 1952,[4] and the boards from the earlier binding were not kept. In consequence, though there is some indication that the manuscript was in a dilapidated state in the sixteenth century, there is no way of knowing whether it was rebound by Parker, when, as Stow records, 'to the end those monuments might be carefully kept he caused them to be well-bound and truly covered',[5] or whether it suffered in the general process of rebinding which Naismith deplored in the eighteenth century. No attempt seems to have been made to check the collation of the manuscript when it was rebound in 1952, but it has been possible to make a partial examination of the composition of the volume, and it may be noted here that the collation given in James's *Catalogue* stands in some need of revision.

The manuscript may be said to contain some twenty-six items,[6] though this is an over elaborate classification, most of them concerned with events in the north. They are, briefly, a *universal history*; extracts from Regino of Prum; Richard of Hexham; a short chronicle to the time of the emperor Henry V; Symeon of Durham's letter to dean Hugh of York; an account of the siege of Durham; the so-called *Historia Regum*; John of Hexham's continuation, arbitrarily divided into two parts by four brief items, the last of which is Ailred's treatise on the battle of the Standard; Ailred's account of the nun of Watton; the accounts of the foundation of St Mary's, York and Fountains; four brief extracts from the *Gesta Regum* of William of Malmesbury; three short anonymous items; the *Historia Brittonum* and *Life of Gildas*. In Blair's view, following M. R. James, these last two sections, comprising the final two gatherings of the manuscript, constituted a separate volume with 'no organic connection'[7] with the major part of the manuscript, and he ignored them in his discussion. This is, however, rather to oversimplify the structure of the manuscript, for while it is

---

[4] 19 February 1952.

[5] M. R. James, [*Descriptive Catalogue of the Manuscripts in the Library of Corpus Christi College, Cambridge*], 2 vols (Cambridge 1912) I p xvi.

[6] For comment on the make-up of the manuscript and on the classification of its contents see appendix.

[7] Blair p 63.

quite clear that the last two items do constitute a separate section within the volume this is not the only division to be discerned.

Apart from the first two folios, which contain miscellaneous later material, including a fifteenth-century list of contents, the manuscript is composed of twenty-two gatherings, mostly of eight folios, consecutively numbered in roman numerals at the foot of the verso of the last folio in each gathering. Gathering XX, which has lost its last four folios, if it ever had them,[8] and the last gathering are not numbered. This overall organisation may be subdivided into at least seven sections. Gatherings I and II comprise the *universal history*; gatherings III to VI Regino of Prum, Richard of Hexham, the chronicle to the time of Henry V, the letter of Symeon of Durham and the account of the siege of Durham; gatherings VII to XVI contain the *Historia Regum* and the first part of John of Hexham, and conclude with the poem on the death of Somerled;[9] gatherings XVII and XVIII comprise the second part of John of Hexham and Ailred's accounts of the battle of the Standard and the nun of Watton; gathering XIX has the foundation accounts of St Mary's, York, and Fountains, and the four extracts from William of Malmesbury; gathering XX, or what is left of it, contains the three brief anonymous items, and gatherings XXI and XXII contain the *Historia Brittonum* and *Life of Gildas*.

Blair drew attention to the peculiarities of this final section which, in his view, marked it out as a separate volume. Much the same, however, can be said of the very first section, the *universal history*. Though of much the same date as the rest of the manuscript it is quite distinct in appearance, the rubrics have been added to it, and the condition of its first and final folios indicate that it existed for a time as a separate manuscript. The fifth section can be distinguished in similar fashion. Containing, essentially, the accounts of St Mary's, York, and Fountains, it is written in double columns of thirty-five lines, and it too shows signs of use as a separate manuscript. With the sixth section it is impossible to be precise, consisting as it does now of only half a single gathering of eight folios, but it can at least be said that there is no direct connection between it and what precedes or follows it. The remaining three sections comprise the greater part of the manuscript – sixteen out of the twenty-two gatherings – and contain most of the historical material of any value. Section two can be distinguished in some respects

---

[8] See Dumville 'The Corpus Christi *Nennius*' p 371.
[9] A further division of materials should perhaps be indicated within this section. See appendix nn 8, 9.

from sections three and four. It is in a different hands to the others, and the irregularity of its gatherings contrasts with the regular eight folio gatherings of the *Historia Regum*. There is, however, an overall impression of unity about these three sections. They are bound together by the rubrics which introduce and conclude the individual items; with minor exceptions they are written in double columns of thirty-six lines and the condition of the first and last folios of the three sections taken together suggest that, for a time, they too constituted a separate manuscript.[10] In short, then, and leaving aside the fragmentary twentieth gathering, MS 139 may be broken down into at least four sections each of which seems to have had a short-lived separate existence. Though the hands vary between and within the sections all are of roughly the same date, and the late twelfth-century numeration of the gatherings, taken together with contemporary marginalia, in more than one hand, in different sections of the manuscript, make it plain that it was then already in the form and order in which we have it now.

The subsequent history of the manuscript in the middle ages is a blank. It can only be said that in the fifteenth century a list of contents and a number of jottings and drawings were added to it, and that at some stage it became necessary to erase the Sawley *ex libris*. Even in the sixteenth century things are not clear, and it is probably best to begin in the comparative clarity of the seventeenth century.

MS 139 is listed and described in three virtually identical seventeenth-century compilations – Thomas James's *Ecloga Oxonio-Cantabrigiensis*, published at London in 1600, Dugdale's description of 1665 preserved in volume forty-eight of his *Collectanea*,[11] and Bernard's *Catalogue* of 1697.[12] Dugdale's and Bernard's descriptions are both derived from James's entry, where the manuscript is described as number 64 at Corpus Christi College. James, in his turn, had probably copied the fifteenth-century list of contents on folio 2^r of the manuscript. The manuscript in its present form has a series of index tags, in arabic numerals up to sixteen, attached to the edges of the folios, and these parallel James's description of the manuscript as one of sixteen items. Up to twelve the tags and James's list coincide, though tags eight and nine are now missing. There, however, things go awry. The present tag twelve has three numbers on it, while tags fifteen and

---

[10] The reference in item 6 to Somerled *qui usque hodie superest* poses some problems here. See appendix n 17.

[11] Oxford, Bodleian MS Dugdale 48 fol 45ᵛ. See appendix.

[12] [E.] Bernard, [*Catalogi Librorum Manuscriptorum Angliae et Hiberniae*] (Oxford 1697) I, 3, pp 131–46, no 1341. 64. See appendix.

sixteen are mistakenly attached to the St Mary's, York, and Fountains items. The other seventeenth-century references to the manuscript occur in Twysden's *Decem Scriptores* of 1652. Twysden knew only of this manuscript as the source for Symeon of Durham and John and Richard of Hexham. He also used it for Ailred's accounts of the battle of the Standard and the nun of Watton, and referred to two other items – Symeon's letter to dean Hugh of York, and to the account of the siege of Durham. In the seventeenth century, then, the manuscript was in its present form, and was already a unique exemplar of certain twelfth-century northern English histories. The record for the sixteenth century is not so straightforward.

There is no comparable listing of the contents of MS 139 in that century, but three writers referred to items in the manuscript in such a way as to leave no doubt as to which manuscript they were consulting. The three were Leland, Bale and Joscelin. John Joscelin (1529–1603) was chaplain and secretary to archbishop Parker (1504–75), and had much to do with Parker's acquisition of manuscripts during the period of his archiepiscopate (1559–75). Joscelin compiled a list of 'the names of those who have written the history of the English people and where they survive' which was printed by Hearne in 1720 in his *Robert of Avebury*.[13] Joscelin's list starts with a series of unnumbered items. Some pages later[14] entries begin to be numbered and the series proceeds as far as number thirty-two, only for numbering to be abandoned again in the later part of the list. The first four items in the list are described as Parker manuscripts; from there until the numbering commences Joscelin is drawing heavily on Bale, and Hearne seems to have indicated this by the kind of type he has used. Once the numbering has begun the references to Bale are scarcely more numerous than those to Twyne, though there are cases where the unacknowledged source must be Bale.

The first four items in Joscelin's list, said by him to be in the possession of Parker, are Felix's *Life of Guthlac*, the foundation accounts of St Mary's, York, and Fountains, and Ailred on the nun of Watton. Joscelin gives their initial lines, and the extracts make it clear that the second, third and fourth items are those preserved in MS 139. The Fountains foundation account, for example, is identified by Joscelin

[13] T. Hearne, *Roberti de Avesbury: Historia de Mirabilibus gestis Edvardi III, et Libri Saxonici, Nomina eorum qui scripserunt historiam gentis Anglorum et ubi exstant. Per J J* (Oxford 1720) pp 269–98. Printed from BM MS Cotton Nero C III fols 208ᵛ–12ᵛ. The manuscript has been refoliated since 1720. See appendix.
[14] *Ibid* p 274.

with the phrase *quomodo Funtanense Coenobium sumpsit exordium*, a title which appears in no other manuscript of the work. Joscelin's order is curious. In the manuscript the work by Ailred precedes rather than follows the other two, and is linked to other items, including Ailred's description of the battle of the Standard, which are not mentioned. Joscelin's list, however, is not notable for its organisation, and it would be unwise to lay too much stress on the eccentricities of order at any point in it.[15] Whatever his shortcomings, however, Joscelin is quite explicit as to how these three works came into Parker's possession. All were given to him by Nicholas Wooton (died 1566), the first dean of Canterbury. Wootton was also dean of York and treasurer of Exeter, and owed his advancement to his political capabilities, being employed by Henry VIII and his successors on various diplomatic missions. Joscelin knew of no other copies of these works.

In the numbered section of Joscelin's list Symeon of Durham's *Historia Regum* and letter to dean Hugh of York, and the works of John of Hexham and Richard of Hexham appear as items 11, 17 and 18. These, too, were given to Parker by Wootton and once again the extracts identify them as the texts in MS 139. Again, the order is curious, but the items recorded by Joscelin demonstrate that the greater part of MS 139 had been given to Parker by Wootton, and make it likely that the whole manuscript was in the archbishop's possession.[16] Joscelin also records, however, that a prebendary of Westminster, Pekyns or Peryns, possessed copies of Symeon of Durham, and John and Richard of Hexham. If this was so then they had vanished by the time that Twysden produced his edition of 1652: he does not even mention that they had once existed. The probability, however, is that Joscelin was duplicating the entries in Bale's list, where virtually identical manuscripts were shown to be at Westminster at a date before Parker had started collecting manuscripts in 1559.

John Bale (1495–1563), despite a rather turbulent career, published two lists of British writers, one in 1548[17] and the other, substantially

---

[15] Similar confusion can be found in Bale's list, items 12–20 in MS 139, for example, being ascribed to Ailred. See appendix.

[16] The items not mentioned by Joscelin, with the exception of the poem by Serlo, and Ailred's account of the battle of the Standard, are either anonymous, or by foreign authors. Ailred's treatise on the battle of the Standard begins a new gathering and lacks a formal rubric. It is introduced in the explicit of the previous item (11). For Joscelin and Bale's lists see C. E. Wright in *Transactions of the Cambridge Bibliographical Society*, I (1949–53).

[17] *Illustrium maioris Britanniae Scriptorum Summarium* (Ipswich 1548, reissued Wesel 1549).

larger, in 1557–9.[18] In the second of these appear all but four of the items in MS 139.[19] Of these, the *Chronicle* of Regino of Prum would find no place in a list of British writers, and items 21–3 are brief, anonymous items. All the items listed by Bale are ascribed, in his *Index*, to Westminster in one of two forms *ex coenobio* or *ex libro*, except for one copy of John of Hexham, said to be in the possession of Nicholas Brigham.[20] The *ex libro* entries, and the Brigham copy, duplicate certain of the *ex coenobio* entries, and might seem to supply evidence for the existence of two copies of the histories of Symeon of Durham, John and Richard of Hexham, and the foundation accounts of St Mary's, York, and Fountains. This apparent double existence of so much of MS 139 must, however, be regarded with suspicion. The extracts from the various items given by Bale, brief though they are,[21] make it certain that the double references to the St Mary's, York, and Fountains accounts are to the same copies – those in MS 139 – and the *ex coenobio* and Brigham references to John of Hexham are virtually identical, even to the misplacing of an annal for 1133. There is a similar, though not absolutely positive, correspondence between the extracts from Symeon of Durham and Richard of Hexham. The doubts thus raised as to Bale's accuracy are reinforced by an examination of the titles and incipits which he gives. In his references to John and Richard of Hexham, for example, there are incorrect titles, and incipits taken haphazardly from the works referred to: in one of the references to Richard of Hexham, the incipit given for *De Bello Standardii* is taken from the middle of the annal for 1138 in Richard's *History*, and in fact comes after the account of the battle.[22]

The best explanation of these inconsistencies and inaccuracies is to be found in the course of Bale's career.[23] In favour while Thomas Cromwell was in power, he went to Germany in 1540, returning on

[18] *Scriptorum illustrium maioris Brytannie Catalogus*, 2 parts (Basel 1557, 1559).

[19] Items 2, 21, 22, 23.

[20] Items 1, 3–10, 12–20, 24–6 are listed as *ex coenobio*, items 3, 4 and 7 appearing twice with this ascription. Items 11, 14 16 are listed as *ex libro*. Items 8a, 9, 8b are listed as *ex collectis* Nicolai Brigham (died 1558).

[21] For example, 'De Funtanensi coenobii, li.i. Anno 1132 ciclus lunaris' (*ex coenobio* entry). 'De Fundatione cenobii Funtanensis' and 'Stephanus . . . scripsit quomodo et a quibus cenobium dive Marie Eboraci fuerit fundatum' (*ex libro* entries).

[22] 'Ea tempestate quidam pestilentem'. See appendix.

[23] Though the essentially alphabetical nature of Bale's list could have caused the duplication of the St Mary's, York, and Fountains references: they appear first under Ailred, and later under Stephen of Whitby and Thurstan. See appendix.

DEREK BAKER

the accession of Edward VI in 1547. The first edition of his *Scriptores* was printed at Ipswich in 1548. In 1552 came his ill-fated appointment to the see of Ossory, but by 1553 he was again on the continent, at Basel from 1553–8, where the second edition of the *Scriptores* was published in 1557–9. On 1 January 1559 he became a prebendary of Canterbury, and he died four years later in 1563. R. L. Poole, in his edition of the *Index*,[24] remarked that it was unlikely that Bale had started collecting notes for his *Scriptores* before his return in 1547, was probably not seriously at work until 1549/50 and finished sometime after September 1557. For the greater part of this time Bale was out of England, and must have relied largely on correspondents and other lists – his use of Leland's collections is well-known. Duplication and inaccuracy on his part, are therefore, quite understandable, and his comments, on these particular authors, may reasonably be taken to indicate their presence at Westminster in MS 139, and only in that manuscript.[25]

It may, too, be possible from the comments of Bale and Joscelin to sketch in a little more of the manuscript's history before it came into Parker's hands. Bale ascribed the texts which comprise MS 139 to Westminster. Joscelin, in a number of places in his list, stated that certain manuscripts were in the possession of 'a prebendary of West Monaster called Pe Ryns', 'a prebendary of Westmonast', 'a Pekyns a prebendary of West'. All these manuscripts duplicate items in MS 139 and consist of the histories of Symeon of Durham and John and Richard of Hexham. William Peryn (died 1558) was a dominican who after two periods abroad (1534–43 and 1547–53) returned at the end of Edward VI's reign to a prebend at Westminster. When Mary restored regular life in England he became prior of the dominican house of St Bartholomew in Smithfield, the first of her revived houses, where he was buried

[24] Bale's autograph and untitled notebook, Bodleian MS Selden supra 64 (Bernard no 3452). Edited by R. L. Poole and M. Bateson, *Anecdota Oxoniensia*, medieval and modern series 9 (Oxford 1902) as *Index Britanniae Scriptorum*. The list is arranged alphabetically not chronologically, with most articles followed by source references. For Poole's description see pp vii–xxvi; the arrangement of the alphabetical scheme is explained on pp xxii–iii.

[25] One apparently serious divergence from the text of MS 139 appears in Bale's extract from the account of the siege of Durham (item 6). He gives the date as 980, the manuscript as 969. The siege, however, is referred to the reign of Ethelred, son of Edgar, who did not succeed until 979. Bale's date, therefore, can be seen as a correction of an obvious error—possibly his own correction since Leland gives 969 in his description of what is demonstrably the same manuscript. See appendix.

on 22 August 1558. Any books of which he had possession would probably have accompanied him to St Bartholomew's, and on his death, or at the beginning of the next reign, could have come into the possession of Wootton who, as Joscelin records, presented them to Parker.

Whatever the confusion of Bale's writings Leland's comments are much clearer, though not without their problems. In vol II of his *Collectanea*[26] Leland gives extracts from a manuscript which in order, contents and marginalia is so similar to MS 139 as to be beyond reasonable doubt the same manuscript. Walbran, however, in his 1862 edition of the *Foundation History* of Fountains abbey[27] asserted that Leland had not seen MS 139, basing his view on what appear to be decisive differences between the extracts from the Fountains material actually given by Leland and the text in MS 139 itself. Had Walbran consulted Leland's actual notebooks[28] rather than Hearne's edition (1770) of them[29] he would not have been misled. For example, the omissions in Leland's extracts which Walbran regarded as decisive are Hearne's and not Leland's. Where words are missing it is because of the dilapidation of Leland's notebook, and this has got worse since Hearne's day, but even now the tops of some of the missing words and letters are visible in the manuscript, and indicate what has been worn away – all of it in agreement with MS 139.[30] In similar fashion the variant readings which Walbran listed all arise from erasures, contractions and textual difficulties in MS 139 which Walbran misread.[31] In addition, Leland quotes the important contemporary footnote[32] to the manuscript text listing a number of cistercian abbots who were monks of Fountains, and remarks of it *haec notata erant in margine codicis*. This is true only of MS 139, and there are a number of other conclusive points of similarity between Leland's extracts and MS 139.[33] There can be no doubt, then, that Leland saw and described MS 139, and further references at another point in Leland's notebook indicate its location in his time. On pages 46–7 of MS Top. Gen. C. 2 are extracts from the *Historia Brittonum*, made available to Leland by Thomas Soulemont. The extracts identify the manuscript as MS 139, and further proof is supplied by Leland's

[26] Fols 301ʳ–20ᵛ. See appendix.
[27] [*Memorials of Fountains Abbey* I, ed J. R.] Walbran, *SS* 42 (1862).
[28] Oxford, Bodleian MS Top Gen. C.2.
[29] See below appendix n 16.
[30] See appendix n 23.
[31] He may not, in fact, have worked on the manuscript itself, see Walbran p lxxi.
[32] MS 139 fol 159ʳ.
[33] See appendix.

own reference to 'the Sawley codex', indicating that the manuscript still possessed its ex libris at that time.[34] The full description of MS 139 in Leland's notebook starts, without any introduction, at the top of folio 301[r] and finishes on folio 320[r], with the last two and a half inches of that side, and the whole of the verso, blank. The subsequent extracts from Higden begin on folio 321[r]. It is, of course, dangerous to argue from the juxtaposition of extracts in the *Collectanea*, but the extracts before folio 301 seem to show Leland moving from Barnwell to Oseney and Oxford, and then to St Albans. The references to Mountjoy, probably the fifth lord (1534–45), also serve to confirm his presence in or near the capital at this time, and make it probable that that is where he saw MS 139.

Leland lists, and quotes from, fourteen of the items which comprise MS 139, but his extracts show that he had the whole manuscript before him.[35] His account opens with references to Symeon of Durham's letter to dean Hugh of York (5), and Symeon's account of the siege of Durham (6). In the first of these Symeon is described as 'precentor', a title which, as Blair has shown,[36] indicates one of the manuscripts ascribed to Sawley,[37] and in this case MS 139. In the second, Leland gives the date '969' in the margin.[38] There then follows an account of the *Historia Regum* (7) with its various sections, corresponding to MS 139, clearly shown,[39] but with one important difference. On folio 309[r] extracts are given from an anonymous life of St Edith which appears nowhere in MS 139. Leland himself, however, distinguishes these extracts from those on either side of them, and they are best regarded as irrelevant to the manuscript being described. The *Historia Regum* is

---

[34] 'ex verbis quae superius scripta sunt coniectura mihi animum subit partem aliquam earum rerum quae in marginibus antiqui exemplaris exarantur autorem ipsum Nennium agnoscere cum Elbodi, qui et alias Elbogudus dicitur, mentionem faciat; et diligentem aliquem lectorem, collatis exemplaribus, ea in marginibus scripsisse, quae *in codice Salleiensis monasterii* [my italics] sensiit deesse.' Thomas Soulemont was French Secretary to Henry VIII from 1532 and Cromwell's Secretary from about 1537. He died in 1541. I owe this reference to Mr Dumville.

[35] It is impossible to separate Symeon's letter (item 5), with which Leland's description now starts, from items 2–4 in MS 139. In view of his reference to the Sawley ex libris it is unlikely that the manuscript that Leland saw lacked item 1, and probable that his notebook has since lost some leaves. See appendix n 16.

[36] pp 75–6.

[37] See below.

[38] See above n 25.

[39] For a detailed account of these sub-sections of item 7 see Blair pp 76–118.

followed by the first part of John of Hexham's continuation (8a), the pieces by Serlo and Ailred on the battle of the Standard (10, 11), the remainder of John of Hexham (8b), Ailred on the nun of Watton (13), the St Mary's, York, and Fountains items (14–16), the anonymous account of Aella's adultery (21) and the *Life of Gildas* (26). The remarkable thing about these extracts is the absence of any reference to the first four items in the manuscript – Bale, for example, recording three of them, and in the order in which we find them in MS 139 – and, in particular, to Richard of Hexham, who appears nowhere else in Leland's collections. The most credible explanation is that here, as elsewhere,[40] Leland's notebook lacks leaves which, in this case, would have recorded the earlier items, and perhaps have indicated where Leland found the manuscript. It is certain that Leland is describing MS 139, and whatever the state of its binding when he saw it the foliation and gatherings do not allow him to have seen Symeon's letter and account of the siege of Durham without having seen the three previous items.

It is, however, probable that MS 139 was in a dilapidated state when Leland saw it, though without affecting its overall shape – Leland consistently refers to it as 'an old codex' – and this is the most likely explanation of the appearance of the life of St Edith in the middle of his description of the *Historia Regum*, possibly at a point where the gatherings divided.[41] At some point in the sixteenth century a number of marginal comments were added to the manuscript, some of them noting the loss of folios from it, not altogether accurately. Whoever the annotator was, and there is some evidence that it may have been Joscelin,[42] he found the manuscript confusing, both in its contents and in its condition, and was concerned to put it in order. This is most likely to have occurred when the manuscript came into Parker's hands. There is evidence that it was dilapidated before he acquired it, and it is likely that it was then rebound without any substantial rearrangement of the contents except the addition of a paper folio concerned to call attention to the similarity of Symeon's and Hoveden's material, and, perhaps, the removal of a misplaced account of St Edith.

---

[40] See Hearne.

[41] See appendix n 8. There are similar comments in Joscelin's list, and the hand appears to be the same.

[42] Corpus Christi College Cambridge MS 66 has a list of contents in the same hand as the list in MS 139, implying that the manuscripts were together in the fifteenth century. It does not, however, follow that both were at Sawley then. Given the similarity of content it is possible that both left Sawley together. I owe this reference to Mr Dumville.

In Leland's time, therefore, before the dissolution, MS 139 was an 'old codex' in the possession of Thomas Soulemont, and in very much the same form then as it is now, and when it was put together in the latter part of the twelfth century. It still had its Sawley ex libris, though this was soon to be erased, possibly on its move to Westminster, and a fifteenth-century list of contents had been added to it.[42] There is no certain indication as to when the book was moved from Sawley, but it is possible to hypothesise. The death of queen Margaret of Scotland on 26 September 1290 led the claimants to the Scottish throne to seek Edward I's adjudication. He for his part, as the historian of Meaux records,[43] wishing to establish beyond doubt his right to act, and his position as superior lord of the Scottish kingdom, ordered a comprehensive investigation of 'ancient chronicles in the archives of churches and monasteries' to identify and present relevant historical evidence. Each house was to assign two monks to the task, and that it was duly, if inconclusively, completed is evident from the account of the assembly at Norham in May and June 1291, and from the catalogue of incidents recorded by Thomas Burton from the early tenth to the later twelfth century.[44] Some of the chroniclers consulted are mentioned by name – Hoveden amongst them – and though MS 139 is not so identified it is difficult to imagine a more relevant and varied collection of texts. Perhaps it was at this juncture that the manuscripts moved from Sawley.

Blair's account of the manuscript distinguished its final two gatherings as a separate volume. Other similar distinctions can be made, and I have suggested that the manuscript is best regarded as a collection of texts, separately copied, and subsequently, though early, combined into a volume which thereafter retained its form, though not its binding. Such a view limits the scope for general conclusions about the manuscript as a whole and imposes caution in attempting to frame them. It is, in fact, necessary to consider the questions of date of compilation and provenance in a sectional, rather than an overall, context in the first instance.

The *universal history*, which comprises the first section of the manuscript,[45] ends with a list of the popes to Calixtus II (1119–24). Like the final section which Blair distinguished, and which can be dated before

[43] [*Chronica Monasterii de*] *Melsa*, [ed E. A. Bond], *RS* 43, 3 vols (1866–8) II p 252. See [F. M.] Powicke, [*The Thirteenth Century*] (Oxford 1953).
[44] *Melsa* II pp 253–4, Powicke p 603. See Walbran p 140 n 2.
[45] Gatherings I–II, fols 3–18.

1166,[46] it is markedly different from the rest of the manuscript. The penultimate section, now, apparently, consisting of only half a gathering,[47] concludes with a vision in which the spirit of Malcolm IV of Scotland appears. The king died in 1165. The fifth section, containing the St Mary's, York, and Fountains material, and the short extracts from Malmesbury's *Gesta Regum* (finished 1125), is of uncertain date.[48] The account of the foundation of Fountains is given in what purports to be a letter of archbishop Thurstan of York written in the autumn of 1132, but there is little doubt that the letter is a later fabrication, written *c* 1145.[49] With the second, third and fourth sections of the manuscript we are on surer ground. The second section,[50] which is in a different hand to the sections which follow it, includes Richard of Hexham's *History*,[51] and the rubric refers to him in the past.[52] Richard was prior of Hexham from 1141 till at least 1154, and was still alive in the period 1161-7. This second section also contains Symeon of Durham's letter to dean Hugh of York[53] and an account of the siege of Durham.[54] In the former, a list of the archbishops of York ends with Roger of Bishops Bridge, archbishop from 1154 to 1181.[55] In the latter, reference is made to a *Sumerlede qui usque hodie superest.*[56]

The third section[57] contains the *Historia Regum*[58] and the first part of its continuation by John of Hexham,[59] an extract from Florence of Worcester,[60] and two poems, one on the battle of the Standard by Serlo,[61] and one on the death of Somerled, in 1164, sometimes mis-

---

[46] Gatherings XXI–XXII, fols 168–82. See Dumville, 'The Corpus Christi *Nennius*' p 371.
[47] Gathering XX, fols 164–7.
[48] Gathering XIX, fols 152–63.
[49] A detailed discussion of this text is forthcoming in *Analecta Cisterciensia*.
[50] Gatherings III–VI, fols 19–53.
[51] Fols 38ʳ–48ʳ.
[52] 'pie memorie'.
[53] Fols 40ᵛ–2ʳ.
[54] Fols 52ʳ–3ᵛ.
[55] In BM MS Cotton Titus A XIX (15th century) the list of archbishops ends with Thurstan (1114–40).
[56] See below appendix n 17. If this is a mistaken reference to the Somerled who died in 1164 (see item 11) then it reinforces the case for the separate compilation, and subsequent combination, of sections 2 and 3 of MS 139 and, incidentally, might suggest that Richard of Hexham was dead by 1164. See *HRH*.
[57] Gatherings VII–XVI, fols 54–135.
[58] Fols 54ʳ–131ʳ.
[59] Fols 131ᵛ–4ʳ.
[60] Fol 134ʳ/ᵛ. Preceded by an erased rubric.
[61] Fols 134ᵛ–5ʳ.

takenly ascribed to Serlo.[62] Leland, followed by Bale, copying the fifteenth-century list of contents in MS 139, but adding to it, refers to Serlo as a monk, and the brother of abbot Radulphus of Louth Park.[63] Ralph was the second abbot of Louth Park and occurs in 1155 and 1176/7. There is, however, no contemporary justification or rubric for this assertion, and it certainly cannot be assumed, as Blair does, that the author of the poem is identical with the monk Serlo who is said to have dictated much of the *Narratio de Fundatione Fontanis Monasterii*.[64] Fortunately the dating of this section of the manuscript does not depend on these relationships. In the *Historia Regum* the annal for 1074[65] contains references to abbot Clement of York (1161–84) and abbot Richard of Whitby (1148–75), and the death of Somerled[66] can be dated to 1164. It is, I think, not possible to achieve greater precision, though Blair argues that the rubrics to the *Historia Regum* can be taken to indicate a completion date of September 1164.[67]

[62] Fol 135r/v.

[63] 'Descriptio Serlonis monachi fratris Radulphi abbatis de Parcho de . . . .' (rubric), 'Descriptio Serlonis monachi metrice de . . . (contents list).

[64] See Blair p 67. It is not possible to sustain the identification of Serlo the poet with Serlo the author of the foundation history of Fountains. The name is common in the twelfth century. A canon of York called Serlo was one of three early recruits to Fountains, would seem to have preceded his namesake at the house, and might be regarded as a more likely poet than the later 'historian of Fountains'. The statement of relationship between a Serlo and abbot Ralph of Louth Park is, however, interesting in the light of the chronicler of Fountains' claim to be related to some of the exiles from St Mary's, York, who founded Fountains. It has not been possible to demonstrate any such relationship from the historical accounts of the foundation and development of Fountains, but this comment in a later twelfth-century cistercian manuscript may embody contemporary knowledge misapplied to the author of the poem on the battle of the Standard. For Serlo of Fountains, and the attempts to give him a literary reputation see [L. G. D.] Baker, '[The] Genesis [of English Cistercian Chronicles. The Foundation History of Fountains Abbey]', I, *Analecta Cisterciensia* 25, 1 (1969) pp 28–32. For abbot Ralph see Walbran p 71 note.

[65] See Blair pp 69–70, 78.

[66] *Ibid* p 68. Dumville, 'The Corpus Christi *Nennius*' p 371, notes that fol 135 is a 'later addition' to gathering XVI, but the folio cannot be as sharply distinguished from the rest of the gathering as he implies.

[67] For Blair's argument see pp 77–8. It is not altogether convincing. It demands that the rubricator be sufficiently alert to describe the *Historia Regum* more or less correctly as spanning the period from the death of Bede almost to the death of Henry I (1129), and sufficiently muddled to calculate the span of time to his own day, and give it as 429 years and four months (not 329 years as given by Blair on p 75). It might seem as plausible to suggest 'ccccxxix' as a misreading of 'mcxxix', the terminal date of the *Historia Regum*. Nor is it altogether satisfactory to identify the inconsistencies of the copyists (See Blair pp 65, 78, and above n 55) with the practice of the rubricator. The rubrics

In the fourth section,[68] the two works by Ailred, on the battle of the Standard[69] and the nun of Watton[70] were probably composed between 1155–7 and 1158–65 (probably 1160).[71] The second part of John of Hexham's continuation of the *Historia Regum*, which is sandwiched between them, ends in 1153, while John first appears as prior of Hexham in 1161.[72]

For these three sections, then, the chronological limits of composition are 1161–4/7 (section 2), 1164–75 (section 3) and after 1161/5 (section 4). The two references to different Somerleds, one living, one dead, each occurring at the end of their respective sections, might suggest, depending on how the first is regarded, that section 2 was completed before section 3. Sections 3 and 4 seem to be bound together by the two halves of John of Hexham's continuation, but the arbitrary division of John's text into widely-separated parts is almost inconceivable in the author's lifetime.[73] There can at the moment be no simple explanation for this treatment, and much still needs to be done to clarify the composition and combination of these central sections of MS 139. It is, however, possible that the copyists of these parts of MS 139 were engaged in compiling a collection of historical materials from a number of sources, some to hand, some borrowed,[74] in a variety of conditions. If John of Hexham's continuation was not a separate work, or a distinct gathering, an unobservant or careless copyist could have continued the *Historia Regum* with the first part of John of Hexham's account[75] and then failed to select or notice the

---

themselves need to be treated with caution. In this context Joscelin's reference to another Durham history which appears to end in 1164 is interesting, and perhaps significant. See below appendix n 52.

[68] Gatherings XVII–XVIII, fols 136–51.

[69] Fols 135^v–40^r.

[70] Fols 149^r–51^v.

[71] Walter Daniel, *Life of Ailred*, ed F. M. Powicke (London 1950) p xcix.

[72] For John of Hexham see *HRH* p 66.

[73] The erased rubric which follows item 8a, if it can be read, may do something to illuminate this question.

[74] It is suggested below that MS 139 should be ascribed, in the first instance, to Fountains rather than Sawley, and one of the early important recruits to the house was Symeon's correspondent, dean Hugh of York, who brought with him a large number of books. These are likely to have suffered in the difficult early years of the house, and, more particularly, in the burning of the house in the course of the York election dispute. The contents of MS 139 may be part of a programme of replacing damaged or destroyed texts, and it may be noted that the so-called foundation charter of Fountains is of much the same date.

[75] To which it might have been attached in the copyists' original.

second part,[76] and this is probably the most likely explanation for their curious arrangement in MS 139. Sections 2, 3 and 4 of MS 139 are given an overall unity by their subject matter, form and rubrics, and it is clear that they were combined into one volume sometime after 1164, and probably before 1175. To suggest September 1164 on an interpretation of the *Historia Regum* rubrics seems to me to be unjustifiably precise on the evidence as it stands, and tends to confuse the composition of these sections with their combination into a separate, but short-lived volume.[77] What can certainly not be said either is that 'this date [September 1164] has a clear significance not so much for item 7 itself, the *Historia Regum*, as for the whole book of which it forms a part'[78] or that 'all the items to the end of the book were written in the form in which we find them in this manuscript not earlier than 1164'.[79] For the penultimate section, containing the vision of Malcolm IV (died 1165), this is demonstrably the case, but for the fifth section in particular there can be no such certainty, though its hand assigns it to the later twelfth century.

In the discussion of MS 139 this same fifth section is of significance in another context. Most commentators, James amongst them, have ascribed MS 139 to Hexham.[80] Mommsen, however, on the grounds of the manuscript's similarity to a Sawley manuscript now split between two Cambridge volumes[81] argued that it should be ascribed to Sawley.[82] Blair indicated difficulties in the Hexham attribution, reviewed the evidence of local interest in Yorkshire, suggested a cistercian scriptorium in Yorkshire and, in agreement with Mommsen, chose Sawley. The subsequent rediscovery of an erased Sawley *ex libris*

[76] This may not even have been to hand when section 3 of MS 139 was being copied.

[77] Blair p 78. Elsewhere (p 70), he suggests *c* 1170 as 'a likely approximation'. See Offler, 'Hexham and the Historia Regum'.

[78] Blair p 78.

[79] *Ibid* p 69. If, as Dumville suggests (see n 66 above) the Somerled poem is an addition to the gathering then the dates for the second section of MS 139 must be extended to 1161-7. It is, however, important to keep the sectional nature of MS 139 clearly in mind when seeking to arrive at an acceptable dating.
Dumville's demonstration that some of the marginalia to the final section of MS 139 must be dated before 1166 is decisive for that section only. Without such clear corroboration for other sections it cannot be extended to them. See 'The Corpus Christi *Nennius*' pp 374-9.

[80] See M. R. James p 323; Blair pp 72-6, 116-18.

[81] Corpus Christi College 66, pp 1-114; Cambridge University Library Ff 1. 27, pp 1-40, 73-252. See Dumville, 'The Corpus Christi *Nennius*' pp 371-2.

[82] Founded 1148.

in MS 139 by the use of ultra-violet light[83] confirmed Mommsen and Blair's conclusions, and might seem to have resolved this question finally. It is, however, not altogether certain that it has.

The fifth section of MS 139 comprises a single gathering (XIX) of twelve folios, the last two of these being a doubled sheet. The greater part of the gathering is occupied by the accounts of the foundation of St Mary's, York, and Fountains, and it is clear that these are all that it was intended to contain. Later the remaining, unused part of the final folio was filled with random extracts from William of Malmesbury's *Gesta Regum*, and the doubled folio was added so that they could be continued. Unlike the double columns of 35 lines of the original folios of this gathering, this additional doubled folio is written in double columns of 36 lines. The added material from Malmesbury has nothing further to contribute to the discussion of the manuscript. The St Mary's, York, and Fountains material does.

The account of the foundation of St Mary's, York, ascribed to Stephen of Whitby, occupies the first three folios of the gathering,[84] and is, it may be suggested, a direct copy of the original.[85] It has only one contemporary marginal addition, at the foot of the verso of the second folio,[86] but the addition is significant. It records the death of earl Alan, a benefactor of St Mary's, and terms him *amicus noster*. Taken by itself such a marginal note would scarcely suggest a cistercian scriptorium for this copy of Stephen of Whitby's account. In fact, however, the same note is to be found within the text on the next folio, and it may be suggested that the scribe was copying a very early St Mary's copy, arguably the original, of Stephen of Whitby's history, and that he first transcribed an existing footnote, recording the death of the first major benefactor of the house, leaving it as a footnote since there was no indicator referring it to a particular place in the text, and then later inserted it into the text when he came to an appropriate place: at the end of the account given of earl Alan, and before a list of benefactors.[87] This copy of Stephen of Whitby could, in fact, have been copied in a cistercian scriptorium, and there are other indications[88] that it was. There is little need to emphasise that Fountains owed its foundation to

[83] Blair p 118.
[84] Fols 152r-4v.
[85] See *Chartulary of Whitby*, ed J. C. Atkinson, SS 69 (1869); *The Chronicles of St Mary's Abbey, York*, ed H. H. E. Craster and M. E. Thornton, SS 148 (1934).
[86] Fol 153va.
[87] Fol 154rb.
[88] See below.

a riot at St Mary's, and that those who seceded from St Mary's included most of the officers of the house and some whose careers in religion stretched back to the first springs of revival of the regular life in the north at Whitby.[89] Their interest, and that of their confreres, in possessing a copy of the foundation account of Whitby is not difficult to appreciate, and if, as seems likely, there was less friction between those who left, and those who remained at St Mary's than twelfth-century polemicists allowed, then the original of Stephen of Whitby's history could easily have been accessible to them.

The other foundation account, that of Fountains, is of no less interest, though it is certainly not the letter of archbishop Thurstan of York which it purports to be.[90] It is written in the same hand as the St Mary's, York, history and is similar to it in every way, except that it shows signs of very careful correction, and has extensive underlining. Its particular interest, in the present context, lies once again in the notes added to it: first, an elaborate dating clause recording the foundation of Fountains on 27 December 1132,[91] and, second, a footnote listing those of the original exiles from St Mary's, York, who became cistercian abbots.[92] From its inclusion of Adam, first abbot of Meaux (founded 1150) some indication of the date of the footnotes can be gained. MS 139 is the oldest surviving copy of this Fountains account, but there is no explicit evidence in it of provenance. The next oldest exemplar is a fine early thirteenth-century copy bearing the Fountains ex libris. It retains its contemporary seal-skin binding and is now in the Bodleian.[93] This copy is contemporary with a wide-ranging activity at Fountains which is visible in the great building works, of which so much still remains, and in the production of a commissioned foundation history of the house – the Narratio de Fundationis already mentioned.[94] To this activity the production of the Bodleian manuscript should probably be related, and it may be regarded as an official copy of the text to be found in MS 139,[95] probably replacing an earlier, less elegant Fountains copy.

[89] See [Derek] Baker, ['The] Foundation [of Fountains Abbey]', NH 4 (1969) pp 29–43; 'The Desert in the North', NH 5 (1970) p 1–11.

[90] See Baker, 'Genesis' and 'Foundation'.

[91] Fol 154vb.   [92] Fol 159r, see appendix n 23.

[93] [Corpus Christi College] D 209.   [94] See n 27 above.

[95] MS D 209, like MS 139, may be divided into a number of distinct sections. The third and final section, comprising gatherings XIII–XVI, fols 92–109, contains, first, the Exordium of Citeaux and then the 'letter of Thurstan'—clearly seen as an English Exordium.

A comparison of the two versions is instructive in a number of ways, and particularly when the footnotes are considered. In the Bodleian copy the footnote in MS 139 listing the names of the abbots is placed in the body of the text, at the point to which MS 139 refers it.[96] The elaborate dating footnote, which precedes the text in MS 139, follows the text in the Bodleian copy. This is a significant difference. It is clear that the dating footnote is intended to precede the account of the foundation of Fountains, and all other medieval copies of this text place it there.[97] The Bodleian copy is eccentric in this respect, and it is an eccentricity which requires explanation. Either the copyist was extremely careless, which is unlikely, or else the mistake arose from the state of the manuscript which he was copying. When MS 139 is considered an explanation suggests itself. In that manuscript the footnotes are additions to a complete and coherent text, and it is clear that MS 139 is the original of these notes.[98] Because they are additions, however, they had to be fitted in where there was room for them. For the list of cistercian abbots this meant beneath the double columns of 35 lines.[99] For the dating clause, however, there was just space at the bottom of the previous folio.[100] Stephen of Whitby's account left seven lines of the second column on the final verso blank. Here the dating clause was inserted, and there is no visible break between it and the previous item. The Fountains account begins at the top of the recto of the next folio,[101] and it would have been easy for a scribe concerned to copy only the Fountains account to have missed the dating clause tagged on to the previous item until it was too late to do anything about it. Once the omission was discovered the dating clause could only be included by placing it at the end, and altering it slightly.[102] It may be suggested, then, that the Bodleian manuscript is not simply a fine copy of an earlier Fountains text, but that it is a direct copy of MS 139 itself. If this hypothesis can be sustained, and the collation of the two texts supplies other evidence which supports it,[103] then important conclusions can be reached about this fifth section of MS 139. If a fine copy of

[96] See MS 139 fol 159ʳ, MS D 209 fol 107ʳ.

[97] See BM MS Cotton Otho C XIV; Oxford Bodleian MS 39.

[98] The rubric to the 'letter of Thurstan' in MS D 209 is followed by a line and a half of erasures which are now totally illegible. It is possible, however, that they represent an abortive attempt to fit in the dating clause, in its proper place, once the omission had been discovered.

[99] Fol 159ʳ.   [100] Fol 154ᵛᵇ.   [101] Fol 155ʳ.

[102] '. . . sicut precedens [sequens] epistola manifeste demonstravit [demonstrabit]'. MS 139 readings in brackets.

[103] Detailed collation will be given in Baker, 'Genesis' III, forthcoming.

the Fountains history, produced at the house itself, and combined in the manuscript with the *Exordium* of Cîteaux, can be shown to have been directly derived from another, substantially earlier copy of the same text then it is reasonable to assume that that earlier copy is itself a Fountains manuscript and, as with the St Mary's, York, history, in all probability a direct copy of the earliest version of the text.

These conclusions apply, of course, only to the fifth section of MS 139 and not necessarily to the whole manuscript. There are, as has been said, indications that this fifth section – and others – of MS 139 had an independent existence, if, probably, only for a very short time.[104] It is possible, however, on other evidence to extend the conclusions reached for this section of MS 139 to other sections of the manuscript.

Blair drew attention to the material of cistercian provenance and interest in the central sections of MS 139[105] in arguing for its production in a cistercian scriptorium, and the evidence he assembled can be supplemented in a number of respects. The footnotes to the Fountains foundation account are, as has been said, distinct from the text itself – additions to it in a different hand, though of very much the same date. They can, however, be related to certain other notes and headings in MS 139 which they resemble in type and hand. In the margins of the *Historia Regum* there are three notes about the monks of Tiron, one written over an earlier note, and claiming that the Tironenses arrived in England ten years before the Savigniacs and one about the Savigniac foundation at Tulketh.[106] To John of Hexham's continuation of Symeon of Durham there are marginalia on the foundations of Byland[107] and Newminster,[108] a note on Richard 'second abbot of Fountains',[109] references to St Bernard and Henry Murdac,[110] a note on their deaths in 1153,[111] and a gloss on David I of Scotland.[112] There is a significant marginal comment to Ailred's account of the battle of the Standard in

[104] See above pp 84–5.

[105] Blair pp 72–4.

[106] For discussion of these notes see G. W. S. Barrow, 'From Queen Margaret to David I: Benedictines and Tironians', *Innes Review* 11 (Glasgow 1960) pp 22–38, repr *The Kingdom of the Scots* (London 1973) pp 188–211. The Tironian notes appear on fols 122vb, 123^r, 130^v. The second of these is written over an earlier note. The Tulketh reference is on fol 128^r.

[107] Fol 132vb.

[108] Fol 140va.

[109] Fol 143^v.

[110] Fol 148^v.

[111] *Ibid*

[112] *Ibid*

which the foundation of Fountains is referred to *vi kal ianuarii*,[113] the only place this date occurs apart from the dating clause added to the Fountains history itself.[114] Finally, the rubric added to the St Mary's, York history is reminiscent of the opening of the *Exordium Parvum*.[115]

It is reasonable, then, on these grounds to group the section of MS 139 which contains the St Mary's, York, and Fountains material with the two previous sections,[116] and to envisage its combination with them not long after their own combination into one volume.[117] The added contemporary rubrics and incipits/explicits further bind them together, and link them with the first two sections,[118] while the contemporary enumeration of the gatherings binds the whole manuscript together.[119] In spite, therefore, of the divisions and differences which can be demonstrated between the sections of MS 139 they can be taken together as a compilation of the later twelfth century in the examination of the provenance of the manuscript.

There can be no real doubt as to the validity of Mommsen's and Blair's arguments for a Yorkshire cistercian scriptorium,[120] and the associated ascription to Sawley is strongly supported. It does not rest simply on the presence in MS 139 of an erased Sawley *ex libris*, of which both Mommsen and Blair were unaware when they wrote. Mommsen drew attention to the close similarity in form, style and contents between MS 139 and another, now divided Sawley manuscript, to which I have already referred,[121] and rightly emphasised that

---

[113] Fol 139ʳ.
[114] Fol 154ᵛᵇ.
[115] Fol 152ʳ. See appendix. Most of these notes are in the same hand, which can perhaps be seen again on fol 168ᵛ in the reference to the abbots of Fountains, see M. R. James p 321.
[116] Gatherings VII–XVIII, fols 54–151
[117] The state of the outside folios of sections 2–4 (fols 19–151), and section 5 (fols 152–63) suggest a short-lived existence as separate volumes—as with section 1 (fols 3–18).
[118] Item 9, the extract from Florence of Worcester, lacks any introduction but is preceded by an erased rubric which may refer to it.
[119] Only gathering XX, which has, apparently, lost its final folio since MS 139 was put together, and gathering XXII, the final gathering, have no numbers. Gatherings I and XXI, which lack their final leaves, are numbered, and were therefore in their present form before the manuscript was put together.
[120] See Blair pp 70–6 for a resumé of the evidence.
[121] Above n 81. See Blair p 76, n 1 for reference to possible palaeographical similarities, but see Dumville, 'The Corpus Christi *Nennius*' p 371 n 4. Dumville has shown that the 'Nennius' portion of MS 66 cannot be dated before 1202–7 (see p 377), but further work on the compilation of this manuscript is needed before this conclusion can be extended.

it was unlikely that such similar volumes should be compiled independently at different centres at the same time. In the absence of any other positive indication of provenance it was not unreasonable to accept the case for Sawley. Now, however, on the basis of the discussion of the Fountains material in MS 139, and its comparison with the early thirteenth-century copy in Bodleian MS Corpus Christi D 209,[122] it seems preferable to attribute them to Fountains, and to suggest that they moved at a later, though still early date, to Sawley.[123] It would not be surprising if Fountains had early possessed some historical materials relating to Durham and the north – dean Hugh of York, Symeon of Durham's correspondent, had been one of the earliest recruits to Fountains (c 1135), and is said to have brought with him numerous books, which were the foundation of a library.[124] Nor was it unknown for manuscripts to move from one house to another legitimately, particularly within a single filiation. Little is known about the early history of Sawley (founded 1148), but that little suggests that it was a poor, insecure and struggling house, and unlikely to have had much of a library.[125] It was the sort of house which might have been expected to have received manuscripts like Corpus 139 and Corpus 66/UL Ff 1.27 when they were duplicated at Fountains by the Bodleian manuscript (Corpus D 209) and Faustina A. V., particularly if the close connection between Fountains and Sawley in the early thirteenth century is taken into consideration.

The thirteenth-century *Narratio de Fundationis* of Fountains ends with a note about Stephen of Easton, abbot from 1247 to 1252. Stephen of Easton had been cellarer of Fountains under two successive abbots, John of Ely (1209–20) and John of Kent (1220–47). In about 1225 he became abbot of Sawley, a charge he occupied for some ten years. By 1236 he was abbot of Newminster, the mother house of Sawley, and the senior of Fountains' daughter houses, and in 1247 he returned to

---

[122] See above pp 100.

[123] Blair (p 74) notes that the text of the *Historia Dunelmensis Ecclesia* in Cambridge University Library MS Ff 1. 27 ranks in date after the Durham and Fountains copies. This latter copy, now BM MS Faustina A.V. 10, was copied at Durham, and had moved to Fountains in or before the early thirteenth century. It is worth noting that none of the Durham copies of the *HDE* refer to Symeon as precentor.

[124] See Walbran p 53. Blair, p 65, refers to two dean Hughs, but Clay is of the opinion that all the references are to the same man. *York Minster Fasti*, ed C. T. Clay, *YAS*, Record Series 123 (1958) 1, p 1.

[125] Sawley was a daughter house of Newminster, itself the first colony sent out from Fountains. See the comments of Walbran pp 62–3 note, 93 n 4,

Fountains itself, dying in 1252. His occupation of the office of cellarer of Fountains during the greatest period of building in the history of the house, his *Meditations on the Joys of the Virgin*, and the concern for his monks which they demonstrate, and his reputation for posthumous miracle-working testify to his ability, talents and quality. It would not be surprising if Sawley had acquired from Fountains major texts bearing on the religious life of the north in the twelfth century in general, and of the cistercians of Fountains in particular, during the abbacy of Stephen of Easton.[126]

Much of what has been suggested here is, of course, conjecture, lacking final proof, but it is not, I think, entirely idle or barren conjecture. Much remains to be done in the elucidation of MS 139 and related manuscripts, and of the problems which arise from them – how are we to regard the so-called *Historia Regum* and its author? How could any copyist divide John of Hexham's continuation so arbitrarily during the lifetime of its author? Why was such interest shown in the foundations of Tiron? When the texts associated and combined in MS 139 are considered it is plain that the sources, materials and methods of ecclesiastical history were as complex and contentious in the twelfth century as they are today.

[126] For Stephen of Easton (Sawley) see Walbran pp 135–6; A Wilmart, 'Les méditations d'Etienne de Salley sur les Joies de la Vierge Marie', *Auteurs spirituels et textes dévots du moyen age latin* (Paris 1971) pp 317–60; Derek Baker, 'The surest road to heaven', *SCH* 10 (1973) pp 55–7.

APPENDIX

This appendix lists the contents of MS 139, analyses its construction, and presents the references made to the manuscript between the later fifteenth century and the end of the seventeenth century. Its main purpose is to elucidate the discussion in the text of the paper, but it may also be taken to indicate the problems of the manuscript, and to suggest areas in which further study is required. In particular, the collation of the manuscript reveals a series of sub-sections each containing a major text or texts, and filled out with a number of short minor works or extracts on the remaining blank folios of each sub-section. Such a technique of compilation opens the way to further consideration of MS 139 itself, and the *Historia Regum* in particular, and suggests that it may be useful and fruitful to compare it and its sub-sections with contemporary manuscripts from neighbouring scriptoria in the north.

I. *Contents*[1]

Item 1 (Tag 1)	Historia omnimoda ab orbe condito ad regnum Davidis, cui subnectuntur nomina pontificum Romanorum a S. Petro ad Calixtum II.
Item 2 (Tag 2)	Cronica abbatis Prumiensis monasterii a Christo nato ad annum 1002.
Item 3 (Tag 3)	Historia piae memoriae Ricardi prioris Hagustaldensis ecclesiae de gestis regis Stephani et de bello Standardii.
Item 4 (Tag 4)	Cronica ab Adamo usque ad Henricum V imperatorem.
Item 5 (Tag 5)	Epistola Simeonis monachi ecclesiae S. Cuthberti Dunelmi ad Hugonem decanum Eboracensem de archiepiscopis Eboraci.
Item 6	De obsessione Dunelmi et de probitate Ucthredi comitis.
Item 7 (Tag 6)	Historia sanctae et suavis memoriae Symeonis monachi et precentoris ecclesiae sancti Cuthberti Dunelmi de Regibus Anglorum et Dacorum et creberrimis bellis et rapinis et incendiis eorum post obitum venerabilis Bedae presbiteri fere usque ad obitum Henrici filii Willelmi nothi.
Item 8a (Tag 7)	Historia Iohannis prioris Hagustaldensis ecclesiae XXV annorum.
Item 9	De Cometa et combustione Londoniarum et aliis iniuriis. [Florence of Worcester]
Item 10	Descriptio Serlonis monachi fratris Radulphi abbatis de Parcho de bello inter regem Scotiae et barones [Carmen Serlonis]
Item 11	Carmen de morte Sumerledi.

[1] The titles given are taken from the manuscript whenever possible. Where no title or rubric is given in the manuscript the content of the item is indicated. No existing enumeration of the items which comprise the manuscript is wholly satisfactory. The fifteenth-century list of contents, and the description by Thomas James are both significantly incomplete. The enumeration by M. R. James is over-elaborate in some respects, and inadequate in others. The enumeration given here retains M. R. James's list and adds to it the extract *De cometa* etc (item 9), and renumbers the *Carmen de Morte Sumerledi* (item 11). This, however, should be regarded merely as an interim measure pending further work on the manuscript. Blair (p 64, n 2) has noted the error in M. R. James's foliation of the manuscript and described the differing paginations employed in the various descriptions of it. At this stage in the study of the manuscript it has seemed best to number the present folios of the manuscript consecutively throughout from 1 to 182. For the fifteenth-century list of contents and the description by Thomas James see below.

Item 12 (Tag 10)   Descriptio venerabilis viri Aethelredi abbatis Rievallis de bello inter regem Scotiae et barones Angliae apud Standardum iuxta Alvertoniam.

Item 8b (Tag 11)   John of Hexham (continued).

Item 13 (Tags 12–14)   Quoddam miraculum mirabile descriptum a viro venerabili Aethelredo abbate Rievall. de quadam sanctimoniali femina de Wattun.

Item 14 (Tag 15)   Quo modo et a quibus cenobium S. Mariae Eboraci fundatum sit, et quantas invidorum perturbationes impulsum sustinuerat, sed Dei protegente gratia magis ac magis auctum et multiplicatum fuerat; autore Stephano eiusdem cenobii abbate.

Item 15   Quo modo Funtanense cenobium sumpsit exordium.

Item 16 (Tag 16)   Epistola Thurstini archiepiscopi Ebor. ad Wilhelmum archiepiscopum Cantuar. de cenobio S. Mariae Ebor. et observantia regulae S. Benedicti in eo.

Item 17   De vita de conversatione Gereberti Papae ⎫ extracts from William of

Item 18   Visio Karoli imperatoris ⎬ Malmesbury

Item 19   Visio S. Maurilii *Gesta*

Item 20   De annulo statuae commendato ⎭ *Regum*

Item 21   Narratio de uxore Ernulfi ab Aella rege Deirorum violata.

Item 22   De eo quod Eboracensis ecclesia nullum dominium super Scotos habere debet.

Item 23   Visio cuiusdam clerici de gloria regis Malcolmi.

Item 24   Eulogium brevissimum Britanniae insulae quod Ninnius Elvodugi discipulus congregavit.

Item 25   Res gestae a Nennio Sapiente compositae.

Item 26   Vita sanctissimi atque doctissimi viri Gildae autore Caradoco Nancarbanensi.

2. Collation[2]

Actual foliation	Gathering	No of folios	Lines (double cols)	Contents
1–2				Fly leaf, ex libris, list of contents
3–11	I	10^3	36 lines	Item 1: Historia omnimoda (3ʳ–18ᵛ)
12–18	II	8^4	36 lines	
19–26	III	8	36 lines	Item 2: Regino of Prum (19ʳ–37ᵛ)
27–34	IV	10^5	36 lines	
35–43	V	12^6	36 lines	Item 3: Richard of Hexham (38ʳ–48ʳ)
44–53	VI	10^7	37 lines	Item 4: Chronicle (48ʳ–50ᵛ)

[2] The collation of the manuscript outlined here differs from that given by M. R. James for gatherings IV, V and XIX. In addition gathering XXI is probably of 8+1 folios.

[3] Lacks the last folio of the gathering.

[4] Lacks the second folio of the gathering.

[5] Lacks the second and third folios of the gathering.

[6] Lacks the fourth, fifth and tenth folios of the gathering. The original fourth and fifth folios of the gathering come between items 2 and 3. Taken together with an erasure on fol 37ᵛᵇ, after the end of item 2, this might indicate that a brief item has been deleted from the gathering.

[7] The prefatory rubric to item 7 has been inserted on the last eight lines of fol 53ᵛᵇ. A more appropriate place for it would have been before the almost continuous series of annals starts in 732, as Blair observes, but where there was no space for it. The placing of this rubric is important in any general discussion of this varied collection of historical materials only conventionally known as the Historia Regum, and, more particularly, in the consideration of those contained in gathering VII. A detailed account of these materials may be found in Blair pp 76–86, and it need only be said here that they comprise a collection all of which antedates the death of Bede, and, as Blair repeatedly observes, sits very uncomfortably even within such an unintegrated work of the Historia Regum which, as its rubric declares, begins with the death of Bede. Perhaps gathering VII should be regarded as a further sub-section of the manuscript, but it is not at present possible to put forward any precise conclusions. While sections 2–4, comprising gatherings III–XVIII, of MS 139 should probably be regarded as the products of a simple programme of copying historical materials evident divisions and differences within these sections make further work on the mechanics of this copying programme necessary. Certainly, if the rubrics are ignored in a first examination of MS 139 its contents suggest a number of scribes copying texts to hand – or as they became available—independently of each other. The erasures which precede item 3 in MS 139, the extraordinary

Collation—*continued*

			37 lines	Item 5: Letter of Symeon (50^v–52^r)
			37 lines	Item 6: Siege of Durham (52^r–53^v)
54–62	VII	8+1^8	36 lines	Item 7: Historia Regum (54^r–131^r)
63–70	VIII	8	36 lines	
71–8	IX	8^9	36 lines	
79–86	X	8	36 lines	
87–94	XI	8	36 lines	
95–102	XII	8	36 lines	
103–110	XIII	8	36 lines	
111–118	XIV	8	36 lines	
119–126	XV	8	36 lines	

treatment of John of Hexham's *History*, and the perplexing description of the *Historia Regum* as being of 429 years and four months all need further consideration in this context.

[8] Fol 61 is a later (16th century) additional parchment folio, inserted in the middle of Bede's annal for 732 – 'Brittones quamvis (fol 61) et maxima ex parte domistico sibi odio gentem Anglorum'. Fol 61^r is blank, fol 61^v contains Roger of Hovenden's prologue *in historiam suam*, and fol 61vb has a note 'Hic Rogerus imitatur Symeonem Dunelmen fere de verbo in verbum ab anno domini 732 ad annum domini 1122'. There is a further note in the same hand at the bottom of fol 62^r, 'Que hic sequuntur sunt in historia Rogeri Hovenden sed hic multo plenius'.

[9] It is possible that a further sub-division of the manuscript should be discerned here. Gathering IX ends with fol 78; gathering X begins with fol 79. In the manuscript the series of annals concludes with the year 957—though its reference to Edward the Confessor means that, in its present form, it cannot be dated earlier than 1042. There follows on fol 78, possibly in a different hand, the rubric 'Sequitur recapitulatio superiorum de rege elfredo. Deinde successio regum per ordinem, qui et qualiter ad regnum pervenerunt anglorum'. Instead, under a further rubric 'De historia Willelmi Malmesbirie', appear four extracts from the *Gesta Regum*. It is only on fol 79^r, at the start of the new gathering, and in a different hand, that the *recapitulatio* begins. It may be that the copyist of MS 139 had before him not a continuous *Historia Regum*, but a collection of historical materials, one text ending with the annal for 957, another containing the annals, largely derived from Florence of Worcester, which begin with the *recapitulatio*. As with gathering XIX, fols 160^r–163, the Malmesbury extracts may have been added to fill up blank leaves at the end of a gathering and section. Much more needs to be done before any final judgement can be made, but it may be remarked that the traditional text of the *Historia Regum* depends entirely on the procrustean placing of the initial rubric in MS 139.

Collation—continued

127–135	XVI	8 + 1[10]	36 lines	*Item 8a:* John of Hexham (131^v–134^r)
			36 lines	*Item 9:* Extract from Florence of Worcester (134^r–134^v)
			36 lines	*Item 10:* Carmen Serlonis (134^v–135^r)
			38 lines	*Item 11:* Carmen de Morte Sumerledi (135^r–135^v)
136–143	XVII	8	36 lines	*Item 12:* Battle of the Standard (136^r–140^r)
144–151	XVIII	8	36 lines	*Item 8b:* John of Hexham (140^r–149^r)
			36 lines	*Item 13:* Nun of Watton (149^r–151^v)
152–163	XIX	10 + 2[11]	35 lines	*Item 14:* Stephen of Whitby (152^r–154^v)

[10] Folio 135 is a separate leaf added to gathering XVI, the final gathering of this particular section of the manuscript. The gathering number at first appeared on 134^v, but it was then erased and inserted, in a different hand, on 135^v. I am grateful to Mr Dumville for calling my attention to this. Item 8a, the first part of John of Hexham, finishes on line 20 of folio 134vb. It is followed by an erased rubric, which originally occupied three lines of the column. It is not at present clear whether the rubric related to the preceding item, or to the following brief extract from Florence of Worcester (fols 134^r–134^v). The last part of fol 134vb and the greater part of fol 135^r is occupied by a poem, in 72 lines, on the battle of the Standard which is ascribed by the prefatory rubric to Serlo, brother of abbot Ralph of Louth Park. The final part of fol 135rb and the greater part of fol 135^v is filled by a poem in 80 lines on the death of Somerled (1164). The next item (12), Ailred's account of the battle of the Standard begins the new gathering (fol 136^r), though the concluding rubric to item 11, the poem on the death of Somerled, serves as an introductory rubric to it. See Blair pp 67–8. The copyist's treatment of John of Hexham's continuation is curious and, for the moment, inexplicable. There is a later copy of the continuation in Paris, Bibliothèque Nationale MS nouvelles acquisitions latines 692, but I have not yet been able to consult this.

[11] An added doubled sheet comprises the final two folios of this gathering. The four brief extracts from William of Malmesbury's *Gesta Regum*, unnecessarily listed as items 17–20, occupy the whole of these additional folios, and such parts of the true final leaf of the gathering (fol 160) as were not occupied by the letter of Thurstan. Clearly this gathering (XIX) and section was intended to comprise only the St Mary's, York, and Fountains foundation accounts (items 14, 16) and, as with gathering IX, the Malmesbury extracts were later additions to fill up

Collation—continued

			35 lines	*Item 15:*[12] Preface to Item 16 (154^{v}) *Item 16: 'Letter of Thurstan'* (155^{r}–160^{r})
			35 lines (36 lines on fols 162–3)	*Item 17, 18, 19, 20* William of Malmesbury extracts (160^{r}–163^{v})
164–167	XX	8[13]	35 lines	*Item 21: De uxore Ernulfi* (164^{r}–166^{v}) *Item 22:* Church of York and the Scots (167^{r}) *Item 23:* Vision of king Malcolm (167^{v})
168–176	XXI	8+1[14]	35 lines	*Item 24:* Nennius, *Eulogium* (168^{r}–168^{v})
177–182	XXII	8[15]		*Item 25:* Nennius, *Res gestae* (169^{r}–178^{v}) *Item 26: Life of Gildas* (178^{v}–182^{v})

blank folios and parts of folios. The first, and longest, of these four extracts extends from fol 160 to 162. See also n 9 above.

[12] There is no reason why this should be listed as a separate item. It consists of a simple, single line rubric at the foot of folio 154va, and an elaborate dating clause at the bottom of fol 154vb, both fitted in underneath the final columns of item 14, and prefatory to item 16, the so-called 'letter of Thurstan'.

[13] Lacks the final four folios of the gathering, and, in consequence, the gathering number (XX). Unlike the other missing folios listed above, which do not affect either the sense of the works included in the manuscript, or the late twelfth-century numbering of the gatherings – see gatherings I and XXI, for example – these folios, or at least the final folio of the gathering, must have been lost between the combination of the various sections into MS 139 and the addition of the fifteenth-century list of contents to the manuscript. At the top of fol 167^{v} there is a late note 'hic desunt septem folia'. Mr Dumville has suggested that there may never have been more than these four single leaves to the gathering, but there are difficulties to accepting this view.

[14] The present first leaf of the gathering is probably an addition to a standard 8 folio gathering. It is in a variety of hands, and its contents include a partially erased reference to the first two abbots of Fountains. This seems to have been overlooked in discussions of the provenance of the manuscripts though it was noted by M. R. James (p 322).

[15] Lacks the sixth and seventh folios of the gathering, and the gathering number.

3. *Fifteenth-century list of contents*

   1 Omnimoda historia cum cronica eiusdem

   2 Cronica abbatis Prumiensis ab incarnatione usque ad annum sequentem m.c.m

   3 Historia Ricardi prioris Haugustaldensis de gestis Regis Stephani et bello standardi

   4 Brevis cronica Adae usque ad Henricum imperatorem filium Henrici

   5 Epistola Symeonis monachi Dunelmiae ad decanum Eboracensem de episcopis eiusdem loci

   6 Historia eiusdem ab obitu venerabilis Bedae usque ad regem Henricum primum

   7 Historia Iohannis prioris Haugustaldensis per modicum tempus sequens

   8 De cometa et combustione Londoniarum et aliis iniuriis

   9 Descriptio Serlonis monachi metrice de bello inter regem Scotiae et barones Angliae

  10 Descriptio sancti Alredi abbatis Rievallensis de bello standardi

  11 Cronica dicti prioris Haugustaldensis

  12 Miraculum descriptum a sancto Alredo abbate Rievallense

  13 De fundatione monasteriorum sanctae Mariae Eboracensis et de Fontibus

  14 Post visiones et narrationes mirabiles et ultimi libri historiae Angliae impertinenter

  15 Cronica Nennii Britonum historiographi

  16 Vita Gildae sapientis

4. Thomas James, *Ecloga Oxonio – Cantabrigiensis* (London 1600) pp 74^b–5^a.

 64 1. Historia omnimoda, cum chronica eiusdem. Pr. *Mundum sine initio*

      2. Chronica Abbatis *Pruniensis*, ab incarnatione, usque ad annum Domini 1002.

      3. Historia *Ric. Prioris Hangustaldensis* de gestis *Regis Stephani*, et bello Standardi.

      4. Brevis chronica *Adae* usque ad *Henricum* Imperatorem.

      5. Epistola *Symeonis* monachi *Dunelmiae*, ad Decanum Eboracensem, de Episcopis eiusdem loci.

      6. Historia eiusdem, ab obitu Venerabilis *Bedae* usque ad Regem H. I.

      7. Historia *Io. Prioris Hangustaldensis*, per modicum tempus sequens.

      8. De Cometa et combustione *Londoniarum* et aliis iniuriis.

      9. Descriptio *Io. Serlonis* Monachi, de bello inter Regem *Scotiae*, et Barones Angliae.

     10. Descriptio *S. Athelredi*, Abbatis *Rievallensis*, de bello Standardi

     11. Chronica dicti Prioris. Athelredi.

     12. Miraculum descriptum ab eodem.

13. De fundatore monasteriorum *S. Mariae Eboracensis*, et de Fontibus.
14. Visiones et narrationes mirabiles, et ultimi libri historiae Angliae impertinenter.
15. Chronica *Nennii* Britonum historiographi.
16. Vita *Gildae* sapientis.

Book II of James's *Ecloga* comprises a series of lists and indices. The component items appear in the categorised lists of works as follows: item 1, II p 74; item 2, II p 74 (retaining the form *Pruniensis*, see also p 98); item 3, II p 74 (retaining *Hangustaldensis*, see also II, p 90); item 4, II p 74 (Chron. brevis ab *Adam* usque ad *H*. Imper); item 8, II p 74; item 9, II p 74 (where the author is again said to be *Io. Serlonis*, see also II p 101); item 10, II p 74; item 11, II p 74 (Chron. *Athelredi*, Abbatis); item 13, II p 75. Items 5–7, 12 and 14–16 are not listed. Though James does not itemise the various components which make up his item 14 one of them does appear on II p 75 under *Scripta quoquo modo pertinentia ad Ecclesias Cathedrales, vel monasteria*, and precedes a reference to his item 13:

p 75^b   Utrum Eboracensis Ecclesia habeat primatum super Scotos.
De fundatore *S. Mariae* Eborac et de Fontibus.

In the chronological list of authors which appears on II pp iii–iv dates are ascribed to some of the authors in James's account of MS 139 as follows: Serlo 1160, Symeon of Durham 1164, Ailred 1166, Richard of Hexham 1190. There is no mention of John of Hexham. Nor does he appear in the subsequent list of authors and their works. In that the *Historia Regum* is not listed under Symeon of Durham, nor is Ailred credited with his account of the Nun of Watton, though a *Cronica* is ascribed to him. There is clearly item 11 in James's list of the contents of MS 139, and as the punctuation of that entry makes clear *Athelredi* is a mistaken addition to the title *Chronica dicti Prioris*, which can only refer to item 7 in James's list, and which is completed by 'Haugustaldensis' in the fifteenth-century list of contents in MS 139.

5. Dugdale MS 48 fol 45^v; E. Bernard, *Catalogi Librorum Manuscriptorum Angliae et Hiberniae* (Oxford 1697) I, 3, pp 131–46, no 1341. 64.
    Both Dugdale's notes on MS 139 and Bernard's posthumous catalogue are derived from James's description, and such differences as appear are either mistakes or insignificant: Bernard item 4 reads 'Adonis', item 5 'Dunelmaei'. In item 11, however, the omission of the full stop after 'Prioris' has the effect of making 'Athelredi' appear as part of the title rather than as the afterthought which it clearly is. Dugdale item 11 reads 'Chronicon Ailredi', and item 13 'De Fundatoribus monasteriorum S. Maria Ebor et de Fontibus'.

6. *References to MS 139:* (a) Leland[16]

fol 30I/Hearne (1715), pp 346–7	*Symeon, monachus et Praecentor Dunelmensis ecclesiae scripsit compendiolum, instar epistolae, de archiepiscopis Eboracensibus, ad Hugonem, Ebora. ecclesiae decanum.
	*Symeon scripsit libellulum de obsidione Dunholmi per Malcolmum, Scottorum regem, tempore Ethelredi regis, filii Edgari, et de comitibus Northumbriae.
	'Sumerledi, qui usque hodie superest, ibi non aderat'[17]
302ᵛ/347	*Ex historia Symeonis monachi, Praecentoris Dunholmensis ecclesiae, quam scripsit de regibus Anglorum et Danorum a tempore Bedae usque ad ultimos annos Henrici primi, regis Angliae; ita tamen ut ante praescriptam historiae inchoationem incipiat a genealogia regum Cantianorum, et vitam Ethelberti et Ethelredi martyrum, et filiorum Eormenredi, qui fuit filius Eadbadli, et frater Erconberti regum Cantiae, scribat, ac praeterea adsuat genealogium regum Northanhumbrorum, multa inserens de abbatibus cum Weremutensis tum Girovicensis coenobii, ac etiam de Beda

---

[16] Bodleian MS Top Gen. C.2 (SC 3118), Leland, *Collectanea* II, fols 30Iʳ–20 This section starts at the top of a new folio and finishes on fol 320ʳ, the bottom 2½ inches and the whole of the verso being left blank. Extracts from Higden begin on fol 32Iʳ. While Leland's extracts make it quite clear that he was describing MS 139 he gives no introduction to it, does not record the first four items in the manuscript and gives, at this point in the notebook, no indication where he saw it. This may be due to the dilapidation of Leland's notebooks after his time, and it is likely that here, as elsewhere, leaves are missing from them. The *Collectanea* were printed by Thomas Hearne in 1715. Hearne's edition is, in general, a close copy of Leland's manuscript, employing a variety of types to present the variations in the original, though on occasion he confuses Leland's main and subsidiary headings. In the abbreviated list given here Leland's main headings are indicated by asterisks.

[17] This comment poses difficulties in dating the manuscript. The Somerled mentioned is not the great Somerled whose death in 1164 is recorded elsewhere in MS 139, but an earlier bearer of the same name, and the date of the incident to which this reference relates makes it unlikely that he was still alive when the copy of Richard Hexham's *Chronicle* in this section of MS 139 was composed. Whether the copyist unthinkingly transcribed the text, leaving the reference to Somerled in, or whether he confused him with the later Somerled it is impossible to say, but either way it raises doubts about the use of this sort of evidence in dating manuscript composition – at least for this manuscript.

	Ex vita S. Ethelberti et Ethelredi
	E genealogia regum Northumbrorum
306ᵛ/353	Ibidem e recapitulatione annorum regis Alfredi ex continuatione temporum per eundem Symeonem
308ᵛ/356	Sequitur in veteri codice[18]
	Integrum caput de genealogia comitum Northumbriae
309ʳ/356	E vita S. Edithae ab incerto autore edita[19]
310ᵛ/357	Adscripta in margine codicis[20]
310ᵛ/358	*Haec, quae secuntur, subscripta erant historiae Symeonis monachi, quae finem fecit anno D 1129. Explicit historia suavis et sanctae memoriae Symeonis, monachi et praecentoris ecclesiae S. Cuthberti Dunelmi, annorum ccccxxix et mensium quatuor
310ᵛ/358	*Continuatio historiae xxv annorum per Joannem, Priorem Hagustaldensem
312ᵛ/360	*Sequitur in veteri codice carmen rithmicum Serlonis monachi, fratris Radulphi abbatis de Parcho, de bello Standartico
	*Sequitur ibidem libellus Alredi Rievallensis abbatis de bello Standardico, data opera a Joanne Priore Haugustaldensi suae Historiae insertus, ex quo (sup. libello Alredi) haec quae secuntur exscripta sunt.
313ʳ/361	*Ibidem est oratio Gualteri Espec ad Anglos pugnatoros, artis et omnium adfectuum plenissima.
	*Oratio ibidem Rodberti de Brus ad David, regem Scottorum.
316ᵛ/365	Quae secuntur ex annalibus Joannis, Prioris Haugustaldensis, sumpta sunt, quemamodum ut supra.[21]

---

[18] In MS 1393 this refers to the annals for 1072–80.

[19] There is no life of St Edith in MS 139, but in Leland's manuscript this reference is clearly separated from what precedes and follows it, and the life of St Edith is referred to a point in MS 139 where the gatherings divide. It is likely that MS 139 was in a dilapidated state when Leland saw it, and that the St Edith material had become included amongst its gatherings, to be removed when the manuscript was put back into order, probably in Parker's time.

[20] This marginal note on the foundation of Furness (1123) in a twelfth century hand occurs on fol 128ʳ of MS 139.

[21] The text of John of Hexham ends, without any explicit, in 1154. In Leland's manuscript the text ends on fol 316ᵛ, only four lines of this folio being used.

317^r/365	*Ex Alredi, abbatis Rievallensis, libellulo de quadam sacerdote impudica Wetadunensis monasterii, a vinculis divinitus post poenitentiam soluta[22]
	*Ex libello Stephani, primi abbatis coenobii Mariani Eboraci, quem scripsit de origine et fundatione eiusdem coenobii
(fol 318 missing)	
319^v/367	*Ex epistola sive libellulo Turstini archiepiscopi Ebor. ad Gul. archiepiscopum Cantuar de origine Fontanensis coenobii per monachos Mariani cenobii Eboraci[23]
320^r/367	*Ex libello incertori autoris de adulterio, quod Aella, rex Deiorum, commisit cum uxore cuiusdam Aernulfi Seafar, ditissimi mercatoris, et Eboracensis.
	in veteri codice erant quaedam fragmenta epigrammaton Henrici archidiaconi

---

Instead of the next item, Ailred's account of the nun of Watton, beginning immediately it does not start until fol 317^r, the start of a new section in the notebook which seems to have had its leaves trimmed, and in consequence has lost the ends of lines.

22 There is a substantial gap of some two inches in Leland's manuscript before the next item. Since the gatherings divide at this point in MS 139, this may be another indication of the dilapidation of the manuscript when Leland saw it. See note 19 above.

23 The subsequent extract, given below, is described by Leland as marginal – [Haec notata] erant [in marg] ine codicis. Where words are missing this is because of damage to the pages of Leland's manuscript, where the extract occurs at the bottom of the folio. It has got worse since Hearne's day, and I have indicated this by the use of square brackets, but part of the missing words at the end of the extract can still be seen: –

> De his tredecim viii abbates fuerunt Ricardus sup olim Mariani cenobii Prior/primus abbas de fontibus Richardus sacrista.2^s. abbas de fontibus/ Robertus de Southwell abbas de Kirkestede Gervasius olim Marianus sup/ prior abbas de Parco Gualterus Eleemosynarius 2 abbas de/Kirkekester Ranulfus abbas de Norwegia Alexander/abbas de Kirkestal Gaufridus Pictor Gregorius Thomas Hai/mo Gamellus monachi obiierunt. Ranulfus Cantor solus recessit/ . . . [eadem] ecclesia venit qui primus abbas de Melsa fuit

In the surviving manuscripts of the 'letter of Thurstan' it is only in MS 139 that this note appears as an addition to the text, and a close comparison of the Leland and MS 139 versions reveal other similarities. Small initials are used for Fountains, and Fountains only, and 'viii' and '2' are used. Leland has 'Kirkekester' and 'Ranulfus Cantor' wrongly, and in MS 139 Kirkstead, on its second appearance, is the only name abbreviated, while 'Radulfus' has a partially erased 'n' contraction, and was originally Rānulfus. At this stage too Leland, as he himself records, could not have seen the *Narratio de fundatione Fontanis monasterii*, and would have had nothing to check the MS 139 entry by: –

320ʳ/368 *Ex libellulo quodam de vita Gildae, autore veteri.[24]

44/45 Ninnius sive Nennius Britannus Eluodugi (Elbodi) discipulus autor fuit Chronici, cuius copiam mihi fecit Thomas Sulmo. Nam ille habebat exemplar non mutilum et sine praefatione ut meum erat

46/47 Ex annotationibus quae inscriptae erant margine antiqui codicis Nennii, quem a Thoma Sulmone mutuo accepi

47/49 Ex verbis quae superius scripta sunt coniectura mihi animum subit partem aliquam earum rerum quae in marginibus antiqui exemplaris exarantur autorem ipsum Nennium agnoscere cum Elbodi, qui et alias Elbogudus dicitur, mentionem faciat et diligentem aliquem lectorem collatis exemplaribus ea in marginibus scripsisse quae in codice Salleiensis monasterii sensiit deesse.

(b): Bale, *Index Britanniae Scriptorum.*[25]

fol 26/p 488 Chronica omnimodae his- li.i. Mundum sine initio toriae[26]   dicimus in tempore
         quia precessit

Durat hoc chronicon usque ad annum domini 1130 fere
Ex coenobio Westmonasteriensi

(fol 159ʳ) De his tredecim viii abbates fuerunt Ricardus prior primus abbas de fontibus, Ricardus sacrista secundus abbas de fontibus Robertus de Sutwelle abbas de Kirkestede Gervasius subprior abbas de parco Walterus elemosinarius iiˢ abbat de Kirkestˢ Rānulfus abbas de Norwegia Alexander abbas de Kirkestal Gaufridus pictor Gregorius Tomas Haimo Gamellus manachi (sic) obierunt Rādulfus [contraction partially erased] cantor solus recessit in cuius loco Adam de eadem ecclesia venit qui primus abbas de Melsa fuit.

[24] The extract ends some two and a half inches from the bottom of fol 320ʳ 'Leland. vel rectius, cu . . . .'

[25] Edited R. L. Poole and M. Bateson (Oxford 1902). Unless otherwise indicated quotations from texts correspond to the text of MS 139.

[26] Probably item 1 in MS 139, though Bale's remark that it extends 'almost to 1130' is reminiscent of the preface to the *Historia Regum*, and his reference to the *chronica omnimoda* follows a reference to 'Chronicon antiquum de primo Saxonum ac Normanorum adventu, sive de eorundem regibus per monachum Dunelmi' – the last three words being an interlineation in the manuscript – and giving 'li.i. Prenotata serie generationum ex primi Anglici generis reges prodierunt'. It seems to be ascribed to the same Westminster manuscript, though there is a change of folio between the two items.

fol 150^v/pp 347–8 Ricardus Hagustaldensis prior, vir pie memorie scripsit

Gesta regis Henrici primi[27]	li.i. Anno verbi incarnati 1135
Gesta regis Stephani	li.i. Anno igitur dominice incarnationis 1136
De bello standardico	li.i. Mox autem aliqui eorum in medio
Chronicon parvum ab Adam[28]	li.i. Adam centum triginta annorum genuit
et alia quedam[29]	Claruit A.D. 1190.

Ex coenobio Westmonasteriensi

fol 157^v/p 348 Ricardus Hagustaldensis prior, vir pie memorie scripsit

Gesta regis Stephani	li.i. Anno verbi incarnati 1135 ab.
De bello Standardii[30]	li.i. Ea tempestate quidam pestilentes
Chronicon ab Adam ad[31] Henricum cesarem	li.i. Adam cxxx annorum genuit Seth, cui super

Ad annum 1190
Ex coenobio Westmonasteriensi

fol 168/p 408 Simeon monachus Dunelmensis, scripsit ad Hugonem decanum Eboracensem

De archiepiscopis Eboraci[32]	li.i. Hec charissime pater et domine Hugo, ecclesie Sancti Petri.
De obsidione Dunelmi[33]	li.i. Anno ab incarnatione domini 980, regnante
p 409 Passiones Ethelberti et[34] Ethelredi	li.i. Anno ab incarnatione dominica 616 qui est

Atque alia nonnulla

the manuscript in Bale's time – there is a marginal comment, in a sixteenth-

[27] This and the two subsequent entries are all references to Richard of Hexham's chronicle, item 3 in MS 139.

[28] A mistaken ascription. This is item 4 in MS 139.

[29] There are in fact no other works.

[30] Part of the work indicated by the previous entry. The reference is taken from the annal for 1138 after the description of the battle.

[31] See note 28 above.

[32] Item 5 in MS 139.

[33] Item 6 in MS 139. There the date is given as 969, and the title has 'obsessione'. See above pp 92, 106.

[34] In the text of the *Historia Regum* in MS 139 these 'Passiones' occur immediately after the main introductory rubric, and not before it as here. The further reference to 'atque alia nonnulla' and the giving of the first line of the Northumbrian royal genealogy as the beginning of the *Historia Regum* may reflect the state of

Historia suavis memorie Simeonis monachi et precentoris
Dunelmi, de regibus Anglorum et Dacorum, et creber-
rimis bellis, rapinis et incendiis eorum post obitum
venerabilis Bede presbyteri fere usque ad obitum regis
primi Henrici, filii Guildhelmi Nothi qui Angliam
acquisivit – id est ccccxxix annorum et quatuor mensium.

		li.i.	In exordio huius operis genealogiam regum Cantuariorum
	Extendit historia usque ad 1130.		
	Ex coenobio Westmonasteriensi		
fol 168/p 409	Simeon Dunelmensis historia de regibus Anglorum	li.ii.	His peractis ex sanctissimi doctoris[35]
	Abbreviationes Guilhelmi Malmesburiensis	li.i.	Non indecens(opinor) si quiddam[36]
fol 106/p 214	Ioannes Haugustaldensis ecclesiae prior scripsit Historiam xxv annorum, ab AD 1130 usque 1156	li.i.	AD 1130 Aschetillus primus prior ecclesiae Haugustaldensis
	De cometa et combustione[37] Londini	li.i.	Anno 1133 Stella cometis octavo
	Descripsit Bellum Scoticum[38]	li.i.	Eodem anno quo mortuus est Petrus Leo, qui inimicitias
	Ex coenobio Westmonasteriensi		
fol 106ᵛ/p 215	Historiam xxv annorum	li.i.	AD 1130 Asketillus primus
	De cometa et signis	li.i.	Anno 1133 stella cometis
	Descriptionem belli standardici	li.i.	Eodem mortuus est Petrus Leo[39]
	Ex collectis Nicolai Brigam		

century hand, to the placing of this material in MS 139. For discussion of this
part of the *Historia Regum*, and particularly for the inclusion of 'Cantuariorum'
in Bale's reference, see Blair pp 78–86.

[35] The reference, which lacks 'gaudiis' after 'peractis' is taken from the beginning
– not line two – of the paragraph immediately following the *Lamentatio Bedae
presbyteri* in the text of the *Historia Regum*. See Blair pp 85–6.

[36] The beginning of the four brief extracts from William of Malmesbury's *Gesta
Regum* which occur on fol 78 of MS 139.

[37] Item 9 in MS 139.

[38] Item 86 in MS 139, the incipit refers to the resumption of John of Hexham's
History.

[39] See n 38 above.

fol 165/p 407	Serlon monachus, frater Radulphi abbatis rhithmo fecit descriptionem belli inter regem Scotie et barones Anglie[40] Ex coenobio Westmonasteriensi	li.i. David ille manufortis, sceptrum tenens
fol 165/p 407	Serlo monachus erat Cluniacensis primum Glocestrie, postea Cisterciensis, et abbas, corpore procerus versificator sui temporis egregius ac fama conspicuus, scholarum magister. Claruit AD 1160 Serlon praefatus monachus scripsit	
	De interfectione Sumerledi[41]	li.i. David rege mortis lege, clauso in
	Ex libro Westmonasteriensi	
fol 40ᵛ/p 13	Ethelredus seu Alphredus abbas Rievalle, Cisterciensis ordinis scripsit	
	De bello inter regem Scotiae et barones Angliae apud Standardium iuxta Alvetonum[42]	li.i. Anno dominice incarnationis 1138 rege Stephano circa
	De quodam miraculo[43]	li.i. miracula domini et manifesta
	De fundatione Eboracensis[44] coenobii	li.i. Quamvis sancta, una, et universa
	De Funtanensi coenobii	li.i. Anno 1132. Ciclus lunaris
	Narrationes mirabiles	li.i. De Ioanne qui et Gerebertus
	Opus praefatum de miraculo, tangit sanctimonialem quandam foeminam de Watton Alia quoque edidit Ex coenobio Westmonasteriensi	
fol 165ᵛ/p 419	Stephanus Withebeiensis monachus, et primus abbas Eboracensis, scripsit quomodo et a quibus cenobium	li.i. Quamvis sancta et una et universalis mater

[40] Item 10 n MS 139.
[41] Item 11 in MS 139. Some attempt is made to clarify the confusion of Serlos in Bales' second edition of his *Scriptores*.
[42] Item 12 in MS 139.
[43] Item 13 in MS 139.
[44] This and the subsequent two items are not by Ailred. See items 14–20 in MS 139.

dive Marie Eboraci fuerit
fundatum.[45]

Ex Westmonasteriensi libro.

fol 174/p 461   Turstinus   archiepiscopus   li.i.   Reverendissimo in
Eboracensis scripsit ad Guil-   Christi charitate
helmum Cantuariensem De
fundatione cenobii Funta-
nensis[46]

Ex Westmonasteriensi libro

fol 138ᵛ/pp 297-8   Nennius Sapiens, Eluodugi discipulus, Eulogium brevissimum Britannie insula congregavit. Alii Apologiam
Nennii Britannorum historiographi, seu historicam
ortographiam mundi nuncupant. Incipit Ego Nennius
Eluodugi discipulus[47]

Res gestas Brittanorum.[48]   li.i.   A principio mundi
usque ad diluvium
anni sunt 2242. Cuius
secundum caput inci-
pit: Britannia insula a
quodam Bruto

Idem cum pseudogilda

Ex coenobio Westmonasteriensi

fol 21/p 53   Caratocus Nancaruan, seu Nancarbanensis, composuit
Vitam Gilde Sapientis[49]

li.i.   Nau fuit rex Scotie
nobilissimus regum
Aquilonalium etc.

Capitula sunt xxix

Ex coenobio Westmonasteriensi

(c): Joscelin, in T. Hearne, *Roberti de Avesbury* etc (Oxford 1720).

No 18/Hearne p 281   Richardus Hagustaldensis, eius loci post dictum
Joannem Praepositus quinquaginta sex annorum
Annales composuit ab anno Christi 1134, ad annum
eius 1190 quo claruit, sub Richardo primo Anglorum
Rege liber unus, qui est de gestis Regis Stephani,
incipit: Anno Christi incarnati 1135.[50]

[45] Item 14 in MS 139.   [46] Items 15/16 in MS 139.
[47] Item 24 in MS 139. Bale's reference should be compared not only with the
manuscript text, but also with the marginalia to this item, noted by M. R. James
p. 321. See also Dumville, 'The Corpus Christi *Nennius*.'
[48] Item 25 in MS 139.   [49] Item 26 in MS 139.
[50] In spite of the missapprehensions in this account, shared by Bale, this is clearly
item 3 in MS 139. Leland has no extant references to Richard of Hexham.

Habet Archiepiscopus Cant. ex dono M^{ri} Wutton and a Pekyns a Prebendary of West.

Et liber alter qui agit de gestis Henrici Secundi, incipit: Anno igitur Dominicae incarnationis 1156. Simeon, Dunelmensis Praecentor ac Monachus historiam quoque composuit de Regibus Anglorum, ab obitu ipsius Bedae usque ad annum ab incarnatione Domini 1130.[51]

No 11/pp 277-8

Claruit anno Domini 1164 quando quidem faciunt eam finivisse historiam quam habet Joan. Netleton Chronicam Dunelmen. Sed an sint alia ab historia Simeonis nescio.[52]

Simeon Dunelmensis finit vere historiam in anno Domini 1129. Annorum 429 et mensium 4.

Habet Archiepiscopus Cant. ex dono M^{ri} Wutton. And a prebendary of West Monaster called Pe Ryns.

Willelmus Gemeticensis Coenobita, patria Normannus, iussus ab Henrico Secundo, Anglorum Rege, ut utriusque patriae Angliae et Normanniae res gestas aeternitati consecravet. Cuius Chronicon de Normannis incipit: Ex quo Francorum gens opus hoc.

Debet poni ante Simeonem Dunelm.

Est scriptor innominatus de Episcopis Dunelmensibus, qui claruit anno Domini 1199.

Idem Simeon de Archiepiscopis Eboracensibus, quod incipit: Haec charissime Pater et Domine[53]

Habet Archiepiscopus Cant. ex dono M^{ri} Wutton. Et abbreviationes Malmesberienses, quod incipit:

Non indecens eam opinor si quiddam[54]

Habet Archiepiscopus Cant. ex dono M^{ri} Wutton.

No 17/p 281

Joannes de Hexham, sive Hagustaldensis Coenobii Praefes, Simeonem Dunelmensem paulo ante praefatum excipiens, eius historiam 25 annis ampliavit, definens in anno Domini 1156. Liber incipit: Anno

---

[51] With a note that most of this will be found in Roger of Hoveden, See above appendix n 8.

[52] This mention of a Durham history ending in 1164 may be relevant to the statement in MS 139 that the *Historia Regum* spans 429 years and four months. See above p. 96.

[53] Item 5 in MS 139.

[54] Part of item 7 in MS 139. See the similar notice by Bale above.

Domini 1130 et definit Asketillus primus. Auctor claruit anno Domini 1160 (1154, sic in lib Archiepiscopi Cant. ex dono Magistri Wutton) sub Rege Henrico Secundo.[55]

Habet Archiepiscopus Cant. and a prebendary of Westmonast.

No 4/p 270   Aelredus Rievallensis descripsit quoddam miraculum mirabile, de quadam Sanctimoniali faemina de Watton, et quodam iuvene, qui eam vitiavit.[56]

Habet Archiepiscopus Cant. ex dono Mr Wutton.

No 2/p 270   Stephanus, primus Abbas Sanctae Mariae, scripsit de fundatione sui monasterii, ostendens, quomodo et a quibus Coenobium Sanctae Mariae Eboraci fundata sit, et quantas invidorum perturbationes impulsa sustinuerit.[57]

Habet Archiepiscopus Cant. Datum illi per Mrm Wutton

No 3/p 270   Turstinus, Eboracensis Archiepiscopus, scripsit epistolam ad Willielmum Cant. Archi-episcopum, in qua ostenditur, quomodo Funtanense Coenobium sumpsit exordium[58]

Habet Archiepiscopus Cant. ex dono Mr Wutton.

---

[55] Item 8 in MS 139.
[56] Item 13 in MS 139. A further reference to Ailred occurs under no 12/Hearne p 278:
> Ealredus Rievallensis (Ethelredum plures vocant) migravit ab hoc seculo anno Christi 1166, sed prius composuit, inter cetera, vitam Edwardi Anglorum Regis, quae incipit: Multis veterum studio fuisse.
> Habet Archiepiscopus Cant.
> De Regibus Anglorum, quod incipit: Quoniam de optimis moribus. In omni scribendi genere similimus hic fruit Divi Barnardo, cui aequalis aetate fuit.
> Habet Joan. Netleton. Petrus Blesensis. Vide in Baleo. Hic Ealredus Rievallensis est senior Joanni Hagustaldo.
[57] Item 14 in MS 139.
[58] Items 15/16 in MS 139.

SOURCES FOR THE EARLY HISTORY
OF THE HUMILIATI

by BRENDA BOLTON

THE task of understanding the significance of any religious movement in its historical context normally depends upon documents being available for description and analysis. In the case of the *humiliati* this is almost impossible.[1] Such documentary evidence as exists for the period 1179 to 1216 comes not from the *humiliati* themselves but from others whose reasons for mentioning them varied considerably – suggestions as to why this is so will be made as the paper develops. Analysing these sources for information about the *humiliati* will thus be difficult. Nevertheless, as these documents cover certain aspects peculiar to the movement, they can be used to indicate such information as the *humiliati* might themselves have given. Indeed, if carefully pieced together, an even more coherent whole can appear on the principle that onlookers see more of the game than the players. The scope of this paper therefore is to examine the sources available in an attempt to show something of the early history of the *humiliati*; bearing in mind all the time, the limitations involved; the inevitable omissions in such accidental or incidental evidence; and the demonstrable bias which will be found to exist. That these documents are few in number and only rarely rich in detail increases the difficulty.

The documents which exist fall into three categories; general papal decrees and letters recorded in the registers of Innocent III;[2]

---

[1] General books and articles on the *humiliati* are few in number. But see A. de Stefano, 'Delle origini e della natura del primitivo movimento degli Umiliati', *Archivium Romanicum*, 2 (Geneva 1927) pp 31–75; E. Scott Davison, *Forerunners of St Francis* (London 1928) pp 168–200; M. Maccarrone, 'Riforma e sviluppo della vita religiosa con Innocenzo III', *Rivista di storia della Chiesa in Italia*, 16 (Rome 1962) pp 29–71 especially pp 46–50; [H.] Grundmann, *Religiöse Bewegungen [im Mittelalter]* (2 ed Darmstadt 1970) pp 70–97, 487–538 and my article 'Innocent III's treatment of the *Humiliati*' in *SCH*, 8 (1971) pp 73–82.

[2] A detailed introduction to Innocent III's letters is given by [C. R.] Cheney, *Medieval Studies and Texts* (Oxford 1973) pp 16–39; there is also a useful general chapter on sources in J. H. Mundy, *Europe in the High Middle Ages 1150–1309* (London 1973) pp 1–21.

contemporary twelfth- and thirteenth-century accounts made by interested observers and chronicles written in the fifteenth century by two members of the conventual *humiliati*. Many of these documents are available in two important printed collections both published in Milan, the *Vetera Humiliatorum Monumenta* compiled between 1766 and 1768 by Girolamo Tiraboschi[3] and the appendix to Luigi Zanoni's work on the movement published in 1911.[4]

When the papal documents are looked at in more detail it will be seen that they themselves fall into two groups. The first of these indicates prevailing papal attitudes varying from hostility to support and based mainly on the *humiliati*'s supposed heterodoxy or orthodoxy. The earliest official mention occurs in Lucius III's decretal *ad abolendam* of 1184 where they are included amongst a whole group of sects classed as heretical.[5] A papal letter of 1199 shows Innocent III asking the bishop of Verona to cease the excommunication of *humiliati* in his diocese until their views had been reconsidered by the papacy.[6] Yet in 1203 an incidental piece of evidence obtained from a local record shows that, at Cerea in the same diocese, the *humiliati* were still being expelled and their goods confiscated by archidiaconal licence.[7] A papal letter of 1214 shows that Innocent, while considering them still orthodox, was forced to admonish them for appearing to have deviated from their original austere and humble life.[8]

The second group of papal documents deals with the acceptance and formal recognition of the *humiliati*. In a letter of 1200 Innocent refers to an earlier request he had made to the leaders of the movement to indicate their willingness to devote themselves to a life of christian piety by presenting *proposita* or short statements of intent.[9] Although these *proposita* have not survived it is possible to deduce their content from Innocent's separate letters to the three orders of the *humiliati* in

---

[3] [G. Tiraboschi] *V[etera] H[umiliatorum] M[onumenta]*, 3 vols (Milan 1766-8).

[4] [L.] Zanoni, *Gli Umiliati [nei loro rapporti con l'eresia, l'industria della lana ed i communi nei secoli xii e xiii]*, Biblioteca historica italia, Serie II, 2 (Milan 1911). The appendix includes the *Chronicle of John de Brera 1421* pp 336-44 and the *Chronicle of Marcus Bossius 1493* pp 345-52.

[5] *VHM* I p 79; Mansi 22 cols 476-8; *PL* 201 (1855) cols 1297-300.

[6] *PL* 214 (1855) col 789. Here the *humiliati* are listed with cathars, arnaldists and poor men of Lyons.

[7] C. Cipolla, 'Statuti rurali veronesi', *Archivio veneto* 37 (Venice 1889) pp 341-5.

[8] *VHM* II pp 156-7; Potthast I no 4945.

[9] *PL* 214 (1855) col 921; *VHM* II p 139.

1201.[10] In giving papal approval to these orders the letters tell us much of what we know about the characteristic features of the movement.[11] These documents, together with comments made by the fifteenth-century chroniclers regarding the fear of some *humiliati* that they would be adjudged as heretics, indicate a preoccupation with the reconciling of the *vita apostolica* and the orthodox views of the Church.[12] Herbert Grundmann, in undertaking a careful exploration of the critical themes underlying the religious movements of the twelfth, thirteenth and fourteenth centuries, concluded that the *humiliati* represented a part of the widespread religious reaction which Chenu has later referred to as the 'Evangelical Awakening'.[13] Grundmann, although pointing out that Innocent's letter to the third order said nothing about the danger of heresy,[14] was the first to suggest that Innocent, when he wrote to the bishop of Verona in 1199, was attempting to achieve a distinction between irrevocable heretics and those who could be drawn back into the church.[15] He referred to Innocent's treatment of the *humiliati* as the first attempt to bridge the gap between the hierarchical church and new religious movements.[16] Perhaps the *proposita* of the *humiliati* convinced Innocent that their views were not heretical which accounts for the omission of a reference to heresy in the letter of 1201.

The documents remaining from this correspondence between Innocent III and the *humiliati* all emanate from the papacy. If, as will be dealt with later, they were indeed literate, then there is every reason to suppose that there was a *humiliati* side to the correspondence. In fact in his letters Innocent asks them to write their responses to his proposals. What then happened to the relevant material? Could there perhaps have been a systematic destruction of *humiliati* writings similar to that which had certainly occurred in Metz in 1199 when the books and vernacular biblical translations of a literate lay group were ordered to

[10] The letters to the third and second orders are dated respectively 7 and 12 June: *VHM* II pp 128–38. The privilege to the first order was sent on 16 June: *ibid* pp 139–48.
[11] The original and strongest branch comprised a group of laymen living at home with their families. These were the tertiaries or third order. The first and second orders were composed of priests and unmarried laymen and women who lived separate and ascetic lives in religious communities.
[12] Zanoni, *Gli Umiliati* pp 341, 350.
[13] [M.-D.] Chenu, ['The Evangelical Awakening'], in his *Nature, Man and Society [in the Twelfth Century: Essays on New Theological Perspectives in the Latin West]* ed and translated by J. Taylor and L. K. Little (Chicago 1968) pp 239–69.
[14] Grundmann, *Religiöse Bewegungen* p 88 note 33.
[15] *Ibid* pp 72–5.
[16] *Ibid* pp 90–1.

be destroyed?[17] We know that Pandulf, papal legate in England, ordered the destruction of all evidence about Magna Carta in 1215 to facilitate the development of an official papal line.[18] Was it also the intention of the church that there should be such an official line in regard to the *humiliati*? Other alternatives could be that the *humiliati* were either illiterate or simply did not wish to express their views in writing.

We should perhaps at this point consider how literate were these early *humiliati*. Although in the opinion of Burchard of Ursperg, a premonstratensian canon, they were *rudes et illiterati* he appears to be alone in this.[19] Other evidence points to a high rate of literacy. In 1199, as we have seen, Innocent III instructed them to write down their *proposita* for him whilst in 1201 he allowed members of the first order to wear a habit *ut laicos litteratos* presumably similar to the habit worn by Italian civil lawyers.[20] Jacques de Vitry, one of the contemporary observers, was of the opinion that almost all of them were literate.[21] If we conclude from this that they were literate we cannot at the same time deduce much about the uses to which this literacy was put. Even if they did not wish to express their views in writing there is no doubt that they wished for formal sanction of their way of life. To obtain this they would need to put something in writing. As with Francis 'some rule however simple must be drawn up'.[22]

We can link the question of their literacy with the permission to preach given to them by Innocent III. His letter to the third order or tertiaries showed his support for them by allowing them to preach and to give their personal witness to the faith.[23] Although he was not prepared to allow them to teach doctrine this was a considerable concession. It will be remembered that it was their insistence on preaching

---

[17] *PL* 214 (1855) cols 695–9; *PL* 216 (1855) cols 1210–14; Potthast I no 781; Grundmann, *Religiöse Bewegungen* pp 97–100.

[18] Cheney, *Medieval Studies and Texts* p 253.

[19] *Burchardi et Cuonradi Urspergensium Chronicon* ed O. Abel – L. Weiland, *MGH, SS* 23 (Hanover 1874) p 377. Burchard was in Italy in 1210 and must have encountered the *humiliati* there: Grundmann, *Religiöse Bewegungen* p 90 note 37.

[20] *VHM* II p 142.

[21] Jacques de Vitry, *Historia Occidentalis* ed F. Moschus (Douai 1597) p 335. I have unfortunately not been able to use the new edition ed J. F. Hinnebusch, *Spicilegium Friburgense* 17 (Fribourg 1972).

[22] J. Moorman, *A History of the Franciscan Order from its origins to the year 1517* (Oxford 1968) p 16.

[23] *VHM* II pp 133–4.

which had first resulted in anathematisation by the decree of Lucius III
in 1184. This authorisation to preach was in direct contravention to the
very fierce legislation of the twelfth century and was in its way unique.
Although episcopal licence was necessary for preaching, Innocent
expressly commanded the bishops not to refuse. Their only concern
was to be the question of place and time.

For reactions to this exceptional privilege we can usefully turn to our
eye-witness observers of the *humiliati*. The anonymous premonstratensian canon of Laon, whose chronicle may be dated at some point
between the third lateran council of 1179 and Lucius III's decree of
1184, recorded the *humiliati*'s refusal to abandon their preaching and
their subsequent excommunication.[24] Burchard of Ursperg of the same
order also mentioned this papal prohibition saying that the *humiliati* by
their preaching were 'thrusting their sickle into the harvest of others'.[25]
This he claimed led to the pope's establishment and confirmation of the
dominicans as the order of preachers. Jacques de Vitry who was the
most detailed, vivid and enthusiastic of the eye-witnesses recorded his
impressions of the *humiliati* first in a letter of 1216 and later in his
Historia Occidentalis.[26] He was convinced of their opposition to heresy
and said that the pope had granted them the right to preach in squares,
open spaces and secular churches. There they 'prudently convinced the
impious from holy scripture and publicly confounded them'.[27] Such a
concentration upon the holy scriptures reflected their wish not only to
live by the gospels but to preach by the gospels. They would be more
concerned in preaching the word than in diffusing biblical texts and
vernacular translations. They would have shown little interest in
writing on doctrinal points of theology and so Innocent's prohibition
on doctrine would not have troubled them. Such a concentration on
preaching the word would mean that they would tend to make use of
oral (rather than written) communication. Preaching the word would
mean to them that the bible was the only necessary written record.

How far was this correct? Innocent had specifically given the *humiliati* the power to witness to the faith and preach on their experience of
christian life but had denied them the right to teach doctrine. But was
he really able to distinguish between theological and moral questions

---

[24] *Chronicon Universale Anonymi Laudunensis*, ed A. Cartellieri and W. Stechèle
(Paris 1909) pp 23–30.
[25] W. Wakefield and A. P. Evans, *Heresies of the High Middle Ages* (New York
1969) p 229.
[26] *Lettres de Jacques de Vitry* ed R. B. C. Huygens (Leiden 1960) pp 72–3.
[27] *Historia Occidentalis* p 335.

as far as their teaching was concerned? It seems likely that they must indeed have touched upon doctrinal issues and that Innocent later became suspicious.[28] The evidence here is lacking. We do not even know whether they stressed one gospel more than another although Innocent in his letter to the tertiaries most frequently cites James.[29] Chenu interprets this acceptance of lay preaching as part of the church's long struggle to give juridical and sacramental authenticity to the apostolic drive amongst not only the *humiliati* but also some waldensians, Poor Catholics and later the franciscans.[30]

Should the definition of lay groups mean that normal life is still carried on in the world? The chronicler of Laon tells us that the *humiliati* considered family life to be of prime importance but it is Jacques de Vitry who again is our main source. He reported that many *humiliati* remained physically in the world with their wives and children while yet humbly abstracting themselves from worldly affairs.[31] Their religious motivation compelled them to live by the work of their hands. The working of cloth involved women as well as men in its production and was operated on a domestic basis. It was thus quite compatible with Innocent's instructions to the tertiaries to remain with their families.[32] In spite of this instruction, the family element in the life of this group is stressed only by contemporary observers who seem to have considered this the distinguishing feature of the *humiliati* and not in the papal documents. Innocent's letter of 1201 to the tertiaries gives more emphasis to the fraternity aspect of their life. This fraternity strengthened vertical as well as horizontal social bonds. It did so by binding the tertiaries together in communal prayer as well as in a mutual assurance society which ensured the provision of material welfare for the sick and needy.[33]

---

[28] Grundmann, *Religiöse Bewegungen* p 81 thinks it unlikely that the *humiliati* had attempted to expound dogma because they were more interested in moral questions but sees a new distinction between clerical and lay sermons.

[29] *VHM* II pp 128–34.

[30] Chenu, *Nature, Man and Society* pp 260–2.

[31] *Historia Occidentalis* p 335.

[32] *VHM* II p 132. For valuable insights into the medieval family see P. Ariès, *Centuries of Childhood* translated by Robert Baldick (London 1973) especially pp 327–99.

[33] *VHM* II pp 132–3. On fraternities see the study by G. Le Bras, *Études de sociologie réligieuse*, 2 vols (Paris 1955–6) II 'Les confréries chrétiennes', pp 418–62; Robert Moore, 'History, economics and religion: a review of the Max Weber thesis' in *Max Weber and Modern Sociology*, ed Arun Sahay (London 1971) pp 82–96. Compare Chenu, *Nature, Man and Society* pp 261–4.

Can we perhaps see here Innocent's wider policies in microcosm? It was greatly in the church's interests to promote these solidarities which cross-cut the family both vertically and horizontally. Such fraternities, although modelled upon the prevalent ideal of the kin-group were not equivalent to the family but rather an alternative. Might it have been a deliberate move on Innocent's part to avoid an over-commitment to kin solidarity which in the context of lombard society with its family feuds, internal tensions and recent patarine past could have proved highly dangerous?[34] In this he may have been successful for after 1216 we hear nothing more of the family groups as a significant feature of the *humiliati* movement. This view is carried further by the chroniclers of the fifteenth century who were instead concerned in writing about the conventual *humiliati* and their place in society.

Various other sources help to throw light on the social composition of the *humiliati*. Zanoni in examining these sources sought to explain their movement as a reaction to social and economic events basing his argument on an incidental account by Humbert de Romans, minister general of the dominicans, who referred to them as *laborantes*.[35] Developing this point Zanoni viewed them as impoverished workers from the lowest stratum of society and so excluded from political influence. There remained for them religious association as their only possible form of organisation.[36] Grundmann however considered that the evidence pointed to a religious reaction in the upper levels of society in a search for the *vita apostolica*.[37] Innocent's letter to the tertiaries about the avoidance of excess[38] and the evidence showing how the *humiliati* organised *schola* seem to bear out Grundmann's view.[39]

A closer examination of the evidence shows that the movement initially at least contained those of good social standing. Jacques de Vitry tells us that it included nobles, powerful citizens, aristocratic matrons and young girls from rich families.[40] Guy de Porta Orientalis, member of one important lombard family and *minister* of the tertiaries is

---

[34] J. K. Hyde, *Society and Politics in Medieval Italy: the Evolution of the Civil Life 1000–1350* (London 1973) pp 120–1. See also the excellent bibliography.
[35] Printed in Zanoni, *Gli Umiliati* pp 261–3; Grundmann, *Religiöse Bewegungen* pp 158–61.
[36] Zanoni, *Gli Umiliati* p 157.
[37] Grundmann, *Religiöse Bewegungen* pp 158–69.
[38] *VHM* II p 132. They were to have only two sparse meals a day, to give back all wrongfully acquired possessions and to give all income in excess of their own needs to the poor.
[39] Chenu, *Nature, Man and Society* p 249 n 12.
[40] *Historia Occidentalis* p 334.

described as *vir nobilis* and *capitaneus*.[41] In northern Italy and especially in Lombardy there was a strong tradition of alienation among the lesser nobility, particularly the *vavassours* who were usually excluded from any positive role in either political or ecclesiastical affairs. Just as some had supported the patarines of the eleventh century or, in the twelfth, the emperor Barbarossa, so some may have been tempted to join the *humiliati* where they would have had a better chance of achieving the eminence denied them in other spheres. We can neither show any consequent antipathies or tension in local relationships nor show that, if they existed, they were being healed by membership of the fraternities of the *humiliati*. The only possible evidence might be that about the name *humiliati* which was given to them by others. We do not know for certain when they accepted the name *humiliati* nor indeed what it implied to them. Both the chronicler of Laon and the fifteenth century *humiliati* chroniclers tell us that their name derived from their plain clothing while Jacques de Vitry elaborates this by citing the example of humility which they displayed. We know from Innocent's letter of 1199 to the bishop of Verona that they were called *humiliati* by the people.[42] Grundmann maintained that those reconciled with the church were not called *humiliati* officially until 1211 or 1214 and stated that they in fact objected to the name.[43] Certainly there is confusion in two papal letters of 1206 when Innocent appears to be using patarine and *humiliati* as alternatives.[44] Jacques de Vitry confirms that this confusion was still deliberately maintained by ill-willed people as late as 1216.[45]

The evidence in regard to the geographical location may also be of help in examining the question of local antipathies and tensions. All of the *humiliati* were to be found in the towns around Milan in northern Italy and there is considerable general evidence to show that these antipathies and tensions were a common feature of life in these towns. Belonging to the *humiliati* therefore may have meant belonging to a fraternity which safeguarded them from the ill-effects of such a social climate.

Using these documents on the *humiliati* in this way gives a reasonably satisfactory picture. Although this may be so it would be wrong to remain content. What further fields of enquiry are open to us? Field work in the *humiliati* towns might produce local records which would

[41] PL 214 (1855) col 921; *VHM* I p 44.
[42] PL 214 (1855) col 789.
[43] Grundmann, *Religiöse Bewegungen* p 89 n 34.
[44] PL 215 (1855) cols 820, 1043.
[45] *Lettres de Jacques de Vitry* pp 72–3.

improve the documentary situation. The techniques of medieval archaeology might also provide another dimension. It is my opinion, however, that what is really needed is a new approach to the existing evidence by using the insights of the social sciences. These would give us fresh awareness of the part played by the *humiliati* in the religious ferment of their time and greater understanding of the way in which the members of this informal religious congregation were able to live devotional lives at grass roots level. If this is done, it would be true to say that 'while few people are asking interesting questions the raw materials for doing so are becoming better understood'.[46]

[46] See the review article by L. K. Little in *Speculum* 48 (Cambridge Mass., 1973) P 345.

UNCOVENANTED BLESSINGS OF
ECCLESIASTICAL RECORDS
(*PRESIDENTIAL ADDRESS*)

by ROSALIND M. T. HILL

THE theme of this volume has been defined as 'the sources, materials and methods of ecclesiastical history'. After the illuminating, fruitful and often racy subjects which have been discussed in earlier volumes in this series, a theme such as this may at first sight appear to be sober to the point of dullness. I hope to show that it is not, and I make no excuse for presenting it. We are historians, knowing that the study of history is a complex affair, demanding a high degree of imaginative understanding and at the same time a great deal of patient, accurate and often very exacting craftsmanship. Before we can understand what ecclesiastical history is about, either we must go back to its sources, with all the problems of time, language and palaeography which that process entails, or we must at least possess sufficient knowledge to enable us to form some reasonable opinion about the validity of the methods used by those who have cleared the ground for us. Not all historians have the time, or indeed the inclination, to edit texts, but all of us are to an increasing extent dependent upon the work of those who do edit them. A medieval scholar might perhaps have compared the two sides of the historian's work, the interpretation of ideas and the transcription or calendering of records, to those two great 'types' of the contemplative and the practical life, the sisters Mary and Martha. The two were interdependent, and they lived in one house. True, it was the spiritually-minded Mary who chose the good part, while Martha's obsession with the practical problems of housekeeping earned her a gentle but unmistakable reproof which historians would do well to take to heart. We are not to become so much engrossed in the finer points of textual interpretation that we lose sight of that historical understanding to which we are called. Yet Martha's part was a necessary, indeed a vital, one; and there is a delightful if unverifiable legend which tells how Our Lord eventually honoured his flustered hostess by granting to her the power to rid the countryside of Tarascon of a destructive dragon, which she quelled with as much thoroughness as she had doubt-less shown in sweeping the blackbeetles out of her kitchen at Bethany. Mary and Martha, symbolically interpreted, were popular figures in the iconography of the middle ages. Both of them had been necessary to minister to Christ in his incarnate life, and both of them were equally necessary to maintain his church and to enable men to understand its message. No-one doubted that Mary's part was the better one, but without her sister she would have starved to death, as Martha without Mary would have sunk into a domestic drudge. Without research, understanding is starved of material; without understanding, research declines into a deadening antiquarianism. Without the light which Mary can bring, Martha's work must be deadly, a mere scrabbling among the records of what is irrecoverably gone, but when she works, as she was intended to work, as her sister's partner, it is she who fills the lamps with oil. Nor, in the minds of medieval commentators, was Martha's part conceived as a life of unrelieved drudgery. She was often represented, as Dante sees Matilda in the *Divine Comedy*, as a girl going out into the woods or fields to gather flowers, while the contemplative Mary sat at home gazing into the depths of her mirror. This imagery shows a most true insight; it is not given to Martha alone to gaze deeply into the nature of things, but there have always been flowers for her to pick by the wayside if she will but look for them.

In the study of history, to take the particular branch of human experience which is our common concern, Martha's work is bound to lie among the sources and materials which contain the records of past events, and the methods by which she interprets them are bound to show the mark of her own strongly practical nature. It is she who keeps the records, edits them and brings them out into the light of day. All historians, even those who are most creative of new ideas and inter-pretations, must of necessity have a strong streak of Martha's practicality in their natures if they are to come to terms with their subject. This down-to-earth realism will show itself most often in the way in which they handle their written sources, for it is above all upon the written word that the study of ecclesiastical history depends. Archaeology, architecture, geography, topography, personal memory, even, of late years, the study of photographs and of the tape-recorder, all have their part, and a steadily increasing part, to pay in the process of historical investigation; but the sources and materials upon which the ecclesias-tical historian's work has so far been based are still, for the most part, manuscript sources, and the methods of his enquiry, despite the admirable advice of the late professor Tawney that 'what the historian needs is not more books but better boots', are likely to encourage him to spend more of his time in the library and the record-office than in the field. If we really want to know about the history of the church and the people who served it, we cannot afford to neglect the archaeologist's spade nor, for the matter of that, the builder's trowel, but for the greater part of our subject we shall be basically dependent upon the written source; we shall have to turn to the people of the past, to the things which they wrote and to the things which other people wrote about them. They may have been, and doubtless often were, wrong in their facts and judgements and muddled in their aspirations; they were, as we ourselves are, blinkered by that partial and fashionable view of truth which is generally the best that can be given to mortal man, but they were nevertheless the people who observed and recorded, as clearly as anyone can, what was going on at the time when they wrote. 'I knew a man,' says Bede in his *Ecclesiastical History*, 'and I wish I had not, who lived in a noble monastery but behaved himself ignobly', and he goes on to tell the story of a brother who, refusing the advice of his ecclesiastical superiors and spurning the rule of his monastery, died in desperation and the certainty that he would be eternally damned.[1] We may well question the validity of Bede's explanation of the terrible dreams which beset his unfortunate craftsman in the course of his last illness, though it is clear that Bede himself gave it in all sincerity. We may quarrel, if we wish, with the strongly religious and didactic temper of mind which impelled a historian to include this particular story in a book on the ecclesiastical history of the English people, but we cannot, I think, reasonably refuse to accept the story as it stands. This thing did happen. It may not have had the precise significance which Bede attaches to it, but the outward facts at least cannot be explained away as a figment of his imagination. In such personal observations we find many links which connect the responses of people, set in very different times and circumstances, to the world in which they find themselves, a thing very comforting to the historian who is trying to grope his way into the minds of other men in other ages. 'I never saw a Peacock spread his tail before this day at Justice Creed's and most Noble it is. How wonderful are thy Works O God in every Being,'[2] wrote parson Woodforde, knowing in all probability little

[1] *HE V*, 14.
[2] *The Diary of a Country Parson*, ed J. Beresford (Oxford 1924) I, p 75.

beyond the name of St Francis, and even less of the unknown Irish scholar who had written, a thousand years earlier, 'A hedge of trees overlooks me; a blackbird's lay sings to me ... The Lord is indeed good to me: well do I write beneath a forest of woodland';[3] but he had in some measure shared their experience. It is in such flashes of personal insight that we come nearest to an understanding of the way in which people's minds could work, whether in the eighth century or the eighteenth, and since the history of the christian church is to a unique extent the history of an individual response to a personal Founder, its sources and records are of necessity bound up with the records of individual experience. Without the records embodied in the New Testament the church would not exist. Without such extremely personal records as the *Confessions* of St Augustine, the *Testament* of St Francis, the prayers of Lancelot Andrewes, the diaries of John Wesley and the letters from prison of Dietrich Bonhoeffer, it would be impossible to understand the direction in which ecclesiastical history was going, for in this field, above all others, history starts from the achievement of individual minds, an observation which no amount of statistical researach or sociological analysis is likely to disprove.

It is above all in the personal writings of individuals that we might expect to find the flowers of Martha's wayside, those 'uncovenanted blessings' of which my title speaks, but they crop up also in the most surprising places, as when St Benedict cuts through the solemn and rather pompous verbiage of the *Regula Magistri*, in its rules about the treatment of late-comers to matins, with the refreshingly practical remark that it is better, in any case, for them to come in, 'for if they stay outside the oratory there will perhaps be someone who either settles down and goes to sleep, or indeed sits by the door and takes the opportunity of gossipping';[4] Theodore of Tarsus pausing in the midst of those judgements which make up the first English penitential to observe that hare's liver, mixed with pepper, is good for the relief of pain;[5] Matthew Paris inserting a note on the behaviour of crossbills into the *Chronica Majora*.[6] In the period of which I can speak with some experience, the middle ages in England, very few individual writings are really dull, and most of them have plenty of such felicities. When however we turn to the routine investigation of whole classes of

[3] G. Murphy, *Early Irish Lyrics* (Oxford 1956) p 4.
[4] *Rule of St Benedict*, cap 43.
[5] A. W. Haddon and W. Stubbs, *Councils and Ecclesiastical Documents*, 3 vols (Oxford 1871) III p 198.
[6] *Chronica Majora*, ed H. R. Luard, RS, 7 vols (1880) *V*, pp 254–5.

administrative, judicial or legal records, then the rewards have to be earned over a long period of time and in the hard way, and there are no short cuts. Such researches are however necessary if we are going to understand the way in which the church worked and lived in any century from the first to the twentieth. As any gardener knows, it is impossible to grow flowers without a good deal of patient digging, weeding and watering, and as soon as the church began to blossom it became painfully apparent that somebody would have to attend to the practical problems of its daily life. Even the apostles themselves, in the first few months of the church's history, seem to have been faced with difficulties in Martha's field: – 'there arose a murmuring of the Grecians against the Hebrews, because their widows were neglected in the daily ministrations. Then the twelve called the multitude of the disciples unto them, and said "It is not reason that we should leave the word of God and serve tables".'[7] In their decision to share the work of the church between apostles and deacons they were laying the foundations of the administrative history of christendom. Whether St Stephen and his six assistants had themselves to struggle upon tablets with such practical considerations as the estimated income from offerings, the price of bread and the probable appetites of widows we have no means of knowing; but certainly somebody had to do it. From the very beginning of its history the church has had to record not only the deeds and sayings of its great men but also the details of its practical administration. Since between the fifth and the fifteenth century the great majority of literate people were clergy (taking the word in its widest sense to include men in orders and monks), these records were on the whole better kept than those of the laity, and more of them have survived.

In the course of my working life I have spent a good deal of time in scratching away amongst administrative records, mostly among the archives preserved in diocesan record offices, and I am constantly surprised by the fact that although the ecclesiastical historians whom I meet there are often very distinguished scholars indeed their numbers are relatively small. Yet it must be clear from the results obtained by people who have worked in this particular field, for example professor Cheney and the late professor Hamilton Thompson, that the possibilities for discovery are simply enormous. Even for the researcher who sticks to a limited field there are good things to be had in abundance. From a study of the register of one bishop, not a particularly out-

[7] *Acts* 6, 1–2.

standing one, Sutton of Lincoln, it is possible to see with great clarity a picture of the life and activities of people in a large area of thirteenth century England, for a bishop's register is the repository of many interesting and not a few peculiar things. But the great majority of registers are still unprinted, and many of them have hardly been used at all. Moreover there are still many people who think that there is not much of interest to be found in a register, and are therefore reluctant to suggest such a field to their promising research-students, so that quantities of excellent material remain unexplored. In the great metropolitan see of York, for example, only two of the registers compiled after 1342 have found editors, and among those which have not yet done so are such promising sources of information as that of archbishop Scrope. The situation is a little better at Canterbury, but even so there is a mass of good material which has scarcely been touched. In the suffragan sees, apart from the activities of the Canterbury and York Society and the Surtees Society, the chance of publication depends not only upon finding an editor of specialised training who is prepared to give up some years of his life to the job, but also upon the finances of local record societies, which are understandably hesitant about using up too high a proportion of their resources in the publication, or even the calendering, of a record in medieval latin for which there is no popular demand.

The possibilities, and the problems, are not confined to registers, or to the medieval period. Whole classes of documents exist whose contents have hardly been investigated at all. Among the ecclesiastical records of York, where I happened recently to have been working in the Borthwick Institute, there are consistory court-books covering the whole span of the years 1417 to 1855; the visitation-records of the diocese, begun in 1567, go on until 1953; there are more than fifty boxes of procters' records, case papers, working papers, notes and correspondence, all of which should be capable of throwing a great light upon the way in which the church has dealt with the tangled but fascinating business of diocesan administration. These are not only unprinted. They are virtually unknown; hardly anyone ever looked at them, although now that Dr Smith has published an excellent catalogue, there is no excuse for this neglect.[8] There is no reason to think that the York records are unique in this respect. Up and down the country such sources of ecclesiastical history exist in splendid profusion, and were it

[8] D. M. Smith *A guide to the Archive Collections in the Borthwick Institute of Historical Research* (York 1973).

not for the work of their devoted archivists and of a very few historians they would exist under piles of dust.

The main reason for investigating these records and for publishing, or at least calendering, their contents is of course to find out how the church as a whole worked in relation to its earthly responsibilities. Great men are atypical – it is in studying the activities of ordinary people that we can see most clearly into the administrative history of a past age. We should not know much about the workings of the twelfth-century civil service if Richard Fitz-Nigel had not by good fortune been moved to write the *Dialogue Concerning the Exchequer*, and we should know very little of the life of an English diocese in the thirteenth century if papal admonitions and the prick of their own consciences had not impelled most bishops of the period to issue synodal decrees and to follow them up with mandates and instructions to see that they were properly observed. It is from the collections kept in ecclesiastical record-offices that we can draw anything from a request for a fifteenth-century archbishop's intervention to ensure the livelihood of university students to the problems of an eighteenth-century meeting of the Society of Friends, concerned with the problem of 'disorderly walking' among its members. Before we can even know what possibilities exist an immense amount of transcribing, editing and calendering will have to be done, and this is a process which takes a long time, demands a great deal of hard work, and is apt to produce the kind of book for which there is a strictly limited sale and very little reward in the way of academic honour and glory. But it is work which I make no apology for recommending. If we are really to understand the history of the church it has got to be done, and to be done thoroughly and properly by people who understand the nature of the material which they are using.

It need not, however, be done in a spirit of grim determination as a means of clearing the way for other and better things. There are flowers for Martha to gather as well as seed-beds for her to dig. A spell of work in a record office is apt to bring its own rewards, not simply in the satisfaction of making accessible sources which have hitherto been wrapped up in the veil of a difficult palaeography (and often, as the knowledge of latin declines in our schools and universities, in a difficult language also), but in those uncovenanted blessings which occur in the course of one's editing. Here I have to confine myself to the pleasures which are to be found in the records of the thirteenth and fourteenth centuries, since they are the ones which I happen to know, but I doubt whether such chance benefits are wholly absent even from the driest of modern administrative documents. Still, a bishop's register is apt to be a particularly enjoyable, as well as a particularly informative, source to use. The registrars who compiled such collections of documents were generally intelligent and thoroughly well-trained people, since a bishop could afford to employ the best man for the job, and a post in his household offered prestige, security of tenure and a good hope of advancement. An editor gets to know his registrar, and often finds that he worked upon highly individual lines. Sutton's registrar John de Scalleby worked out for himself a complicated system of cross-referencing by means of marginal drawings (he had a lively pen) in which, for example, a crozier stood for business in the Court of Arches and a scholar's head with its distinctive cap stood for letters relating the university. While registrars tended, to the despair of modern editors, to leave gaps in the records – giving us, for example, all the stages of an interesting story except its conclusion – they also put in much which would have got lost in the system of a modern filing-cabinet. John de Scalleby was on one occasion so much exasperated by the endless subterfuges used by the chancellor and regent-masters of Oxford university in their efforts to escape from the jurisdiction of the bishop of Lincoln that he added his own comment to one of the bishop's letters on the subject – 'Care must be taken not to give way too much to the university people for they have begun to rear themselves up in the spirit of pride.'[9]

As for the bishops themselves, an extraordinarily lively picture of their daily routine, as well as of their more unusual activities, emerges from the recorded texts of their official correspondence. There were the constant travels round the diocese, or further afield on the king's service or in response to a metropolitan or papal command, often in bad weather and sometimes under threat of hostile invasion or the attacks of local 'sons of Belial and satellites of Satan'. There was the reception of endless letters of petition or complaint, and sometimes of the petitioners themselves, brimming with *relationes querelose sive lachrymose* which had to be investigated and dealt with. There were the records of their relations with brother-bishops, relations which were not always as brotherly as they should have been. When, for example, archbishop Melton of York tried to carry out a perfectly lawful diocesan visitation of the tenements of Northallerton and Allertonshire, held by Lewis de Beaumont, bishop of Durham, de Beaumont was so much (and according

[9] *LRS* 48, p 10.

to his metropolitan so unreasonably) enraged that he 'prepared himself in an unbridled way with a stiff neck and arm outstretched for violence, with no small army of excommunicated robbers and thieves, to rush out upon us or to lie in ambush for us, threatening to kill us and our people'.[10] There were dealings with puzzled people of tender conscience, such as an unfortunate woman who believed herself bound by a vow to maintain in perpetuity a priest to pray for her husband's soul, although the wretched fellow had died leaving her nothing except his debts,[11] or the prioress of Fosse whose response to bishop Sutton's attempts to induce her to withdraw her resignation was a burst of such 'astonishing weeping' that he was compelled to give in and let her have her way.[12] There were records of personal charities, such as the practice (apparently and most surprisingly unique at the time, but perhaps other instances remain to be discovered) employed by bishop Langley of Durham of using his power of granting indulgences in such a way as to raise money for disconsolate grass-widows who were trying to scrape up the ransoms for husbands taken prisoner in the French or Scottish wars.[13]

To investigate a register which has not been printed, or even to work carefully through one which has, is like putting your hand into a lucky-dip from which almost anything may emerge, and the reader finds himself constantly impelled to challenge his own and other people's historical pronouncements in the light of this new material. The register of bishop Dalderby of Lincoln gives a good deal of sober information about the trial of the templars in England and their subsequent fate, which may be used as a salutory commentary upon the wilder stories which circulated about the order in France. The *Diverse Littere* which form a considerable section of the register of archbishop Melton of York contain, among many other good things, a full and extremely lively account of the unsuccessful attempts made by the papal legates, the archbishop himself and their respective messengers to convey to Robert Bruce the letters which contained the formal notice of his excommunication.[14] The registrar of bishop Wakefield of Worcester, recently edited, shows that despite all the evidence of wycliffite agitation in the west midlands during the reign of Richard II, the diocesan bishop was taking the whole lollard problem very calmly, and scarcely

---

[10] *Register of William Melton*, fol 489ᵛ.
[11] *Ibid* fol 449.
[12] *Rolls and Register of Oliver Sutton, Stow Roll*, m. 2.
[13] *SS* 169 (1970) p 77 and *SS* 170 (1970) p 19.
[14] *Register of William Melton*, fol 500ᵛ.

troubling to do anything about it.[15] The register of bishop Braybrooke of London, a rather younger contemporary of Wakefield, shows that whatever the satirists may have written about greedy chantry-priests who flocked to London for good pickings, the actual number of such men who came in from other dioceses was negligible, and that in London itself the bishop (a conscientious man) and his clergy were complaining that it was difficult to find good candidates to fill positions in chantries when the pay offered was so wretchedly poor.[16] We have constantly to be turning back to the sources and raw materials of our history if we are to avoid the dangers of trying to swamp the particular in the general, and to fit upon the infinite diversity of human life a systematic pattern which it will not endure.

I cannot do much more here than indicate some of the things which may be found in a very small corner of a very large field. I am not qualified to speak of any records beyond those concerned with the middle ages in England, and even here the proportion which I know at first hand is exceedingly small, but I have tried to indicate some of the lines along which I think fruitful research might be undertaken, in the hope of catching the imagination of some of the rising young medievalists. When it comes to the records of the seventeenth century and still more to those of the last hundred years, the problem is much greater. I once heard a learned man from the Public Record Office estimate, terrifyingly, that in the course of the hour's lecture which he had just delivered some sixty-seven feet of bookshelves had been silently filled by the growth of public records, a fact which set the mind reeling. The microfilm will, mercifully, reduce some of this actual bulk, but it will not lessen the burden upon the conscientious researcher. Of course, not all public records are ecclesiastical records – far from it – but even the encroachments of the secular state have left a good deal of ecclesiastical administration untouched, and people today write more lengthily, if not always more sensibly, than their ancestors did in the middle ages. The divisions of the christian church in the post-reformation period have produced many different sets of records where formerly the system of administration was, in western Europe at least, fairly unified, and whatever happy results the present move towards reunion may bring, it does not appear that a reduction in verbiage is likely to be

---

[15] W. P. Marrett, *A Calendar of the Register of Henry Wakefield, Bishop of Worcester 1375–95* (Worc Hist Soc, 1972).
[16] *Register of Robert Braybrooke*, fols 109 and 163.

among them. Somebody, and presumably the ecclesiastical historians of the future, will have to do a great deal of hard work in sorting, calendering and generally clearing the decks before the history of christendom in the twentieth century can satisfactorily be written. We are acquiring new techniques which may help us to deal with some of the donkey-work, but for two reasons I am rather sceptical about the value of the computer for any but a rather simple and straightforward kind of historical investigation. In the first place, by the time really adequate material has been provided from which to establish a programme most of the research has already been done. In the second, as my title suggests, I think that half the interest and nearly all the fun of historical research lies in its tendency to produce uncovenanted blessings, things which you do not expect to find, and which no amount of preliminary theorising about the subject would have suggested that you were at all likely to find. The computer should have its place, and a very useful place, in dealing with the sheer bulk of standardised records which is one of the daunting products of cheap printing and the type-writer, and it may well be supplemented by other and more sophisticated aids to the memory and wit of man. Still, I doubt whether the traditional methods of research into the problems of ecclesiastical history are likely to undergo a fundamental change in response to new technical equipment. Research has always been directed towards two ends – what the researcher himself wants to find out and what, if he is one of Martha's disciples, he wants to make accessible to other and probably better scholars than himself. In this problem of accessibility we are brought up against the question of the relationship between historians, librarians and archivists; and there is only one possible answer. We are one team, runners in one race, '*et quasi cursores vitai lampada tradunt*'.[17]

If we think that the history of the church is worth preserving then we must go back to our sources whenever we can lay our hands on them, and we must work in the fullest possible collaboration with those whose job it is to preserve them. Our materials lie ready to our hands – the problem is one of 'too much' rather than 'too little'. Our methods must take account of all the new possibilities of technical help as they appear, but fundamentally methods cannot change very much, since they are based upon the historian's insatiable curiosity and his determination to dig out the truth of what really happened – not the things which he thinks should have happened in order to present a tidy picture or to prove a desirable conclusion.

[17] Lucretius, *De Natura Rerum*, II, 79.

There is one last quality which historical work should possess, and that is the quality of enjoyment. Historians should thoroughly enjoy their work, and in fact most of them clearly delight in it, not simply believing the study of ecclesiastical history to be a valuable activity in itself, but really enjoying the process of finding out about it and discussing it with one another. Martha's work begins in the kitchen but it should not end there. She is the one who gathers flowers as she goes on her way.

MISLEADING MANUSCRIPTS: WYCLIF
AND THE NON-WYCLIFFITE BIBLE

by MICHAEL WILKS

THE precise nature of Wyclif's connection with the production of the first English bible[1] is shrouded in mystery, a subject for the fierce controversy and debate that is possible only where ignorance and uncertainty prevail. To begin with, there is an almost total absence of reliable contemporary evidence. The first statements explicitly attributing authorship to Wyclif do not occur until the generation after his death. Of these, the earliest is that of the chronicler Henry Knighton, whose contacts with early lollardy might make him appear to be a more reliable source than most.[2] Writing perhaps in the mid-1390s, Knighton referred back to the year 1382 as the time when Wyclif translated the gospel, which Christ had given to the clergy and doctors of the church, into the tongue, not of the angels, but of the Angles. He accused Wyclif of trying thereby to make the gospel easily available to the literate laity – or, as he viewed the matter, of scattering the pearl of biblical wisdom so that it might be trampled on by the swine.[3] There is however no other reference to Wyclif as translator

---

[1] For details of previous translations of individual books of the Bible in England see [M.] Deanesly, [*The*] *L[ollard] B[ible and Other Medieval Biblical Versions]* (Cambridge 1920) especially pp 302–18; or the convenient list in H. Hargreaves, 'From Bede to Wyclif: Medieval English Bible Translation', *BJLR*, 48 (1965–6) pp 118–40 at 118–20. Compare Sir W. A. Craigie, 'The English Versions (to Wyclif)', *The Bible in its Ancient and English Versions*, ed H. Wheeler Robinson (2 ed Oxford 1954) pp 128–45 at 134–7; F. F. Bruce, *The English Bible: A History of Translations* (2 ed London 1970) pp 10–11; G. Shepherd, 'English Versions of the Scriptures before Wyclif', *CHB*, II (Cambridge 1969) pp 362–87.

[2] As canon of the augustinian house of St Mary of the Meadows at Leicester, he was not only in the heart of lollard country, but must have been acquainted with Hereford and Repingdon, and probably Swinderby: Deanesly, *LB*, p 239.

[3] Knighton, [*Chronicon*, ed J. R. Lumby], 2 vols RS (London 1889) II, pp 151–2, 'Hic magister Iohannes Wyclif evangelium, quod Christus contulit clericis et ecclesiae doctoribus . . . transtulit de latino in anglicam linguam, non angelicam, unde per ipsum fit vulgare et magis apertum laicis et mulieribus legere scientibus quam solet esse clericis admodum literatis et bene intelligentibus, et sic evangelica margarita spargitur et a porcis conculcatur.' This section of the chronicle (from 1377) terminates at 1395, which presumably indicates the date

147

during the parliamentary controversies of 1395–7 about the legality of vernacular bibles,[4] nor in the revival of the dispute at Oxford in 1405.[5] The subsequent condemnation of biblical translation by archbishop Arundel in 1407 mentioned only translations 'made in the time of the said John Wyclif or since';[6] and it was not until 1411 that the archbishop told John XXIII (in a covering letter to a list of 267 wycliffite errors being forwarded to the pope) that Wyclif himself had maliciously instigated the practice of translating the scriptures into his mother tongue.[7] Even this does not have the unambiguous attribution contained in Hus's statement of the same year that Wyclif had actually translated the whole latin bible into English, and Hus himself acknowledged that this was only what the English said.[8] But enough had in fact been said to establish a tradition: there had been a Wyclif bible.

It is true enough that manuscripts of the whole bible in English were in existence by 1400. Many of these manuscripts clearly represent the version thought to have been prepared by Wyclif's erstwhile secretary, John Purvey, and published together with an introductory tract on translating the bible into English about 1396. This version need not concern us here, except to notice that Purvey refers in his *General Prologue* to a previous translation of the bible into English, with an implication that it was in need of correction – although not to the extent, he remarks, of many ordinary latin bibles.[9] It has generally

---

of composition: V. H. Galbraith, 'The Chronicle of Henry Knighton', *Fritz Saxl Memorial Essays*, ed D. J. Gordon (London 1957) pp 136–45.

[4] Deanesly, *LB*, pp 282–3; [H. B.] Workman, [*John Wyclif*] (Oxford 1926) II, pp 193–4, 343–5.

[5] Deanesly, *LB*, pp 293–4; Workman, II, p 169.

[6] Wilkins, III, p 317, '*Ne quis texta s. scripturae transferat in linguam anglicanam*. Statuimus igitur atque ordinamus ut nemo deinceps aliquem textum sacrae scripturae auctoritate sua in linguam anglicanam vel aliam transferat per viam libri, libelli aut tractatus, nec legatur aliquis huiusmodi liber, libellus aut tractatus iam noviter tempore dicti Iohannis Wycliffe, sive citra compositus sive in posterum componendus, in parte vel in toto, publice vel occulte.'

[7] Wilkins, III, p 350, 'novae ad suae malitiae complementum scripturarum in linguam maternam translationis practica adinventa'; compare Deanesly, *LB*, p 238; Workman, II, pp 186–7 (correcting the date from 1412).

[8] Cited Deanesly, *LB*, p 240; Workman, II, p 187.

[9] '. . . for no doubt he shall find full many Bibles in Latin full false . . . and the common Latin Bibles have more need to be corrected, as many as I have seen in my life, than hath the English Bible late translated': see further Deanesly, *LB*, pp 255 *et seq*. The high standard of Purvey's work as a translator has been stressed by Hargreaves, 'The Latin Text of Purvey's Psalter', *Med A* 24 (1955) pp 73–90; 'The Marginal Glosses to the Wycliffite New Testament', *S[tudia] N[eophilologica]*, 33 (Uppsala 1961) pp 285–300; 'The Wycliffite Versions', *CHB*, II, pp 387–415 at 407–13.

been accepted that the material evidence for this earlier version consists primarily of three manuscripts, two now at Oxford and the other at Cambridge, all of them remarkable in that they appear to suggest a change in the identity of the translator at Baruch 3:20. Bodley 959, written in four or five different hands, stops short at Baruch 3:20 itself. Bodley Douce 369 covers the whole Bible, but contains a break at the Baruch passage with a note: *Explicit translacōm Nicholay de herford.* Whilst the other, Cambridge, manuscript (University Library MS Ee.i.10, an 'abridgement' of the latter part of the old testament) also notes at Baruch 3:20: 'Here endiþ þe translacioun of N and now bigynneþ þe translacioun of j and of oþere men.'[10] The 'N' is presumably Nicholas Hereford, one of the most prominent of Wyclif's circle at Oxford; but the 'j' could relate to Wyclif, Purvey or to somebody else altogether. Moreover, the text of the translation up to this Baruch passage is one of an extremely literal nature, but is far less literal afterwards. Accordingly, the nineteenth-century editors of the wycliffite bible, Forshall and Madden, working mainly on the basis of the two Oxford manuscripts and accepting Bodley 959 as the original manuscript of the first translation, argued that Nicholas Hereford must have translated the old testament up to Baruch in this very literal fashion whilst at Oxford, but had broken off when he left England in 1382 to appeal against his condemnation at the papal curia. The work had then, therefore, to be finished by others, in particular by Wyclif himself, and they had done so in a much less literal style of translation.[11]

In assuming that Bodley 959 was the original manuscript, Forshall and Madden completely ignored the point that the existence of a number of different hands posed a serious problem for this interpretation, and this discrepancy has since opened up the way for more recent scholars, notably the swedish linguistic experts, Fristedt and Lindberg,

[10] Hargreaves, *CHB*, II, p 400, amending the reading given by him in 'An Intermediate Version of the Wycliffite Old Testament', *SN*, 28 (1956) pp 130–47 at 133. As Hargreaves comments (p 146), it is not clear why such an abridgement should have been made—although John Rylands Library English MS 89 provides another example—and it is even more difficult to understand why the writer should have copied in a note about Hereford stopping at Baruch which could have had no obvious relevance to his own work.

[11] J. Forshall and J. Madden, *The Holy Bible: made from the Latin Vulgate by John Wycliffe and his Followers*, 4 vols (Oxford 1850) I, p xvii; also F. D. Matthew, 'The Authorship of the Wycliffite Bible', *EHR*, 10 (1895) pp 91–9. Deanesly initially accepted that the translation was by 'Wyclif and his circle' (*LB* p 251), but in *The Significance of the Lollard Bible* (London 1951) pp 3–5, suggested that Wyclif merely inspired the work and that the chief translator was Hereford. Bodley 959 was still accepted here as the original manuscript.

to demolish the Forshall-Madden thesis very thoroughly. Bodley 959 can no longer be regarded as the original manuscript of the first translator. On the contrary, it is a copy of a much corrected version:[12] either the last of a whole series of earlier but no longer extant manuscripts,[13] or at least a fair copy of a heavily revised original draft translation.[14] Either way it is unlikely to be earlier than the last decade of the fourteenth century.[15] This in turn casts doubts upon the existence of a break in the work of translation at Baruch 3:20 caused by Hereford's supposed visit to Rome in 1382. It has been suggested by Lindberg that the break might equally well have been due to Hereford's reported recantation between 1387 and 1391[16] – whilst Fristedt would reject the notion of a break altogether: it is certainly a very odd place for a

[12] [S. L.] Fristedt, [*The*] *W*[*ycliffe*] *B*[*ible*, 2 vols (Stockholm 1953–69)], I, pp 76, 113; 'The Authorship [of the Lollard Bible]', *S*[*tudier i*] *M*[*odern*] *S*[*pråkveten-skap = Stockholm Studies in Modern Philology*,] 19 (Stockholm 1956) pp 28–41 at 31; [C.] Lindberg, [*MS. Bodley 959: Genesis—Baruch 3.20 in the Earlier Version of the Wycliffite Bible*], 5 vols (Stockholm 1959–69) I, pp 21–3; III, pp 29–32; IV, pp 18–19.

[13] Fristedt, *WB*, also 'The Dating [of the Earliest Manuscript of the Wycliffite Bible'], *SMS, ns*, I (1960) pp 79–85 at 84–5. As he points out (*WB* I, p 43), this would mean that 'we are not in possession of a single document which is indubitably by the pen of Wycliffe, Hereford or Purvey.' That there was a considerable variety amongst the manuscripts of the English bible by 1400 is suggested by the introduction to an early fifteenth-century wycliffite concordance to the new testament in English: discussing synonyms of the word 'church', the author comments, 'Now it may be so þat in sum Newe Lawe is writen in sum text þis worde *kirke* & in þe same text & in a noþer book is written þis word *chirche*': cited A. McIntosh, 'Some Linguistic Reflections of a Wycliffite', *Franciplegius: Medieval and Linguistic Studies in honor of F. P. Magoun*, ed J. B. Bessinger and R. P. Creed (New York and London 1965) pp 290–3 at 291; and now printed in S. M. Kuhn, 'The Preface to a Fifteenth-Century Concordance', *Speculum*, 43 (1968) pp 258–73.

[14] Lindberg, II, pp 7, 29–31; III, 32–3: all the scribes were working off the same original manuscript and making a fair copy of revisions to it. Thus Bodley 959 is 'the translator's authorised copy, based on his own first version, and written out by several scribes who were also guided by him in revising the text.' In V, pp 95–6, he suggests that it may be Hereford's copy of his own original together with an intermediate Oxford version, in effect making this a third version.

[15] Fristedt, *WB*, I, pp 11–15, 146, was initially prepared to accept the Forshall-Madden dating to before 1390, but has subsequently re-dated to *c* 1400: 'The Dating', pp 84–5. Lindberg also oscillated between *c* 1390 and *c* 1400 (III, p 33; IV, pp 30–1), but has now settled for the latter: V, pp 55, 61, 95.

[16] Lindberg, II pp 30–2; III, p 33; V, pp 95–6: this means that the completion ot the translation of the whole old testament cannot be placed before 1390 af the earliest. The original idea of a break in 1382 is still to be found with E. Delaruelle, *L'Église au temps du Grand Schisme et de la crise conciliaire* (Paris 1962) p 969.

translator to stop work, virtually in mid-sentence. He would argue that Bodley 959 is an incomplete manuscript, which simply stops short in the form that we have it at the end of a folio, and that a similar break in other manuscripts must have other explanations.[17] This can hardly be said to provide a convincing reason for the existence of rubrics stipulating that Hereford was the translator up to this point. But it would indicate that there might originally have been a complete literal translation of the old testament, which is now no longer available.[18]

This point aside, however, both writers seem to agree with each other in accepting that these old testament manuscripts provide the key to the genesis of the Wyclif bible, and offer a basis for discussing Wyclif's own part in its production. According to Fristedt, they show that the work of translating the whole bible into English was undertaken at Oxford[19] early in the 1370s by a group of wycliffites centred on Queen's College, with John of Trevisa playing a prominent part,[20] and

[17] Fristedt, *WB*, I, p 145; II, p xlvii: this led to the scribes of later manuscripts changing to a different one at this point, I, pp 86–8. A comparison can, he suggests, be made with Bodley Douce 369, which is not a single work but a fifteenth-century binding together of two separate parts. Craigie, 'The English Versions', p 139, appears to accept that the break in Bodley 959 is due both to] it being the end of the folio and to Hereford stopping the work of translation here.

[18] Fristedt, *WB*, I, pp 107, 135, 145; 'The Authorship', p 31: support for this belief in a complete version of the whole bible translated on strictly literal principles is provided by Christ Church MS E.4.

[19] Fristedt, *WB*, II, pp lxiii–lxiv, although he had earlier rejected the theory of an 'Oxford idiom' (I, pp 39–50, 91) and identified the dialect of the original literal version (I, pp 95–8, 118, 145–6) as being that of Leicestershire, which might indicate Lutterworth, but with some northern idioms, which he first attributed to derivations from Wyclif, but subsequently explained by the argument that Hereford was himself a Yorkshireman too: 'The Dating', p 80. Lindberg identifies the dialect of the original translation and of the various scribes of Bodley 959 as being that of the north-west Midlands: see the detailed discussion in I, pp 13–15, 23–5; II, p 18; III, pp 16–18, 33; IV, pp 30–1; V, p 98; whereas M. L. Samuels, 'The Dialect of MS Bodley 959' = Lindberg, V, pp 329–39 (App. I) prefers the central Midlands; but both would accept a Leicester location.

[20] Fristedt, *WB*, II, pp xlviii–xlix, lxiii–lxiv, revising I, pp 1, 6–7, 118. The case for Trevisa's participation, originally suggested by Caxton, rests primarily on his remarks in *Dialogue between a Lord and a Clerk upon Translation* of the mid-1380s in favour of putting the bible into English, and on the fact that he was at Queen's college for a number of years which coincide with the residence there of Hereford and, to a lesser extent, Wyclif himself. Trevisa and Hereford were members of the southern group of masters who were expelled during the north versus south conflict in the college during 1376–80, and in 1378–9 they carried away a number of books from the college library which might well have been useful to someone translating the bible. See further H. J. Wilkins, *Was John*

was completed at Lutterworth by Hereford and his assistants, possibly Repingdon and Brut,[21] by 1383. It was then revised by Wyclif and Purvey, who objected to the numerous errors and excessively literal character of this first draft, and who therefore produced a 'first revision' or 'intermediate version'[22] (perhaps with further assistance from Hereford) during the course of 1384.[23] In all this Wyclif himself was well to the fore. He can be assumed to have initiated and inspired the project, laying down rules of procedure for the translators to follow, supervising and correcting their work,[24] even if he personally wrote little of the actual original text.[25] Eventually Purvey, seeking to achieve a clearer and more readable translation, must be accredited with a second revision of the whole bible in the middle years of the 1390s.[26]

Lindberg on the other hand regards the first part of the old testament as the work of Hereford in the years between 1384 and 1387,

---

Wycliffe a Negligent Pluralist?: John de Trevisa, his Life and Work (London 1915) pp 100–12; D. C. Fowler, 'John Trevisa and the English Bible', *Modern Philology*, 58 (Chicago 1960–1) pp 81–98.

[21] Fristedt, *WB*, I, pp 115–17; compare Lindberg, IV, pp 30–1. Walter Brut seems to have been a literate layman: at his trial in 1393 he, or an associate, reproached Hereford for his ignorance of latin grammar: see Workman, II, p 337.

[22] The idea of an intermediate version, for which see Hargreaves, 'An Intermediate Version', especially p 145, was previously put forward by E. W. Talbert, 'A Note [on the Wyclyfite Bible Translation]', *University of Texas Studies in English*, 20 (1940) pp 29–38, mainly on the basis of Huntington Library MS HM 134. Fristedt, originally working independently of Talbert, first accepted Talbert's evidence ('The Authorship', pp 28, 33–40), but subsequently rejected it on the grounds that the Huntington MS contained passages from Purvey's version of *c* 1396, and so must be dated after 1400: 'The Dating', pp 81–2.

[23] Fristedt, *WB*, I, p 145. Talbert suggested a continuous process of revision between 1384 and 1395: 'A Note', p 38.

[24] Fristedt, *WB*, I, pp 136, 141–8; II, pp xi, lxiv, lxvi; compare 'The Authorship', p 35. He argues that the same rules were applied to the lollard translation of the pseudo-Augustinian tract *De salutaribus documentis*: I, pp 43–8; II, *passim*; also 'New Light on John Wycliffe and the First Full English Bible', *SMS*, ns, III (1968) pp 61–86. That Wyclif himself conceived the idea of translating the Bible into English is also maintained by P. A. Knapp, 'John Wyclif as Bible Translator', *Speculum*, 46 (1971) pp 713–20.

[25] Fristedt, *WB*, I, pp 95–105, 115–17; II, pp xlviii–xlix, lx–lxi, lxiv–lxvii; compare 'The Authorship', p 37.

[26] Fristedt, *WB*, I, pp 8–9, 140–1. According to this it was Purvey's departure from the literal method in his second revision which explains the need for the *General Prologue*—he was conscious of the need to justify the new method (I, p 137)—and also accounts for Arundel's condemnation, aimed against the revision rather than the original translation: a straight word for word translation might have been tolerated, but not one which set out to make the bible intelligible to all (I, pp 142–3).

that is to say, in the period immediately after Wyclif's death.[27] On the assumption that the translators began at the beginning, this would effectively exclude Wyclif from any direct connection with the wycliffite Bible – as had already been argued by a number of English historians.[28] But Lindberg thinks this so improbable that he has steadily come to the conclusion that Wyclif had already translated the new testament first around 1380[29] (and without help from Trevisa[30]), leaving Hereford to carry on and do the old testament after 1384 – a task which Hereford performed so badly without Wyclif present to guide him that Purvey was later obliged to revise Hereford's old testament up to the point where it stopped at Baruch, and then complete the remainder of the old testament himself[31] about 1390.[32] Whichever version of these diametrically opposed Stockholm stories is preferred, the modern scandinavian account of the Wyclif bible accepts that it remains Wyclif's to a very considerable extent.

No one can reasonably mourn the demise of the superficially plausible and deceptively simple Forshall-Madden interpretation: but we may express regret that a quarter of a century of intensive technical scholarship has only managed to replace it with a situation of excruciating complexity, so that general bewilderment now prevails. We may notice straight away, however, one glaring inconsistency in the swedish approach to the problem. All the elaborate superstructure about the place of Wyclif in the preparation of the English bible is deduced from

---

[27] Lindberg, II, pp 30–2; III, p 33.

[28] Workman, II, pp 157, 160–2, allowed that Wyclif instigated the translation of the old testament, and the literal quality of the original version was due to his intention that there should be a sentence by sentence translation, but the work was carried out by Hereford first, and then Purvey, and Wyclif himself had no hand in it. But Wyclif was dissatisfied with the result, as shown by his refusal to use it, and set Purvey to the task of revising it. Much the same position was adopted by H. E. Winn, *Wyclif: Select English Writings* (London 1929) pp 7–9; also G. Leff, *Heresy in the Later Middle Ages*, 2 vols (Manchester/New York 1967) II, pp 512 n 3, 578, 591.

[29] Lindberg, II, pp 30–2; III, p 33; V, pp 92, 95. The possibility that translation of the new testament preceded that of the old testament was considered by Forshall and Madden, I, pp xv–xvii; compare Craigie, 'The English Versions', pp 139–40.

[30] Lindberg, II, p 32, who rules Trevisa out on the grounds of dialect. However relevant this may be in an old testament context, it does not necessarily preclude his involvement in translation of the new testament.

[31] Lindberg, III, p 32; and see also S. H. Thomson, *Europe in Renaissance and Reformation* (London 1963) p 175: Wyclif began translating the bible between 1380 and 1384, leaving Hereford and Purvey to complete and revise the work, which was finished by 1388.

[32] Lindberg, II, pp 30–2; III, p 33; IV, pp 30–1.

manuscripts which make no reference to Wyclif whatsoever and which contain within themselves not a shred of real evidence that he was in any way connected with them. These manuscripts have been studied on the presupposition that they represent a Wyclif bible: whereas, if taken without this prior assumption, there would be no intrinsic reason for mentioning Wyclif in this context. Because, in other words, a tradition has existed since the 1390s, namely, that there *was* a Wyclif bible, it is taken for granted that English bible manuscripts must in some way or other illustrate this tradition. If the tradition is ignored, the manuscripts as such can offer no grounds for thinking that Wyclif participated in their production. The only firm conclusion that can be reached amidst this morass of supposition about the manuscripts is that there was an English bible – a matter which was never in doubt. The secondary question of whether Wyclif and/or his followers should be related to it cannot be approached on a manuscript basis: it can only be considered from what we know independently about Wyclif and early lollardy.

Since Wyclif regarded the old testament as a mere prelude, and sometimes a misleading one, to the evangelic law of the new testament,[33] he might naturally have preferred to have the new testament available in English first. It is a pity therefore that so much erudition should have been devoted to this less important section of the bible, especially when genuine evidence exists for thinking that the new testament was in fact available before the old testament, and that Wyclif might have approved of this order of procedure. His own statements clearly indicate that some biblical texts in English were in existence by 1383, but we notice that he always refers here specifically

---

[33] In the *De veritate sacrae scripturae*, 10 (I, pp 218–21) he attacked the 'sophists' who argued that the old testament was not part of scripture: it had to be accepted as canonical, and Christ himself had said that he came to fulfil the old law, not destroy it. But Wyclif's own use of it was decidedly selective, and he was quite prepared to use the pauline principle that the foundation of the church constituted a new age operating on different principles, so that the new apostolic law swept away mosaic ordinances, when it was convenient for him to do so: see for example his refusal to use the old testament to justify warfare in *De civili dominio*, II, 17, pp 247–8, and his denunciation of arguments for papal absolutism based on old testament passages like Jer. 1:10, as in *De potestate papae*, 11, p 273. This did not however deter him from finding 'right' examples in the old testament, for example, 11, p 275; compare *De Ecclesia*, 7, pp 143–4. His overall position does not seem to have changed much from his initial discussion in chapters 7 and 8 of the *De mandatis divinis*, in which he concluded that the old testament contained certain basic truths in conformity with the new testament, but was far from being of equal standing with the *lex evangelica*. All references are to the Wyclif Society editions.

to the gospels, or at least the *lex Domini*, and nowhere mentions an old testament or a complete bible in English. It may also be of significance that the earliest attribution of biblical translation to Wyclif, that of Knighton, only accuses him of having translated Christ's gospel and other parts of the new testament in 1382. There is no positive reason for thinking that a new testament was produced any earlier than this. It is only during 1382 that passages begin to appear in Wyclif's works to justify knowledge of the gospels in English, and here it could very well be argued that they refer only to preaching the biblical texts in English rather than to an actual translation itself.[34] As has been noted, the celebrated case of William Smith, the 'parchemyner' of Leicester, who later confessed to having written books in English since 1381 or 1382 *de evangelio et de epistolis et aliis epistolis et doctoribus* only refers to new testament material, and could be books *about* the gospel and epistles rather than *of* the biblical texts.[35] It was not until the end of this year, 1382, that Wyclif began to urge that the laity should be able to study the gospel in English for themselves;[36] and not until the middle of 1383 do we at last have a direct statement by him that the lay lords can do so,[37] with all its implications that some sort of translation must have been ready. Finally, in 1384, we hear from Wyclif that codices of an English new testament are being burned.[38]

[34] The first indication seems to be *Sermones*, III, 45, p 384 (June 1382) where he argues that pronunciation of the gospel is no more important than the language it is written in provided the right meaning is retained. *De nova praevaricantia mandatorum*, 1, pp 116–17 (late 1382 or early 1383) refers only to pamphlets preaching biblical truths in English; whilst *De triplici vinculo amoris* 2, p 168 (late 1383) mentions only writings in English and queen Anne of Bohemia's possession of Czech and German translations of the bible: Buddensieg's editorial note is surely correct against Deanesly, *LB*, p 248, in that there is no specific reference here to an English bible. *Of Mynistris in þe Chirche*, ed Arnold, p 293 (about September 1383) merely suggests that the gospels should be known and expounded in English; and similarly *Opus evangelicum*, III, 31 and 36 (II, pp 15 and 132) of 1384, but incorporating earlier material, refers to English preaching.
[35] K. B. McFarlane, *Wycliffe and English Nonconformity* (repr Harmondsworth 1972) p 125, with reference to Knighton, II, p 313. For the re-dating of this see A. Hudson, 'A Lollard Sermon-Cycle [and its Implications]', *Med A*, 40 (1971) pp 142–56 at 152 n 1.
[36] *De amore* = *Ep* V, p 9 (late 1382); *Speculum saecularium dominorum*, 1, pp 74–5 (1382–3).
[37] *Expositio Matt. XXIV*, 8, p 378, 'quia temporales domini . . . possunt tamen ex Dei gratia studere Christi evangelia in lingua eis cognita'.
[38] *De contrarietate duorum dominorum*, 2, p 700, 'dyabolus . . . faciat comburi codices de lege Domini. Lingua enim sive hebraea sive graeca sive latina sive anglica est quasi habitus legis Domini'; and see also 8, p 711, accusing the friars of arranging 'quod libri ewangelici et sensu catholici declarati populo comburantur.'

None of this does more than indicate that Wyclif was aware in his last two or three years that an English new testament existed, and that he gave a rather limp measure of approval to it. There is nothing to suggest that he had a hand in it himself. Otherwise we should have to account for a most uncharacteristic reticence on his part. Considering the extent of his writings at this period, he seldom refers, and then only in passing, to something which one might have supposed would be very close to his heart – a means by which all should be able to understand the bible. How can one explain this unaccustomed modesty? There is no such diffidence when he was talking about the importance of the sermons which he devised for his 'poor priests' to preach.

Since we do not know what this early English new testament was like, it is difficult to say. But much of the difficulty would indeed disappear if our swedish experts are correct to the extent of suggesting that it was a very literal type of translation made on the traditional model, which the lollards would subsequently have to revise extensively. Its very literalness would be the best possible argument for it *not* being a Wyclif bible. The dominant tradition of medieval biblical translation, based on Jerome's discussion of this highly specialised task, was one which assumed that every word of the sacred text was itself sacred, and that even the very order of the words was a divine mystery which made it imperative to preserve this in the translation. The faithful exponent had to make word correspond to word, and there was little scope for an idiomatic expression of what the translator thought the divine author had meant.[39] This might render the meaning almost unintelligible in places, but this was particularly appropriate for use by university masters and the educated clergy generally. The word for word system provided for greater academic accuracy, was of more value for the purposes of debate, and had the immense advantage that it was still possible to make use of the standard latin glosses on the vulgate text in which each individual word was annotated. The 'construe' method produced a work to suit experts, and it is not surprising that the wycliffites should prefer to revise a translation of this type rather than attempt a new one altogether. Insofar as the Wyclif group was a university élite there was hardly likely to be dissatisfaction with the English bible on this score. Wyclif had himself remarked often enough that

[39] W. Scharz, 'The Meaning of *Fidus Interpres* in Medieval Translation', *JTS*, 45 (1944) p 75.

not one syllable of scripture was lacking in significance.[40] But Wyclif's opponents were academics too, and a bible which would have been of equal value to them (given that they could have ignored the canonical prohibition on bible translations[91]) would not have been Wyclif's conception of a good translation. What he wanted was an English bible which would bring out the real essence of the gospel teaching – and so prove his enemies to be falsifiers of scriptural truth.[42] If he had a bible, he would need one which would explain what it meant as it went along.

It only confuses the issue to maintain that Wyclif wanted the bible to be a new legal code to set against the canon law of the papacy and its supporters, and therefore would have welcomed a word for word translation as producing the verbal accuracy needed in a code of law.[43] This not only overlooks the point that the bible had always been regarded as the lawbook *par excellence* of the hierocratic system itself,[44] but also assumes quite unjustifiably that Wyclif was an exponent of *sola scriptura* in the sense of wishing to make the higher law of the bible into an instrument of everyday usage, replacing both human traditions and the positive law itself. On the contrary, however, Wyclif continued to treat the bible, divine law, as very much a higher and therefore – in a fundamental sense – unwritten law, quite unsuitable for general lay use. This can be seen in his incessant demands for reliance on the literal sense of scripture. For what Wyclif meant by the literal *sense* had little

---

[40] *De Ecclesia*, 1, p 10: the statement 'in tota scriptura non ponitur vel una sillaba sine sensu' is in fact a tautology in that scripture is itself to be defined as those parts of the bible which have a right 'sense'.

[41] *Decretales*, V, vii, 12, which derived from Innocent III's condemnation of waldensians in Metz who were translating the bible into French for use in unauthorised preaching: see *Reg.*, I, 141–2 (*PL* 214 (1855) cols 695–9).

[42] See for example the long attack on the papalists in *De Ecclesia*, 3 pp 48–56, demanding that their actions should be judged against the bible truly understood, and concluding, 'Quae enim posset esse maior adulteratio verbi Domini quam intelligere ipsum ad sensum diaboli iuxta quem defendatur esse haereticum et blasfemum . . . ?' Similarly *De veritate sacrae scripturae*, 7, especially pp 141–2, 148, 158–9, for the argument that those who misinterpret scripture are falsifying it, and so can be accused of saying that scripture is largely untrue: 'Ex istis videtur quod magna pars scripturae foret falsissima . . .'

[43] Deanesly, *The Significance of the Lollard Bible*, pp 8–9; Knapp, 'John Wyclif as Bible Translator', p 714; W. Mallard, 'John Wyclif and the Tradition of Biblical Authority', *Church History* 30 (Chicago 1961) pp 50–60 at 57.

[44] Compare the very pertinent remarks of W. Ullmann, 'The Bible and Principles of Government in the Middle Ages', *La Bibbia nell'alto medioevo: Settimane di studio del Centro italiano di studi sull'alto medioevo* 10 (Spoleto 1963) pp 181–227, 331–6.

enough to do with literal *translation*. One must never confuse the two things. By literal, Wyclif meant true, conforming to the inner divine content of a biblical statement: he was always concerned with what he thought to be the meaning behind the words, not with the words themselves – let alone the ink and parchment which gave them visible form and made them legible.[45] Words were signs, essentially vehicles for righteousness, and their supreme function was to convey the true sense, to carry a correct understanding of Christ's teaching with them.[46] The bible was a *via regia*, a highway to truth, and as with all road systems it was necessary to have guidance along the right way. The underlying assumption here was that translation meant understanding, and understanding entailed exposition by those qualified to interpret the words rather than actual reading by the faithful of the texts themselves – even if they could read and could even afford the cost of having their own bible. Certainly all were to know the scriptures,[47] but by this Wyclif primarily had in mind that all were to know them by being taught what they ought to mean, not by using their own eyes. The reading of texts was a job for the priest rather than the layman (unless perhaps he was a lord), and the priest would then retail to his audience what he thought they should know, taking care to explain and gloss what was being said as he went along. For Wyclif the good priest still stood between the Word and man. His technique for getting the bible 'read' was the sermon or the tract, the explanation of a text by one qualified to reason rightly about it. The sermon was itself the best 'translation' of the bible,[48] the handing on or transfer (*translatio*) of the

---

[45] *De veritate sacrae scripturae*, 6 (I, pp 107–8), 'Nam, sicut ostendi alibi de lgee Dei, est praeter codices vel signa sensibilia dare veritatem signatam, qaeu potius est scriptura sacra quam codices. Unde solebam describere scripturam quod sit sacra veritas inscripta . . .', and more extensively pp 114–16: the same distinction applies in reverse to heresy: 7 (I, p 140). See also *Trialogus*, III, 21, pp 238–9; *De civili dominio*, III, 1, p 4, 'codices aut habitus corporales vel ritus sensibiles non sunt christiana religio, licet sint quandoque per accidens eius signa.'

[46] For example *De veritate sacrae scripturae*, 3 (I, p 44); 16 (II, pp 5, 15, 19–20, 32).

[47] Note the use of phrases like *De Ecclesia*, 7, p 146, 'scrutetur homo totam scripturam . . .'; p 156, 'Sed scrutetur fidelis evangelium . . .'; and therefore 'nam mille sunt fideles qui habent immediate a Deo fidem scripturae independenter ab illo [papa], etiam plus quam ipse', *De potestate papae*, 10, p 261; also *De officio regis*, 4, p 72.

[48] There is an excellent illustration of this principle in Trevisa's *Dialogue*: 'Also the gospel and prophecye & the right feyth of holy chirche must be taught and preched to Englysshe men that conne no latyn. Thenne the gospel and prophecye and the right feyth of holy Chirche must be told hem in englysshe, and that is not don but by Englysshe translacon, for such *englysshe prechyng is very*

divine truths behind the written words. We might reasonably infer that the wycliffite vernacular sermons were much more closely akin to what he wanted than any translation in the modern sense of the word. The question of the actual authorship of the English sermons raises its own problems, but the most significant thing about them in this context is that the lengthy passages of the bible which do get translated in the course of them bear no resemblance to any other known version. The translator of the English sermons did not have, or did not wish to have, a bible translation to work from. He preferred to make his own – and his own mistakes and corrections.⁴⁹ By the time he had finished his work on the sermons, he had produced his own 'selected passages of the New Testament in translation', selections which were so extensive that they may be regarded as forming their own abridged version of the bible.⁵⁰ Why should he be anxious for more, for the whole Bible in translation? He had already produced what he thought most important for the benefit of the laity, and had, by putting it in sermon form, ensured its right presentation. This discrepancy between the English sermon version and the so-called Wyclif bible is again a clear indication that Wyclif had nothing to do with the preparation of the latter. The English sermons were not only contemporary, but the translator was working off the manuscripts of Wyclif's latin sermons before these were revised and augmented.⁵¹ This argues for someone, or a group, close to Wyclif, even if it was not Wyclif himself; and the very fact that the alleged early Wyclif bible did not employ the same language means that this first English bible was not a creation of Wyclif's immediate circle in its initial recension. On the contrary, the bible translators may themselves have made use of the English sermons.⁵²

Future research into the sources should therefore be concerned with the question of a non-Wyclif bible, not of a Wyclif or even a wycliffite one. It is possible that Wyclif's emphasis on the sense of scripture as

---

translacon, and such englyssh prechyng is good and nedefull, thene englyssh translacon is good and nedefull.' See Wilkins, p 95; Fowler, pp 97–8.

⁴⁹ As originally pointed out by [T.] Arnold, [*Select English Works of John Wyclif*], 3 vols (Oxford 1869–71) in notes to I, p 71 and II, p 13.

⁵⁰ Workman, II, pp 176–7. Fristedt, *WB*, I, pp 7, 106, glosses rather unconvincingly over this point. A similar situation arises with Chaucer's translations: see now W. M. Thompson, 'Chaucer's Translation of the Bible', *English and Medieval Studies presented to J. R. R. Tolkien*, ed N. David and C. L. Wrenn (London 1962) pp 183–99.

⁵¹ The translator used the 3-part version of the *Sermones* written (as a single work) by Wyclif in 1381–2, not the 4-part compilation of 1384.

⁵² The suggestion is made by Arnold, II, p 345 note.

opposed to undue interest in the words apparent in the *De veritate sacrae scripturae* of 1378 is a pointer to the period when the work of translating the bible into English began. But we can only assert with any confidence that some sort of English version of the new testament had been made available by 1382. We do not know who was responsible for it, nor where it was produced. John of Trevisa, working at Oxford, may still have as good a claim as any to be considered, but we can only be convinced that it was not Wyclif, and that this early version was not an authentic wycliffite production. To this was apparently added an old testament at a later date, on which Nicholas Hereford and a certain John seem to have been engaged at some stage. But by this time the work of providing an English bible for general consumption had become very much a group activity, and the text underwent a process of continuous revision which in due course led to the Purvey version in the 1390s, but is unlikely to have stopped there. There was in other words a takeover of an originally independent English bible project by the wycliffite movement in the decade or so after Wyclif's death, one more example of the way in which early lollardy moved fairly rapidly away from the original standpoint of its founder in the direction of a more radical, populist, lay-centred church. English bible revision and multiplication was just the sort of work which would be appropriate to and, I suggest, was appropriated by the wycliffite missionary school or rival *universitas* which Wyclif appears to have established after his virtual expulsion from Oxford, the intensely active and well-staffed headquarters, a veritable 'Centre for Lollard Studies', combining a wycliffite library and publishing house, whose existence has been revealed recently by Dr Anne Hudson's profoundly important and very exciting investigation of early lollard literature.[53] This may have been located in the Leicestershire area, although not necessarily at Lutterworth itself,[54] and this is precisely the area to which we may look

[53] 'A Lollard Compilation and the Dissemination of Wycliffite Thought', *JTS*, ns, 23 (1972) pp 65–81, especially 75–80; 'Some Aspects of Lollard Book Production', *SCH*, 9 (1972) pp 147–57, especially 155–7; also 'A Lollard Sermon-Cycle', pp 145–6, 150.

[54] It is possible that this was at Oxford itself ('A Lollard Compilation', pp 73, 75) but the alternative suggestion of the Braybrooke area ('Some Aspects', pp 155–6; compare the remarks on dialects, 'A Lollard Sermon-Cycle,' pp 149–50) may prove to be a more fruitful one, since this was the land of Thomas Latimer, known to be one of the lollard knights, and a notorious lollard centre in the early fifteenth century: see K. B. McFarlane, *Lancastrian Kings and Lollard Knights* (Oxford 1972) pp 195–6.

for the provenance of the Oxford and Cambridge bible manuscripts. But these manuscripts themselves, however significant for the study of late fourteenth-century lollardy, derive from a late stage in the history of biblical translation, and can only be peripheral to the prime question of the relationship between Wyclif and the first English bible.

THE SERMON LITERATURE OF
POPE CLEMENT VI[1]

by DIANA WOOD

MAXIMUS *sermocinator verbi Dei* is the description of pope Clement VI, formerly Pierre Roger, given by a fourteenth-century French chronicler.[2] Others of the pope's compatriots were equally fulsome in their adulation. An Italian chronicler, perhaps an ex-student at the university of Paris, where Pierre Roger had been a master in theology, records:[3]

> . . . gratissimus fuit sermocinator. Quum cathedram concionaturus aut disputaturus ascendebat, tota Parisiorum Civitas, ut eum audiret, accurrebat. Proh quam eleganter sermocinabatur!

In Prague, Clement's ex-pupil, the emperor Charles IV, remembered the grace with which he had been infused through listening to one of his master's sermons over twenty years before.[4] Even the English joined this chorus of praise. Thomas Walsingham paid tribute to Clement as a man of singular culture,[5] while Walter Burley lauded his teaching skill, his oratory, and his legendary memory.[6] By the early

[1] I should like to thank Dr Margaret Harvey for discussing this paper with me in its early stages, and Dr Michael Wilks for his kindness in reading the draft and for much help and encouragement. I also thank the university of East Anglia for generous grants towards microfilms.
[2] Aymeric de Peyraco, *Chronicon*: cited in S. Baluze, *Vitae Paparum Avenionensium*, ed G. Mollat, II (Paris 1927) p 422.
[3] *Historiae Romanae Fragmenta*, ed L. A. Muratorius, *Antiquitates Italicae Medii Aevi*, III (Milan 1740) cap xii, p 344.
[4] *Vita Karoli Quarti Imperatoris ab ipso Karolo conscripta*, ed J. F. Böhmer, *Fontes Rerum Germanicarum*, I (Stuggart 1843) p 235: 'Placuit autem michi predicti abbatis facundia seu eloquencia in eodem sermone, ut tantam contemplacionem haberem in devotione ipsum audiens et intuens, quod intra me cepi cogitare dicens: *Quid est quod tanta gracia michi infunditur ex homine isto?* Cepique demum sui noticiam, qui ad me multum caritative ac paterne confovebat, de sacra scriptura me sepius informando'.
[5] Thomas Walsingham, *Historia Anglicana*, ed H. T. Riley, *RS* 28, I, i (London 1863) p 254.
[6] Walter Burley, *Epistola dedicatoria ad Commentarium in VIII libros Politicorum Aristotelis*, ed A. Maier, 'Zu Walter Burleys Politik-Kommentar', A[*usgehendes*

fifteenth century Clement's sermons were regarded as models. Several of them appear, abbreviated and anonymous, as part of a treatise on preaching by Paul Koëlner, canon of Ratisbon, written some time before 1420.[7]

The pope's reputation is evidenced by the number of his sermons still extant in both fourteenth and fifteenth-century manuscripts. The latest list, by professor J. B. Schneyer, gives the incipits of 101 sermons.[8] If we add to these some which have been attributed to Clement, and others, of which we have only fragments, to be found in a commonplace book he kept in his early Paris days,[9] the total is over 120. The total number of manuscripts given by Schneyer is 79. In fact, it can now be shown to be over 90, and is still increasing. And the manuscripts are far-flung – from Uppsala to Venice; from Barcelona to Warsaw.

Was Clement's reputation justified? He set his own standards. The touchstone of sermon eloquence was beauty. And for him truth was beauty. A sermon, like the human body, was beautiful if it had 'the truth of existence, the height of greatness, the virtue of efficacy, and the clarity of intelligence'.[10] Falseness and baseness, vanity and obscurity – these were the evils to be banished from the sermon.[11] He lamented

---

mittelalter gesammelte] A[*ufsätze zur*] G[*eistesgeschichte des 14 Jahrhunderts*], I (Rome 1964) pp 95, 96.

[7] Oxford, Bodleian library, MS Laud Misc 432, fols 120r–263v. Part of the treatise appears also in Munich MSS lat. 19539, fols 45r–9v and 13431, fols 1r–6r; Trèves MS 327, fols 95r–101r, and Graz MS Univ. 348, fols 80r–7r. All the manuscripts are fifteenth century, Graz MS Univ. 348 being the earliest, written *c*1420. Munich 19539 is the only one to acknowledge Clement VI: see Th.-M. Charland, '*Artes Praedicandi*'. *Contribution à l'histoire de la rhétorique au Moyen Age* (Paris/Ottawa 1936) p 74.

[8] J. B. Schneyer, *Repertorium der lateinischen Sermones des Mittelalters*, pt iv (Münster, Westfalen 1972) pp 757–69. On Clement's sermons in general see [G.] Mollat, 'L'oeuvre oratoire [de Clément VI]', *Archives d'histoire doctrinale et littéraire du Moyen Age*, III (Paris 1928) pp 239–74; P. Schmitz, 'Les sermons et discours de Clément VI', *RB*, xli (1929) pp 15–34; [A.] Maier, 'Der Literarische [nachlass des Petrus Rogerii (Clemens VI) in der Borghesiana]', *AAG* II (Rome 1967) pp 255–315, 503–17.

[9] Vatican MS Borghese 247. For description see Maier, 'Der Literarische', pp 308–13 and her *Codices Burghesiani Bibliothecae Vaticanae, Studi e Testi*, 170 (Rome 1952) pp 295–301.

[10] [Paris, Bibliothèque] St G[eneviève MS] 240, fol 162r: '. . . unde videtur michi quod inter cetera eloquium dicitur habere pulchritudinem ex quattuor, secundum similitudinem pulchritudinis corporalis: primo quando habet veritatem existentie, secundo quando habet sublimitatem eminentie, tercio quando habet virtuositem efficacie, quarto quando habet claritatem intelligentie. Eloquium enim merito dicitur pulchrum.'

[11] St G 240, fol 162v: 'Falsitas autem vilitas, vanitas et obscuritas debent esse extranea a sermone. Et ideo quando remota sunt, sermo pulcher est'.

that from the mouths of many of his verbose contemporaries issued forth *falsitas quam veritas, vilitas quam honestas, vanitas quam utilitas, obscuritas quam claritas* making their sermons deformed rather than beautiful.[12] Such rhythm and assonance are characteristic of Clement's own compositions, and must occasionally have lent them what we should regard as beauty. Typical too is the scholastic division of the sermon text into phrases or words, the subtle explanation of each of these, and their use as the foundations of each section of the work. Throughout the sermons there is constant repetition, frequent play on words, and endless quotation. All these things, coupled with his undoubted personal magnetism, led to Clement's medieval reputation for eloquence.

At a distance of some six centuries we may regret that Clement did not heed his own preaching. His sermons are equally verbose, unrelieved by *exempla*, and overladen with citations. His delight in displaying his own learning is inexhaustible, often leading to the very *obscuritas* he deplored in others. As a student at Paris he had edited the works of Bernard,[13] something which his later sermons reflect. As pope he could afford to pay research assistants: the rubric of a Paris manuscript shows that he ordered the compiling of a dictionary of quotations from Ambrose, but the scribe, possibly tiring of the task, never got beyond the letter G.[14] Professor Mollat uncharitably suggests that the reason for the proliferation of clementine manuscripts is that other ecclesiastics liked to plunder the pope's quotations for their own compositions.[15] Occasionally Clement's elegiac pieces merit the accusation of bad taste. He delivered a sermon in consistory when he imposed processes on the unknown murderers of prince Andrew of Hungary, first husband of the lascivious Joanna of Naples. Contemporaries disagreed about Andrew's character: at best he was ineffectual and childish, at worst he

---

[12] St G 240, fol 162v: 'Et quia hodie prohdolor in multis verbis prelatorum etiam magnorum ista quattuor vel eorum alterum se immiscent, quia frequenter in ore eorum invenitur potius falsitas quam veritas, vilitas quam honestas, vanitas quam utilitas, obscuritas quam claritas. Idcirco eorum verba turpitudinem potius quam pulchritudinem habent'.

[13] Paris, Bibliothèque Nationale MS nouvelle acquisition latin 2627: *Bibliothèque de l'Ecole des Chartes*, 124 (1966) pp 153–4: 'Incipit liber primus exceptionum collectarum de diversis opusculis b. Bernhardi ... editus ab episcopo Petro Senonensi [Clemens VI, papa]'.

[14] L. Delisle, *Inventaire des Manuscrits de la Bibliothèque Nationale: Fonds de Cluny* (Paris 1884) Appendix V, p 387: 'Bartholomei de Urbino, compilatio ex dictis sancti Ambrosii, facta jussu Clementis VI, ordine alphabetico, usque ad litteram G inclusive'.

[15] Mollat, 'L'oeuvre oratoire', p 268.

was vicious.[16] Yet Clement compares his murder with the passion of Christ; and some of the comparisons are hardly to Christ's advantage. Andrew was more sinned against than Christ, because although both were killed by their own people, the jews had not recognised Christ as their true king. Both were of tender age, but Andrew more so than Christ.[17] And so it goes on. Another example occurs in the funeral oration for cardinal Napoleon Orsini, where Clement puns embarrassingly on the name of the deceased. He takes the *leon* from Napo*leon*, and, changing the *Ors*ini to *Urs*ini arrives at 1 Samuel, 17, 36: *Leonem et ursum interfeci.*[18] Such laboured puns, the artificiality of structure, the tedious assonance, and the sheer length of his discourses, however appealing in the fourteenth century, do not ensure Clement a wide public today.

Why, then, are the sermons read? The value of the consistory collations as a record of facts has long been recognised. The pope's lurid descriptions of Andrew's murder still ranks as one of the official accounts. Sometimes Clement will supply us with evidence of personal motives: for example, he admitted that a French cardinal had been promoted purely as a result of pressure from the French royal family.[19] The pulpit sermons often contain tirades against contemporary abuses – the worldly ambitions and lax morals of the clergy. This is somewhat paradoxical when one remembers Clement's own reputation, however undeserved, as the most notorious of the Avignon popes. An aspect of Clement's discourses which merits more attention, however, is their value as a source for papal theory. The collations expand the abbreviations of papal correspondence and complement them. In so doing they reveal Clement as a pope in the traditional hierocratic mould. Three examples should suffice. In 1344 Clement created a prince of the Canary Islands. The chronicles and correspondence about it imply that his

16 For conflicting interpretations see E. G. Léonard, *La Jeunesse de Jeanne I*er, *reine de Naples, comtesse de Provence* (Paris 1932) I, p 257.

17 St G 240, fol 363v: 'Sed videtur michi quod licet multi legantur in scriptura prodicionaliter interfecti, tamen nullius mors, nullius occisio fuit ita similis morti Christi sicut mors nostri Andree. . . . Primo quidem ratione patientis passus est enim Christus. Passus est noster Andreas, qui habent similitudinem quo ad tria. Primo quo ad teneritudinem complexionis. Uterque enim in etate tenera, sed Andreas in magis tenera. . . . Tercio quantum ad celsitudinem dominationis. Uterque enim Rex, et uterque a suo Populo interfectus. Sed videtur prima facie quod etiam in hoc homicide Regis Andree gravius peccaverunt. Iudei enim licet Christus esset Rex verus, eorum tamen eum non cognoscebant in regem'.

18 St G 240, fols 403v–8r.

19 Mollat, 'L'oeuvre oratoire', pp 270–1.

main concern is for the conversion of the islands, and that he is simply acceding to a request in bestowing the crown. But from the collation preached on the creation of the new office[20] we learn that Clement's true motive is the overtly political one of increasing his own *imperium* by increasing the lands directly under papal control.[21] In 1343 a roman embassy requested the pope to return to Rome. Needless to say Clement had no intention of doing so, but in the discourse he delivered in reply he tried to dupe the Romans by enmeshing himself in a web of argument and counter-argument. Some of this is based on the familiar idea that a bishop is married to his see. Clement admitted that he ought to go to Rome for the 'appropriation' of his see – literally the taking possession – because Rome is the *propria sedes* of the supreme pontiff and successor of Peter. Indeed, this is why he is called roman pontiff, or roman bishop.[22] But Clement then reverses his position. It can be argued that Rome is not the *propria sedes* of the pope. After all, the spouse of the universal church does not have his own particular see. The pope is the spouse of the universal church; therefore the pope does not have his own particular see. And thus Rome cannot be his *propria sedes*.[23] Extreme papalists had said much the same.[24] Later in the sermon Clement returns to the marriage theme. Although the bridegroom loves his bride, he ought, when necessity demands it, to withdraw himself from her presence and transfer himself to another; and he cites the example of how Jacob was compelled to desert Rachel for Leah.[25] In other words, the pope is obliged to travel throughout the universal church. But it must not be thought that Clement is advocating a general policy of episcopal adultery. Far from it: only the pope is allowed to transfer himself from one see to another.

[20] St G 240, fols 336v–43v.

[21] St G 240, fol 337v: 'Secundo dico quod hic concurrit fidei nostri imperii dilatatio copiosa vel gloriosa'.

[22] St G 240, fol 148v: 'Roma est propria sedes summi pontificis et successoris Petri. Unde vocatur Romanus pontifex, Romanus episcopus'.

[23] St G 240, fol 148v: 'Sed arguitur contra, videtur quod Roma non sit propria sedes papae. Probatur sic: sponsus universalis Ecclesie non habet propriam sedem; sed papa est sponsus universalis Ecclesie; ergo non habet propriam sedem. Et sic secundum istum modum Roma non est sua propria sedes'.

[24] For examples see M. J. Wilks, *The Problem of Sovereignty in the Later Middle Ages* (Cambridge 1963) pp 401–7.

[25] St G 240, fol 149v: 'Ergo quamvis sponsus sponsam diligat debet tamen cum oportunitas exigit, dimissa presentia sponsa, ad alia transferre. Et de hoc habemus figurum Gen xxx° quod quamvis Patriarcha Jacob diligeret Rachelem, velut sponsam valde dilectam formosam et valde pulchram, oportuit tamen ipsum de beneplacito Rachelis descendere ad Lyam ...'.

When the tempest raged in the ocean, only Peter went out on to the waves, according to Matthew 14, 29. The other disciples remained in the ship, to show that the roman Pontiff who stands in the place of Peter, ought to visit different areas to bring peace to all those committed to him and to still tempests. The other prelates should remain, just as in the ship, in their own churches – *in propriis ecclesiis* – to which they have been ordained and deputed.[26]

The third example is the most famous of Clement's political collations, that preached on the approbation of the election of Charles of Moravia as *rex Romanorum*.[27] It is based on 1 Kings 1, 35, *Salomon sedebit super solium meum, et ipse regnabit pro me*. Solomon, of course, is Charles, and the point that it is not *the* throne, but *my* throne, that is, Clement's throne, is laboured throughout the discourse. 'Shall I renounce this throne and this seat?' he asks rhetorically. 'Certainly not. He shall reign for me when he reigns for my honour and that of my see. When he reigns on my behalf he will totally direct his rule to the honour of God and the Holy See.'[28] The traditionally authoritarian nature of this is obvious, and is reflected not only here, but in Clement's collations as a whole.

The fourteenth-century historian generally reads the consistory collations: his fifteenth-century colleagues might be more interested in the pulpit sermons for saints' and red-letter days. Since 1923, when Finke published his work on the council of Constance,[29] isolated examples of Clement's sermons have been recognized in manuscripts containing conciliar sermons. Finke himself found one, and unknowingly published extracts from a second.[30] Recently professor Schneyer has identified as many as fourteen of Clement's sermons in a manuscript from

---

[26] St G 240, fol 150r: 'Item tempestate in mari existente solus Petrus exivit ad fluctuationes maris. Mt. xiiiio [22–9]. Alii discipuli remanserunt in navi, ad denotandum quod Romanus pontifex, qui stat in loco beati Petri, debet ad diversas partes accedere, ut possit sibi commissarum omnium [*sic*] sedare et tollere tempestates. Alii vero prelati remanent velut in navi in propriis ecclesiis, quibus sunt ordinati et deputati'. The latin appears to be corrupt at this point, but a comparison with a later recension of the sermon in Cambridge, Peterhouse MS 265, fols 166r–73v at fols 169r/v reveals identical wording.

[27] *MGH Const*, VIII, no 100, pp 143–63.

[28] *Ibid* pp 151–2.

[29] [H.] Finke, [*Acta Concilii Constanciensis*], II (Münster 1923). The standard work on preaching at Constance is P. Arendt, *Die Predigten des Konstanzer Konzils* (Freiburg im Breisgau 1933).

[30] Finke, pp 370–1. The incipits of the two sermons are: 'Filius noster iste protervus et contumax', Deut. 21:18–19, and 'Ortus est sol', Ps 103:22.

St Paul in Lavant, in Austria.[31] There are, in fact, three more than Schneyer realized: indeed, he edited one of them without recognition. This is the famous discourse delivered by Pierre Roger at Vincennes in 1329, and the edition supplied by Schneyer presents a slightly shortened version of the fourteenth-century original.[32]

The St Paul manuscript is the best one: it is followed jointly by one from Klosterneuburg[33] and one from Krems, described by Vidal, although without mention of Clement.[34] Both sermon-collections were compiled by Coloman Chnapp (died 1443), a canon of Klosterneuburg,[35] and contain the same six Clement sermons in the same order. Using two reliable fourteenth-century manuscripts to provide models of Clement's sermons,[36] and comparing their wording with that of the Klosterneuburg conciliar manuscript, with versions of allegedly conciliar sermons edited by Walch,[37] Mansi,[38] and Schneyer,[39] and with descriptions of manuscripts wherever these are sufficiently full, it is possible to find twenty-one of Clement's sermons masquerading as conciliar pieces, distributed in fourteen conciliar manuscripts.[40] There may well be more.

---

[31] [J. B.] Schneyer, 'Konstanzer Konzilspredigten. [Eine Ergänzung zu H. Finke's Sermones – und Handschriftenlisten]', Z[eitschrift für die] G[eschichte des] O[berrheins], 113 (Karlsruhe 1965) pp 361–88; 'Konstanzer Konzilspredigten: Texte', ZGO 118 (1970) p 99, and 'Neuaufgefundene Konstanzer Konzilspredigten', *Annuarium Historiae Conciliorum* II (Amsterdam 1970) pp 66–77.

[32] Schneyer, 'Konstanzer Konzilspredigten: Texte', pp 100–9, from Stift St Paul (Lavant) MS pap. 29 fols 88v–96r. The best manuscript version is St G 240, fols 328v–34r. The discourse has been printed several times, the best edition being Durand de Maillane, *Les Libertez de l'Eglise Gallicane prouvées et commentées*, III (Paris/Lyons 1771) pp 460–79.

[33] Klosterneuburg Stiftsbibliothek MS 82.

[34] [J. M.] Vidal, ['Un recueil manuscrit de sermons prononcés aux Conciles de Constance et de Bâle'], *RHE*, 10 (1909) pp 493–520. The number of the manuscript is not given.

[35] Vidal p 494.

[36] St G 240 and Klosterneuburg Stiftsbibliothek 204.

[37] [C. W. F.] Walch, *Monimenta* [*Medii Aevi ex bibliotheca Regia Hanoverana*], I, fasc 3 (Göttingen 1759) pp 29–57; fasc 4 (Göttingen 1760) pp 47–71.

[38] Mansi 28, cols 906–7.

[39] Schneyer, 'Konstanzer Konzilspredigten: Texte'.

[40] The manuscripts are: Berlin, Staatsbibliothek, Lat 632, fols 46 *et seq* (See Finke p 480). Erlangen, Universitätsbibliothek 534 fols 194r–7v; 203r–6v; 257r–60r. Hanover MS used by Walch, *Monimenta*, fasc 3, pp 29–57; fasc 4, pp 47–71. Karlsruhe: Reichenau 23, fols 146v–53v. Klosterneuburg, Stiftsbibliothek 82, fols 91v–108v; 112r–18r; 130r–3r. Krems, fols 119r–42r; 147r–54v; 168v–72r (See Vidal). Kremsmünster 4, fols 216v–28v. Lübeck, Stadtbibliothek theol 59, fols 181 *et seq*. Nürnberg, Stadtbibliothek, Solg 48.2, fols 180r–9r. St Paul (Lavant) pap 29, fols 88r–130v; 206r–302r. St Paul (Lavant) pap 31 fols 300r–,

The obvious questions are: were they preached, and, if so, when, by whom, and why? The answers can be only tentative at this stage. Finke, unaware of the Clement connection, identified the preachers of two sermons; and Vidal a third. John of Seravalle, bishop of Fermo, preached one, on John the Evangelist, on 27 December 1416;[41] Theodoric of Münster delivered another, on 6 January 1417;[42] while the third was repeated by John Zacharie, professor of theology at the university of Erfurt, on All Saints' day of an unknown year.[43] Walch edited a sermon of Pierre Roger on saint Nicholas and called it an anonymous oration on clerical vices preached at Constance on 6 December 1415.[44] 'Clerical vices' is the salient point, for the majority of the eleven pulpit sermons in the group contain references to clerical abuses. This makes plausible their use at Constance, concerned as it was with reform. Moreover, they all lack historical references, abound in quotations, and would have applied equally well in any year.

The second group comprises two funeral orations – one of them the lion-and-bear piece for Napoleon Orsini.[45] The sermons appear together in three conciliar manuscripts.[46] In the Klosterneuburg version no attempt has been made to adapt the wording, despite the fact that both sermon texts play on the names of the dead cardinals, and that these names, together with the texts, recur throughout the sermons.[47] But their significance seems to have escaped Coloman Chnapp, who

---

15r. Stettin, Mariengymnasium 33, fols 66 et seq (See Finke pp 368, 371). Stuttgart, Württembergischen Landesbibliothek, HB I 116, fols 100v–4r. Vienna, Pal. 4958, fols 345r–50v.

[41] Finke p 480. Incipit: 'Hic est discipulus ille,' John 21:24. The sermon appears in Klosterneuburg 82, fols 130r–3r and in this version corresponds with the wording of Klosterneuburg 204, fols 62v–8v.

[42] Finke p. 482. Incipit: 'Reges eorum ministrabunt tibi,' Is. 60, 10. It is edited by Walch, Monimenta fasc 4, pp 47–71, and in this version agrees with Klosterneuburg 204, fols 165r–72r.

[43] Vidal p 500, no 28. Incipit: 'Sufficiat nobis quia omnis multitudino sanctorum est et cum ipsis est Dominus,' Num. 16:3. The sermon appears in Klosterneuburg 82, fols 96v–102r, the wording of which agrees with that of St G 240, fols 41v–9v.

[44] Walch, Monimenta, fasc 3, pp. 29–57. Incipit: 'Talis decebat ut esset nobis Pontifex,' Heb. 7:26. The printed edition corresponds with St G 240, fols 284v–90v.

[45] St G 240, fols 403v–8r. Incipit: 'Leonem et ursum interfeci,' 1 Kings, 17, 36, fols 244v–7v. Incipit: 'Tempus tribulationis est Iacob et ex ipso salvabitur,' Jer. 30, 7.

[46] St Paul (Lavant) 29, fols 262r–72r; Klosterneuburg 82, fols 91v–6v; Krems, fols 119r–26r.

[47] See n 45 above.

simply labels each piece 'exequies for a certain cardinal'.[48] The subject matter of the discourses was sufficiently innocuous to have been applied to any deceased cardinal, and might even have suited cardinal Zarabella, who died on 26 September 1417.

The final group, an amorphous one of eight political collations, is the most problematical. The Vincennes discourse of 1329 is unlikely to have been repeated, since it was aimed at Philip VI Valois, and the historical references remain in the conciliar version.[49] Then there is a christmas sermon preached at the beginning of the Hundred Years War,[50] which condemns the alliance of Louis of Bavaria with England. It is just conceivable, given the alignment of the English and German nations in opposition to the French at Constance, that the sermon could have been reused, although this is unlikely. The remaining six collations are all connected with the deposition of Louis of Bavaria from the emperorship and the elevation of Charles of Moravia in his stead. Two of them are of considerable interest. The first is the collation Clement preached when he deposed archbishop Henry of Mainz for favouring Louis.[51] It occurs in five conciliar manuscripts, and part of it was edited by Mansi with the revealing comment *in contemptu concilii* which, with its papal-hierocratic tone, it certainly is.[52] Both he and Finke thought that it applied to John of Nassau, archbishop of Mainz, and was preached by Martin V or one of his adherents.[53] John was a partisan of John XXIII, and in 1417 charges were brought against him for helping the ex-pontiff to escape from prison.[54] At such a time the sermon might have fitted him. The second collation is Clement's sermon in approbation of Charles of Moravia. There is no evidence that this was preached, and it appears as an isolated clementine composition in only two conciliar manuscripts, both of them obscure.[55] What is significant is that it was still read in the fifteenth century. One of Martin V's first official acts as pope was to scrutinise the personal qualities and election of Sigismund and to grant him approbation as *rex Romanorum*.[56] The words of confirmation used by Martin V for Sigismund are similar to

[48] Klosterneuburg 82, fols 91v; 93v.
[49] See n 32 above.
[50] St G 240, fols 334v–6r. Incipit: 'Ortus est sol', Ps 103:22.
[51] Mansi 28, cols 906–7.
[52] *Ibid* col 907.
[53] *Ibid* col 907; Finke p 371.
[54] Cerretanus, *Liber gestorum*, ed Finke, II, p. 298.
[55] St Paul (Lavant) 31, fols 300r–15r; Kremsmünster 4, fols 216v–28v.
[56] Fillastre, *Gesta Concilii Constantiensis*, ed Finke, II, p 163.

those used by Clement VI for Charles.[57] Even after Constance this part of the hierocratic theory was still being applied, which could account for interest in Clement's collations.

To sum up, it seems probable that the pulpit sermons for saints' and red-letter days were plagiarised wholesale, that the funeral orations could have been reused, but that the consistory collations, with one exception, were read rather than repreached. The slur cast on the integrity of some of the holy fathers of Constance is considerable. We cannot be certain how they came to commit their literary theft, but given the fact that Clement's sermons so often appear anonymously in manuscripts – even at times in contemporary preaching manuals – it is possible that the conciliarists did not recognize the works of the *maximus sermocinator verbi Dei*. Imagine the dismay of these fifteenth-century revolutionaries had it been revealed to them that they had copied from the work of one of the most hierocratic popes of the fourteenth century.

[57] Compare *ibid* with Clement VI, *MGH Const*, viii, no 100, p 163. On the history of the papal approval of imperial candidates see E. Feine, 'Die Approbation der Luxemburgischen Kaiser in ihren Rechtsformen an der Kurie', *ZSR, KA* 27 (1938) pp 364–97.

THE COMPILATION OF A LATE
FOURTEENTH-CENTURY PRECEDENT BOOK—
REGISTER BRIAN 2

by ROY M. HAINES

AMONG the episcopal registers housed at the county record office in St Helen's, Worcester,[1] is a neatly written paper book, which though it bears no medieval title, has often been described as the second volume of bishop Brian's register.[2] As has been pointed out recently,[3] it was taken to be such by the county historian, Treadway Nash, and also by Reginald Lane Poole when he examined the Worcester records for the Historical Manuscripts Commission.[4] On the other hand, it is now common knowledge among those acquainted with the registers that this is a misnomer. My intention here is to examine the manuscript in more detail and to suggest the manner of its composition and the sources from which it is derived.

The book is in a larger format than is usual among the parchment registers.[5] It comprises four quires, for which signatures remain.[6] The first three have eight sheets, the fourth apparently seven. Small strips of parchment on which writing can be seen (from some theological

---

[1] I am grateful to Miss Margaret Henderson, the deputy archivist, and her assistants for their courtesy during the preparation of this paper. My thanks are also due to Mrs B. E. Johnston who made me so welcome at the cathedral library.

[2] *II° Domini Reginaldi Brien* is written on folio 4 (arabic). This is the blank leaf before the *primo fol.* which precedes the initial quire. The same (?) post-medieval (seventeenth century?) hand prefaces the index (fol 1) with the title *IIo Domini Reginaldi Brien*, to which has been added *Hen. Wakefield et Simon. de Monteacuto.*

[3] W. P. Marett, [A] *Calendar of [the] Register [of Henry] Wakefeld [Bishop of Worcester 1375–95,]* Worcs. Hist. Soc. (Worcester 1972) p xiii.

[4] T. Nash, *Collections for the History of Worcestershire*, 2 vols (1781–2) II, p xcv; HMC 14th Rept, App pt viii, p 204: 'There is some confusion in the registers of bishops Montacute, Bryan, and Wakefield, portions of the first and third being inserted in the register of bishop Bryan, part ii'.

[5] It measures approximately $11\frac{1}{4} \times 15\frac{3}{4}$ inches, as against the $9\frac{1}{4} \times 13\frac{3}{4}$ inches of *Register Brian 1.*

[6] In arabic numerals.

treatise?) have been used to strengthen the spines. Four folios were added at the beginning to provide room for the index and some preliminaries.[7] The present binding – uniform with that of the episcopal registers – apparently dates from the 1820s, when the deputy registrar, Henry Clifton the younger, was collating the diocesan records.

The original foliation (roman numerals) runs from one to forty-seven and ends in the third quire. In the final quire – after a number of blank leaves – are written *acta* of the purgation process of a clerk imprisoned at Worcester on a charge of rape during bishop Brian's rule (1352–61).[8]

It is not difficult to assign an approximate date to the manuscript, particularly as it is written in a single hand throughout.[9] The scribe prefaces by far the greater number of entries with 'H etc.' or 'Henricus etc.'. It is a reasonable assumption that he was at work during the episcopate of Henry Wakefield (1375–95). True, he often fails to pen that bishop's name or initial, but copies instead the 'R', 'Reginaldus', 'W' etc. of his exemplars, thus leaving valuable clues as to their whereabouts. None the less, his intention remains clear. It may be surmised that had his mind not wandered during the copying, all the entries would have purported to come from Wakefield's time – with the possible exception of any added after that bishop's death.[10]

Another inconsistency lets slip more precise information. Ordinarily the scribe omits specific dates, but just occasionally he copies them mechanically. One such date – 14 January 1388/9 – provides a *terminus a quo* for the writing of the subsequent folios and possibly for the book as a whole.[11] It cannot be that this entry was added later, there being no break in the text or change of ink.

Revealing too, is an entry dated 20 March 1395/6, the first year of the episcopate of Wakefield's successor, Tideman de Winchcombe

---

[7] Index and preliminaries, 4 fols and 4 stubs; 1 (fols ii–xvii); 2 (fols xviii–xxxiii); 3 (fols xxxiiii–xlvii) plus one blank folio, 52); 4 (fols 54–69: 60–9 written on). Quire 4 probably comprises 7 sheets plus 2 fols at end (the binding is too tight for close examination); '.ii.' at foot of fol 68 is in the usual place for the quire signature. There are only two entries on fol i^r (primo fol) and one on the dorse.

[8] Arabic foliation runs 1–69, 53 being missed between the third and fourth quires. The *acta*, dating from 1354/5, are at fols 60–9: compare *Register Brian 1*, fols 8^v, 112^r.

[9] Including the index and marginal rubrics. Compare Marett, *Calendar of Register Wakefield*, pp xiii–xiv.

[10] Against this it could be urged that the entries from *Registers Reynolds* and *Montacute* are consistently *not* ascribed to Wakefield. But these really form an appendix, as it were.

[11] Fol xv^r.

(1395–1401).[12] This has the appearance of being a later insertion, for the ink is of a slightly different shade and the folio, even with it, is by no means filled up. All the same, this entry figures in the index, which must therefore have been written out subsequently. There is no evidence of fictitious dating elsewhere and hence no reason to postulate it here.

In short, the compiler may have begun his task in 1389 – or a little before – and finished it in or about 1396. It is conceivable that the *acta* were entered later, as they are not indexed. Alternatively, the final quire could have been written before the index, but only attached to the precedent book as an afterthought. Clearly it forms no part of an overall plan.

The hand of *Register Brian 2* is a distinctive one. Moreover, it occurs in conjunction with a fairly uncommon 'tadpole' sign – a triangle of three dots with subtended tail.[13] In this hand is written the register of bishop Tideman's vicar general, Master Richard Wyche,[14] as well as other material in Tideman's register, notably much of the ordination lists.[15] Without a doubt the same scribe penned the initial nine folios of *Register Wakefield*, a substantial part of the remainder, and many of the marginal rubrics.[16] Here too, the 'tadpole' sign is in evidence. He was even responsible, it would seem, for the first folio of *Register Lynn* (1368–73) and much else besides. If such is the case, he spent some thirty or more years in the registry.

It is not possible to say whether Wakefield's registrar was the scribe. His hand has not been identified, nor indeed do we know his name. But presumably so time-consuming a project was undertaken with his knowledge and subject to his direction.

Despite the apparent regularity of the index, with its fairly consistent emphasis on the general rather than the particular, it would be wrong to conclude that the compiler made a careful selection of documents to fit prearranged categories. Minor exceptions are provided by the prefatory forms (first three folios) which may be untraceable since they are not sufficiently specific. Much the same can be said of the initial entries on folio xiii, prefaced in the text by the heading *Diverse littere exeuntes de registro episcopi*, of the *Indulgencie* at folio xxvi[r], and of the

---

[12] Fol xxxv[v].   [13] ·ı·
[14] *Register Tideman*, fols 1–12[v]. The register proper begins at fol 15.
[15] Fols 67[r] *et seq*.
[16] This is the editor's 'hand A', but much of the writing ascribed by him to 'hand D' is in fact by the same man, whose hand thus emerges as the principal one in *Register Wakefield*. See Marett, *Calendar of Register Wakefield*, p xii; *Register Wakefield*, fols 1–9[r] and, for instance, fols 42[r] *et seq*, 60[r] *et seq*, 128[v], 156[r] *et seq*.

forms interpolated at folio xxxv^r under the title *Sentencie generales.* These apart, there is scant evidence of categorisation. On the contrary, a far more pedestrian method of working can be reconstructed by setting the index and text against the corresponding exemplars in the episcopal registers.

It can be assumed that at the time of the precedent book's compilation bishop Wakefield's register was in loose quires, so we would not expect it to be treated in quite the same way as completed registers. In fact there is little doubt that very few entries belong to his episcopate. Perhaps only the one mentioned above.

The most recent completed register available to the compiler would have been that of bishop Lynn (1368–73), so it is no surprise to find that after a few preliminary forms the precedent book proper begins on folio iiii with an extract from the initial folio of that register.

What the scribe did – or it could have been someone in authority over him – was to work steadily through a register marking items with a small cross for subsequent copying in whole or in part. Thus, in *Register Lynn* it is possible to follow his course from the first to the forty-third folio. The resultant extracts occupy six folios (iiii–ix) of the precedent book.

Having dealt with Lynn's register the scribe added an entry which I have not been able to trace. Working backwards, he took up the next register – William Wittlesey's (1364–8), beginning in the same fashion at the first folio and progressing steadily through to the thirty-third. This time the scheme is not fully sustained, for there are a number of intrusions, including the *diverse littere* and entry from Wakefield's register commented on above. Putting aside Wittlesey's act book the scribe turned to that of bishop Barnet (1362–3). The succession of the extracts from the latter is a little irregular, since after folio 27 there is a reversion to folios 22 and 2. Although the original order of folios in *Register Barnet* has been upset,[17] this does not seem to account for the irregularity.

The procedural pattern now becomes confused. We would expect the compiler to have turned to bishop Brian's register (1352–61) and to have worked his way through it. He did begin on it, but after extracts culled from the early folios and the thirtieth come a whole spate of entries apparently dating from Brian's episcopate, but not identifiable in his register. This could be because there *was* at one time a second volume which provided the material. Alternatively there may have

[17] The arabic foliation is in considerable disarray.

been some loose files in the registry or a temporary paper book. Here, at any rate, is the sole element of justification for the title subsequently bestowed on the precedent book.

Thus the source or sources of all or most of the 'mainly Brian' documents entered between folios xxii and xxvii must have been lost, though copies of a few of them may also exist among the muniments of the cathedral priory.[18]

By folio xxviii the system is reestablished. The compiler at that juncture was working on the latter part of *Register Brian* between folios 68 and 104. There are, it will be admitted, some untraced – and possibly untraceable – interpolations, among them the entry from Tideman's period already mentioned.

After *Register Brian* one looks in vain for the compiler's path through the preceding registers. Despite many likely documents in those of Thoresby and Cobham and the impressive size of Bransford's, the scribe seems to have passed them by. There are some seemingly telltale crosses in the Bransford register, and in some of the others, but these were ignored at the writing up stage, if indeed they are the compiler's.[19]

What happened was that the compiler skipped the forty years from Brian's register to that of Reynolds (1307–13). He plunged *in medias res* at folio 60, but soon settled down to his normal method of working folio by folio. The last eight entries in the precedent book are taken from the second volume of Montacute's register (1333–7), which of course, follows rather than precedes that of Reynolds.

Altogether, over 70 per cent of the material has been traced to the episcopal registers in the manner described.

It may be hypothesised that the compiler embarked on his forbidding task of working backwards through the act books in order to provide a comprehensive series of extracts for the information and guidance of his fellow clerks in the registry, both present and future. Initially all went well, but as the magnitude of the operation dawned on him his resolution failed, or the time available slipped by. The end-product is in essence a selection of material from the latter half of the fourteenth century, or more precisely, from the registers of bishops Brian, Barnet,

[18] For example, pope Clement VI's bull concerning the use of the mitre by the prior of Worcester. This is in the *Liber Pensionum* (fol 51^r), from which it is printed by W. Thomas, *A Survey of the Cathedral Church of Worcester* (London 1737) App. 110, p 125. Other items on this topic are in the *Liber Albus*.
[19] Even in the registers heavily drawn upon by the compiler there are crosses against items which were not copied.

Wittlesey and Lynn, with a minor contribution from those of Reynolds and Montacute in the earlier half of the century.

It is more accurate to describe *Register Brian 2* as a precedent book than a formulary, though the two are not always carefully distinguished. It does, of course, contain many common forms, though by no means anything like the full range of those in regular use in an episcopal registry of the time. What is more, many of the extracts are highly particular.

The index is by no means infallible. In fact at one stage the indexer continues at variance with his own text for several folios. The marginal rubrics were added to the text after its completion and seemingly during the compilation of the index. But index and rubrics do not invariably coincide. Sometimes the latter have been omitted altogether. In a number of instances the index is misleading with respect to the contents of individual entries and the scribe was not sufficiently alert to avoid the mechanical addition of *Romana* to *curia* in the case of a licence for an oratory within the diocese.

What purpose did the book serve in practice, then? It bears no traces of repeated consultation. The folios are not thumbed, soiled, or – with rare exceptions[20] – annotated, although a few index notes occur on the dorse of the ultimate folio (69). The rounding off at the corners arises from the friable nature of the paper, and no doubt, from the fact that the limp covers which once served as binding afforded inadequate protection to such vulnerable areas. Lack of systematic arrangement detracts from the book's value as a source of reference. Even so, there is no obvious reason why clerks in search of a precedent or a form should not have examined it in the first instance, rather than ploughing straightway through the mounting pile of episcopal registers. It has the further advantage of consistent legibility.

Today the immediate importance of *Register Brian 2* stems from the fact that it contains copies of a small group of documents not to be found elsewhere. Also, perhaps, it reveals the type of material which a fourteenth-century Worcester registrar deemed worth copying for posterity. At a personal level it marks the culmination of the lengthy career of a dedicated registry clerk. Whether anything strictly comparable has survived elsewhere remains to be seen.[21]

[20] For example, fols xxv^v, 61^v.

[21] During discussion of this paper it was pointed out that a York 'formulary' (*Register Neville 2*, 1374–88) has features in common with *Register Brian 2*. David M. Smith has noted it in *A Guide to the Archive Collections in the Borthwick Institute of Historical Research* (York 1973) p 10, no 13, but I have not had an opportunity to examine the manuscript.

Register Brian 2

appendix

contemporary index to *Register Brian 2*
with the addition of identified sources

Bishops and/or registers referred to are abbreviated as follows:

Walter Reynolds (1307–13)	Reyn.
Simon de Montacute (1333–7)	Mont.
John de Thoresby (1349–52)	Thor.
Reginald Brian (1352–61)	Brian
John Barnet (1362–3)	Barn.
William Wittlesey (1364–8)	Witt.
William de Lynn (1368–73)	Lynn.
Henry de Wakefield (1375–95)	Wakef.
Robert Tideman de Winchcombe (1395–1401)	Tidem.

folio	entry	source (fols)
i	Commissio vicarii generalis	
	Alia super eadem	
	Commissio ad expellendum penitentes	
ii	Commissio ad inquirendum super statu monasterii	
	Alia commissio super eodem	
	Alia commissio super eodem	
	Revocacio commissionis huiusmodi et ad prefigendum diem visitacionis	
iii	Commissio ad petendum clericos convictos	
iiii	Commissio ad instituendum	Lynn 1r
	Readmissio et reintegracio[22] ad ecclesiam etc.	Lynn 3v
	[Oldebury capella][23]	Lynn 4r
	Induccio ad archidiaconatum	Lynn 7r
	Mandatum directum clero ad obediendum	Lynn 7r
	Readmissio et reintegracio[24] ad ecclesiam	Lynn 16r
	Prefixio prioris Minoris Malvernie	Lynn 20r/v
	Prefixio prioris Wygorn'	Lynn 20v
v	Prefixio magistri sancti Marci Bristoll'	Lynn 21r
	Commissio ad levandum et colligendum .l. mille libras	Lynn 32v
vi	Alia commissio super eodem	Lynn 32v/3r
	Mutacio de ecclesia in capellam	Lynn 33r/v

[22] A 'd' subsequently interlined here and below to make *redintegracio*.
[23] This is the rubric from the text. The index omits the reference.
[24] See n 22 above.

folio	entry	source (fols)
	Commissio ad levandum procuraciones cardinalium	Lynn 37v/8r
vii	Alia super eodem	Lynn 38r/v
	Alia super eodem	Lynn 38v
viii	Certificatorium super huiusmodi mandato	Lynn 38v/9r
	Mandatum ad plene solvendum subsidium huiusmodi	Lynn 40 r
	Commissio ad audiendum confessiones	Lynn 41r
	Commissio ad levandum bona defuncti	Lynn 41v
	Commissio ad sequestrandum bona iuxta capitulum 'Ad compescendas' etc.[25]	Lynn 42r
	Mandatum presbitero ad deserviendum cure	Lynn 42r/v
	Mandatum ad denunciandum excommunicatos et ad citandum abstrahentes fugientes ecclesias	Lynn 42v
ix	Citacio detinencium bonorum defuncti cum sequestracione eorundem	Lynn 42v
	Commissio ad procedendum in causa matrimoniali	Lynn 43r
	Commissio ad mandandum rectori ad residenciam et ipsum amovendum	Lynn 43r
	Licencia ad celebrandum in capella	Lynn 43v
	Commissio ad inquirendum super pollucione ecclesie cum inhibicione etc.	Lynn 43v
x	Citacio auctoritate apostolica	
	Ordinacio sive examplificacio cum citacione de ecclesia de Westbury	Witt. 1r/v
xi	Constitucio procuratoris in curia Romana	Witt. 2v
	Citacio ad prestandum obedienciam	Witt. 3r
	Commissio ad admittendum et constituendum cum potestate sequestratoris	Witt. 4v
	Commissio ad recipiendum professionem	Witt. 4v
	Commissio ad proficiendum priorissam	Witt. 5r
xii	Mandatum religiosis mulieribus in genere	Witt. 7r
	Confirmacio ordinacionis in domo religiosorum facte	Witt. 7r
	Ordinacio inter Stodeley et Cokehulle super sepultura apud Spernore	Witt. 7v
	Indulgencia	Witt. 8v
xiii[26]	Mandatum ad monendum abbates quod non	

[25] Clement. 2, 6, c. 1.
[26] Heading: *Diverse littere exeuntes de registro episcopi.* This and the first three entries are in darker ink.

folio	entry	source (fols)
	permittant religiosis vagare	
	Mandatum visitacionis	
	Mandatum missum abbati ne aggrevat canonicos suos propter querimoniam factam episcopo	
	Indulgencia	Witt. 8v
	Diffinicio super percepcione decimarum	Witt. 7v
	Inquisicio super valore ecclesie appropriate et de valore vicarie eiusdem	Witt. 8r
	Composicio inter rectorem de Rysindon Magna et abbatem et conventum de Belvero	Witt. 8r
xiiii	Littera indulgencie pro audientibus evangelium 'Missus est angelus Gabriel'	Witt. 8v
	Littera sequestracionis pro cancella de Westbury	Witt. 11r/v
	Prefixio priorisse de Pynley	Witt. 12v
	Commissio et ordinacio capelle de [Hen]ley	Witt. 17r
xv	Inhibicio religiosis ne faciant privaciones	[temp. Wakef.]
	Commissio ad cognoscendum in causis[27]	Witt. 18v
	Commissio ad levandum procuraciones nunciis sedis apostolice	Witt. 18v
	Admissio religiosorum ad ecclesias curatas	Witt. 24v
	Permutacio etc.	Witt. 26r
	Prefixio priorisse	Witt. 27r
	Indulgencia pro confessionibus tempestive in Quadragesima[28]	Witt. 29v
xvi	Mandatum ad puplicandum litteras apostolicas	Witt. 29v/30r
	Citacio ad quemlibet presentatum quod dimittat ecclesiam etc.	Witt. 31r
	Sequestracio decimarum super orta desencione	Witt. 31r
	Alia super eodem	Witt. 31r
	Sequestracio pro decima silve cedue	Witt. 31r
	Commissio in causa mortuarii	Witt. 31v
xvii	Commissio ad procedendum auctoritate apostolica	Witt. 31v/2r
	Commissio pro processionibus faciendis racione pestilencie	Witt. 32r
	Commissio custodie bosci de Malverne	Witt. 32r

[27] 'John Dunclent' is substituted for 'John de Swyneshed' in the copy.
[28] MS 'xla'.

folio	entry	source (fols)
	Commissio ad procedendum auctoritate apostolica	Witt. 32r
	Littera testimonialis super purgacione clerici incarcerati	Witt. 32r
	Licencia rectori de manso habendo	Witt. 32v
xviii	Composicio pro capella de Norton in parochia de Kemsey	Witt. 32v
	Composicio super lampade ardere debente in ecclesia de Lye	Witt. 32v/3r
	Alia littera super capella de Norton	Witt. 33r
	Commissio auctoritate apostolica	Witt. 33r
	Commissio ad reconciliandum cimith[er]ium	Witt. 33r
	Licencia concessa vicario ad peregrinandum ex causa ad curiam Romanam	Witt. 33r
	Commissio ad admittendum et cognoscendum in causis	Barn. 6r
xix	Commissio ad corrigendum et puniendum	Barn. 6r
	Collacio ecclesie iure devoluto	Barn. 8r
	Commissio ad cognoscendum et procedendum in causis et corrigendum et puniendum	Barn. 8r
	Commissio ad levandum decimam	Barn. 9r
	Concessio pensionis episcopi Wyg' racione nove creacionis	Barn. 10v
	Commissio ad inquirendum de salario presbiter[orum]	Barn. 12v
	Mandatum pro decantacione 'Mater ora fil[ium]'	Barn. 14r
	Commissio ad audiendum confessiones	Barn. 14v
xx	Alia commissio pro salario presbiterorum	Barn. 17v
	Mandatum pro diebus festivis	Barn. 17r
	Mandatum ad convocandum clerum	Barn. 20v
	Absolucio ad instanciam excommunicacionis[29]	Barn. 21r
	Commissio ad exponendum causas convocacionis	Barn. 22r
	Commissio ad levandum subsidium caritativum etc.	Barn. 22r
	Prefixio priorisse	Barn. 27r
	Commissio ad monendum capellanum ad deserviendum cure	Barn. 22v
xxi	Revocacio relig' de audiendo confessiones	Barn. 2r/v

[29] Correctly *a sentencia excommunicacionis*.

folio	entry	source (fols)
	Monicio rectoris ad residenciam	Barn. 2v/3r
	Commissio ad exequendum litteras aposto-licas[30]	Brian 3r
	Commissio ad audiendum confessiones	Brian 5v
	Commissio ad inquirendum de fama incarcerati	Brian 8v
xxii	Prefixio prioris Minoris Malvernie	Brian 3or/v
	Ordinacio sive composicio per abbatem de Wynch' et rectorem de Aldrynton	
xxiii	Ordinacio de domo sancti Wolstani iuxta Wygorn'	
xxiiii	Monicio rectoris ad residenciam	
	Littera vicario non curanti residere	
	Procuratorium diversorum episcoporum ad curiam Romanam	[temp. Brian]
	Citacio religiosi vagantis	
xxv	Dispensacio super solempnizacione matrimonii contra interdictum ecclesie init'	[temp. Brian?]
	Commissio apostolica super negocio huiusmodi	[temp. Brian?]
	Sequestracio ecclesiarum etc.	[temp. Brian]
	Declaracio super usu mitre[31]	[temp. Brian]
	Alia super eodem[32]	[temp. Thor.]
	Notificacio in negocio predicto[33]	[temp. Brian]
xxvi[34]	Indulgencia	
	Alia indulgencia	
	Alia indulgencia	
	Alia indulgencia	
	Alia notificacio super negocio predicto	
	Mandatum ad inquirendum de vacacione hospitalis	
	Commissio cum certificatorio super negocio purgacionis clerici incarcerati	[temp. Brian]
	Littera testimonialis super eadem purgacione	[temp. Brian]
xxvii	Relaxacio sequestri	
	Littera directa fratribus ad obediendum etc.	

[30] 'John Wyshangre of Gloucester' becomes 'John Broun of Gloucester' in the copy.

[31] Bull of Innocent [VI] reciting that of Clement [VI]. See *Liber Albus*, fols ccxli r/v.

[32] *Liber Pensionum*, fol 51r; *Liber Albus*, fol ccxliv. Compare *Register Wittlesey*, fol 2r: bull of Urban [V] recapitulating the concession of Clement [VI] *inter alia*.

[33] *Liber Albus*, fol ccxliv.

[34] Heading: *Indulgencie*.

folio	entry	source (fols)
	Commissio ad absolvendum solempnizantem matrimonium extra ecclesiam parochialem	
	Sentencia contra iniecentes manus violentas in clericum	
	Sentencia generalis	[temp. Brian]
xxviii, xxix, et xxx	Dimissio super appropriacione ecclesie de Campeden	Brian 68v (lxxxi)/ 69r (lxxxiiii)
xxxii[35] [recte xxxi]	Mandatum pro pecunia procuratorum curie levanda	Brian 70r (lxxxv)/ 70v
	Item pro procuracionibus cardinalium etc.	Brian 77v/8v
xxxiii	Alia super eodem	Brian 78v
	Alia super eodem	Brian 79r
xxxiiii	Alia super eodem	Brian 81v/2v
xxxv[36]	Sentencia generalis contra impedientes bona defuncti	
	Alia contra iniecentes manus in clericum	
	Alia contra diffamatores	
	Alia contra detentores librorum, cartarum etc.	
	Alia super eadem	
xxxvi [recte xxxv v.]	Mandatum pro indulgencia concessa etc.	[temp. Tidem.]
xxxvii [recte xxxvi]	Commissio ad exequendum litteras aposto-licas	Brian 82v
	Alia citacio[37] super eadem	Brian 82v
	Commissio ad levandum procuraciones cardinalibus nunciis sedis apostolice debitas	Brian 83v/4r
xxxviii [recte xxxvii]	Alia super eodem	Brian 84r
	Sentencia generalis contra iniecentes manus in clericos	Brian 86r
	Indulgencia ad orandum pro regina	Brian 86r/v
	Indulgencia ad orandum pro pace	Brian 90v
xxxix	Ordinacio inter vicarium et rectorem et	

[35] Rubrics have not been added to the text, making it difficult to disentangle these entries.

[36] Heading: *Sentencie generales*. The five subsequent entries are in a lighter shade of ink and interrupt the previous one, which is continued below them against a sign corresponding to that at the foot of fol xxxiiiiv (with the injunction *vadas ad hoc signum*).

[37] Correctly *certificacio*.

folio	entry	source (fols)
[*recte* xxxviii]	eius parochianos sancti Andree de Wyche[38]	Brian 93v/4r
xl [*recte* xxxix]	Sentencia generalis contra asportantes bona de maneriis etc.	Brian 94v
xl [sic]	Sentencia generalis contra detinentes pentecostales debitas et legatas sacriste Wyg'	Brian 96r
	Monicio ad monendum clerum ad defensionem regni	Brian 96r/v
	Littera contra Scodales	Brian 104r
xlii	Littera contra rectorem homicidam	Reyn. 60r/v
[*recte* xli]	Sentencia generalis contra comitem Sorrie	Reyn. 37r
	Citacio in genere pro bonis defuncti	Reyn. 48r/v
[*recte* xlii]	Sentencia generalis contra infringentes libertates ecclesiasticas	Reyn. 49v/50r
	Absolucio de excommunicato liberando	Reyn. 51r
	Item contra rectorem homicidam	Reyn. 60r
	Inquisicio super statu domus domus sancti Marci Bristoll'[39]	Reyn. 64v/5r
xliii	Licencia alicui ad construendum oratorium in curia Romana [sic]	Reyn. 87r
	Citacio super augmentacione vicarie	Reyn. 86v
	Inhibicio pro domo religioso	Reyn. 96r
xliiii	Monicio ad dedicandum ecclesias	Mont. 2, 1v/2r
	Commissio cum infirmacione ad petendum clericos incarceratos	Mont. 2, 2r
	Sentencia generalis contra iniecentes manus in clericum	Mont. 2, 2v
xlv	Commissio ad audiendum purgaciones clericorum	Mont. 2, 4v
	Sentencia generalis contra infringentes parcum domini	Mont. 2, 5v
xlvi	Littera ad orandum pro rege	Mont. 2, 7v
	Sentencia pro raptu cuiusdam monialis	Mont. 2, 8r
xlvii	Littera mutue vicissitudinis obtentu	Mont. 2, 8r/v

[Unindexed]

| 60–9 | [*Acta* concerning the purgation of John de Waddesworth, clerk, indicted for rape.] | [temp. Brian] |

---

[38] *Sancti Andree de Wyche* added.
[39] *Domus sancti Marci Bristoll* added.

THE LETTERS OF THE UNIVERSITY OF
OXFORD ON WITHDRAWAL OF OBEDIENCE
FROM POPE BONIFACE IX

by MARGARET HARVEY

IN this paper I shall discuss two letters apparently sent in 1399 by the university of Oxford to Richard II, in answer to the king's request for advice on whether to withdraw obedience from pope Boniface IX in an endeavour to end the great schism.[1] There has been a controversy about which letter represents the official view of the university, and this argument has largely arisen, I suspect, because hitherto one of the letters has been studied in its printed form which is incomplete and does not give a true idea of its arguments. I will also consider how these letters are to be seen in the context of the final stages of Richard II's policy on the schism.

The background to the letters is as follows: From 1394 the French and English were drawing closer together politically and part of their agreement concerned an attempt to end the schism.[2] The French intended to persuade their pope, Benedict XIII, to resign, and wished to persuade the English to urge the *via cessionis* on the roman pope Boniface IX. When consulted about this method of ending the schism, however, the university of Oxford refused to accept it. In a letter which enjoyed wide diffusion, dated 17 March 1396, the Oxford masters said that a general council was the only practical solution to the schism, though they did not say who was to call it.[3] If there were no other way to bring unity to the church than for a pope to resign, he would have to do so, but the masters did not believe that there was no

---

[1] I wish to thank professor H. S. Offler for his help in transcribing the vatican manuscript referred to below and for reading and criticising this paper in draft. I also thank Dr V. I. J. Flint. I hope shortly to publish the vatican text.

[2] These events have been described in [N.] Valois, [*La France et le Grand Schisme*] III (Paris 1901) pp 1–187; [E.] Perroy, [*L'Angleterre et le Grand Schisme*] (Paris 1933) pp 361–87; [J. J. N.] Palmer, [*England, France and Christendom*] (London 1972) pp 194–7, 218–22.

[3] [G.] Ouy, ['Gerson et L'Angleterre'], in *Humanism in France at the end of the Middle Ages*, ed A. H. T. Levi (Manchester 1970) pp 56–79, for the Oxford reply. I owe this reference to Dr J. Catto.

other way and they doubted whether resignation by Boniface would bring unity.[4] Withdrawal of obedience (and the masters were sure it would come to that) was probably schismatic.[5] Richard did not follow this advice. As part of the treaty which included his marriage he made an agreement with the French on 5 November 1396. He bound himself to send ambassadors jointly with the French to both popes to tell each that the allies had decided that resignation was the best method of ending the schism and requiring each to resign so that a new pope could be elected by michaelmas 1397. The written agreement makes no mention of Richard's obligation if the popes refused to resign.[6] Opinion in France was in fact divided about the next step and the French clergy in August 1396 had voted to postpone the use of coercion (withdrawal of obedience was to be the coercion) against Benedict until the effect of the joint embassy should be known.[7] The joint embassy, now also including some Castilians, went to Rome and Avignon in the summer of 1397. Neither pope was at all enthusiastic, and both allowed the deadline for resignation to pass, so on 27 July 1398 the French withdrew their obedience from Benedict XIII.[8] Was Richard II obliged to follow suit and withdraw from Boniface IX? All modern writers on the subject are agreed that he was so obliged and only disagree about why the English did not withdraw. It has usually been argued that Richard either could not overcome the scruples of his clergy (already evident in 1395/6) or that he went back on his obligations in return for favours from Boniface.[9] Recently however Dr Palmer has suggested that the usual explanation will not do.[10] He thinks that in 1398/9 Richard was still willing to try to force the resignation of Boniface, though he may

[4] Ouy p 66 '... datus pastor cederet iuri suo nec esset alia via qualiter humana ratione comprehendi posset ad unitatem verissimilis; quis tunc ambigeret quin vera caritas pastorem in hoc casu scientem hoc aut sine dubitatione credentem ad cedendum efficaciter inclinaret?'

[5] Ouy p 60 '... cessio coacta foret nostro iudicio via ad pacem difficillima, tum quia in papa iusto foret iniusta, tum quia non posset fieri verissimiliter nisi per brachium seculare, et forte non nisi per bella, vel saltem per substractionem obediencie; que quidem substractio a papa iusto reos scismatis argueret substrahentes.'

[6] Perroy pp 414–15; F. Ehrle, 'Neue Materialien zur Geschichte Peters von Luna', *Archiv für Literatur-und Kirchen-Geschichte*, 6 (Freiburg-im-Breisgau 1892) p 243; *Chronique du Religieux de St Denys*, ed M. L. Bellaguet, *Collection de Documents inédits sur l'histoire de France*, II (Paris 1839) p 447.

[7] Valois pp 104–7.

[8] Valois pp 183–4.

[9] Perroy pp 383–4.

[10] Palmer and especially his article 'England and the Great Western Schism', *EHR* 83 (1968) pp 516–22.

have been hesitating to press the matter too hard, for diplomatic reasons
. . . essentially because the French had not kept their part of the bargain
made in November 1396. Dr Palmer thinks that it was the lancastrian
usurpation which spoiled the plan for forcing papal resignation by
withdrawal of obedience.

In spite of what modern writers have said, however, it does not seem
certain that Richard was obliged by his agreement with France to use
any kind of coercion on the pope. It is true that the French government
believed that Richard had bound himself to withdrawal and in August
1398 an embassy came from France to England to persuade Richard to
fulfil what the French considered to be his part of the agreement of
November 1396. In the instructions of the French ambassadors it was
stated that Richard had agreed in 1396 to withdraw obedience if the
popes would not co-operate with the joint embassy.[11] This is the chief
evidence that Richard had made such a promise and from such a source
the evidence must be suspect. The instructions tell us more about what
the French believed Richard to have done than about what Richard
himself believed, and there is no doubt that in the minds of contemporaries it was one thing to support free resignation as a means to end the
schism and quite another to contemplate forcing the pope to resign by
complete withdrawal of obedience. It is worth noting here an exchange
between the leading French opponent of withdrawal Pierre Ravat,
bishop of St Pons, and Simon Cramaud, patriarch of Alexandria, the
leading spokesmen for the French government's point of view, during
the debate among the French clergy in June 1398 at the third council of
Paris which eventually withdrew obedience. Ravat said that *in cedula
Regis Anglie est verbum libere cessionis*.[12] One supposes that he was referring to the agreement of November 1396. Cramaud, whose main task
at the council was to manipulate opinion onto the government side,
replied that Ravat had got it wrong.[13] The *cedula* did not talk of free
resignation *sed voluit simpliciter cum Rege Francie prosequi cessionem*.[14] If

---

[11] Perroy pp 416–18.
[12] Mansi 26, col 848.
[13] Valois pp 148–87 for the third council. See also [H.] Kaminsky, 'The politics
[of France's subtraction of obedience from Pope Benedict XIII, 27 July 1398,]'
Proceedings of the American Philosophical Society, 115, 5 (Philadelphia 1971) pp
366–97; Kaminsky, 'Cession, subtraction, [deposition: Simon de Cramaud's
formulation of the French solution to the Schism,]' *Studia Gratiana*, 15 (Bologna
1972) pp 295–317. I am most grateful to professor Kaminsky for supplying
copies of these papers and for answering my questions.
[14] Mansi 26 col 861.

Cramaud had been able to refer to a concrete agreement by Richard one can be certain that he would have done so.

It is most probable, therefore, that when Richard received the French embassy in August 1398 he was bound only to support papal resignation as a means to end the schism but not to any means of enforcing resignation now that both popes had refused to resign freely. The French ambassadors brought with them a letter from the university of Paris to Charles VI advising him to withdraw obedience,[15] and a letter from Charles VI justifying the step he had taken.[16] Richard proceeded to consult Oxford and Cambridge about the morality and legality of withdrawal of obedience, just as he had earlier consulted Oxford about resignation.

Hitherto no-one has doubted that both universities rejected the French policy out of hand and would only consider a general council as a possible means to end the schism, and even then only a general council called by their own pope. It is the aim of this paper to suggest that early in 1399 Oxford was preparing to modify its opinion, perhaps under royal pressure, and was not by any means as conservative as has hitherto been thought.

The same is not true of Cambridge. Richard summoned that university in November 1398 to give an opinion, and duly received a reply dated 24 January 1399.[17] Professor Ullmann has printed this in full.[18] The masters were only prepared to consider two solutions to the schism: joint uncoerced resignation or a general council called by their pope.

The answer of Oxford is much more of a puzzle. Richard called on that university for advice but there are two writs of summons. The first, identical with that to Cambridge and sent in November 1398, asked for a final response by 12 February 1399.[19] This was followed by further writs to individuals including three bishops and several theologians and canon lawyers, dated 2 January and ordering them to meet the university on 27 January and give their advice and consent on the

---

[15] [C. E.] Du Boulay, [*Historia Universitatis Parisiensis*] (Paris 1668) IV pp 845–7.
[16] [O.] Raynaldus, [*Annales Ecclesiastici*] (Lucca 1752) VIII pp 13–20; Du Boulay pp 853–62.
[17] [W.] Ullmann, ['The University of Cambridge and the Great Schism'] *JTS*, ns 9 (1958) p 55.
[18] *Ibid* pp 68–75.
[19] T. Rymer, *Foedera* (London 1709) VIII p 62; C[*alendar of*] C[*lose*] R[*olls, Richard II*], VI (London 1927) p 354; BM MS Cotton Cleopatra E II, fol 236 (modern copy).

matter.[20] All 29 individuals named in the writs had been, or were still, at Oxford and some were very distinguished.[21]

To add to the problems there are two letters which have passed for the official reply of the university, and scholars have for long argued about which letter is definitive. It is these two letters which chiefly concern me here.

The surviving copy of one letter is contained in volume 25 of the Spanish volumes in the vatican archive collection known as the *Libri de Schismate*, a collection of documents concerning the schism made by the cardinal Martin de Salva and assembled by 1404.[22] The letter was printed by Raynaldus, and as far as I have been able to discover all those scholars who have discussed it have done so from the printed version.[23] This is unfortunate because, as Raynaldus made clear, the printed version is incomplete. It does however contain the dating clause, 5 February 1399, and states that the letter is sent to the king by the regent and

[20] *CCR* pp 367–8, printed in full in *Reports on the Dignity of a Peer*, III (London 1826), Appendix to the first report pp 763–4; BM MS Cotton Cleopatra E II, fol 236ᵛ (modern copy). Cambridge was sent a reminder on 6 January, Ullmann p 56.

[21] The names are John Trefnant, D.C.L., bishop of Hereford; John Trevaur, D.Cn and C.L., bishop of St Asaph; Henry Beaufort, bishop of Lincoln; Thomas Chillenden, D.Cn.L., prior of Christ Church, Canterbury; Thomas Bekenham, B.Th., prior of St Augustine's Canterbury; William Welde, D.Cn.L., abbot of St Augustine's, Canterbury; Geoffrey de Pykering, abbot of Byland; Philip Repingdon, D.Th., abbot of Leicester; John Borard, D.Th., prior of Christ Church, Hants; Thomas Neville, prior of Winchester; Thomas Montague, B.C.L., dean of Salisbury; John Shepey, D.C.L., dean of Lincoln; Ralph Tregisiow, D.C.L., dean of Exeter; John Shirborne, D.Th., chancellor of York; Robert Rygge, D.Th., archdeacon of Barnstaple, former chancellor of the University; John Huntman, D.Th., chancellor of Lincoln; John Play, MA, former fellow of New College, Oxford; John Balton, D.Th. of Balliol College; William Middleworth, former fellow of Merton and Queen's Colleges; John Kynyngham, D.Th., prior provincial of the carmelites; William Siward, D.Th., former prior provincial of the dominicans; John Hynkley, D.Th., O.S.A.; John Shillyngford, D.C.L. who held various posts in ecclesiastical courts; John Barnet, D.C.L., Lic.Cn.L., official of Canterbury; John Elmer, D.C.L., official of Winchester and former warden of New College, Oxford; Richard Drayton, B.Cn.L., official of Bath and Wells; William Clynt, MA, fellow of Merton College; Michael Kympton, O.S.A., of Merton priory; and Nicholas Fakenham, D.Th., provincial minister of the franciscans. The careers of all those named can be traced from A. B. Emden, *Biographical Register of Oxford Graduates to 1500*, 3 vols (Oxford 1957–9).

[22] Vatican Archives Arm. LIV vol 25 fols 268–73ᵛ, for the letter. The whole collection is described M. Seidlmayer, 'Die spanischen Libri de Schismate des Vatikanischen Archivs', *Gesammelte Aufsätze zur Kulturgeschichte Spaniens* Series I, 8 (Münster 1940) pp 199–262.

[23] Raynaldus pp 35–7.

non-regent masters of Oxford. The text of the copy is very corrupt and even in the heavily edited parts printed by Raynaldus the letter is very difficult to understand.

The surviving copy of the second letter is contained in the Bodleian manuscript Digby 188.[24] This is an incomplete manuscript of the early fifteenth century.[25] It is made up of polemical works on withdrawal of obedience and is anti-French. The letter which concerns us is addressed to Richard by *cetus unanimis Universitatis Oxoniensis studii*.[26] There is no dating clause but the writer or writers had read the French king's edict withdrawing obedience (which is quoted word for word in order to refute it) and the letter from the Sorbonne to the French king (which is also quoted).[27] The occasion for writing is said to be the king's order to read and consider these.[28] The letter however refers back to previous letters for the university's plan for a general council,[29] and on the vital matter of the practicalities of the council (who was to call it, for instance refers to *ipsa [via] sub modo et forma competentibus in nostre parvitatis epistola secunda taxata*,[30] and gives no details itself. These details are supplied in the vatican letter and it seems most likely that that is the *epistola secunda*, the first being that of 1396. There are some reasons for wondering whether the Digby letter was a private pamphlet rather than an official letter. Chief among these is its unfinished state, but another is that in places it addresses the king in a somewhat hectoring tone.[31] All the writings in the manuscript, but especially this letter, are very badly copied and in places do not make sense.

[24] W. D. Macray, *Catalogi Codicum Manuscriptorum Bibliothecae Bodleianae, Pars Nona, Codices a . . . Kenelm Digby* (Oxford 1883) pp 200–1. The MS belonged to Digby's tutor, Thomas Allen, who died in 1632.

[25] The final item fols 62–6 is an incomplete disputation against withdrawal, addressed to a king. The first item fols 1–46 is a dialogue between *Rex* and *Unitas*. *Rex* consists of the French king's letter on withdrawal, see note 16 above. The MS may be Flemish in origin. At the end of the Oxford letter fol 61ᵛ is written 'god laet goet wesen'. But it must have been in England in the mid-fifteenth century, since there are scribbled references to cases in the English ecclesiastical courts on fly leaves, for example fol 67ᵛ to Matilda abbess of Sion, 1445.

[26] Fol 47–61ᵛ.

[27] From fol 53ᵛ extensive quotations from the edict of the French king. Fol 61 contains a reference to the promise of the Parisians to defend themselves.

[28] Fol 47 'perlectis siquidem iuxta vim et formam vestri solempnis edicti duabus epistolis, altera inclitissimi regis francorum patris vestri, alia Parisiensis studii . . .'

[29] Fol 53 'ostensa enim est eis in nostris epistolis prioribus veritatis via cum sua practica'.

[30] Fol 59ᵛ.

[31] Fol 48 has many examples (including that of king Uzzia, 2 Chron. 26, 19) of the dire results of kings usurping the role of priests.

Professors Jacob,[32] Perroy,[33] and Ullmann[34] have disagreed about the relation between these letters, but I think that the full contents of the vatican letter, especially the parts not printed by Raynaldus, show that it was the official reply of the university. The Digby letter, if it is official, must have been written shortly after the vatican one, and mainly provides further arguments against forced resignation and in favour of obedience to lawful superiors. A general council is the answer to the schism, but for the practicalities we are referred to earlier letters. The agenda was to be the papal title and the evils resulting from the schism. The university of Paris had offered to argue the matter.[35] Oxford was prepared to send twelve theologians to prove her point.[36] The vatican letter is a different matter and historians have only failed to realise this because they have not seen that Raynaldus printed only those parts where Oxford discussed its main idea – a general council instead of withdrawal of obedience, which is condemned. The general council was to be called by Boniface and, if Benedict attended, the chief item on the agenda was to be the papal title. It is not surprising that these parts of the letter made it look as if the university had not moved an inch since 1396 and as if the chief differences between this version and the Digby one were stylistic only. In fact the differences are much greater than that.

First of all the university begins its reply, after the usual lamentation about the schism, by saying that of the ways to end the schism the most suitable were free resignation or a general council *sub debitis et competentibus mediis practicande*.[37] This was a modification. In 1396 the masters had been most reluctant to support even the free resignation of Boniface, though very much in favour of it for Benedict XIII, of course.[38] By 1399 resignation of both popes had become royal policy, and Oxford gives every indication of accepting it in theory. Nonethe-

---

[32] [E. F.] Jacob, [*Essays in the Conciliar Epoch*] (3 ed Manchester 1963) p 64.

[33] Perroy pp 386–7 n 3.

[34] Ullmann pp 61–2 n 1.

[35] Du Boulay p 847 'cui si res exigat, suas rationes, colores atque motiva tempore congruo dabimus.'

[36] Digby 188 fol 61 'istarum conclusionum contrarias murmurunt et affirmunt ac se probaturos promittunt amici nostri parisienses doctores, qui si suis promissis immobiliter stare disposuerunt ... si saltem vestri regalis culminis nutus precesserit, signabimus de nostris tironibus xii doctores electos in clericali militia sufficienter probatos qui contra quorumlibet adversariorum insultuum iacula iudicio contradicionis bello ubi et quando dixeritis clipeos defensionis apponent parati.'

[37] Fol 268v.

[38] Ouy p 58.

less, it is pointed out that when the royal embassy had gone to both popes (in the joint embassy of 1397) and Boniface had been requested and Benedict summoned to resign, neither had been willing. Hence Oxford assumes for the rest of the letter that resignation is not at present a practical possibility.

Raynaldus began his extracts with the next section,[39] where Oxford points out that she opposes the French method of achieving resignation because of its doubtful legality and because there were other possible methods of ending the schism. Oxford compared the policy of Benedict (who offered discussion) with that of Boniface (who, they said, offered a general council)[40] to the detriment of Benedict. But the king of England was not resorting to the dubious French methods but was looking for a canonical method of ending the schism. At this point Raynaldus again omitted a passage which would have helped to end a puzzle for historians. The university stated that the king had asked its advice on how to act over the French letters and continued:

> ad cuius iussionis imperium, congregatis eciam nobiscum venera-
> bilibus patribus dominis Edmundo Exon' episcopo cancellario
> Anglie, Enrico Lincolen', Johanne Eroffroden et Thoma Carliolen'
> episcopis et aliis venerabilibus prelatis et doctoribus, in univer-
> sitatis vestre cathedra dignissime sublimati, prefatas epistolas in
> communi dictorum patrum, prelatorum et doctorum audiencia
> legi fecimus . . . ad huiusmodi consilium unanimiter condecendi-
> mus: quod utique via consilii generalis sicut eciam iam dudum ad
> mandatum regium requisiti literis nostris patentibus vobis scripsi-
> mus, est via pro cedando tam gravi scismate canonica. . . .[41]

We are almost certainly being referred back to the 1396 letter here. The passage as a whole shows that the vatican letter was the product of a meeting between certain bishops and doctors and the whole university. How satisfactory if the bishops named here: Stafford the chancellor, Beaufort, Trefnant and Merk, were the same as those named in the individual writs of summons for the meeting of 27 January 1399. Unfortunately only Beaufort and Trefnant received writs. Nonetheless we may be dealing with the same meeting, with the

---

[39] Raynaldus pp 35-6; fols 269-71.
[40] F. Bliemetzrieder, *Das Generalkonzil im grossen abendlandischen Schisma* (Paderborn 1904) pp 138-9 n 3; L. Suarez Fernandez, *Castilla, el Cisma y la Crisis Conciliar* (Madrid 1960) p 216, for a letter from Henry of Castille dated 10 September 1397, saying that Boniface offers a council.
[41] Fol 271.

chancellor to represent the view of the government and Merk replacing Trevaur.

The university makes it clear that the only other policy which would be generally approved by the clergy was free resignation and this was passed over because it was clearly not acceptable to the rival popes.[42]

Having omitted these interesting details, Raynaldus[43] began again at the point where the university discussed the practicalities of a general council. The solution was to be offered again to the rivals by ambassadors. If Benedict's supporters accepted a council, Boniface, as the true pope, was to call it and cite his rival. If the other side attended, the chief item on the agenda was to be the papal title. If the other side refused to attend, Boniface was to ask the princes on his side to persuade the secular supporters of the other side to compel Benedict and his cardinals to submit to the judgment of the council. If the secular supporters of Benedict refused to do this the supporters of Boniface could use force. It was not surprising that scholars have thought after this that Oxford was putting forward a rigidly conservative and totally unrealistic solution. In fact however Raynaldus here omitted a passage which introduced important modifications into the plan for a general council called Boniface. In some ways this is the most interesting passage in the whole letter.

The university asked what if the rivals, duly summoned *sub districcione consilii se clarificare recusent?* Then, it says:

> ... cum pro tam gravi scandalo et animarum periculo removendis [et ad] hinc inde favencium consciencias serenandum non appareat via securior veritatis et fidei difenssiva, tunc reges et principes Christiani, subvercionem fidei non inmerito formidantes, mutuis exortacionibus, consiliis [et] assensu prelatos et clerum suorum regnorum pro celebrando generali consilio et dolendi scismatis fomento penitus [e]xstirpando, prout sacri canones senciunt et declarant, auctoritate ecclesie faciant convenire.[44]

If the supporters of Benedict insist obstinately on their chosen method there is another way:

> ... quod videlicet de singulis diocesibus utriusque obediencie una

---

[42] Fol 271r/v 'nec alia in toto clero reperi poterit, nisi sit via ultronee cessionis practicanda tamen cum modo et formis competentibus; quam tamen, cum sit per utramque partem contendencium refutata, sub silentio pretermittimus'.

[43] Raynaldus pp 36–7.

[44] Fol 272. The parts in square brackets are my additions.

persona sufficiens et idonea, sue de singulis regnis, patriis et aliis dominiis, que in temporalibus de facto superiores non recognoscunt vel non admittunt, due tres vel quatuor huiusmodi persone per totum clerum eligantur et in loco tuto et competenti insimul adunate potestatem habeant inveniendi, eligendi, providendi et assumendi viam quamcumque rationabilem, per quam presens scisma sedari poterit et terminari. Quam quidem viam sic per eos aut [MS ac] maiorem partem eorundem inventam, assumptam et electam et utrique contendencium per viam exortacionis oblatam, valeant omnibus viis et modis canonicis ulterius persequi eciam usque ad finalem conclusionem eiusdem.[45]

The political powers concerned and the clergy were to undertake to abide by the decision of these delegates, but there was a very important proviso:

personis per nostram obedienciam eligendis detur onus et mandatum ... quod ad viam coacte cessionis aut obediencie subtractionem a domino nostro pape directe vel indirecte, publice vel occulte, non consensient, et quod ad maiorem securitatem huiusmodi persone coram suis dominis spiritualibus et temporalibus quod ad premissa, ut premittitur, non consensient, iuramentum prestent ad sancta dei ewangelia corporale. Et nichilominus antequam ad hoc medium procedatur, consulimus quod dictus dominus noster papa per serenitatem regiam consulatur et eius benevolencia et consensus sit specialiter requirendus[46]

If the other side would not accept they were to be left to perdition.

Raynaldus, having omitted all this, then printed the end of the letter where the university begs the king not to desert the obedience of Boniface which he had accepted in full parliament with his clergy and people and which he had given his royal word that he would foster.[47]

The major differences between the vatican letter and its predecessor of 1396 and the limitations of the edition of Raynaldus should now be clear. It is now certain that the vatican letter was the product of a meeting between certain bishops and doctors and the university, called by the king. The practicalities of its chosen method, the general council, were now much more clearly envisaged. The first possibility was a

[45] Fol 272v.
[46] Ibid
[47] Fol 273r/v; Raynaldus p 37.

perfectly orthodox general council called by Boniface, but the university was prepared to consider much less normal methods. There was
either a general council called by christian kings and princes to discuss
ending the schism or a clerical gathering which was not quite an orthodox general council because not called by the pope, though it would
seem that the initiative here was to be clerical, with the support of the
secular powers. The consent of Boniface was to be sought but the
meeting was to have the final say in ending the schism *viis et modiis
canonicis*: an important proviso.

This was a major alteration of view for Oxford, but there seems
little doubt that the plan for a clerical gathering came in the first place
from France and was probably presented to the English for the first
time officially by the French diplomats who arrived in England in
autumn 1398. The originator of the French plan had been Simon
Cramaud, who had included ideas about a meeting of both popes and
their cardinals in a treatise on withdrawal of obedience (late 1396), a
copy of which he sent to England. Cramaud put his plan forward in a
much modified form at the third council of Paris in July 1398.[48] In the
instructions of the French ambassadors the plan appeared as follows:[49]
The French clergy were said to have advised the king that certain of the
clergy needed to assemble with the two rival popes and the cardinals
of both sides to advise how resignation was to be put into effect, how
peace in the church was to be achieved and how to have an undoubted
pope. The French church had already chosen its delegates (at the third
council of Paris).[50] The king of England was now asked to follow suit.
The assembly would have the power of a general council and therefore
power to act for the church. The kings were to give their delegates full
powers, even to act against the rival popes if they refused to appear. The
ambassadors were to point out that since the English had already agreed
that resignation was the best method of ending the schism, and had
earlier talked of a general council, this plan met the wishes of both sides.

This must be the scheme which the king asked Oxford to consider.
In drawing up a version of the scheme in the first place Cramaud almost
certainly had in mind (among many other considerations) the Oxford
objections to resignation in the letter of 1396. In his treatise he had
rejected a general council but pointed out that the letter from the

---

[48] Valois pp 163–4; Perroy p 385; Kaminsky articles cited above note 13. Evidence
   that Cramaud sent his treatise to England from the speech by P. Ravat, bishop
   of St Pons, at the third council of Paris, Mansi 26 col 886.
[49] Perroy p 418.
[50] Kaminsky, 'The Politics', p 383 and notes.

university of Paris which Oxford was refuting talked of resignation without going into practicalities and Oxford said that *nuda cessio* would not suffice to end the schism. He points out that practicalities have now been considered and outlines some possibilities for a meeting of the cardinals and both popes concluding *et ego credo quod domini Exonien [sic] numquam tempore quo fecerunt istam epistolam audiverunt istam practicam.*[51] Equally the Digby letter suggests that the writers had read Cramaud, though, if so, there he is firmly refuted.[52]

Evidently the vatican letter does not accept any version of the French plan completely. It was in any case a plan for putting resignation into practice, and Oxford was against forced resignation. But Oxford was prepared to go some of the way to coerce Boniface if he refused to call a general council himself. If it came to a clerical gathering and he refused to consent, one can only suppose that the meeting would go ahead without him, even though the English delegates were forbidden to discuss withdrawal of obedience. This was not a great concession to the French but it was something. One will never know what Oxford (or Richard II) envisaged as the next step. If the Digby letter is an official product of the university, it is really a reinforcement of the plea for a general council and against enforced resignation. It does not advance the debate at all. It is possible that if the diplomatic contacts with France had continued, something like the council of Pisa might have been achieved in 1400.[53] As it was, on 29 May 1399 Richard sailed for Ireland and set in train the events which brought Henry IV to the throne and with him a change in policy.

[51] Balliol College, Oxford MS 165 B p 77. Quoted in part by Jacob p 69 n 3, but without realising that the work is by Cramaud. See now R. A. B. Mynors, *Catalogue of the Manuscripts of Balliol College, Oxford* (Oxford 1963) p 164. Professor Kaminsky is about to produce an edition of this treatise. See meanwhile his article 'Cession, Subtraction', esp pp 297 and 310.

[52] Cramaud presents many arguments in favour of withdrawal which appear again in Digby, to be there refuted. Kaminsky, 'Cession, Subtraction', p 302 notes that the treatise became a kind of manual for both sides at the third council of Paris.

[53] Suggestion by Kaminsky, 'The Politics', p 397.

ECCLESIASTICAL JURISDICTION IN ENGLAND 1300—1550: THE RECORDS AND THEIR INTERPRETATION

by DOROTHY OWEN

> In my own district once there used to be
> A fine archdeacon one of high degree,
> Who boldly did the execution due
> On fornication and on witchcraft too
> Bawdry, adultery and defamation
> Breaches of wills and contracts, spoliations
> Of church endowments, failure in the rents
> And tithes and disregard of sacraments,
> All these and many other kinds of crime
> That need have no rehearsal at this time,
> Usury, simony too. But he could boast
> That lechery was what he punished most[1]

The picture drawn by Chaucer in the *Friar's Tale* is a little journalistic, not to say sensational, and it deals with only some aspects of the ecclesiastical jurisdiction of his day, yet it leaves us in no doubt as to the importance of the courts, and of the way in which they were regarded in some quarters. Perhaps the picture was overdrawn, and true only of the half century or so within Chaucer's own knowledge. On the other hand it has recently been demonstrated that these same courts furnished some at least of the excuses for royal and parliamentary action at the outset of the reformation,[2] and there seems to be good reason for a closer look at them in this context. Most of all, however, for those whose principal interest is the quality of medieval life, it is desirable to consider the institution during the whole period for which there is some sort of continuous record of its working, that is, for the years

---

[1] *The Canterbury Tales*, trans N. Coghill (rev ed London 1972) p 311.
[2] M. Kelly, 'The submission of the ordinaries', *TRHS*, 5 ser, 15 (1965) pp 97–120, and [M.] Bowker, 'Some archdeacons' court books [and the commons' supplication against the ordinaries of 1532'], [D. A.] Bullough and [R. L.] Storey, [*The Study of Medieval Records*] (Oxford 1971) pp 282–316.

covered by my title. There is no doubt that such a study should reveal a considerable section of the public and private life of the time, and while in the limits of this paper I can do no more than skim the surface of my material I hope that I shall persuade others to make further and deeper studies.

There are plenty of difficulties about this study. It is scarcely comparable with the fearsome task sketched by Sir Steven Runciman, yet it has its own peculiar pitfalls. Who exercised jurisdiction in the church? Through what organs was it exercised? What law was administered in the courts? Above all, where are the records of the courts? There have been several attempts to give a comprehensive answer to the first of these questions, probably the best-known being Stubbs' appendix to the *Report of the Ecclesiastical Courts Commission* in 1883.[3] This is not the place to dwell on the early history of the courts, and it is enough to say here that by 1300 they were well established in England. By this date one can see a regular pattern of courts, which, with minor divergences, was to endure until well after the reformation, and it is with this established judicial system that I am concerned today.

The *Sext*[4] laid down that since the bishop was known to have ordinary jurisdiction in his whole diocese, there was no doubt that he might freely sit in judgment, either in person or through another, to hear causes belonging to the ecclesiastical court in every place not exempt from that jurisdiction, and we may begin with the diocesan courts based on that authority. By 1300, of course, no bishop any longer decided on the merits of all causes submitted to him, nor did he personally punish all crimes brought to his notice. Certain matters were, it is true, reserved for personal decision by himself or a member of his household, in his 'court of audience', which functioned as and when it was needed. The surviving records of such courts have usually been incorporated into the episcopal register and many published editions of registers contain audience material. Very occasionally, however a separate register was kept, and has survived. Lambeth manuscript 244,[5] for example, and Canterbury cathedral manuscript F₂ A.36[6] are both

---

[3] *Report of the Commissioners appointed to inquire into the Constitution and Working of the Ecclesiastical Courts* (London 1883) i, pp 21–51.

[4] *Sexti Decret.* lib. 1, tit. xvii, c. vii.

[5] I hope to publish an edition of this register for the Canterbury and York Society.

[6] C. Donahue and J. P. Gordus, 'A case book from Archbishop Stratford's Audience Book', *Bulletin of Medieval Canon Law*, ns 2 (Berkeley 1972) pp 45–59.

Canterbury audience act books of the early fourteenth century, and there is a register of inhibitions and acts of bishop Martival of Salisbury which is a record of his audience proceedings.[7] Hamilton Thompson published extracts from a Lincoln audience book for the years 1446 to 1449, and Mrs Bowker has edited a later audience book for the same diocese.[8] Reservation of heresy prosecution to the bishop probably gave added importance to these audience courts from the late fourteenth century, and Dr Hudson has just demonstrated that sometimes, at least, separate record was kept of heresy hearings.[9]

No surviving record suggests that audience business, outside the provincial courts, was extensive or onerous, and there seems no doubt that most of the bishop's criminal jurisdiction was delegated to one or more commissaries, while the contentious jurisdiction was exercised by an official. Practice varies very much with the size and complexity of the diocese, and generalisation is full of pitfalls, but it seems reasonably fair to say that in a medium-sized diocese a commissary, who is also sometimes called a corrector, exercised criminal jurisdiction, proved a few wills, and heard some contested causes, in 'chapters' which were held at frequent intervals in various centres.[10] The official, on the other hand, decided most of the contested causes, and proved more wills, in his consistory court, which usually had a single fixed meeting place. In larger dioceses, such as Exeter or Lincoln, large numbers of advocates, proctors, apparitors, notaries and scribes were attached to the consistory, and by the fourteenth century these courts had become important business centres in the lay world around them. Professor Morris and Mrs Bowker have of course demonstrated that the picture I have drawn is not true for the large and complex diocese of Lincoln, but it appears to hold good for Canterbury, Ely, Durham, Exeter, Hereford, Rochester and Wells, for all of which there is substantial evidence for chapters and consistory.[11]

[7] This will form the last volume of the Canterbury and York edition of Martival's register, and is in the press.
[8] [A. H.] Thompson, [*The English Clergy and their Organisation in the later Middle Ages*] (Oxford 1947) pp 206–46; [M.] Bowker, [*An*] *Episcopal Court Book* [*for the diocese of Lincoln*], LRS 61 (1967).
[9] Anne Hudson, 'The Examination of Lollards', *BIHR* 46 (1973) pp 145–9.
[10] D. M. Owen, 'The records of the bishop's official at Ely', Bullough and Storey, pp 189–205; R. W. Dunning, 'The Wells Consistory court in the Fifteenth century', *Proceedings of the Somerset Archaeological and Natural History Society*, 106 (Taunton 1962) pp 54–61; A. T. Bannister, 'Visitation returns of the diocese of Hereford in 1397', *EHR*, 44 (1929) pp 279–89, 444–53.
[11] C. E. Morris, 'The commissary of the bishop in the diocese of Lincoln', *JEH*, 10 (1959) pp 50–65, and 'A consistory court in the middle ages', *JEH*, 14 (1963)

All of these courts dealt with the bishop's subjects throughout his diocese, but a parallel system, confined to specific sections of the diocese, existed almost everywhere. With a few exceptions, Chichester, Hereford, Worcester and Carlisle, there were in every diocese one or more archdeacons, each of whom had a jurisdiction which he too exercised through an official in a consistory, and in perambulating chapters, with functions very similar to those of the bishop's courts. In Lincoln, London and Norwich there were also episcopal commissaries in each archdeaconry, and it is often difficult to see where their authority ends and that of the archdeacon's official begins. Fragmentary records of these indeterminate courts survive at Lincoln from the early fourteenth century,[12] and by the end of the next century there are considerable records for various London and Norwich courts and for Buckingham, Bedford and Leicester. Much of the material printed by archdeacon Hale in his *Precedents and Proceedings in Criminal Causes* is drawn from London courts, A. P. Moore has printed long and valuable extracts from the Leicester records, and Mrs Bowker has recently analysed some Bedford and Buckingham records.[13]

On an even smaller scale, chapters or courts were held by rural deans for correction and probate, although, except where no archidiaconal court existed, they may have had a somewhat shadowy existence, especially in the later medieval centuries. At Hereford and Carlisle, where there were no archdeacons, rural deans were regularly accounting for the profits of their jurisdiction during the fourteenth and fifteenth centuries, and elsewhere there is no doubt that suitors would be tempted to prove wills, and even to start contentious causes, in these small local courts, in preference to a distant, and possibly hostile

---

pp 150–9; Bowker, 'Some archdeacons' court books'. For lists and locations of episcopal archives see D. M. Owen, *Records of the Established Church in England* (London 1970), and *Archives*, 10 (London 1970) pp 53–6; see also [B. L.] Woodcock, [*Medieval Ecclesiastical Courts in the diocese of Canterbury*] (Oxford 1952).

[12] L[incolnshire] A[rchives] O[ffice] Dean and Chapter MS A.1.19; compare A. Gransden, 'Some 13th century records of an ecclesiastical court in the archdeaconry of Sudbury', *BIHR*, 32 (1959) pp 62–9.

[13] *Special and General Reports made to His Majesty by the Commissioners appointed to inquire into the practice and jurisdiction of the Ecclesiastical Courts* (repr London 1856) pp 582–9; [W. H.] Hale, *A Series of Precedents and Proceedings in Criminal Causes 1475–1640*, ed R. W. Dunning (Edinburgh 1973); [A. P.] Moore, ['Proceedings of the ecclesiastical courts in the archdeaconry of Leicester'], *AASR*, 28 (1905–6) pp 117–220, 593–662; Bowker, 'Some archdeacons' court books'; C. A. McClaren, 'An early sixteenth century act book of the diocese of London,' *Journal of the Society of Archivists*, 2, no 7 (London 1968) pp 336–40.

archidiaconal or episcopal consistory.[14] At Ely, where there was no archdeacon for the Isle, and the nearest consistory was at Cambridge, the
two rural deans of Ely and Wisbech were in the habit of taking cognisance of 'matrimonial and other important causes'[15] in the fourteenth
century, and it is possible to parallel this elsewhere.

Traces of a similar tendency to flock to any efficient, all-purpose,
local court can be seen in the evident popularity of the courts of liberties
and peculiar jurisdictions. There can have been few dioceses where one
could not find a peculiar or liberty which claimed exemption for its
subjects from archidiaconal or even from episcopal jurisdiction, so that
appeals from its courts would go directly to the provincial courts, or
even to Rome. In the diocese of York, for instance, there were peculiar
courts of the dean and chapter and of several dignitaries and prebendaries of York, of the bishop and the prior and convent of Durham, of
the collegiate churches of Beverley, Ripon and Southwell, and even of
a few parishes such as Snaith. The subject of the relations and exemp-
tions of peculiar jurisdictions is most complicated and no one has so far
satisfactorily disentangled it for the whole country. Failing a good
modern directory of peculiar jurisdictions, one must go to nineteenth
century reports on ecclesiastical courts to discover them, or to manuals
compiled for the genealogist. A relatively large number of the medieval
records of these peculiar courts has survived, and is known from transcripts or extracts. Because of this many modern assumptions about the
nature of medieval courts has in fact been drawn from the activities
of small, all-purpose courts which are very unlike the larger and better
organised business of archidiaconal and episcopal consistories. Some of
these courts, like those of the Salisbury and Lincoln cathedral chapters
in the fourteenth centuries, seem to be concerned solely with correction,
although the Rochester peculiar of Isleham and Freckenham, where the
parochial chaplain was the judge, certainly heard contentious causes.
Larger liberties, especially in compact populous areas like Ripon or St
Albans, had multi-purpose courts where summary corrections for
fornication, or refusal to join a rogationtide procession, are followed
by full hearings of matrimonial, defamation, and perjury causes. These

---

[14] J. H. Parry, *Registrum Johannis Gileberti episcopi Herefordensis*, CYS, 18 (1915)
p. 36; Carlisle Joint Record Office MS DRC2/7, 8, 21; E[ly] D[iocesan] R[ecords]
MS D 2/1, fol 153.A fragmentary court book of a Worcester decanal court for
the year 1300 has been published by F. S. Pearson, *Collectanea*, Worcestershire
Historical Record Society 29 (Worcester 1912).

[15] This was forbidden by the canons of the provincial council of Oxford, 1222,
F. M. Powicke and C. R. Cheney, *Councils and Synods* (Oxford 1964) p 113.

last were much used at Ripon by the mercantile community for the recovery of small debts. Quite the busiest of all these courts, so far as records have survived, was that of the abbot of Whalley in the twenty-three years before the dissolution. Here, summary corrections were dealt with in 'general chapters', while causes of tithe, matrimony, defamation, perjury and probates were heard in 'particular courts'. The records of this court are slightly amateurish and unpractised, by comparison with the tidy, business-like book kept by the official of the 'archdeaconry' of St Albans in the mid fifteenth century, although this, too, is out of the ordinary in its inclusion of administrative acts.[16]

The boundaries of these various jurisdictions were often uncertain, and since, from the view-point of the owner of the jurisdiction, it was essential to retain all possible sources of profit, resistance to encroachments was very strong. St Wilfred's liberty was particularly vulnerable, and complaints of attacks on its officers 'modo guerrino' and of the evasion of defendants beyond its borders, were very frequent. There had in fact been similar disputes between archdeacons and bishops, most of which had been resolved by the early fifteenth century, and the struggle between the Canterbury prerogative court and the episcopal courts was to continue until the sixteenth century.[17]

The provincial courts as places of direct appeal, or for the 'tuition' of an appeal to Rome, completed the legal pyramid. I do not propose to discuss the courts of Canterbury in any detail, since Miss Churchill and Mr Woodcock have already described their working, and, apart from two audience books, and the long series of diocesan court records used by the latter, only strays resulting from sede vacante jurisdiction, and inhibitions from other courts, still survive.[18] For York we are on firmer ground. Here, too, there is an audience (chancery) court, the registers of which begin in 1525, probates were dealt with in the exchequer

---

[16] H. M. Chew, *Hemingby's Register*, Wiltshire Archaeological and Natural History Society, Records Branch, 17 (Trowbridge 1962) nos 308–9; LAO, Dean and Chapter MS A.2.31; [J. T. Fowler], *Acts of Chapter [of the Collegiate Church of St. Peter and St. Wilfred, Ripon, 1452–1506]*, SS, 64 (1875); C. Johnson, *Registrum Hamonis de Hethe*, 1, CYS 48 (1948); A. M. Cooke, *Act book of the ecclesiastical court of Whalley 1510–1533*, Chetham Society, ns 44 (Manchester 1901); Hertfordshire Record Office MS ASA/1AR, Register Stonham, briefly described by C. E. Hodge in *LQR*, 49 (1933) pp 269 *et seq.*

[17] I have discussed some of these disputes in *John Lydford's Book*, Historical Manuscripts Commission and Devon and Cornwall Record Society, forthcoming.

[18] I. J. Churchill, *Canterbury Administration*, Church Historical Society (London 1933); Woodcock, pp 6–14; 'Dean and Chapter of Canterbury', *HMCR*, 5 (London 1876) pp 426–62; 'acts, inhibitions and other proceedings in ecclesiastical courts occur in every division of the *Carte Antique*'.

court, and the consistory heard causes of first instance from the diocese, tuitions, and appeals from the province. We are particularly fortunate in the survival of part at least of the court papers from as early as 1310, and of consistory act books from 1417, with a few earlier strays.[19] Much of what I shall say later is drawn from these York cause papers, with additional material from the published records, from Lichfield, Rochester, Ely, and Hereford court books, and from several formularies and collections of cause papers.[20]

I cannot, therefore, pretend to attempt more than a partial survey of the late medieval courts in the limits of this paper. Moreover, I shall not discuss either the machinery of appeal or the activities of papal judges delegate, for professor Brentano and Miss Sayers have already treated these topics and others are at work on them.[21]

The law administered in the courts under review is that of the universal church, clarified and interpreted by a succession of commentators and by the specific pronouncements of English provincial and diocesan synods.[22] There is room however for an investigation of the development of the law within England, and here a detailed study of pleadings, like that professor Helmholz is conducting, points the way for other students. A survey of formularies, like John Lydford's notebook, and its close relative manuscript Harley 862, will reveal a number of informal counsels' opinions in specific causes, which can be related to actual pleadings in similar causes. At the same time it will be necessary to look at the schooling and careers of lawyers and court officials, who sometimes must have disseminated the results of new thinking picked up in their schools, but more often preserved the old practices and beliefs imparted by their masters. At the same time we need more detailed studies of individual courts, such as Mr Woodcock made at Canterbury, if we are to form a complete picture of medieval jurisdiction.[23]

[19] R. Brentano, *York Metropolitical Jurisdiction and Papal Judges Delegate* (University of California 1959); D. M. Smith, *A guide to the Archive Collections in the Borthwick Institute of Historical Research* (York 1973) pp 52–61.

[20] I am very grateful to Mrs Gurney and her staff at York for the facilities they have afforded me, and also to Miss Penelope Morgan, Mr F. B. Stitt, Mr P. Walne and Dr Felix Hull for permitting access to collections in their care.

[21] [J. E.] Sayers, [*Papal Judges Delegate in the Province of Canterbury 1198–1254*] (Oxford 1971).

[22] F. W. Maitland, *Roman Canon Law in the Church of England* (London 1898) *passim*; C. R. Cheney, *English Synodalia of the Thirteenth Century* (new imp Oxford 1968) *passim*.

[23] A start has been made by Dr R. Houlbrooke's Oxford D Phil thesis 'Church courts and people in the diocese of Norwich 1519–70' (1970), and Mr C. A. McClaren's M Litt thesis (1972) on a London vicar general's book.

The causes which came to the courts fall easily into the civil and criminal divisions to be seen in secular courts. Correction by the judge, in right of his office, for the health of the defendant's soul, corresponds to the secular criminal jurisdiction. It was usually initiated by the 'mere office of the judge', after a presentment at a visitation, or a denunciation by a clerk, neighbour, or court official. This is of course the sort of court Chaucer was thinking of, and it is the side of the church courts best known to the sixteenth century. The causes were usually dealt with by a brief oral procedure, in which the accused man was cited to answer personally to the charge before the judge. He might produce evidence to refute the charge; if this was accepted he was then dismissed. He might confess, and receive penance, or he might seek to prove his innocence by the oaths of four, six or eight compurgators, who were his compeers in age, sex and status. In any case the proceedings were brief, and large numbers of such causes could be dealt with, as the London and Whalley records show, at each sitting of the court. It is hard to decide whether any court, even the largest of the commissarial chapters, devoted any special sessions to office business. There is no evidence for the York courts before the sixteenth century, but in all the other surviving records earlier than 1530 office hearings are intermingled with probate and a few contested causes. Liber B of the Ely consistory, which like the Rochester court books was regarded as a probate register, contains record of general chapters held by the official of Ely and the dean of Wisbech in the deanery of Wisbech, in the years 1460 to 1479.[24] Most of the causes heard are prosecutions, such as one of John Reynold of Byrdisdrove in Leverington who was fined 6s 8d (to be divided between the bishop's alms and the Leverington fabric fund) because he confessed to being 'a common chatterbox in church, who, though often warned, will not be silent'. It is a type of correction very familiar in the sixteenth century. A longer and more elaborate cause was the prosecution of Robert Everard and Thomas Bytham, who have failed to carry out the terms of a will of which they are executors. They say in defence that the testator bequeathed £10 to buy a new cross for Leverington church, but the churchwardens there refused the legacy and have demanded instead a house belonging to the testator to convert into a gild hall. The executors therefore seek to be exonerated from the terms of the will, and the official allows this and dismisses them. Obviously the churchwardens, or even the defendants, have promoted this 'friendly' action and this sort of 'promoted office' cause

[24] Cambridge University Archives, Consistory probate records, liber B, fols 1–99.

is very frequent. Many of the usury and will forgery charges which figure in the Norwich courts of the early sixteenth century[25] seem to have been inspired by a second party who was the real plaintiff, and in all these causes the procedure, apart from the start of the cause, was like that of the contested causes. A good example appears in the first Ely court book, when in 1378 articles supplied to the judge against John rector of Kingston by his parishioners, and alleging non-residence and dilapidation, began a full office prosecution.[26]

More than twenty years ago, professor Hamilton Thompson, in publishing a fragment of a Lincoln audience court record, suggested that it was primarily 'a court of correction for serious offences' and Mrs Bowker finds that the bulk of her material is divided between the important corrections which fall into the categories reserved by prelates for their own judgment, and difficult matters referred to the bishop from a visitation. The brief Worcester record, for two months in 1349, which appears in Wolstan de Bransford's register, consists almost entirely of reserved corrections of clerks and prosecutions of laymen for attacks on church property, and Hamo de Hethe's court is much the same.[27] Martival's fuller record suggests that his audience court was much more active. Many of the offenders with whom it dealt were clerks who had failed to amend their ways after an earlier correction. A characteristic defendant was the litigious rector of Oaksey, who was also prior of the hospital of St John in Cricklade. The articles against him alleged non-residence at Oaksey and waste at Cricklade, a breach of his oath to the bishop to abjure the company of the sisters in the hospital, participation in a case in a secular court despite his oath to keep away from hundred courts, and neglect of an excommunication laid on him for violence to a laybrother of the hospital. There are also prosecutions for theft of tithe sheaves, which begin with inquisitions to discover the names of guilty men, and end like the Oaksey cause, with a confession on oath and a petition for absolution. Some of the matrimonial causes in this court began as correction, like that of a marriage celebrated without banns, where the guilty parties confessed and were allowed then to prove that their marriage could be regarded as valid because no impediments existed.

[25] E. D. Stone, *Norwich Consistory Court Depositions 1499–1512 and 1518–30*, Norfolk Record Society, 10 (Norwich 1938).

[26] EDR MS D2/1, fol 106ᵛ.

[27] Thompson, pp 55–6; Bowker, *Episcopal Court Book*, p x; Hethe, pp 197, 237–9; R. M. Haines, *A calendar of the register of Wolstan de Bransford, bishop of Worcester 1339–49*, Worcestershire Historical Society, 4 (Worcester 1966) pp 504–9.

An important tithe cause began with the presentment of a layman at visitation for non-payment of tithes, by the parochial chaplain who was collecting them, and *ex officio* articles were used by the bishop to implead the officers of St Nicholas' hospital Salisbury for refusal to admit a man to an almsman's place there.[28]

Heresy prosecutions seem always to have come to the bishop's or archbishop's hearing, and when lollard activity was at its height during the first half of the fifteenth century, and again in the early sixteenth century, special sessions must sometimes at least have been held. Extracts printed by Foxe and Wilkins appear to be drawn from act books of such sessions which have not always survived; the list of what he calls 'authenticated trials for heresy prior to 1533', which Stubbs included in his evidence to the ecclesiastical courts commission, is revealing of the sort of record that has survived. Norwich and Lich-field material of this kind has been used and Dr Hudson, as we have seen, has recently discussed them again. Almost all fifteenth century bishops' registers contain a few heresy causes along with other audience material: at Ely, for example, two folios of bishop Gray's register are taken up with a lollard prosecution of 1457.[29] The procedure here, and elsewhere, was adapted from that of promoted office: the articles are replaced by specific charges of heretical speaking, writing or preaching, the defendants confess or deny the charges, submit, receive penance, and read or speak an abjuration. The whole process is usually recorded in full. A very early example of the same type, which records the pro-secution by bishop Braybroke of William Thorp in 1395, was copied by Lydford into his notebook, and there are scattered extracts to be found in *Fasciculi Zizaniorum*.[30]

Even the fullest and most professional records of audience procedure seem to be a little amateurish and as late as the early sixteenth century Atwater's book shows some hesitation and uncertainty in the manner of record. At their fullest the books are chronological records of inter-mittent sessions, each beginning with a formal heading giving judge, place and date, and with marginal flags of the defendant's name or parish. Some of the more difficult or important office causes, and all of the instance business, is narrated in full. Martival has elaborate and con-fusing narratives of a series of matrimonial causes, though even here the

[28] Martival, v, nos 137, 50, 34, 57.
[29] EDR MS G1/5, fols 130ᵛ–133ᵛ.
[30] Lydford, nos 206, 209; W. W. Shirley, *Fasciculi Zizaniorum magistri Johannis Wyclif, cum tritico*, RS 5 (1858) pp 318 *et seq*.

service of the court was so unsure that a few of the relevant entries were put, presumably by mistake, into the register of divers letters.

Plenary procedure, whether in promoted office, or in contested (instance) causes seems to be the source of many later complaints about delays and excessive fees, the memory of which was still very much alive, as readers of David Copperfield are aware, in the early nineteenth century.[31] The procedures of the courts were those drawn from the roman law, which had become usual throughout the western church long before the time we are concerned with, wherever lawyers trained in the civil and canon laws were employed. Causes opened with a request from the plaintiff (*pars actrix*) to the registrar of the court for the citation of the defendant (*pars rea*) to answer a charge. The citation was served by an apparitor, its service was certified to the court, and proctors were appointed, and admitted to speak for each party. The libel containing the plaintiff's case was then produced and read in court, after which, if the action was plenary, the defendant could make procedural or material exceptions to it, on the value of which the judge must decide before the cause could continue. If the exceptions were refused the court moved forward to the *litis contestacio* in which the plaintiff's case was again propounded and the defendant denied its points *seriatim*. This denial or *contradiccio* could be a lengthy business, and so might the next stage, when oaths *de calumnia* and *de veritate dicenda* were sworn by both parties; it was possible for either side to refuse the oaths.[32] The plaintiff, once they were taken, proceeded to prove his case. The articles of his libel were once more read over, the defendant answered 'yes' or 'no' to each, and witnesses were named, cited, sworn, and deposed to the truth of each point. The depositions they made were usually taken down in writing, and copies supplied to the defendant, who might then except against the character of the deponents or the truth of their depositions, proving his exceptions by a further series of depositions. Finally, when the plaintiff was satisfied that his case was established, he moved for a 'term to propound all acts' and this was followed by a petition for sentence. The sentence repeated the substance of the libel, and accepted or rejected the plaintiff's proofs. A final term was assigned for the taxation or assessment of costs.

The characteristic record of this litigation is a chronological journal of the court's acts, in which the stages reached in all actions, and the

---

[31] L. Lefebre, 'Procédure', *DDC* 7 (1965) cols 285–96; Woodcock, part ii, *passim*; Sayers, pp 42–99.
[32] BM MS Harley 862, fols 189–91, 39ᵛ.

terms assigned (hence the name 'assignation books') are briefly noted. Such books contain no record of the pleading, and in my experience the outcome of a cause can rarely be known, because the sentence is not copied, unless it is abandoned, or goes to arbitration. Not all entries mention the type of cause under way, and at the best one can only count up the numbers of different types of cause begun in a certain period, learn something about the litigants, and perhaps a little about the peculiarities of court practice. A characteristic entry may be taken from a record of the Lichfield consistory sitting on 15 May 1464.[33] On that day fifteen contested causes and two corrections, were at various stages, and the usual note for each reads like this: 'Tateley in a cause, of perjury (*fidei lesionis*) between Peter Tateley of Drayton in Hales, the plaintiff, appearing by Croftes, and David Williamson of the same, defendant, appearing by Calton, in the term for conclusion of the cause (to propound all acts) the judge decided, with the parties' agreement to end the cause, and decreed the next court day as the term for sentence.' The York consistory registers are of this type, which of course was the usual practice almost everywhere, for everything except simple correction, by the middle of the sixteenth century. Smaller or less well organised courts, like Ely in the late fourteenth century, and the various peculiar courts, include copies of libels, articles, and even a sentence or two, and this practice continued at Leicester until at least 1550. The court notaries ought all to have written, distributed to parties, and retained originals of, citations, libels, exceptions, depositions, and all the other necessary documents of a cause, for this was required by the thirty-eighth canon of the fourth lateran council.[34] How far the canon was observed it is impossible to say. Certainly the multiplication of copies of documents added to the costs of a cause and the official of Ely at any rate was ready to admit oral pleading, and to decree that a written libel need no longer be demanded, but only a summary petition for entry in the acts.[35] This perhaps explains why Ely and other courts have no sign of cause paper files and many documents copied into their registers.

Even at York it is clear that not all the cause papers can possibly have survived, yet enough certainly remains to provide a fair survey of the habits of the court, and of the causes it heard. I am still not sure, after more than a year's intermittent study, that I can reconstruct the practice

[33] Lichfield Joint Record Office MS B/C/1, fols 3ᵛ–5.
[34] Mansi, 22 (1778) cols 1022–3.
[35] EDR MS D2/1, fols 57,ᵛ 65, 82, 162ᵛ.

in this, or indeed, in any other medieval court, but I hope that I can give others some impetus to continue the study. Papers survive for 377 causes in the period 1304 to 1435. Of these, 300 originated at York: 43 per cent matrimonial, 20 per cent tithe and offerings, 10 per cent defamation, 9 per cent testamentary, and 6 per cent perjury. There are also 57 appeals from lower courts and 20 requests for tuition during an appeal to Rome. The period covered is too long, and the gaps are too obvious, to make comparisons with other courts at all helpful, yet it might perhaps be worth mentioning that at a later period of the fifteenth century Mr Woodcock found 800 causes introduced in his Canterbury court in fifteen years.[36]

The light thrown by the York papers varies considerably and probably the most informative are the appeals, where the initial document recites most of the proceedings in the lower court. Incidentally this remains true of a number of scattered narratives or 'compiled acta', probably copies made for a party in an appeal, which can be found in the archives of cathedrals, colleges, or private families which were parties to a cause, or have succeeded to a party. J. C. Cox has printed a number of scattered narratives or 'compiled acta', probably copies made for a party in a Lichfield tithe cause, two appeals concerning the tithe of Altcar are now in the Lancashire record office, and many other examples could be quoted. No doubt the archives of the court of Arches once contained large numbers of these processes, forerunners of the seventeenth century process books described by Miss Slatter.[37]

Without the help of such a narrative, however, a good deal can be learned from the usual papers, and from other sources, about the conduct of a cause. The initial citation, reciting the names of judge, plaintiff, and defendant, was served by an apparitor (the summoner), and might well be met with disapproval. Defendants who disappeared into vacancy before the apparitor's coming were all too familiar, but truculence, and even violence, were regularly recorded, and might be

---

[36] At Rochester in 1347–8: 30 instance causes and 123 corrections; 30% matrimonial, 23% tithe, 17% each probate and defamation, 10% perjury and 3% usury. At Ely in 1374–81: 177 instance and 70 corrections; 33% defamation, Whalley 1510–38: 29 instance, 250 corrections; 45% matrimonial, 17% each, tithe and probate, 14% defamation, 7% perjury.

[37] J. C. Cox, 'Ancient Documents relating to tithes in the Peak', *Journal of the Derbyshire Natural History Society*, 5 (Derby 1883) pp 129–64; Lancashire Record Office MSS DDC1, 1050, and DDM 19/11, partially printed in *Transactions of the Historical Society of Lancashire and Cheshire*, 82 (Liverpool 1930) pp 136–61, and 101 (1949) pp 47–62; M. D. Slatter, 'The records of the court of Arches', *JEH*, 4 (1954) pp 139–53.

countered with an excommunication for contempt. An Exeter notary recorded in a formulary[38] an attempt by Robert Woller to serve an inhibition from the court of Arches on William Wenlok, in the church of St Mary the Virgin at Oxford. He said in the vulgar tongue 'Mayster I mooste serve yow as I have servyd your felows. By the auctoritie of this mandement I inhibitt yow'. While he was speaking Robert Grenewod came up with a wrathful face, pushed him backwards, and pulled Wenlok away through the north door of the church. Woller followed them and Grenewod cried 'Ye owe not to obey his mandement. Lewde Jacke. Go piss with thy mandement'.

Assume the citation has been served, and the proctors nominated, the plaintiff's case is then revealed. At York, formal libels seem not to have been used, or at least, have not been preserved. For the substance of the cause it is necessary to rely on the proctor's statement of the positions or articles which he proposes or intends to prove. Usually, however, the libel was composed with great care to suit the particular needs of the cause. Lydford and the Exeter formulary include large numbers of libels to suit a variety of disputes. In a cause concerning burial fees, for example, there were at least four ways of stating the case.[39] Allegations, or delaying exceptions against the libels, could be equally varied. Again there are few of them at York, but the formularies include numerous examples from the compilers' own practice. The usual form of exception alleges that each article of the libel is '*vagus, obscurus et nimis generalis*', and petitions for its re-presentation in a more precise form.

Once this hurdle is passed, and the *litis contestacio* reached, it seems to have been the York habit to set out the gist of the plaintiff's case in the positions for proof. These were often very long, especially in tithe causes. An appeal of 1321 brought by the prior and convent of Durham against an archdiaconal claim to visit their churches,[40] measures twenty-four inches and contains one hundred and fifty positions, many of them of a rather trite and obvious nature:

> He alleges that the said prior and convent are rectors of the said church,
> That they have been so for the aforesaid time,
> And so individually for each of the said churches and chapels,

[38] BM MS Harley 862, fol 20. This early fifteenth-century compilation uses much Exeter material and is drawn largely from the practice of two Devon notaries, John and Robert Stephen, but it includes causes from Wells, Lincoln, Oxford and Salisbury.

[39] *Ibid* fols 49–53.   [40] Y[ork] B[orthwick] I[nstitute] MS CPE 13/21.

That the said religious are publicly held to be rectors of the said
  church,
And so individually for each of the said churches and chapels.

The positions are plainly the central record of the cause at York;
often they have notes of assignations and lists of deponents, and they
are carefully and professionally drawn up.[41] This was obviously not so
at Ely, where they are regularly said to have been delivered *oretenus*.
On occasion the actual positions serve as interrogatories to be put to
the deponents, but more often an expanded version with some explanation, was produced. Even with this it was clearly necessary, unless the
deponents were clerks, and even when they were, to translate the
questions; where this occurred the depositions mention the fact. It was
particularly desirable in complicated tithe or offering causes, where the
proof depended on an accurate knowledge of topography. An appeal
of 1394 by the inhabitants of Stoke Bardolph from the sentence of the
commissary general condemning them to pay tithe to Gedling, where
proof turned on the precise line of the parish boundaries, called for the
explanation of the positions *in vulgari* to all deponents, including several
parochial chaplains.[42]

Depositions are in many ways the most obviously attractive and
accessible part of the records of the courts, as Dr Purvis and others
have demonstrated, and it is all too easy to be seduced into quoting
them. Certainly they throw a lot of incidental light on social customs
and attitudes, dress and occupations, and even topography, and are
inexhaustible sources for information about parochial life and ecclesiastical administration. I am particularly fond of the depositions made
to prove the age of a nun who was kidnapped from her convent in
1425, apparently because she was an heiress and a desirable marriage
parti. The prioress brought a charge of infraction of ecclesiastical liberties against the kidnappers, who in return attempted to prove that their
victim was not old enough to be professed, and therefore could not be
a nun. In support of their contention they had assembled ten women
who were all inhabitants of the nun's native village, and who remembered her birth and baptism because they too were pregnant at that
time and bore children, whom they name and describe, and all too
many of whom seem to have died.[43] Then there is the matrimonial
cause of 1432 in which the plaintiff seeks to prove that he was elsewhere

[41] YBI, MSS CPE 15, 17, 19, 25.
[42] YBI, MS CPE 208.
[43] YBI, MS CPF 89.

at a time when he had allegedly promised marriage to the defendant, and calls four witnesses, including a monk of St Mary's York, to prove that he spent the night drinking and horse trading, in the Lion in Pontefract together with the monk, who was his uncle.[44] One could go on for ever. Yet it is important to remember that the depositions throw very little light on the cause for which they are made, and are frequently directed, with great repetitiveness sometimes, to proving a single proposition, the age of an heiress, the line of a parish boundary, or the ownership of a piece of land. Because of the ingenuity of proctors in detecting flaws in the proofs offered, depositions needed to be increasingly detailed and circumstantial; at York accurate times are given (*circa primam pulsacionem horologii*) in the early fifteenth century, and details of clothes worn by parties in a divorce suit are mentioned as early as 1370.[45]

Depositions were not all, of course, intended to prove the plaintiff's cause, and they can be very misleading if one does not realise that they are sometimes supporting the defendant's exceptions. With the declaration of the names of the plaintiff's witnesses, or after they had deposed, it was open to the defendant to except against them, and if necessary, to prove his exceptions by his own witnesses. The defendant in a Leicester defamationcause of 1524, for example, excepts against four of his opponent's witnesses, one because he is uncle to the plaintiff, two others because they were within the degrees of consanguinity with him, and the fourth because she had married her present husband despite a prior contract with another man, and must therefore be unreliable.[46] The deposition itself might be discredited by an exceptor who showed it to be wrong in details. In the Altcar tithe cause during its first hearing at Lichfield the defendants had said 'Note that the witnesses have spoken falsely in saying that Depull divides Hasall from Walton, because it is a rivulet which lies wholly within Walton parish'.[47]

When the plaintiff responds to the exceptions he may produce a further set of witnesses and yet more depositions, so that the prospect seem illimitable. Indeed the ingenious proctors obviously prided themselves on the number and unpredictability of their devices, and in the later fourteenth century two consistories, those of Exeter and Ely, found it necessary to warn their proctors against undue use of these

---

[44] YBI, MS CPF 104.
[45] YBI, MSS CPF 33, 62; CPE 248.
[46] Moore, p 626.
[47] Lancashire Record Office MS DDM 19/11/A.

tactics.[48] The formularies include a number of examples which were presumably legitimate gambits, and in any case the judges seem, so far as it is possible to tell from assignation books, to have moved fairly quickly to the conclusion of the cause. Before that point was reached they might even have persuaded the parties, or allowed them, to go to arbitration. Large numbers of instance causes of all types, but especially those involving tithes, or perjury, ended in this way in the Whalley and Leicester courts, but only one example has so far appeared at York, a perjury dispute of 1383,[49] which had arisen from a breach of an agreement about dilapidations, and it was clearly a case for an agreed settlement, and assessment of damages.

Failing an arbitration, the definitive sentence brings the cause almost to a close, the last stage being, as we have seen, the taxation of costs. Presumably proctors retained the 'taxed bills' of costs until they had received their wages, for very few of them have remained with the other papers in the York causes, and there is plenty of evidence of the assiduity of proctors in recovering costs from their masters. One list of fees has been noted, in a tithe cause of 1390.[50] The defendant's costs were: citation, 2d, certificate of citation, 1d, Alan of Newark, advocate, 3s 8d, Hugh of Roberton, advocate, 3s 10d, Roger Ragenhill, advocate, 13s 4d, John Staunton, proctor, 16s, examination of 10 witnesses, 10s, copies of examinations, 5s, 2 copies of the sentence, 4s, apparitor 8d, writing the execution of the sentence, 2s 6d, various expenses coming and going, 22s, other necessary expenses, 10s. This compares with a total of £3 3s 9d in a Lincoln cause of 1440, with £50 spent by the sacrist of Ely in promoting a tithe cause in the court of Arches in 1416, and with Mr Woodcock's quotation of 35s 2d in a cause heard at Canterbury in 1491.

It is time now to look at the nature of some of these instance causes and to try to consider how they throw light on the world of their time. Let us look first at causes which directly concern the clergy and ecclesiastical rights, and which one might expect, mistakenly perhaps, to take up most of the courts' attention. There is no doubt about the large numbers of tithe and offering causes heard at York and elsewhere, during the fourteenth and fifteenth centuries. A number of them are no more than disputes as to which parish could claim tithe from an

---

[48] EDR MS D2/1, fol 62ᵛ; F. C. Hingeston Randolph, *Register of John de Grandisson*, ii (Exeter 1897) pp 807–8.
[49] YBI MS CPE 132.
[50] YBI, MS CPE 177; LAO, MS Ben 3/78; Ely Dean & Chapter, sacrist's roll, 1416; Woodcock, pp 135–6.

outlying mill, such as that inconveniently situated on the boundary between Leeds and Rothwell, or from the fishery of a stretch of the Trent. Causes of this sort can of course provide some surprising information, like the deposition of 1401 which alleged that the parish of Crayke was clearly separated from its neighbours 'by a round hedge surrounding the whole parish in circular fashion'.[51] After 1384 the first causes about brushwood (*silva cedua*) occur at York, and they continue in some numbers. On the other hand there are relatively few attempts to claim personal tithes.[52] A dispute of 1368 at Birstall which concerns tithe of iron working between Batley and Birstall 'where Adam Fraward has two hewers *anglice* clivers, working there every week', is of this type and so are the persistent squabbles in the last decade of the fourteenth century, about tithe of coal 'a quodam puteo *anglice* cole-pitte' at Silkstone.[53] These attempts to extract personal tithes seem to have died away and I have seen few fifteenth century examples. Two Ely specimens, concerning fairly small matters, have some significance perhaps. In 1379 Simon Williameson, a barber of Holy Trinity, Cambridge, was accused of failing to pay tithe of his curtilage and of the gain of his business and craft. In 1380 William Milner of Littleport was accused in similar terms and his reply is recorded. He confessed that he was a sailor, exercising the craft of sailing, and that, although he was a parishioner of Littleport, he had never paid tithe there. He was sent off to estimate his receipts from sailing, but failed to re-appear and disappears from the record.[54]

Another closely related cause is that concerning burial offerings, which resulted usually from a testator's desire for burial in a friary or hospital in preference to his parish church, and which was generally brought by the incumbent of the parish against his executors, or against the friary or hospital which declined to share the profits of the burial. Other examples, arising perhaps from increasing pressure or redistribution of population, arise when the incumbent or proprietor of a parish church seeks to prevent burials in the churchyard of an outlying chapel, as the rector of Grantchester did with Coton, which had long ceased to be described as a chapel.[55]

Other attacks on clerical property which became frequent in the

[51] YBI, MSS CPE 50; CPF 10.
[52] N. Adams, 'The judicial conflict over tithes', *EHR*, 52 (1937) pp 1–22; A. G. Little, 'Personal tithes', *ibid* pp 67–88.
[53] YBI, MSS CPE 98, 162, 234.
[54] EDR MS D2/1, fols 114ᵛ, 145.
[55] EDR MS A/6/1, p 53 and BM MS Harley 862, fol 197.

troubled economic and social conditions of the late fourteenth century
are reflected in the dilapidation causes which are brought as promoted
office against incumbents or dignitaries such as the provost of Beverley
for waste of manors in 1380, and the rector of Harthill in 1397 for
dilapidation of his chancel.[56] There are also instance causes begun by a
new incumbent or dignitary against the executors or other representatives of his predecessor. In 1366 there was a cause of this sort to recover
the cost of repairs of buildings belonging to the see of Bangor, and in
1401 the executors of bishop Tydeman of Worcester were sued for
dilapidations of the entire temporalities of the see.[57] There are even
attempts, by inhabitants of outlying hamlets and chapelries, to bring a
dilapidation cause against the incumbent or religious house responsible
for the upkeep of a chapel needing repair, as was done by the men of
Paull, against the vicar of Skelling, in 1424.[58]

More frequently, however, discontented chapelries brought causes
of 'withdrawal of service' against the responsible authority, as the
inhabitants of Hatfield Chase did in 1365 against the vicar of Thorn.[59]
There are so many of these disputes, and of tithe causes concerning the
inhabitants of outlying settlements, that it is difficult not to see in them
a reflection either of a marked rise or shift in population, or of a shrink-
age in the real income of the church, which has led to an exploration
of all possible sources of income.

To turn now to some of the specifically lay causes heard by the
church courts: as we have seen, a considerable proportion of the York
business was matrimonial and this is equally true of other courts, so that
it would be easy to turn this paper into a *chronique scandaleuse*. However,
the whole subject of matrimonial litigation is being thoroughly
examined by theologians and canonists and I do not intend to devote
any but the most superficial attention to it.[60] Depositions in matrimonial causes can of course throw a lot of light on social habits, and
even on demography. I want to quote one or two lines about a certain
Agnes de Donbarr, alias White Annays, who in 1360 was the defendant
in what seems to have become a bigamy cause. It had been difficult to
discover Agnes' movements (and her marriages) and this was because,
according to a deponent who was himself a Peebles man, but had settled

[56] YBI, MSS CPE 123, 230.   [57] BM MS Harley 862, fols 148ᵛ, 209.
[58] YBI, MS CPF 150.   [59] YBI, MS CPE 90.
[60] M. Sheehan, 'Formation and stability of marriage in fourteenth century
England', *Medieval Studies*, 33 (Toronto 1971) pp 28–63; R. H. Helmholz,
'Adjuration *sub pena nubendi* in the church courts of medieval England', *The
Jurist*, 32 (1972) pp 80–90, and a forthcoming book.

at Thorp Arch near York she 'frequently changed her mode of speech, pretending sometimes to be a southerner, sometimes a northerner, and sometimes a Scot, pronouncing English words in the manner of the Scots'.[61] I do not propose, either, to say much about testamentary causes, for they too are a subject in themselves, and, in any case seem to be outside the usual proctorial practice.

It is otherwise with defamation and perjury causes, which figure prominently in the smaller courts, and must have been, outside correction matters, and probate, the way in which the average person encountered the courts. Defamation causes occasionally arise from a correction or from a general sentence, promulgated in the local synod, against defamers. The plaintiff seeks from the court a sentence of excommunication against his opponent, who, he alleges, has defamed him, and proceeds to proof of his allegation in the usual style. He may also, if the allegation is one of crime, seek to purge himself of the imputation of the crime. John Grawnge, a priest at Ripon, in 1454 of his own volition sought to purge himself of a charge of incontinence, and having succeeded, brought a defamation cause against the spreader of the rumour.[62] Many of these causes are trite enough, and much like that brought by William Reynold against James Cressen of Wisbech, who said to him before witnesses 'Tu es a morder man et occidisti Hamond Porfrey de Wysbech'. There are other, more significant accusations like that brought by Marion Chyldyrhoke of Wisbech against John Everard, who had attempted to prove that she was of villein status, and belonged to his manor of Fitton Hall, or the report in St Albans in 1433 that a priest in the town had defamed a spiritual son by revealing his confession.[63] The York defamation causes mostly concern the town population, and are of more substance, the proof is elaborate, and their depositions detailed and informative. In a cause of 1327 where the plaintiff had been defamed of theft, there are descriptions of business meetings among the business community in the carmelite friary at York,[64] and this can be paralleled elsewhere. In general, however, the accusations are petty enough, and one can see that a summoner would find it easy to play on personal spites in a small community, and multiply the causes in his court.

[61] YBI, MS CPE 87.
[62] *Acts of Chapter* p 33.
[63] Ely consistory probate, liber B, fols 65ᵛ, 66; Hertforshire Record Office MS ASA/1AR, fol 76.
[64] YBI, MS CPE 22.

Perjury causes are much more unpredictable. Two-thirds of the Ripon perjury business is concerned with the recovery of small debts, and entirely secular in content. At Lichfield, however, there are a number of substantial clerical causes. The dean of the collegiate church of Tamworth, for example, brought a charge of *fidei lesionis* against the two chaplains of the church, for detaining offerings contrary to their oath of obedience. On the other hand a secular gild might bring a similar charge against a refractory member as the wardens of the smiths' gild at Coventry did against a locksmith called Thomas Marton.[65] Similar charges were brought at Wisbech by aldermen or keepers or religious gilds at about the same time. A century earlier, in 1376, a chantry priest who tried to recover arrears of salary from a parochial gild at Stow Quy, found himself defender in a perjury suit for alleged breach of his agreement with the gild, and this use of the law was one which occurred to York employers of conducts in a time of labour shortages.[66] On the whole, however, the York perjury causes, like those in Ripon, were of a secular nature, the parties were citizens of York and the disputes concern debt recovery, failures to implement contracts for the supply of timber, wool or building stone, or to make payment for bitumen or woad supplied by the plaintiff, or to carry out building work.[67]

The value of these actions is demonstrated by the number of times in which they end in a compromise, or arbitration, which probably is the effect desired by the plaintiffs. The proximity of the York court undoubtedly made it a useful mercantile tool, in the absence of a convenient secular tribunal, just as the Ripon and Whalley courts served their localities, and causes of breach of contract or debt which in the southern province probably went to Chancery or King's Bench were conveniently dealt with at home.

Charges of usury, though fewer, were perhaps used by laymen in the same way, though they more often appear in corrections than as contested causes. One such contested cause has however turned up at Ely in 1378.[68] Richard Bytering, a Wisbech chaplain, lent £18 to Robert Wardale, who agreed to pay him £1 per year for three years and then to repay the principal sum. Robert carried out the terms of the agreement, but then brought an action for the recovery of the

---

[65] Lichfield Joint Record Office MS B/C/1/2, fol 16.
[66] EDR MS D2/1, fols 43ᵛ–44ᵛ; YBI, MS CPE 194, CPF 82.
[67] YBI, MSS CPE 180, 199, 204, 224; CPF 1, 52, 77, 80.
[68] EDR MS D2/1, fols 126–8.

three pounds interest, on the grounds that they were the profits of usury. The judge found the libel non proven, and the parties agreed to an arbitration, yet the defendant felt himself still threatened by the charge, and purged himself.

Religious and collegiate owners of tithes are among the most active promoters of causes for the recovery of tithes, mortuaries and burial offerings. There is however a surprising number of examples of groups of parishioners who bring actions against incumbents, hired priests, or religious houses, for failure of service, neglect of buildings, and breach of contract. There is even a case where the churchwardens and parishioners of Teversham sue a carpenter for failing to finish a repair. What is even more marked is the frequency with which one cause led to another in all these courts, as it did with the chaplain of Quy. A matrimonial cause involving three parties at Wilburton gave rise to a long series of prosecutions for clandestine celebrations of marriage, and the whole business was of sufficient general interest for an Exeter notary to copy it into his formulary.[69]

The part played by the officers of the court or the proctors and advocates in the promotion of litigation like this is rather difficult to assess. No doubt Chaucer was describing something that was common knowledge in his own day, but I have seen no evidence that similar provocation was likely in contested causes. It is true that the defamation cause against a priest who repeated a confession may have been 'inspired' and so may the Wilburton prosecutions, but these were at least concerned with serious matters of principle, and not based on spite. I suppose that the proctors in Ely causes who demanded written libels on their employers' behalf may have been acting in the interests of their fellow officials and certainly they were quick enough to bring actions for the recovery of their own fees. Perhaps there is some significance, too, in the fact that plaintiffs bringing suits against court officials seem to lose their cause, as did Agnes Pateshull, who brought a charge of prior contract against Hugh Candelsby, archdeacon's registrar, in the Ely consistory in 1376.[70] Probably proctors and advocates and registrars were suitable targets for malicious prosecutions, and there is what is obviously such a case at York in 1411, when one of the advocates of the court was cited as defendant in a matrimonial cause.[71] He wrote to John Ragnal seeking his help: –

[69] *Ibid*, fols 123, 82v–85; BM MS Harley 862, fol 199.
[70] EDR MS D2/1, fol 57v.
[71] YBI, MS CPF 63.

Dear brother, I earnestly entreat you to be good enough to represent me yourself, or find a good substitute, in our court next Monday, and ask for the postponement of my business, because I must be at Newcastle with my master. In case you cannot influence the judge in my favour, have ready an exception declining the jurisdiction of the court. Also be good enough to ask Robert Ragnal's help and favour for me.

Yours, Thomas Cleveland.

The plaintiff's cause was of course lost.

I have asked, rather than answered questions in this superficial survey. It will be seen that the field is wide, that a great deal remains to do, but I hope that I may have indicated, despite the technical difficulties involved, some ideas of the rewards that are to be gained.

THE GREEK CHURCH UNDER THE TURKS:
PROBLEMS OF RESEARCH

by STEVEN RUNCIMAN

HISTORICAL research is full of surprises and shocks. It may produce the blessings of which professor Hill has so eloquently reminded us; but it can also leave the student thwarted and disappointed. We cannot know when we embark on a subject what uncharted reefs and contrary currents are going to impede our course. A few years ago I rashly set out to work on the subject that the late professor Iorga called *Byzance après Byzance*. I hoped to tell of the fate of the Greeks and their neighbours in the orthodox christian world when they passed under the absolute rule of the infidel ottoman sultan, during the centuries when they were tended by the orthodox patriarchate of Constantinople: to which one could apply, far more accurately than to the papacy, Hobbes's description of 'the ghost of the Roman Empire sitting crowned upon the ruins thereof' – but the ruins were miserably dilapidated and the crown did not fit. I decided not to attempt a full history of the social life of the christian minorities nor a detailed discussion of theological developments but to concentrate my study on the central organisation of the patriarchate itself. Even so it proved to be a daunting task.

If I may use professor Hill's analogy, the rôle of Mary was not easy. It cannot ever be easy to interpret the religious beliefs and habits and reactions of another people living in another age, especially when they are subjected to capricious and oppressive masters. My orthodox friends tell me, kindly but firmly, that no one can truly understand the orthodox church unless he has been born and brought up in it. Sympathy and study are not enough. That may be true; but it may also be true that a sympathetic objectivity can provide a useful perspective. But there are bound to be pitfalls. As for the rôle of Martha, this is a house in which she may have tidied up all the rooms, but she has then locked some of them up and lost the keys.

Of the great churches of christendom the orthodox church is the

worst documented as regards its history, especially during the period
from the mid-fifteenth to the early nineteenth century, the period that
the Greeks call the *Tourkokratia*, the rule of the Turks. We are not too
badly informed about the church in byzantine times, though there is
not the rich documentation that illumines the church in the medieval
west. So long as a christian emperor reigned in Constantinople the
history of the church was an essential part of the history of the empire.
The byzantines, whatever their faults may have been, were genuinely
religious. They were deeply devoted to their church and deeply interested in it. At least from the eighth century onwards, every byzantine
historian and chronicler dealt fully with church affairs. He was not
always objective. He freely omitted what might not be pleasing to the
authorities of the time or what did not suit his own tastes and views.
But the sins of the byzantine historians were sins of omission, not of
commission; and it is usually easy to allow for their prejudices. Moreover, under the christian emperors ecclesiastical records were well kept.
Reqorts of the numerous synods or of imperial decrees concerning the
church were freely copied in order that the fellow-patriarchates and,
until the later middle ages, Rome might be informed of them; and
copies were sent to the chief hierarchical and monastic centres of the
empire and to the daughter-churches. In educated circles works of
theology and religious exegesis were eagerly read; and lives of the
saints were produced in profusion and always had a wide circulation.
In consequence many of them survived. Every byzantine monastery
was required to have a library whose upkeep was, officially at least,
supervised by the authorities; and there were numbers of wealthy laymen who collected books. It is remarkable that though Constantinople
itself, where the imperial record-office and the greatest libraries were
situated, was twice pillaged, once by the crusaders and once by the
Turks, and its incomparable collections of manuscripts were burnt or
scattered, yet so much material has survived, especially ecclesiastical
material. The byzantines cared about their libraries, their books and
their records. In the thirteenth century, after the crusader sack of
Constantinople, the scholar Nicephorus Blemmydas was sent round
neighbouring countries to recover what he could of the scattered
documents; and after the Turkish sack in 1453 cardinal Bessarion, the
last great byzantine-born scholar, had agents travelling through ottoman territory to buy up whatever manuscripts survived, and he
employed copyists to copy the rarer manuscripts that he possessed or
could borrow for the purpose. The result of his labours can still be seen

in the Marciana Library in Venice. Some documents survived because they had been stolen by the Venetians during the crusader sack of 1204. (The crusaders themselves preferred destruction to theft.) Again, though in the course of subsequent centuries the great monastic libraries were destroyed by the Turks, yet a number of old manuscripts were rescued by the monks as they fled away. Much seems to have perished unrecorded when finally the Greeks were ejected from Anatolia in 1922/3. But a few records were then brought to Greece; and most of the contents of the important medieval library of Soumela, near Trebizond, were preserved by the Turks and, after spending some decades in the cellars of the Turkish parliament house at Ankara, are now available to scholars. Other older manuscripts were preserved because western travellers in the eighteenth and nineteenth centuries found them neglected in decaying Greek monasteries and hastily bought or stole them before they distintegrated. But nearly all these rescued records deal with the older centuries, before the fall of Constantinople. No one bothered himself much about the later records.

Thus when we come to the history of the Greek church after the fall of Constantinople the picture is sadly different. The Greeks had become a minority race, second-class citizens who were anxious to draw as little attention to themselves as possible. Few of them could be found willing to write the history of their enslaved condition. Education decayed, as their new masters were not prepared to allow christian schools to flourish. The patriarchate of Constantinople, to which the sultan had handed over the internal administration of the orthodox *millet* (to use the Turkish term for the orthodox community or 'nation'), was continually and increasingly short of money. It could not afford to employ the armies of studious and efficient scribes that had worked for the emperor; and, indeed, not many such scribes were available.

The patriarchal records, which should have been the chief source for a history of the church under the Turks, are remarkably meagre. The patriarchate itself is not to blame for this. It was the rallying-point for the orthodox christians, and it took its duties seriously. It had its officials, headed by the *protonotarius*, whose duty it was to see that the records were properly kept. But not only did impoverishment and the decline of education hamper him in his task; the history of the patriarchal buildings added further difficulties. When sultan Mehmet II conquered Constantinople he took over the great church of Saint Sophia and the patriarchal palace and offices. When he created a new

225

patriarch, Gennadius, the patriarchate was allotted the church of the Holy Apostles, the second great cathedral of the city. But it was in a poor condition and was set in a district handed over to Turks who resented its occupation by the christians. The patriarch could neither protect it from them nor afford to repair the buildings. With the sultan's consent he moved to the smaller church of the Pammakaristos, which was in a district allotted to the Greeks; and he used the adjoining convent buildings as his offices. But in 1586 sultan Murad III arbitrarily annexed the Pammakaristos and turned it into a mosque. The patriarch suddenly found himself with nowhere to go. He was temporarily lent the small church of St Demetrius Kanavou, which belonged to the patriarch of Alexandria; but it is uncertain where the patriarchal officials and archives were housed until the church of St George in the Phanar was taken over and offices were built round it. This work was only completed in 1614. Doubtless many documents were mislaid or jettisoned during the intervening years. It is significant that there were several Greek historians writing in the sixteenth century who clearly made use of the patriarchal records, but in the seventeenth century there were none until we come to Demetrius Cantemir, whose history of the ottoman empire was compiled at the very end of the century and whose information about the Greeks seems to have been derived almost entirely from tradition or from hearsay. Eighteenth century historians seem to have been able to use patriarchal records; but many of these records are now lost. This is chiefly the result of fires. There was a bad fire in the middle of the sixteenth century, another in the mid-eighteenth century, and two in the nineteenth century. The last occurred in 1941; but fortunately by then most of the records that had so far survived had been published, notably by Michael Gedeon in the 1890s. When I looked through the patriarchal archives in the 1960s I came across very little that had not been already published or described; and some of what had been published seemed to be missing.

The archives of the eastern patriarchates provide very little help. When I asked for permission to see those of the patriarchate of Antioch I was politely informed that I would find nothing there which would interest me. The records only concerned the internal affairs of the patriarchate, and most of them were in arabic. It is true that at that moment the Syrian government was strongly xenophobe; and the patriarch, whose actual residence is in Damascus, may well have thought it impolitic to encourage a western visitor. But the impression that I gained from an earlier visit to that somewhat slipshod and impoverished institution inclines me to believe that I did not miss much. On that occasion I accompanied the poet George Seferis, who was then Greek minister to Lebanon and Syria and had been asked by his government to enquire politely why the Antioch patriarchate was receiving so much money from the Soviet Union. 'Why?' replied the patriarch. 'Because no one else has ever offered me any money.'

I must also confess that I have not seen the archives of the orthodox patriarchate of Alexandria. A number of interesting documents from it were published about a century ago by the Russian scholar Uspensky; and I am reliably told that what remains unpublished is only of local interest. The seat of the patriarchate was moved from Alexandria to Cairo early in the seventeenth century; but from the mid-sixteenth to the mid-eighteenth century the patriarch spent most of his time in Constantinople and presumably kept many of his records in offices next to his church of St Demetrius Kanavou, the church which he lent temporarily to his brother of Constantinople. But an earthquake followed by a fire in the early eighteenth century severely damaged the church and the surrounding buildings, and many of the patriarchal archives must have perished then.

In contrast, the orthodox partiarchate of Jerusalem still possesses one of the great libraries of the world. The archival material is naturally mainly concerned with local affairs; but as these include matters of wider interest, such as the ownership of the holy places, they have some bearing on the general history of orthodoxy. There seems, however, to be little there that has not been published by Russian or Greek scholars of the nineteenth century. It is worth noting that the one great Greek ecclesiastical historian during the ottoman period was a patriarch of Jerusalem, the peloponnesian Dositheus Notaras. But we cannot tell how much he depended for his work on the Jerusalem library or on libraries in Constantinople or Moldavia, where he had spent much of his life. He certainly added books and manuscripts to the Jerusalem library, as did his nephew and successor, Chrysanthos.

The Greek monastic libraries, especially those on Mount Athos, are at first sight more promising. Fire has been the chief enemy there, and, as regards the older manuscripts, the acquisitive habits of travellers from the west. But great numbers of records survive, most of them concerned with the administration of the monasteries and monastic estates. For anyone who is studying the social and economic history of the Greek countryside under the Turks they are invaluable, as they are for the history of the Holy Mountain itself; but they do not tell us very much about the patriarchate. There are also a number of theological manuscripts, though few of great interest. The contents of the libraries have now been almost all of them catalogued, though much remains unpublished.

The rock monasteries of Meteora similarly contain rich libraries, from which much has been stolen. The important historical manuscripts there have been published early in this century by the Greek scholar, Nicholas Bees; but most of them concern the later middle ages. There is a splendid library in the monastery of St John on Patmos, but its archival material is unimportant. The monastery of Megaspilaion in the Peloponnese had a good library, which was almost entirely destroyed by fire in 1936, without ever having been catalogued.

The rather meagre ecclesiastical records to be found in Bulgaria and Serbia contain little of more than local interest. Romania, however, is a far more fruitful area. The princes of Wallachia and Moldavia were autonomous vassals of the sultan and were in a position to provide valuable help to the Great Church of Constantinople. The link became closer when the Greek merchant families which began to emerge in the later sixteenth century, the so-called Phanariots, realised that they could invest their wealth safely and profitably in the principalities, and that by judicious marriage-alliances with the princely and noble families there, all of whose members were eager to marry for money, they could acquire power and influence and even a princely throne. Indeed, by the eighteenth century, when the native dynasties had died out, the thrones were reserved for the Phanariots. The princes frequently made gifts of cash or of landed estates to the patriarchate of Constantinople, and they were particularly generous to the patriarchate of Jerusalem. Greek universities and seminaries were founded in the two capitals, Bucarest and Jassy, and libraries were built up there. Romanian church records and the records of the great Greco-Romanian families, especially the Mavrocordato family (which claimed descent both from Othello and Desdemona and from Fabius Maximus Cunctator) contain valuable information, above all for the seventeenth and eighteenth centuries. They are now being collected and catalogued by the Romanian state; and it is to be hoped that they will soon be easily available. The more important of them are already published in a vast series begun in the 1870s by the Romanian scholar, de Hurmuzaki, and continued in this century by Iorga and Papadopoulos-Kerameus.

Numbers of Russian documents concerned with the Constantinopolitan patriarchate were brought to light and used by Russian ecclesiastical historians in the nineteenth century. I do not know what more there may still be in Russia nor how accessible such records are. Church history is not a very fashionable subject in modern Russia.

Ottoman records contain little about the christian minorities. To judge from them, the Turkish authorities were only interested in the taxes that they could raise from them. Imperial *firmans* confirming the election of bishops or permitting the erection or restoration of churches seem to have been handed over to the beneficiaries without any copies being kept. The library of the *Vakif*, the Pious Foundations, contains some particulars about the transformation of churches into mosques. I shall talk later about records dealing with the relations of the orthodox with the other churches of christendom.

When we come to the Greek histories and chronicles of the period, the ground seems very barren to anyone used to the historical writings of the byzantine world. They fall into two groups. The first dates from the mid-sixteenth century. Thanks to the work of his friend and correspondent, the protonotary Theodore Zygomalas, the lutheran scholar Martin Crusius received and published two histories, which he called the *Historia Politica* and the *Historia Patriarchica*, which both deal in a complementary manner with the period from 1453 to 1578. The former is a version, with additions by Zygomalas, of a chronicle known as the *Ekthesis Chronicôn*, which exists in several manuscripts. Crusius ascribes it to a certain Malaxus, who may have been only the copyist. The latter seems to be a version, with a few additions, of an unedited chronicle in the patriarchical library, traditionally ascribed to Damascenos the Studite, metropolitan of Arta, and now usually called the *Chronicle of 1570*. The problem of the authorship and interrelationship of these chronicles is a matter only of academic interest. They seem to be reliable historical sources and were so regarded by Zygomalas and his patron the patriarch Jeremias II, both of them men of great learning. The chronicle attributed to Dorotheus of Monemvasia, who probably never existed, is a version of the *Patriarchal Chronicle*, embellished by the author's prejudices, in particular his dislike of the patriarch Jeremias II. For the early years, till the death of Mehmet the Conqueror, we have the *Chronicon Majus* of Sphrantzes, which modern research has shown to have been written in its present form in the mid-sixteenth century by Macarius Melissenus. For a number of reasons I believe it to be based on a genuine work by Sphrantzes, at least from 1452 onwards, with easily detectable additions which do not detract from its historical value. The brief verse chronicle by Hierax covers the same early period, without adding anything of value to our knowledge. More interesting is the verse chronicle of archbishop Arsenius, which deals with Jeremias II's negotiations with the Russian church and his journey to Moscow.

For the seventeenth century, which is, I think, the most interesting century of the period, we have no contemporary Greek historian. The controversies of the time did, however, produce a number of theological works of great historical importance. In particular there were the statements on doctrine, such as the *Confessions* of Cyril Lucaris, of Peter Moghila and of Dositheus, all of which had an immense effect on the history of the church. Demetrius Cantemir, who was born in 1671, was certainly collecting material for historical works, chiefly from Turkish sources, before the end of the century. But his only work to survive, his *Ottoman History*, which was written in latin, was completed much later, when he was in exile in Russia; and it survives because his son, who was Russian ambassador in London, brought the manuscript there, and it was translated and published by an English clergyman, Nicholas Tindal. Dositheus of Jerusalem, who was born in 1641, must have written most of his *History of the Church of Jerusalem* before 1700. But it was only published in 1715, eight years after his death. Neither tell us much about the church of Constantinople during the seventeenth century. Cantemir is primarily concerned with Turkish affairs: while Dositheus, though he deals with the whole history of the orthodox church, is chiefly interested in refuting Roman errors and in exposing the wickedness of the jesuits.

For the eighteenth century there are three important Greek historians. Kaisarios Dapontes wrote in about 1780 a *Chronicle* which covers the period from 1648 to 1704; but it is sketchy and is of doubtful reliability. Far more useful is his *Historical Catalogue*, which goes from 1700 to 1784, and is especially valuable when he is dealing with events that occurred in his own life-time. Almost as useful, and rather more entertaining, is the *Ecclesiastical History* of Georgios Makraios, dealing with the period from 1750 to 1800, the period of his own life. He had his quirks and prejudices, which need to be watched. The third, Hypsilantis, wrote a chronicle which stretches from 1453 to 1780. It is not particularly valuable for the earlier centuries but contains useful information about the eighteenth century.

The rise of Greek nationalism at the end of the eighteenth century produced a flood of pamphlets and works of propaganda, which are of great interest in showing the temper of the time. Nearly all of them are highly critical of the patriarchate.

Not many private letters have survived. E. Legrand's magnificent *Bibliographie Hellénique* mentions all the known correspondence that dates from the sixteenth and seventeenth centuries. There are a number of eighteenth-century letters in the Romanian archives; and the letters of Dapontes have been published. None of them are of great importance. The letters of Cyril Lucaris to his foreign friends exist because they were published abroad.

The scarcity of Greek writers till the late eighteenth century is undoubtedly connected with the difficulty of having works in Greek printed. There was no Greek printing-press in Constantinople or anywhere in the ottoman provinces till then. Cyril Lucaris when patriarch had tried to set one up in 1627 with the help of the English ambassador, but the attempt was foiled by the jesuits, in alliance with the French ambassador. Greek works had to be printed abroad, chiefly in Venice, until Greek presses were set up in the principalities, in Bucarest and in Jassy, the most active being the Jerusalem Press at Jassy, founded by the patriarch Dositheus early in the eighteenth century. Most of the works published there were theological or educational; but it meant that Dositheus's own works could be published; and the presses were in general an encouragement to Greek writers.

It can thus be seen that a history of the patriarchate under the sultans which was based purely on Greek and oriental sources would leave many gaps unfilled. Fortunately these sources can be supplemented by a number of western sources, many of which are very enjoyable to read. In the diplomatic archives of the powers who kept embassies in Constantinople there are numerous references to the christian minorities, as there are in the archives of the English Levant Company. The venetian records, and those of the Greek church in Venice, are particularly helpful. When once the jesuits began to operate in the Levant, in the late sixteenth century, they sent back a sequence of extremely well-informed though usually hostile accounts of events at the patriarchate. It is no exaggeration to say that our most useful information for the history of the church in the sixteenth century comes from German authors and for the seventeenth century from English authors. I have already mentioned that two basic chronicles of the sixteenth century were first published by Martin Crusius (Kreuz) of Tübingen. They appeared as a section of his great work *Turcograecia*, published at Basle in 1584 and supplemented by a shorter work, *Germano-Graecia*, published the following year. The protonotary Theodore Zygomalas not only sent him the manuscripts of the two chronicles but also, with the help of the patriarch Jeremias II, supplied a large amount of additional information for which Crusius had asked. Crusius had been put in touch with Zygomalas by the lutheran chaplain to the ambassador from the Hapsburg court to the Sublime Porte, David von Ungnad, who happened to be a lutheran. The chaplain, Stephen Gerlach, spent many years in Turkey and later published his own very interesting diary. His successor, Salomon Schweigger, also published a diary of his life in Turkey. But, as he disliked the Greeks and had as little as possible to do with them, he does not give us much useful information. Gerlach's good relations with the patriarchate led the lutheran divines at Wittenberg to attempt to make some sort of religious union with the orthodox. These negotiations, in which the lutherans were gently snubbed by the patriarch, are only recorded in German lutheran sources. The patriarch presumably kept copies of the lutheran proposals and his replies, but those copies must have perished long ago. When an early-eighteenth century Greek scholar, Gedeon of Cyprus, wished to publish Jeremias II's letters, he had to use the German publication.

The protestant churches were interested in allying themselves with the orthodox against Rome. The lutherans achieved nothing; but the anglicans hoped for a better response. It is from English sources that we owe most of the details that we have about the most remarkable patriarch of the seventeenth century, Cyril Lucaris. The foundation of the Levant Company at the end of the previous century led to the establishment of English colonies in the sultan's dominions; and they had their chaplains, who usually took a friendly interest in the local christians. It was one of these chaplains, Thomas Smith, who gathered together all the information that he could find about Cyril and published in his *Collectanea de Cyrillo Lucario*, which appeared in 1707. Smith had only arrived in Constantinople in 1668, thirty years after Cyril's death; but he clearly had access to both English and Dutch embassy papers, to an unpublished life of Cyril by the savoyard Antoine Leger, calvinist chaplain at the Dutch embassy in Cyril's time, and to a brief published life by Hottinger, a friend of Leger's. He had talked with Edward Pococke, who had been chaplain at Aleppo and, incidentally, the first great English arabist, and who had known Cyril and been in Constantinople at the time of his death. In addition to Smith's excellent book there is information about Cyril, apart from references in a few calvinist tracts and the hostile accounts given by the catholic scholars, Allatius and Arnaud, and the jesuit records. It is true that the huguenot Aymon published a hotch-potch of information about Cyril in 1708, which included some of his letters. But his account is not nearly so careful and well-edited as Smith's.

Smith had already published, in latin in 1676 and in English in 1780, a well-informed, critical but not unsympathetic account of the Greek and Armenian Churches as he knew them. A later chaplain, John Covel, who later became master of Christ's College, Cambridge, also published in 1722, towards the end of his life, a book on the Greek church. But he disliked the Greeks, though he considered himself to be the leading authority on their religion: about which, indeed, he had amassed much information when serving in the Levant, in the intervals of making a fortune out of the silk-trade. Far deeper understanding was shown by Sir Paul Ricaut, whose account of the Greek church was published in 1680. Sir Paul had been consul at Smyrna. His book, like Smith's, is not uncritical of the church; and, though he was a layman, he had perhaps a better grasp of its difficulties. Another layman, Sir George Wheler, who travelled extensively in Greece in 1670, made many informative and friendly remarks about the church in the book that he wrote on his travels, as did his companion, the Frenchman Spon. The later abortive attempts of the anglicans, especially the non-jurors, to achieve some sort of union with the orthodox are, again, only known to us from English sources.

On the whole, travellers to the Levant in the seventeenth century showed a sympathetic interest in the Greeks and their church. In the eighteenth century, especially during its later decades, and in the first decades of the nineteenth century, the number of western travellers increased; but almost all of them regarded the Greek church with disapproval. Their books are often entertaining to read; but we would have a strange view of the church if we depended only on them. To the educated man of the time, with his rationalistic outlook, the church seemed to be steeped in superstition and to be a betrayal of the classical Greece that he so much admired. It is true that what most of the travellers saw was dirty monasteries and ignorant priests and monks in the poorer provinces; and it was not admirable. The provincial clergy were reacting against the somewhat tactless attempts of the patriarchate to reform the church while at the same time it extracted all the money that it could from the faithful; and the Greek provinces were out of touch with the genuine spiritual revival that was taking place in

Romania and Russia. And soon the whole atmosphere was made stormier by the movement towards Greek independence, which was led by anti-clerical Greeks, though passionately supported by the provincial clergy, and which put the patriarch, who on his accession had to swear allegiance to the sultan and to promise to see that the orthodox *millet* remained orderly and loyal, in a difficult position. Travellers who met the educated Greeks in Constantinople and the Romanian principalities were not much better impressed: though Dr Walsh, who was chaplain at the British embassy in Constantinople at the time of the Greek rebellion, does show an understanding of the problems of the patriarchate.

Without the help of the western sources it would be impossible to write a history of the Great Church of Constantinople in captivity. Even so, there are gaps which cannot be filled. For instance, it is impossible to establish beyond all doubt the dates and even the sequence of the various patriarchs. Perhaps this is not surprising, as there were so many of them. The custom, established before the end of the fifteenth century, of paying on every patriarchal election a fee to the sultan, known as the *peshkesh*, made the sultan eager to have as many elections as possible. A few patriarchs were put to death on flimsy charges of treason. More often the Holy Synod would be ordered to depose a patriarch, though he might later return to the throne. Cyril Lucaris was seven times patriarch, and on one occasion he was re-elected after only one week. The system was at its worst in the seventeenth century, a century for which we have few patriarchal records and no contemporary Greek historian. From 1595 to 1695 there seem to have been sixty-one patriarchal reigns; but it is impossible to sort them out with certainty. Meanwhile the *peshkesh* grew in size, the climax coming in 1726, when Callinicus III paid roughly 5,600 gold pounds for his election, and died of joy the following day. There are other gaps. Details about the patriarchal finances are scrappy and not always consistent. All that we can say for certain is that they continually deteriorated. Details about the administration of the patriarchate are similarly incomplete.

Had I been writing purely about the theology of those centuries, research would have been easier. The material is plentiful; for there was always room for another theological work in a monastic library, though many of the works remain unpublished. It would have been easier to write an account simply of the social and economic life of the Greeks of the time, with the help of Greek monastic records and a number of ottoman sources, as well as the papers of the various Levant Companies. But the history of the patriarchate itself is often clouded over, with clouds that I found impenetrable. Maybe a more ingenious researcher would have been able to clear away some of the mist. I can only say that though I often felt that it was beyond my powers to describe adequately and accurately the story of the Great Church in captivity, the effort earned its rewards. At times there was high comedy to be extracted from it. More often there was tragedy. But there was always the interest that is to be found in the study of men and women who try to maintain a religious life in a cruel and oppressive world. I hope that my studies gave me a wider knowledge and a wider understanding; and I hope that they may have helped to enlighten a handful of readers.

JOHN STRYPE AS A SOURCE FOR THE STUDY OF SIXTEENTH-CENTURY ENGLISH CHURCH HISTORY

by W. D. J. CARGILL THOMPSON

ECAUSE he was not a medievalist John Strype does not find a place in David Douglas's classic study of the golden age of English antiquarian scholarship, *English Scholars 1660–1730*.[1] Yet in terms both of his output and of his influence on the subsequent development of the study of English church history Strype is arguably one of the most important scholars that the age produced. Even to-day, nearly 250 years after his death, the twenty-five volumes of his works in the Clarendon press reissue of the 1820s are still a standard source for the study of English church history in the sixteenth century and it is difficult to open a book dealing with any aspect of the English reformation, which does not have its quota of references to Strype. At the same time, as any one who works on the period knows, Strype's standing as an ecclesiastical historian is ambiguous. If, on the one hand, he is widely quoted, on the other, he is frequently attacked for his mistakes and his works are notoriously full of pitfalls for the unwary. It is therefore perhaps appropriate, in a volume devoted to 'the Sources, Materials and Methods of Ecclesiastical History', to consider, first, what is Strype's value to-day as a source for the study of the English reformation and, secondly, the question of his reliability as a church historian. The two questions, one should stress, are distinct, although they are not unrelated.

As a scholar Strype belongs in the antiquarian tradition of the late seventeenth and early eighteenth centuries. He was born in 1643, the youngest son of a prosperous Dutch merchant who had settled in London and married an English wife and who died while Strype was a child.[2] After receiving his education at St Paul's school and Jesus and

---

[1] David C. Douglas, *English Scholars 1660–1730* (2 ed London 1951).
[2] For the details of Strype's life, see *DNB; Biographia Britannica* (London 1747–66) VI, i, pp 3847–50. The latter contains an interesting account of the circumstances of Strype's appointment as minister of Leyton (p 3847, n A).

St Catharine's colleges, Cambridge, he took orders in 1666 and almost the entire remainder of his life – from 1669 until his death in 1737 at the age of ninety-four – was spent as minister of the parish of Leyton in Essex, a post which he combined for many years with that of lecturer at nearby Hackney. Strype's father had left him in comfortable circumstances[3] and he was able to devote his life to the study of ecclesiastical antiquities – in particular, to collecting and transcribing records relating to the history of the English reformation. Although he had been gathering materials for many years, Strype's first historical work, the *Memorials of Thomas Cranmer*, was not published until 1694, when he was already over fifty. But thereafter he emerged as one of the most prolific scholars of the age. The life of Cranmer was followed by the lives of sir Thomas Smith (1698), bishop Aylmer (1701), and sir John Cheke (1705). Then in quick succession came the first part of the *Annals of the Reformation* (1709), the lives of Grindal (1710), Parker (1711) and Whitgift (1717–18), his edition of Stow's *Survey of London* (1720) and the three volumes of *Ecclesiastical Memorials* (1721), covering the history of the reformation in England during the reigns of Henry VIII, Edward VI and Mary – all published in the short space of twelve years. Finally, between 1725 and 1731, when he was in his eighties, he brought out three further volumes of the *Annals,* carrying the narrative down to 1589 and the records to the death of Elizabeth.

Strype's professed aim as an historian was to base his work on original sources. As he put it in the preface to the second edition of the *Annals,* 'My relations of things are not hearsays, nor taken up at second hand, or compiled out of other men's published writings; but I have gone as near the fountain-head as possible; that is, to archives, state-papers, registers, records, and original letters, or else to books of good credit printed in those times; directing more surely to the knowledge how affairs then stood.'[4] Although by modern standards Strype's scholarship was defective, he was an indefatigable collector of records and he had access to all the major collections of his own day, as well as to many smaller private collections. Among the more important collections that he used were the State Paper office, the Cotton library (before the fire), the Petyt manuscripts now in the Inner Temple, archbishop Parker's manuscripts at Corpus Christi college, Cambridge, and the

---

[3] See the extract from the letter of Strype to Dr Samuel Knight, 19 January 1729, printed in *Gentleman's Magazine* (London 1791) i, p 223.

[4] [John] Strype, *Annals [of the Reformation and Establishment of Religion, and other various occurrences in the Church of England, during Queen Elizabeth's Happy Reign],* 4 vols in 7 (Oxford 1824) I, i, p vii.

registers of the archbishops of Canterbury at Lambeth, while in the early years of the eighteenth century he acquired the entrée to the Harleian library, then in process of formation.[5] Apart from those collections that he explored himself, he corresponded with scholars such as Thomas Baker, Ralph Thoresby and bishop Moore, who sent him transcripts of documents, while, as his reputation grew, strangers would write to him volunteering to lend him papers in their possession.[6] In addition, he built up an important collection of original manuscripts of his own, which provided him with much of the material that he used.

Strype's two most important coups were the acquisition of the papers of John Foxe, the martyrologist, and of that part of lord Burghley's papers which had passed into the possession of Burghley's secretary, sir Michael Hickes, and thence by descent to Hickes's grandson, sir William Hickes of Ruckholt – both of which he used extensively in his works. Both these collections came into Strype's ownership under somewhat dubious circumstances. The Foxe papers were originally lent to Strype in the 1680s or 1690s by his friend, William Willys of Hackney, the cousin and executor of sir Richard Willys, 1st baronet, who had married Foxe's great-granddaughter, Alice. Strype retained possession of them and, after the death of the second baronet, Foxe's last surviving descendant, in 1701, he treated them as his own private property.[7] Later, between 1709 and 1711, he sold the bulk of them to Robert Harley and they are now among the Harleian manuscripts in the British Museum.[8] The history of the Burghley papers is similar,

---

[5] Strype was granted permission to use the Harleian library on 26 May 1707; see [*The Diary of Humphrey*] *Wanley* [*1715–1726*, ed C. E. and Ruth Wright], The Bibliographical Society, 2 vols (London 1966) I, Intr, p xxi.

[6] Strype's correspondence, which contains numerous letters from contemporaries relating to his historical collections, is preserved in the Baumgartner MSS in the Cambridge University Library. See *A Catalogue of the Manuscripts preserved in the Library of the University of Cambridge* (Cambridge 1856–67) V, pp 1–159.

[7] J. F. Mozley states that the Willys family 'lent' the Foxe papers to Strype, J. F. Mozley, *John Foxe and his Book* (London 1940) p ix; and this appears to be confirmed by Strype's own remark in the preface to his *Cranmer* (1694) that 'I have been conversant in what remaineth of the papers of John Fox, communicated to me by the favour of my good friend William Willys, of Hackney, Esquire,' [John] Strype, [*Memorials of the Most Reverend Father in God Thomas*] *Cranmer, [Sometime Lord Archbishop of Canterbury*], 2 vols (Oxford 1840) I, pp xiii–xiv. Later, however, in a statement made after all the parties concerned were dead, he claimed that they 'were given me long since by Mr Will. Willis of Hackney deceased, who was Executor to Sr Richard. Willis Kt. yt married ye Heir of Foxes Family'; see [Cambridge University Library, Baumgartner MSS, Patrick Papers, vol 40, no 7], 'Mr Strypes Case' [August 1714] p 4.

but rather more complicated. Ruckholt, the seat of the Hickes family, was in Strype's parish of Leyton and sir William Hickes allowed Strype to make extensive use of them. In or about 1682 Strype persuaded Hickes to sell them to the printer, Richard Chiswell (who published the *Memorials of Cranmer* in 1694), who undertook to publish them from transcripts to be prepared by Strype.[9] In the event, the edition was never published and, after Hicke's death in 1703, the manuscripts remained in Strype's possession until his own death in 1737, when they were sold by his executors to the antiquary, James West. Eventually, after West's death in 1772, they were purchased by lord Shelburne, afterwards first marquess of Lansdowne,[10] so that they too, like the Foxe manuscripts, are now in the British Museum.

What gives Strype's works their lasting value as a source for the study of the English reformation is that he did not simply use this mass of documentary material as the basis for his own narrative: he made a point of reprinting original records wherever possible, with the result that his works are an important repository of the raw materials of tudor church history. It might be assumed that in the 250 years since Strype's death much of this material would have found its way into print in some other form. But surprisingly this is not the case. Although most of the collections that Strype used are familiar to modern historians, the greater part of the documents that he prints has never been properly edited since his own day. To cite only one example, whereas the Burghley papers at Hatfield have been excellently edited in the *Calendar of the Manuscripts of the Marquis of Salisbury* published by the Historical Manuscripts Commission,[11] no attempt has been made to publish the Burghley manuscripts in the Lansdowne collection, for which the only guide is the *Catalogue of the Lansdowne Manuscripts*, published in 1819. Consequently, for many important documents relating to the tudor period Strype's works are still the most accessible printed source and it is not surprising that scholars frequently tend to

---

[8] See *Wanley*, I, pp xxi–xxii, and C. E. Wright, *Fontes Harleiani*, British Museum Bicentenary Publications (London 1972) p 321. The remainder of the Foxe papers, which Strype retained in his possession, were sold with the Burghley papers and are now in the Lansdowne collection.

[9] The exact details of this transaction are obscure. For Strype's version of this episode, see 'Mr Strypes Case'.

[10] *A Catalogue of the Lansdowne Manuscripts in the British Museum* (London 1819) preface, p ix.

[11] Historical Manuscripts Commission, *Calendar of the Manuscripts of the Most Hon. The Marquis of Salisbury, K.G., &c., preserved at Hatfield House, Hertfordshire*, in progress (London 1883–) vols 1–8.

quote these documents from Strype instead of going back to the originals in the British Museum or elsewhere. In addition, Strype also preserves the texts of some documents which he was lent by private individuals but which have since disappeared.

Unfortunately, by modern standards Strype has considerable deficiencies as an editor and transcriber of documents. In the first place, his treatment of records tends to be haphazard. Following a practice adopted by bishop Burnet in his *History of the Reformation*,[12] he usually prints the longer and more important documents in appendices, which fill a substantial part of each volume. But he also prints many documents in the text. When the records are given in the appendices, they are generally printed more or less verbatim, although on occasion he omits passages either because of the length of the document or because he did not consider it sufficiently interesting to transcribe in full. On the other hand, when he cites a document in the main body of his narrative, his practice varies. Sometimes, particularly if it is short, he prints it in full. On other occasions, he paraphrases it or turns it into *oratio obliqua* or only gives abbreviated extracts, so that – although the gist of the document may be recorded – it is not in a form which can easily be used by the modern scholar who wishes to quote from it.

Secondly, his system of references is, by modern standards, extremely vague. Although there are exceptions, he usually only cites the collection from which a document comes. For example, an item from the Foxe or Burghley papers may be cited simply as *MSS. Foxii* or *MSS. Burghlian.* or sometimes just as *MSS. ecclesiast. penes me.* However, this is an inconvenience rather than a serious drawback, since it is usually possible, with the aid of the relevant library catalogue, to track down the item that Strype is referring to without too much difficulty.

A much more serious fault is that, although Strype prided himself on the care he took in copying manuscripts,[13] in practice his transcriptions are frequently inaccurate and sometimes misleading. As anyone who has had occasion to check Strype's printed version of a document against his original source will know, S. R. Maitland was hardly

---

[12] In the preface to his *Cranmer*, Strype claims to be modelling himself on 'a good practice first begun by Mr. Sumner of Canterbury' in his *Antiquities of Canterbury*, (i.e. William Somner, *The Antiquities of Canterbury. Or a Survey of that Ancient Citie, with the Suburbs, and Cathedrall*, London 1640) *Cranmer*, p xv.

[13] See John Strype, *Ecclesiastical Memorials, relating chiefly to Religion, and the Reformation of it, and the Emergencies of the Church of England, under King Henry VIII, King Edward VI, and Queen Mary I*, 3 vols in 6 (Oxford 1822) I, i, preface, pp xii–xiii.

exaggerating when he wrote, in a devastating critique of the first volume of the Ecclesiastical History Society's edition of the *Memorials of Thomas Cranmer*, of 'Strype's loose, inaccurate, mode of copying, and his great liability to mistake'.[14] Words are often misread; phrases and passages are omitted without any indication that this is the case; occasionally, even, documents are conflated to the confusion of subsequent readers of Strype's works.[15] On the other hand, as Maitland himself pointed out in the same review, part of the explanation for Strype's frequent inaccuracies lies in the fact that in many cases he had made his original notes and transcripts several years before he came to prepare his material for publication, with the result that by that time 'he had in a great degree forgotten what they were about, and whether they were extracts, abstracts, or full copies'.[16] Consequently, as a general rule, one can say that Strype is likely to be more accurate when he is quoting from manuscripts in his own possession, such as the Foxe or Burghley papers, than when he is relying on notes and transcripts compiled several years earlier; but even in the case of the Burghley papers I have found from my own experience that mistakes are not infrequent. The conclusion to be drawn from this is that it is always hazardous to assume that the text of a document printed in Strype is reliable and it is advisable, wherever possible, to check Strype's version against the original. Fortunately, this is not such a daunting task as might appear at first sight, for most of the documents Strype used are readily accessible and it is usually possible to identify a specific item without great difficulty.

It is as a general historian, however, that Strype's weaknesses are most pronounced and in some respects more dangerous: for, owing to the enormous prestige which his works enjoyed in the eighteenth and nineteenth centuries, his statements have often been accepted uncritically by later church historians and many traditional misconceptions about the English reformation turn out on investigation to have been fathered by Strype.

Some of Strype's limitations as an historian are those of his age. In the first place, like most seventeenth-century antiquaries, he was an undiscriminating collector of facts and this is compounded by the fact that he followed the contemporary convention of writing his histories

---

[14] [S. R.] Maitland, *Remarks [on the First Volume of Strype's Life of Archbishop Cranmer, recently published by the Ecclesiastical History Society]* reprinted from the *British Magazine* (London 1848) p 4.

[15] For examples from Strype's *Cranmer*, see Maitland, *Remarks*, pp 5 *et seq.*

[16] *Ibid* p 10.

in the form of annals. In Strype's works, the materials are assembled not by topic but by year, with the result that a great deal of miscellaneous information tends to be jumbled together with little attempt at organisation, while conversely no attempt is made to follow an issue through if it involves events falling in different years. While it would be anachronistic to blame Strype for not breaking away from the annalistic tradition, it undoubtedly helped to encourage the magpie element in his nature which led him to treat the accumulation of facts as an end in itself.

Secondly, he was a man of strong prejudices, which are always close to the surface in his writings. Above all, he was a staunch and complacent anglican. He was sublimely convinced that the English reformation had been brought about by the direct intervention of divine providence and in a sense he saw the function of his books as being to inculcate in his readers a due sense of gratitude to the Almighty for his benevolence in establishing the church of England. 'He that readeth and weigheth this history', he writes in the preface to the *Annals*, 'will see great reason to acquiesce in the reformation of our church, and to be a peaceable and thankful member of it; and be convinced what a mighty hand of God overruled in this blessed work, and overthrew all opposition before it.'[17] Not surprisingly he was strongly anti-catholic. More significantly, he tended to be equally anti-puritan. When writing about the controversies of Elizabeth's reign, his sympathies are always with the establishment, while the puritans are depicted as innovators and trouble-makers. An interesting study could, in fact, be made of Strype's use of language, for his vocabulary reflects his prejudices. Episcopacy, for example, is 'the ancient wholesome government used in' the church.[18] Whitgift is 'this vigilant and industrious Prelate',[19] 'our useful Bishop',[20] or 'our careful Archbishop'.[21] By contrast, the puritans are 'the innovators',[22] 'this faction',[23] 'the malecontent party';[24] Cartwright is 'the great ring leader of disorders and disturbances' in the

---

[17] Strype, *Annals*, I, i, p viii.
[18] *Ibid* I, ii, p 372.
[19] [John] Strype, [*The Life and Acts of John*] *Whitgift*, [*D.D., the third and last Lord Archbishop of Canterbury in the Reign of Queen Elizabeth*], 3 vols (Oxford 1822) I, p 227.
[20] *Ibid* p 213.
[21] *Ibid* p 530.
[22] Strype, *Annals* I, ii, p 372.
[23] *Ibid.*
[24] Strype, *Whitgift*, I, p 347.

university of Cambridge;[25] Robert Beal is 'one of the heads and patrons of this disaffected party',[26] and so on.

Strype's biases, however, are so obvious that they can easily be guarded against. A much more serious failing – since his mistakes are not always immediately apparent – is that as an historian he was both careless and given to indulging in speculation. On the credit side, it should be said that Strype frequently uses some such phrase as 'if I mistake not' or 'as I conjecture', when he is putting forward his own suppositions, and sometimes his guesses are right. But often they are wrong – and they are wrong because he was hasty and did not take sufficient care in reading his sources. In his critique of the Ecclesiastical History Society's edition of the *Memorials of Thomas Cranmer*, S. R. Maitland assembled a long list of factual mistakes which were directly attributable to Strype's slipshod handling of Cranmer's *Register*.[27] Many of these mistakes are trivial – such as giving the wrong name or the wrong diocese for a bishop involved at a consecration or declaring that a fact is omitted from the *Register*, when it is clearly mentioned – but, especially when taken together, they indicate how unreliable Strype can be on points of detail.

Some of Strype's errors, however, are more serious, because they came to be widely accepted by later historians and they have bedevilled the subsequent interpretation of sixteenth-century English church history. In many cases these errors are due to the fact that Strype misread or misunderstood his original sources. Since I have mainly used Strype as a source for the elizabethan period, I would like to cite two classic instances from the *Annals* and the *Life of Whitgift* – his account of the making of the elizabethan prayer book and his treatment of Richard Bancroft's Paul's Cross sermon.

In the first volume of the *Annals* Strype prints two documents, which have since become famous – *The Device for alteration of religion, in the first year of queen Elizabeth* and the letter, attributed to Edmund Guest, concerning a proposed revision of the prayer book.[28] Strype believed – wrongly, as we now know – that the *Device* represented the official programme which was adopted for the settlement of religion at the beginning of Elizabeth's reign and he, therefore, assumed, as a matter of course, that the committee of divines named in the *Device*

[25] *Ibid* p 38.
[26] *Ibid* p 301.
[27] Maitland, *Remarks*, esp pp 9–13.
[28] Strype, *Annals*, I, ii, Appendix, pp 392–8 and pp 459–64.

for revising the prayer book was actually appointed and that it was this group which drew up the 1559 prayer book.[29] To be fair to Strype, he did not originate this idea which can be traced back through Burnet to Camden. [30] But so convinced was he that the *Device* was followed that at a later stage he gives a vivid description of how 'great pains had been used in reviewing of the old Common Prayer Book' and 'in this business the divines, Dr. Sandys, Dr. Bill, and the rest above mentioned, were diligently employed at sir Thomas Smith's house in Westminster'[31] – a claim for which there is not the slightest evidence, although it was generally accepted on Strype's authority until quite recently. (Incidentally – and this is typical of Strype's capacity for making minor errors – Sandys was not one of the divines named in the *Device*, whom, in fact, he lists correctly on an earlier page.)[32] At the same time, Strype had also come across among the Parker correspondence at Corpus the unsigned and undated letter, commenting on proposals for a revision of the prayer book, which he attributed to Edmund Guest, and he, therefore, jumped to the conclusion that Guest must have been added to the committee of divines, named in the *Device*, at Cecil's instigation and 'that the main care of the revisal and preparation of the book lay upon that reverend divine, whom I suppose Parker recommended to the secretary to supply his absence'.[33] The precise significance, date and even authorship of this letter are still a matter of debate among historians and it would take too long to discuss the matter in detail here.[34] What is quite clear, however, from the text of the letter is that, whatever proposals it does refer to, it does not refer to the prayer book which was established by the act of uniformity. Consequently, there is no evidence to show that Guest – if he was the writer of the letter – was involved in the making of the 1559 prayer book, as finally drawn up – much less that he was the principal author of it, as Strype has misled generations of historians into supposing.

[29] *Ibid* I, i, pp 74–6.

[30] Gilbert Burnet, *The History of the Reformation of the Church of England*, 4 vols in 7 (Oxford 1829) II, i, pp 754–7, and II, ii, pp 459–64; William Camden, *The History of the Most Renowned and Victorious Princess Elizabeth, Late Queen of England* (4 ed London 1688) p 16.

[31] Strype, *Annals*, I, i, p 119.   [32] *Ibid* p 75.   [33] *Ibid* pp 120–1.

[34] The most recent scholar to investigate the problem is W. P. Haugaard, who considers that Guest was the author of the letter but that it relates to an earlier scheme by Elizabeth for adopting the 1549 prayer book as the basis of the 1559 settlement. See W. P. Haugaard, *Elizabeth and the English Reformation* (Cambridge 1968) p 109 and 'The Proposed Liturgy of Edmund Guest', *Anglican Theological Review*, 46 (Evanston 1964) pp 177–89.

The case of Bancroft's Paul's Cross sermon is very similar. In an earlier article some years ago I showed that the origins of the popular belief that Bancroft's sermon represented the first statement by a post-reformation anglican divine of the *jure divino* theory of episcopacy can be traced back directly to Strype's account of the sermon in the *Life of Whitgift* and the *Annals*: for, although Strype did not go as far as later writers, he was the first person to state that Bancroft had asserted that bishops enjoyed their authority by divine right.[35] Significantly, earlier historians, such as Heylin and Collier, had not interpreted Bancroft's sermon in this way. Strype was led to do so, partly because he had apparently not read the sermon itself, but mainly because he once again carelessly misinterpreted a piece of documentary evidence. In this case, he rashly assumed that a syllogism by sir Francis Knollys, attacking an unnamed preacher for maintaining that bishops enjoyed their superior authority '*iure divino*', must refer to Bancroft's sermon, when, in fact – as he should have observed – it explicitly referred to a sermon preached on a different date.[36]

What these examples show – and they could be multiplied endlessly – is that it is dangerous to take any statement by Strype on trust or to cite him as an authority unless one can corroborate his remarks from another source. For even when, as is usually the case, his statements appear to be founded on solid documentary evidence, there is always a strong possibility that he may have misinterpreted his sources or introduced some error that was not in the original. Even on minor points of fact, where it might seem reasonable to assume that he would be reliable, there is no guarantee that this is the case and, indeed, there is a considerable statistical likelihood that he will make a mistake. Thus, as a general rule, one should never quote an unverified statement by Strype as authoritative, for his accuracy can never be taken for granted. For the same reason, it is important, when reading older books on sixteenth-century English church history, especially those written in the nineteenth century, to check their sources, for in many cases they contain misstatements which ultimately derive from Strype.

So far my remarks may appear to have been mainly critical. Yet, in summing up, it is important to stress how much the modern historian of the English reformation owes to Strype. Strype may not have been a very accurate scholar and he may have misled posterity by his mis-

---

[35] W. D. J. Cargill Thompson, 'A Reconsideration of Richard Bancroft's Paul's Cross Sermon of 9 February 1588/9', *JEH*, 20 (1969) esp pp 253–6.
[36] *Ibid* pp 255–6.

takes, but more than any other historian he laid the foundations for the modern study of sixteenth-century English church history through his collections of original records and documents and the measure of his achievement is the extent to which his books are still quoted to-day. Ideally, what is needed is a new annotated edition of Strype, such as S. R. Maitland called for over a hundred years ago,[37] which would correct his errors, provide accurate texts of the documents he cites and give adequate references to the sources he used. However, this would be a formidable undertaking and it is unlikely that, even with the resources of modern scholarship, it will ever be carried out. Meanwhile, even in their present form, his works remain an unrivalled source of documentary material and miscellaneous information relating to the English reformation, provided that they are handled with proper care.

---

[37] S. R. Maitland, *Notes on Strype* (Gloucester 1858) which contains a draft pro-spectus which he had compiled some years earlier for a new edition of Strype's *Works*, which was never published.

THE RECUSANT VIEW OF THE
ENGLISH PAST

W. B. PATTERSON

THE English roman catholic, or recusant, community of the late sixteenth and early seventeenth centuries has proved to be of considerable interest to historians in recent years for political, economic, and social reasons.[1] But the community was intellectually important, too, having produced theological and devotional works which had a considerable impact upon the reading public, protestant as well as roman catholic, in England and on the continent.[2] The recusants, however, were not content to argue their case on the basis of theology and the scriptures, but turned, as cardinal Baronius and cardinal Bellarmine were doing during these years, to the evidence of history. It was by no means the least of their achievements – though it is one which has been little noted – that they developed a distinctive view of their nation's past and helped to launch an intensive investigation of some of the most important problems in English ecclesiastical history.[3]

The theoretical foundation for their work may be said to have been laid in the earliest years of the reformation era by Thomas More, bishop John Fisher, and, paradoxically, king Henry VIII. It was in the anti-lutheran writings of these Englishmen that the view was developed

---

[1] John Bossy, 'The Character of Elizabethan Catholicism', *PP*, 21 (1962) pp 39–59; Lawrence Stone, *The Crisis of the Aristocracy, 1558–1641* (Oxford 1965) pp 725–45; Patrick McGrath, *Papists and Puritans under Elizabeth I* (London 1967) pp 57–72, 100–24, 161–204, 253–99.

[2] Some of their more significant contributions are noted in A. C. Southern, *Elizabethan Recusant Prose, 1559–1582* (London 1950). For a detailed list of their English writings, see [*A Catalogue of Catholic Books in English, Printed Abroad or Secretly in England, 1558–1640*, ed A. F.] Allison and [D. M.] Rogers (Bognor Regis 1956).

[3] The fullest treatment of their importance in the historical area – treating mainly their views on antiquity – is in [Pontien] Polman, *L'élément historique [dans la controverse religieuse du XVIᵉ siècle,]* Catholic University of Louvain, Dissertations in Theology, ser 2, vol 23 (Gembloux 1932) *passim*. See also George H. Tavard, *Holy Writ or Holy Church: The Crisis of the Protestant Reformation* (London 1959) pp 131–6, 210–44.

that the scriptural record could only be adequately understood in the light of the teachings and practices of the church, especially in ancient times. Even before the outbreak of the reformation, More had advocated, in a way which strongly suggested the influence of his humanist interests, that one should pay the closest attention to the writings of the ancient fathers in formulating a 'positive theology'.[4] Later, in the course of his controversy with the protestant William Tyndale, he went on to argue that God's revelation to his people was not restricted to what was contained in the pages of the scriptures, but had been continued in the church, under the guidance of the Holy Spirit.[5] In a rather similar way, Henry VIII viewed antiquity as a guide to the apprehension of christian truth when he stressed, against Luther's *Babylonian Captivity of the Church*, that the practices and beliefs which Luther viewed as modern inventions because they were not described in the scriptures, could be traced back to the earliest times, and were thus of apostolic or even dominical authority.[6] Fisher, in defending the king against Luther's subsequent reply, attempted to go even further in finding support for catholic doctrines in the fathers, councils, and traditions of the early church.[7] Among all three, the conviction was strong that history provided an arsenal of evidence which could be used to defend the church against protestant attacks. Recusant writers fully shared this conviction, even when it seemed that their citadel, at least in England, had been all but overrun.

The particular interpretation which was to underlie the historical publications of recusant writers was also developed in Henry VIII's reign, though by a famous exile from the henrician court. Reginald Pole, a cousin of the king's, who had found himself rather uncomfortably involved in presenting Henry's marriage case before the Sorbonne for judgement in 1530, received permission in 1532 to leave England for the continent.[8] Henry subsequently solicited Pole's views on the

[4] See [André] Prévost, *Thomas More*, [*1477–1535, et la crise de la pensée européenne*] (Paris 1969) pp 131–41, 363–7. More's advice was contained in a letter to his friend Martin van Dorp, in the Netherlands, in 1515.

[5] Prévost, *Thomas More* pp 167–96, 233–87. See, for example, *The English Works of Sir Thomas More*, ed W. E. Campbell and A. W. Reed, II: *The Dialogue concerning Tyndale* (London 1931) pp 63–128.

[6] Polman, *L'élément historique* pp 293, 352. Henry VIII's *Assertio septem sacramentorum adversus Martin. Lutherum* (London 1521) is dated 12 July 1521.

[7] For Fisher's defence of the king against Luther's attack, which had appeared in Wittenberg in 1522, see Edward Surtz, *The Works and Days of John Fisher* (Cambridge, Mass. 1967) pp 11–13, 320–36.

[8] For Pole's life and the circumstances of his departure from England, see Wilhelm Schenk, *Reginald Pole: Cardinal of England* (London 1950) pp 1–30, and Dermot

validity of his marriage to Anne Boleyn, an event which had plunged him into what seemed to be intractable difficulties with the papacy. Pole's reply did not come until 1536, and was both longer and more outspoken than the king had expected.[9]

In his reply, Pole came, almost at once, to what was for him the heart of the matter, namely 'this new dignity which you have just taken, which no one before had usurped: the attributes and the title of supreme head of the Church of England'.[10] Such a headship was manifestly impossible, being contrary to the establishment of the church by Christ on the foundation of the apostle Peter, and to the affirmation by the church that the petrine supremacy belonged to the roman pontiffs, as Peter's successors. Moreover, the action which Henry had taken threatened immense harm to the church in England.[11] When Pole finally took up the question of the king's marriage, he stated frankly that the king had tired of the wife with whom he had lived for twenty years, and had experienced a 'lamentable passion' for a young woman. She, having learned by the example of her sister how quickly the king left his mistresses, contrived to put herself in a stronger position as his wife. The divine law which the king had cited as an impediment to his marriage with queen Catherine was merely a pretext.[12] Henry's reign, which had begun so promisingly, was now threatened by disorder and the problem of an uncertain succession. Even more serious was the fact that the king had 'rendered uncertain the dogmas of our faith', with the most dangerous consequences.[13] Returning to the king's pretended title, Pole declared it was particularly inappropriate for one who had pillaged and despoiled the church, as Henry had done, and had tortured and executed the church's faithful servants. In truth, Pole declared,

---

B. Fenlon, *Heresy and Obedience in Tridentine Italy: Cardinal Pole and the Counter Reformation* (Cambridge 1972) pp 24–44.

[9] Pole's treatise was sent to the king in May 1536; the first printed edition was issued in Rome in 1539. Other editions were published in Strasburg in 1555 and in Ingolstadt in 1587. For a modern edition with critical apparatus, see [Reginald] Pole, *Défense de l'unité de l'église, [en quatre livres,]* ed Noelle-Marie Egretier (Paris 1967).

[10] [Reginald] Pole, *Pro ecclesiasticae vnitatis defensione, [libri quatuor, in quibus conatus est maximo studio Ecclesiae Romanae Primatum constabilire]* (Strasburg 1555) fol 1; *Défense de l'unité de l'église* p 51.

[11] Pole, *Pro ecclesiasticae vnitatis defensione* fols 1–51; *Défense de l'unité de l'église* pp 51–205.

[12] Pole, *Pro ecclesiasticae vnitatis defensione* fols 53ᵛ–54ᵛ; *Défense de l'unité de l'église* pp 212–16.

[13] Pole, *Pro ecclesiasticae vnitatis defensione* fols 56–8; *Défense de l'unité de l'église* pp 220–5.

there were two churches, and Henry had shown himself to be the head, not of that of Christ, but that of Satan. For the sake of England and of christendom, Henry should return to the faith and obedience of the true church of Christ.[14]

Pole's treatise on the unity of the church suggested not only an interpretation of the origins of the English reformation, but a view of its significance in relation to the centuries of English history which had gone before.[15] The development and elaboration of this understanding was the work of recusant writers whose investigations spanned the centuries between the time of Christ and the decisive events of the sixteenth century. By the study of history, these writers felt, the nation could find its way back to the heritage of faith and practice which some of its leaders had so perversely rejected.

Pole's brief account of the circumstances surrounding the beginning of the reformation in Henry VIII's reign was greatly expanded later in the century by Nicholas Sanders, one of a remarkable group of exiles from England during Elizabeth's reign. Sanders was a militant opponent of the queen and her religious policies and had tried, during the reconvened council of Trent, to secure her excommunication and deposition. He ended his life in 1581 in a vain attempt to foment a rebellion in Ireland which would overthrow the English government. Sanders's account of the English reformation was left unfinished at his death, but was continued and prepared for the press by a fellow priest, Edward Rishton. Sanders's and Rishton's *De origine et progressu schismatis anglicani* appeared in Cologne in 1585, and subsequently in Rome. Translations were published in French, German, Italian, and Spanish. The *Anglican Schism* became, on the continent, a standard work.[16]

Sanders's account of the English reformation of the sixteenth century was related within a broader historical framework, though the earlier centuries were only briefly described. Christianity had come to Britain,

---

[14] Pole, *Pro ecclesiasticae vnitatis defensione* fols 58–60, 84–96; *Défense de l'unité de l'église* pp 225–31, 305–42.

[15] The importance of Pole's treatise for the development of the roman catholic view of the English reformation is discussed in B. H. G. Wormald, 'The Historiography of the English Reformation', *Historical Studies*, 2, ed T. Desmond Williams (London 1958) pp 50–8.

[16] For Sanders's career and his work as a theologian and historian, see Thomas McNevin Veech, *Dr Nicholas Sanders and the English Reformation, 1530–1581*, University of Louvain, Publications in History and Philology, ser 2, fasc 32 (Louvain 1935), and [Nicolas] Sanders, *Rise and Growth of the Anglican Schism*, ed and trans David Lewis (London 1877) pp xiii–xxix. For an account of the movement of English Catholics abroad, see Peter Guilday, *The English Catholic Refugees on the Continent, 1558–1795* (London 1914).

he said, in the first and second centuries, and had been firmly planted among the pagan Anglo-Saxons by the roman mission led by Augustine. From the conversion of king Ethelbert to almost the twenty-fifth year of the reign of king Henry VIII, or for nearly a thousand years, the roman catholic faith had been the religion of England. Now that faith had been suppressed, and attempts made to introduce in its stead the zwinglian and calvinist heresies, the first under king Edward VI, the second under queen Elizabeth. How was it possible for such beliefs to be promulgated in a land formerly faithful to the catholic church? The explanation was to be found in the schism of Henry VIII.[17]

The picture given of king Henry in Sanders's pages is unflattering, to say the least, though Sanders does see in his character some appealing features. Henry is given credit for trying to preserve many of the fundamental catholic doctrines of the faith even after the rupture with Rome, and he is described as honouring the holy sacrament to the end of his life. What led him astray was his desire to put away his lawful wife, Catherine, having been tempted to do so by a suggestion put to him on the instigation of cardinal Wolsey, who wanted to conclude a French marriage alliance. The idea fell on fertile ground, but with un-expected consequences; Henry was attracted to Anne Boleyn, and became determined to marry her. To accomplish this end, he went to absurd lengths, involving himself in bigamy, and ultimately taking England away from the roman communion. Sanders believed that the match with Anne was all the more reprehensible, as well as being un-canonical, because Henry had had sexual relations with Anne's sister and with her mother as well. He even reported as fact that Henry was the father of the young woman he proposed to marry.[18]

If Henry does not come out of Sanders's story untarnished, neither do a number of his contemporaries, whether of a protestant or catholic persuasion. The great bulk of the catholic clergy and laity of England are found to be at fault for having acquiesced in the king's declaration of supremacy over the English church. But if much of the nation was involved in apostasy, there had been some, at least, who had remained faithful. Sanders's work is in part a catholic martyrology, chronicling the brave deaths of those who refused to acknowledge the royal

---

[17] [Nicolas] Sanders, *De origine ac progressu schismatis anglicani* (Cologne 1585) Sig. a iiij–a v verso; *Rise and Growth of the Anglican Schism* pp cxlv–cxlvii.
[18] Sanders, *De origine ac progressu schismatis anglicani* pp 14–16; *Rise and Growth of the Anglican Schism* pp 22–5.

supremacy. Prominent among these martyrs was Thomas More, formerly the lord chancellor of England, in whom Sanders saw remarkable qualities. He was a layman – but such a layman as the nation had never seen before. All England, said Sanders, mourned the death of Thomas More, regarding the blow of the executioner 'as having fallen not so much upon the martyr of Christ as upon itself'.[19] With More, the reader is led to believe, far more had been eclipsed than a single choice spirit and valiant believer.

Sanders saw the very form of the succession after Henry as a divine judgement on the schism. In order to show how unworkable a royal headship over the church actually was, God allowed Henry's successor to be a mere boy, unable to govern himself, let alone the church and nation. That ruler's successor was a woman – and a woman, according to Paul himself, was unable to speak with authority in the church. Under the young king Edward VI, the ecclesiastical affairs of the nation were quickly in chaos, according to Sanders's account, with outbreaks of iconoclastic vandalism and the introduction of a variety of heretical opinions from abroad. English catholics now began to recognise how pernicious the schism actually was, and wished they had opposed it more resolutely from the beginning. When Mary, the daughter of Catherine of Aragon, came to the throne, she showed her good sense by rejecting at once the profane title of ecclesiastical supremacy, leading the way to a reconciliation of the nation with Rome. But parliament was unwilling to alter the succession to the throne to prevent the accession of Elizabeth, even though she was legally a bastard and thus, in Sanders's view, had no legitimate right to rule. Elizabeth's coming to the throne, followed by the reestablishment over the church of the royal supremacy and the reintroduction of protestantism, marked the last stage in England's degradation. 'Then came the hour of Satan,' wrote Sanders, 'and the power of darkness took possession of the whole of England.'[20]

Sanders and Rishton made clear that, in their opinion, Elizabeth was guilty of crimes which made her deserve the deposition decreed by pope Pius V. She had persecuted loyal catholics, allowed calvinist beliefs and practices to be introduced into the English church, and

[19] Sanders, *De origine ac progressu schismatis anglicani* pp 77–81; *Rise and Growth of the Anglican Schism* pp 120–6.

[20] Sanders, *De origine ac progressu schismatis anglicani* pp 106–42; *Rise and Growth of the Anglican Schism* pp 167–233.

[21] Sanders, *De origine ac progressu schismatis anglicani* p 158; *Rise and Growth of the Anglican Schism* p 261.

banished the ancient nobility from her council – raising up in their place obscure subjects of heretical belief. Yet the two writers were not entirely discouraged by prospects for the future. When Elizabeth came to the throne, 'the very flower of the two universities, Oxford and Cambridge, was carried away, as it were, by a storm, and scattered in foreign lands'. But now, from abroad, a rich harvest of literary works was being gathered, 'to be sown again in the barren lands of England, there to grow at last, so we hope, to be the salvation of all its people'.[21]

Sanders was not the only catholic exile to see appealing and saintly qualities in Thomas More. English catholics seem, from an early date, to have treasured memories of his life and death, and many of these recollections found their way into print. William Roper, the husband of More's daughter Margaret, stated, for example, that he had lived for sixteen years in More's household, and had 'at the request of divers worthy friends, put downe in wryting, such things touching the same, as I can at this present well call to remembrance (having through my negligence, forgotten many other very notable passages thereof) to the end that all should not utterly perish to posterity'.[22] Thomas Stapleton, a former fellow of New College, Oxford, and a prominent member of the English catholic communities at Louvain and Douai, provided detailed information to his readers about More, based upon the recollections of members of his household and of his circle of friends who had become fellow-exiles with Stapleton on the continent.[23] In addition to Roper's life, which was not published until 1626, though it had circulated in manuscript for more than seventy years, and to Stapleton's, which was published in 1588, there were manuscript lives by Nicholas Harpsfield and by one now known only as 'Ro: Ba:', as well as a life of More written by a descendant, now presumed to be his great-grandson, Cresacre More, which was published about 1630.[24] The readers of these works were invited, as it were, to

[22] William Roper, *The Mirror of Vertve in Worldly Greatnes: Or, The Life of Syr Thomas More Knight, Sometimes Lo. Chancellour of England* (Paris [St. Omer] 1626) preface.
[23] See Thomas Stapleton, *The Life and Illustrious Martyrdom of Sir Thomas More, Formerly Lord Chancellor of England*, trans Philip E. Hallet (London 1928) pp x, xv–xvi. On Stapleton's distinguished academic and literary career, see Marvin R. O'Connell, *Thomas Stapleton and the Counter Reformation* (New Haven, Conn. 1964) pp 26–51 and *passim*, and Michael Richards, 'Thomas Stapleton', *JEH* 18 (1967) pp 187–99.
[24] Nicholas Harpsfield, *The Life and Death of Sʳ Thomas Moore*, ed R. W. Chambers, E[arly] E[nglish] T[ext] S[ociety] (London 1932); Ro: Ba:, *The Lyfe of Syr Thomas More, Sometymes Lord Chancellor of England*, ed Elsie Vaughan Hitchcock

see the beginnings of the English reformation through the experiences of one who had suffered and had been martyred for his loyalty to the catholic church. Stapleton's life of More was a part of a work entitled *Tres Thomae* – the other two Thomases being, significantly, Thomas the Apostle, and Thomas Becket, saint and martyr.[25]

The interpretation of the English reformation provided by Pole, Sanders, and the biographers of More was placed within the context of earlier English history by several roman catholic writers during the late sixteenth and early seventeenth centuries. As early as 1565, Thomas Stapleton published a translation of the venerable Bede's *Ecclesiastical History of the English People*, written in the eighth century, in which he pointed out the significance of the work for the century of the reformation. Stapleton suggested, in a dedication of the work to queen Elizabeth, that if she would be pleased to read this translation of Bede, she would see

> the misse informations of a fevve for displacing the auncient and right Christen faith, as also the way and meane of a spedy redresse that may be had for the same, to the quietnesse of the greater part of your Maiesties most loyal and lowly subiectes cõsciences.[26]

Here was described, said Stapleton, the faith in which the realm had been christened and which had been continued for almost a thousand years, 'to the glory of God, the enriching of the crowne, and great welth and quiet of the realme'.[27] The argument of the protestants, Stapleton noted, was that a millenium of church history had been marked by 'a corrupted faith, traded up in superstitions, blindnesse, and idolatry', but this view seemed to him theologically as well as historically absurd.[28] Stapleton claimed, on the authority of Bede, that a great number of catholic beliefs and practices condemned by the

---

and P. E. Hallett, EETS (1950); Cresacre More, *The Life and Death of Sir Thomas Moore, Lord High Chancellour of England: Written by M.T.M. and Dedicated to the Queens Most Gracious Maiestie* ([Antwerp, *c* 1630]). For the identification of the author and probable date of publication of the last work see Allison and Rogers. Also Cresacre More, *The Life of Sir Thomas More*, ed Joseph Hunter (London 1828) pp xvii–lxi.

[25] Thomas Stapleton, *Tres Thomae: Sev, De S. Thomae Apostoli rebus gestis; De S. Thoma Archiepiscopo Cantuariensi & Martyre; D. Thomae Mori Angliae quondam Cancellarij Vita* (Douai 1588).

[26] [*The*] *History of the Chvrch of Englande*, [*Compiled by Venerable Bede, Englishman*, trans Thomas Stapleton] (Antwerp 1565) Sig. *2 verso–*3.

[27] *History of the Chvrch of Englande* Sig. *3.

[28] *Ibid* Sig. *3 verso.

protestants had been known in England from the time of the conversion of the Anglo-Saxons. Moreover, as he argued in a lengthy appendix to the work, entitled *A Fortresse of the Faith*, the religion planted by Augustine was the same as that of Christ and the apostles.[29] Thus, for Stapleton, the scriptures and the traditions of the church were all of a piece, and the only real break in continuity, as far as the church of England was concerned, was that which had occurred as the result of the reformation of the sixteenth century.

The case for continuity which Stapleton had developed was further worked out by the jesuit Robert Parsons, in *A Treatise of Three Conversions of England from Paganisme to Christian Religion*, published in 1603. Parsons argued that the inhabitants of the island of Britain had been converted to christianity not once but three times, and that each time they had received the 'Christian faith from Rome, and by Romish preachers'.[30] He admitted that the evidence for the first planting of christianity in Britain was scanty, but he appeared to find credible that Peter himself had come to Britain, after the jews had been banished from Rome, and he accepted the traditions which linked other apostles to Britain in the first century. In the second century the second conversion had followed, when king Lucius, of whom Bede had written, sent to pope Eleutherius the request that christian missionaries be sent to Britain.[31] The third, of course, was the result of the mission of Augustine, at the end of the sixth century. Parsons could thus speak of a considerably longer period than other catholic apologists for the duration of the catholic faith in England. Unfortunately, his argument also involved him in accepting uncritically any tradition, however dubious, which linked early christianity in Britain to the bishop of Rome.

Parsons was more effective in his critique of John Foxe's *Actes and Monumentes*, the major English protestant work which attempted to relate the ecclesiastical history of the sixteenth century to that of earlier

[29] The work has a separate title page: *A Fortresse of the Faith, First Planted amonge Vs Englishmen, and Continued Hitherto in the Vniuersall Church of Christ, the Faith of Which Time Prostestants Call, Papistry* (Antwerp 1565). The argument here is more theological than historical, and is based upon an understanding of the church as a divine institution, guided by the Holy Spirit, and visible to the world.

[30] [Robert] Parsons, *A Treatise of Three Conversions [of England from Paganisme to Christian Religion: The First vnder the Apostles, in the First Age after Christ; The Second vnder Pope Eleutherius and K. Lucius, in the Second Age; The Third, vnder Pope Gregory the Great, and K. Ethelbert in the Sixth Age]* ([St. Omer] 1603) p 1. For Parson's career, see John E. Parish, *Robert Parsons and the English Counter-Reformation*, Rice University Studies, 52, 1 (Houston 1966) *passim*.

[31] Parsons, *A Treatise of Three Conversions* pp 3, 76–9, 149–50.

times. In tracing the succession of true believers down through the ages, Foxe had, according to Parsons, produced a misshapen and highly misleading book. He had taken from Eusebius and other ancient writers the accounts of martyrdoms suffered in the general persecutions under the emperors, though these men were generally considered catholic saints and heroes. For long stretches of time, Foxe could cite little real evidence to support his case, devoting a mere seventy pages to the first thousand years of church history. He had mistakenly made Wyclif into a protestant.[32] Finally, his martyrs and confessors of the sixteenth century were no more in agreement on matters of faith than the various foreign divines brought into England under king Edward VI. To drive this point home Parsons listed, in a separate part of the treatise, the large number of sects which he found represented among Foxe's martyrs.[33]

Foxe's book of martyrs had also been attacked by Nicholas Harpsfield, who devoted the final section of his *Dialogi sex*, published in 1566, to this subject. Harpsfield, a member of New College, Oxford, had gone into exile at Louvain during an earlier phase of the reformation while the young king Edward was on the throne, and had returned to fill responsible ecclesiastical posts under queen Mary. Early in Elizabeth's reign he was put into the Fleet prison, where he remained until or shortly before his death in 1575. Despite his imprisonment Harpsfield managed to carry out an ambitious programme of writing and research, though it was many years before some of his works were published.[34] *Dialogi sex* took Foxe to task for unjustly claiming as protestants many who were not, and emphasised – as Parsons was to do – the lack of agreement on matters of belief which these men and women exhibited. Harpsfield also spoke scornfully of the idea of the church of England as a middle way in religion. Since Henry VIII's time, he observed, protestants as well as catholics had been persecuted and even executed by the new ecclesiastical establishment. 'Thus a cer-

---

[32] *Ibid* pp 302, 436–7, 488–9, 507.

[33] *Ibid* pp 574, 590. The section in which these sects are listed has a separate title page: *The Third Part of a Treatise, Intituled: Of Three Conversions of England; Conteyninge, an Examen of the Calendar or Catalogue of Protestant Saints, Martyrs and Confessors, Devised by Iohn Fox, and Prefixed before His Volume of Acts and Monuments*([St Omer] 1604).

[34] For Harpsfield's career, see R. W. Chambers, 'Life and Works of Nicholas Harpsfield', in his edition of Harpsfield's *Life and Death of Sr Thomas Moore* pp clxxv–ccxiv. Harpsfield's *Treatise on the Pretended Divorce between Henry VIII and Catherine of Aragon*, apparently written during Mary's reign, was first published by the Camden Society, ed Nicholas Pocock, in 1878.

tain new and middle religion has been found between Lutheran perfidy and Catholic truth, which punishes equally Lutherans and Catholics.'[35]

Harpsfield's most important contribution to catholic historiography in this period was, however, his large-scale history, written in prison and not published until 1622, in which he traced the course of the church's growth and development in Britain from the beginning down to the early sixteenth century. Here he described, on the basis of a substantial number of literary sources, what he considered to be the catholic heritage of the English people: saints, martyrs, missionaries, poets, kings, crusaders, scholars, the universities, the monastic orders, the great episcopal sees. Significantly, he concluded his account of the archbishops of Canterbury with William Warham, Cranmer's predecessor. Thomas Cranmer, he had observed elsewhere, was the first man elevated to Canterbury who was unorthodox on the question of the primacy of the pope.[36] In 779 folio pages, Harpsfield's *Historia anglicana ecclesiastica* was his final answer to Foxe.[37] It was in this history, he said in effect, that the real church of the English people was to be found, not in Foxe's procession of heretics and sectaries. Harpsfield devoted a separate section to Wyclif in order to clear up a number of matters which he felt Foxe had obscured. Wyclif's ideas were complex and distinctive, needing careful analysis. Their influence, however, had clearly been disastrous. In Wyclif's wake, floods of heresies and civil commotions had washed over England and across much of Europe.[38] Wyclif's followers had professed many errors, which Harpsfield enumerated, and their descendants were still endeavouring to extinguish the catholic church in England. Foxe, in Harpsfield's eyes, had glorified a movement which threatened to destroy what had been built up in England over many centuries. As if to prove this point, Harpsfield listed in an appendix the monasteries and other ecclesiastical institutions suppressed in England since the beginning of the schism.[39] Harpsfield's history, written in latin for an international audience, remained for many years the most detailed and scholarly overall account of the church in England before the reformation.

---

[35] [Nicholas] Harpsfield, *Dialogi sex*, [*contra svmmi pontificatvs, monasticae vitae, sanctorvm, sacrarvm imaginvm, oppvgnatores, et psevdomartyres,*] ed Alan Cope (Antwerp 1566) pp 802–4, 904–9, 996 (quotation found on the last page).

[36] *Ibid* p 985.

[37] [Nicholas] Harpsfield, *Historia anglicana ecclesiastica* [*a primis gentis svsceptae fidei incvnabvlis ad nostra fere tempora dedvcta, et in qvindecim centvrias distribvta*] (Douai 1622).

[38] *Ibid* pp 661–732. This section is given a separate title: *Historia Wicleffiana.*

[39] *Ibid* pp 741–79.

Harpsfield's ecclesiastical history summed up the viewpoint of catholic writers in an era in which the church of England was being restructured under the influence of the protestant reformation and along lines determined by royal policy. What had these writers achieved? They had, in the first place, suggested in compelling terms that England's medieval past was to be taken seriously, and that the rich cultural heritage of the middle ages was something of which the nation could be justly proud. This was an emphasis which had been lacking for the most part, in humanist and protestant historiography, and was not really prominent even in the works of the English antiquaries. English catholic writers thus helped to lead their countrymen towards a fresh appreciation of the middle ages. In the second place, the recusant writers had described in considerable detail the circumstances of the nation's break with the see of Rome, and had made this appear to be a final, tragic chapter in the otherwise heartening story of a church which had flourished since the early centuries of the christian era. In spite of the formidable difficulties which they encountered in conducting historical research and publishing and distributing the fruits of their labours, these writers had been able to get before the reading public in England – and on the continent – an interpretation of the course of ecclesiastical history in England which was coherent and persuasive, and more fully elaborated than anything the anglicans had yet produced.

Among anglican writers, John Leland, John Bale, and Matthew Parker had been concerned, as recent writers have pointed out, to exhume and analyse the surviving sources of the church's past. Later, James Ussher brought his formidable learning to the task of investigating the early history of christianity among the Britons and the Irish.[40] The elizabethan Society of Antiquaries had devoted several sessions to early evidence of christianity in Britain.[41] John Foxe, of course, had reached an enormous readership with his work, which described the suffering of believers of all estates of life in the reformation era, and linked these episodes with those involving confessors and martyrs in earlier centuries. More than any other protestant work, Foxe's *Actes and Monumentes* had helped to fix a view of the English reformation

---

[40] F. J. Levy, *Tudor Historical Thought* (San Marino, Calif. 1967) pp 79–166; May McKisack, *Medieval History in the Tudor Age* (Oxford 1971) pp 1–49; R. Buick Knox, *James Ussher, Archbishop of Armagh* (Cardiff 1967) *passim*.

[41] *A Collection of Curious Discourses Written by Eminent Antiquaries upon Several Heads in Our English Antiquities*, ed Thomas Hearne, 2 vols (London 1771) II, pp 155–72.

among English readers.[42] Yet the work was, as catholic writers frequently pointed out, relatively thin on the history of the English church prior to the fourteenth century. Furthermore, in its overwhelming emphasis on persecutions and martyrdoms it did relatively little to unravel the complexities of the reformation settlements or to explain the workings of those human agencies which had made the settlements possible.

There were, in addition, other works by anglicans in the early seventeenth century which dealt with the historical problem of the English reformation. Sir Edward Coke, the celebrated statesman, judge, and commentator on the common law, devoted the fifth part of his *Reports* to the 'Kings Ecclesiasticall Law', and here he dealt with a number of the legal and historical aspects of the religious settlements of the sixteenth century. The burden of his argument was that the statute passed in the first year of Elizabeth's reign, which established her jurisdiction over the ecclesiastical estate, did not establish any new right of the crown, but declared what had existed from ancient times, as was indicated by its title: 'An Act restoring to the Crowne the auntient Iurisdiction over the state Ecclesiastical and Spirituall'.[43] The anglican clergyman Francis Mason took up the problem of the succession of bishops in the church of England, arguing in his book *Of the Consecration of the Bishops in the Chvrch of England* that 'the Church of England had alwayes Bishops to conferre sacred Orders, according to the ordinary and most warrantable custome of the Church of CHRIST'.[44] He contended further that the church's theology of ordination was – despite the claims of roman catholics – that of the primitive church. Mason's fellow-clergyman Richard Mocket also produced a treatise, mainly, it seems, for the information of foreigners, which described how the church of England was organised and governed, and what were its standards of belief. The work included discussions of the royal supremacy, canon law, and episcopal jurisdiction, and was published

---

[42] J. J. Mozley, *John Foxe and His Book* (London 1940) pp 118–74; William Haller, *Foxe's Book of Martyrs and the Elect Nation* (London 1963) pp 140–233.

[43] Edward Coke, *The Fift Part of the Reports of Sʳ Edward Coke, Knight, the Kings Attorney Generall: Of Diuers Resolutions and Iudgements Giuen vpon Great Deliberation, in Matters of Great Importance & Consequence by the Reuerend Iudges and Sages of the Law; Together with the Reasons and Causes of Their Resolutions and Iudgements* (London 1605) fol 8 and *passim*.

[44] Francis Mason, *Of the Consecration of the Bishops in the Chvrch of England, with Their Succession, Jurisdiction, and Other Things Incident to Their Calling, as also of the Ordination of Priests and Deacons* (London 1613) Sig. A3 verso. The sub-title of the work indicates that it is an answer to the 'Slanders and Odious Imputations' of Bellarmine, Sanders, Harding, Allen, Stapleton, and Parsons.

with accompanying historical documents.[45] Yet it remained true that as late as the middle of the seventeenth century no anglican writer had yet come forward to relate the story of the English reformation fully and frankly, and to set that history within the framework of a detailed account of the church in Britain from the earliest times.

The anglican reply to the historical arguments of the recusants did not come until the second half of the seventeenth century, when the *Church History of Britain*, by Thomas Fuller, was published, followed by the history of the English reformation by Peter Heylyn, and of the early church in Britain by Edward Stillingfleet.[46] Gilbert Burnet's three-volume history of the English reformation dealt further with the sixteenth century from a rigorously protestant point of view, and included documents of permanent interest and value. This prolific era in anglican historiography culminated with the monumental works of John Strype and Jeremy Collier in the early eighteenth century.[47] The anglican works of this era owed a great deal to the antiquarian movement in their methodology, form, and point of view.[48] Yet it is difficult to resist the conclusion that they owed a good deal as well to the stimulus provided by the recusant works of an earlier era. Thomas Fuller, at least, was not unappreciative of the achievement of the recusants. He said of Harpsfield's *Historia anglicana ecclesiastica* that it was 'no less learnedly than painfully performed; and abating his Partiality to his own Interest, well deserving of all posterity'.[49] This assessment might equally well be applied to other important writings by recusant historians.

[45] Richard Mocket, *Doctrina, et politia Ecclesiae Anglicanae, a Beatissimae Memoriae Principibvs Edovardo Sexto, Regina Elizabetha stabilitae, et a Religiosissimo & Potentissimo Monarcha Iacobo, Magnae Britan. Ec. Rege continuatae* (London 1617). For the circumstances which caused James I to withdraw his support from the book, see Bertha Porter, 'Richard Mocket', *DNB* 13, p 538.

[46] [Thomas] Fuller, *The Church History of Britain, [from the Birth of Jesus Christ, untill the Year M.DC.XLVIII]* (London 1655); Peter Heylyn, *Ecclesia Restavrata: Or, The History of the Reformation of the Church of England* (London 1661); Edward Stillingfleet, *Origines Britannicae: Or, The Antiquities of the British Churches* (London 1685).

[47] Gilbert Burnet, *The History of the Reformation of the Church of England*, 3 vols (London 1679–1715); John Strype, *Memorials of the Most Reverend Father in God, Thomas Cranmer, Sometime Lord Archbishop of Canterbury* (London 1694), *Annals of the Reformation and Establishment of Religion, and Other Various Occurrences in the Church of England; During the First Twelve Years of Queen Elizabeth's Happy Reign* (London 1709), and other volumes; Jeremy Collier, *An Ecclesiastical History of Great Britain; Chiefly of England: From the First Planting of Christianity, to the End of the Reign of King Charles the Second*, 2 vols (London 1708–14).

[48] David C. Douglas, *English Scholars, 1660–1730* (2 ed London 1951) pp 195–221.

[49] Fuller, *The Church History of Britain* bk IX, p 143.

THEOLOGY AS A BASIS FOR POLICY
IN THE ELIZABETHAN CHURCH

by DAVID J. KEEP

THE enigma of Elizabeth's faith and personality continues to fascinate historians. Her actions are fully recorded: the rejection of her father's title in favour of 'Supreme Governor', and the passing of the act of uniformity in 1559 which almost, but not quite, restored the form of religion authorised under her brother. Elizabeth had chosen between London and Rome, but at the same time she made gestures towards Spain and Germany. Her church was staffed partly by returned exiles, partly by scholars like Matthew Parker, who had remained at their desks under Mary. The archbishop had to build up the numbers and quality of the clergy, and create a new church. Henrican catholicism was dead beyond recall. The work of Knox in Scotland was about to diminish the standing of the crown. The exiles had tasted independence in church government, though in a still corporate view of society this was to remain an anabaptist heresy. Parker had to use these men to establish a church as close as possible to the desires of his mistress, which were never made explicit. A study of contemporary theological works is a vital guide to the nature of this church.

The elizabethan church was protestant, though it was ten years before Elizabeth was excommunicated. It had its martyrs, lovingly recorded by John Foxe. It had no founding father, however, no reformer who had established a system of hermeneutic. Cranmer had blended a reformed liturgy with a catholic hierarchy, and there remained a greater variety of tradition and opinion in England, let alone Wales and Ireland, than in the city-states of the Rhine. When Parker issued his *Advertisments* in 1566 at the suggestion of the queen, this attempt to control clerical dress led to dissent. It also brought home to the hierarchy the slender nature of the support for their discipline, especially as Elizabeth never gave direct approval to these regulations. The historian can easily trace the precedents for Parker's rules, and follow the consequences. He should also examine the rationale for them, even if, to parody Anselm, it turns out to a *Fides quaerens justificationem*.

The question of clerical uniform seems very trivial in the total gamut of christian belief and practice, but it isolated two vital issues: the nature of the royal supremacy in the church, and the nature of the ministry. The language of bishop Sandys, 'popish habits', and Jewel, 'vestiges of popery' indicates that there was a basis for the fears of the Oxford radicals, Humphrey and Sampson, that this was the restoration of sacerdotalism. To the scrupulous there is nothing indifferent in the practice of religion. Yet when the archbishop in the name of the queen made a rule, the clergy had to obey. Jewel, Bilson, Cooper and Hooker accepted and defended the royal supremacy. Even Grindal, who sympathised with clerical prophesyings, dared only petition the queen: '... that you would refer all these ecclesiastical matters which touch religion, or the doctrine and discipline of the church, unto the bishops and divines of your realm, according to the example of all godly Christian emperors and princes of all ages.'

The anglican church, then, existed by royal consent. Its defenders fought for support '... by the whole course of the scriptures, and by the undoubted practice of the primitive church'.[1] Contemporary support was also desirable, though, to rally dissident supporters and to emphasise England's place in the true catholic church which, it was hoped, was replacing the corrupt roman church. Calvin was clear that the state was involved in religion: 'Thus all have confessed that no polity can be successfully established unless piety be its first care, and that those laws are absurd which disregard the rights of God, and consult only for men.'[2] He had earlier expressed his preference for Aristotle's aristocracy as a form of government, but allowed that God had appointed which countries should be kingdoms, and which free states. His claim to the right to excommunicate, which involved loss of citizenship, meant that the genevan system gave potentially the greater power to the church. Moreover, Elizabeth did not forget Knox's tract *against the monstrous Regiment of Women*, which unfortunately coincided with her accession, and which she believed to be approved by Calvin. Time has increased the importance of Geneva. Zurich, where the exiles had been 'a community of scholars', was more important at the time. In order to understand anglican theology, it is essential to look at the writings of Zwingli's successor, Henry Bullinger, who was chief minister 1531–75.

[1] Quoted from Claire Cross: *The Royal Supremacy in the Elizabethan Church* (London 1969) pp 63, 28.
[2] *Institutes* IV, p 20.

Bullinger became a key figure in the vestarian controversy when his letter of 1 May 1566 to Humphrey and Sampson was published without his consent.[3] His writings were well-known in England, and from 1573 Thomas Cooper, bishop of Lincoln began to require the reading of the *Decades* as a penance. In 1577 this was made a weekly exercise for all clergy in the diocese below the MA degree, and an English translation was published. In 1583 bishop Middleton of St Davids ordered that a copy be put in every parish church, and in 1584 Whitgift repeated Cooper's order for the province of Canterbury. I suspect that as dean of Lincoln he may have advised Cooper, and come to know the *Decades* as chaplain to Cox at Ely. Bullinger's correspondence, including some seventy unpublished letters, is well-known as a source for the period. This does not show him as influential in church policy, and his invitation to defend the queen against the bull of 1569 was less official than Dixon implied. The editors of the *Parker Society* were right to give such weight to his writings, however, as there is no theologian who so accurately mirrors the anglican settlement. Bullinger was a prolific writer, and no-one since A. J. Van 't Hooft in 1888 has attempted to survey his complete theology. It is possible to discern major themes from the *Decades* and occasional writings, and we are able to appreciate what his students and friends would have learned. This should have made the Oxford dissenters chary of seeking his support in their dispute with Parker.

Bullinger discussed the role of the state at greater length than Calvin. He preached four sermons on the sixth commandment in answer to anabaptist dismissal of civil government. One of these was translated as a tract by 'J F' in 1549. His argument was similar to Calvin's: 'But the catholic verity teacheth, that the care of religion doth especially belong to the magistrate; and that it is not in his power only, but his office and duty also, to dispose and advance religion. For among them of old their kings were priests; I mean, masters and overseers of religion.'[4] He proceeded to describe the role of Melchizedek, Joshua, the kings of Judah and the christian emperors at Byzantium. It is important to note Bullinger's concept of the continuity of revelation from Adam. Christianity was both *The Old Faith*, a tract published in 1537, and Plato's *Das Höchste Gut*, a manuscript of 1520 published by Staedtke in 1955. Bullinger was correct in condemning the pope for assuming

[3] Material on Bullinger is taken from my unpublished thesis *Henry Bullinger and the Elizabethan Church* (Sheffield 1970). References to the *Decades* are to the four volume edition edited by Thomas Harding (Cambridge 1849–52).

imperial power, but both catholics and anabaptists were more 'evangelical' in confining their claims to the recorded words of Jesus. His pupil Erastus worked against the calvinist Olevianus at Heidelberg 1560–70, and when his writings were published in 1589, the term erastian was adopted in Britain to describe a subservient church. This is unfair to Bullinger and his pupil. They argued that the ruler had as much a divine commission as the minister. Bullinger used a tortuous etymological argument to demonstrate this, but his sincerity is not in doubt: He is referring to Isaiah 49:22–3.

> I will in the end add also the prophecy of the prophet Esay, whereby it may appear, that even now also kings have in the church at this day the same office that these ancient kings had in that congregation which they call the Jewish church. There is no doubt but that they ought to be accounted true Christians, which being anointed with the Spirit of Christ, do believe in Christ, and are in the sacrament made partakers of Christ. For Christ (if ye interpret the very word) is as much to say as 'anointed'. Christians therefore, according to the etymology of their name, are anointed. That anointing, according to the apostle's interpretation, is the Spirit of God, or the gift of the Holy Ghost. But St Peter testifieth, that the Spirit of Christ was in the kings and prophets. And Paul affirmeth flatly that we have the very same Spirit of faith that they of old had; . . . [5]

The teaching of the *Decades* was particularly relevant to England as the second and third volumes were dedicated to Edward VI and the marquess of Dorset. Volume two was split and issued in March and August 1550 in order that Bullinger might encourage the young king in his reformation of the church, and demonstrate to the English the danger of the council of Trent, which was retrogressive and unrepresentative. The king would find felicity:

> . . . if throughout your whole realm, you dispose and order religion, and all matters of justice, according to the rule of God's holy word; if you decline not one hair's breadth from that rule, but study to advance the kingdom of Christ, and go on (as hitherto you have happily begun) to subvert and tread under foot the usurped power of that tyrannical antichrist. [6]

[4] I, pp 323–4.
[5] *Ibid* pp 326–7.
[6] *Ibid* II, p 14.

The second preface reaffirmed the royal right to dispose of national affairs by the Word of God, without reference to the council:

> But now, that it is lawful for every christian church, much more for every notable christian kingdom, without the advice of the church of Rome and the members thereof, in matters of religion depraved by them, wholly to make a reformation according to the rule of God's most holy word ... Therefore Christians, obeying the laws and commandments of their prince, do utterly remove or take away all superstition, and do restore, establish, and preserve the true religion, according to the manner that Christ their prince appointed them.[7]

Bullinger argued that the rulers were the guarantors of true religion. He saw himself as the servant, colleague and friend of the Zurich council. The essence of religion was the proclamation of the word of God, which to him was so vital that he read the apostles' creed, as 'I believe the Holy Catholic Church', which so became a mechanism for preaching rather than a corporate identity. He expounded his doctrine of the church in the fifth *Decade*:

> The chief and principal points of the godliness of the church of God are, the sincere teaching of the law and the prophets, of Christ and the apostles; faithful prayer offered unto her only God through Christ alone; a religious and lawful administration and receiving of Christ's sacraments.[8]

Both here, and in his study of the ceremonial law in the third *Decade*, he stressed the continuity with Israel which, like the church, included good and evil. There was an underlying unity which should not be destroyed for the sake of ceremonies. Provided there were no doctrinal errors, the church could be as varied in its practices as the primitive church had been. Hence it was logical that he should approve of the 'royal' injunctions, even if the English clerical dress were more priestly than he would have chosen. He warned the dissenters against provoking the queen into expelling them from the ministry and appointing less sound pastors. In 1566 most of the clergy conformed. By 1596 Bullinger was forgotten, and there was a growing body of dissent.

Here, then, is a senior and widely respected protestant divine who clearly spelt out the responsibility of rulers in church affairs, what might

[7] *Ibid* III pp 119–20.
[8] *Ibid* IV, p 479.

be called the 'divine duty' of kings. Bullinger had written a preface to Henry VIII in 1538, and though the king took no notice, his children and lady Jane Grey were educated by tutors like Richard Cox and Roger Ascham, who were zealous reformers, and well aware of the potential roles of their pupils. Elizabeth was not unfamiliar with the teaching of Bullinger when she sent him a chalice in 1560. Although this influence is not explicit, I have indicated the use of his writings until the 1580s. Helmut Kressner in *Schweizer Ursprünge des anglikanischen Staatskirchentums* (Gütersloh 1953) traced the parallels between Hooker and Rudolf Gualter, who was pupil, son-in-law, colleague and successor to Bullinger. Emerging from the reformed theologians is a kind of protestant feudalism, a covenant with God and people, which developed into the social contract. This is implicit in Hooker's eighth book, which was not published until 1648, and in Hobbes *Leviathan*, which failed to please Charles II. James I confused the idea of 'divine duty' with 'divine right', which was twice to lead to the expulsion of the Stuarts. The monarch was supreme, so long as she did what was right. This was as clearly grasped by the young Elizabeth as the young Victoria!

In this paper I have attempted to offer a line of defence for the elizabethan settlement, not simply as the best available between Rome and Geneva, but as a positive system based on a clear exposition of the bible. This does not emerge from the compromises of the commons, or the swingeing satires of puritan pamphleteers. It is clear only in the theological writings of the time. Nor is it sufficient to read the elizabethan apologists. I suggest that their doctrines were clearly formulated in Zurich, emerging in effect with the independence of the city, which had long disregarded the German bishop of Constance. Bullinger, like Zwingli, taught that the total responsibility of the government cannot be divided. I offer this as a model of an important approach to the study of ecclesiastical history. We properly concern ourselves with the minutiae of dates and connections, of wills and statutes, but are sometimes in danger of forgetting that there is a body of faith behind these. In this instance we are able to see the elizabethan bishops as honourable christians seeking to establish the peace of Jerusalem, rather than as time-servers who were willing to cut their consciences, as well as their coats, to the whim of their mistress.

POPULAR PIETY AND THE RECORDS OF THE UNESTABLISHED CHURCHES 1460–1660

by CLAIRE CROSS

JOHN FOXE in his long account of 'the grievous affliction of good men and women in the diocese of Lincoln', based on Lincoln episcopal records for 1521, gave over a quarter of a page to the Colins family of Ginge, near West Hendred in Berkshire. At a time of wholesale detection of lollards, when episcopal officials had succeeded in getting neighbour to inform against neighbour, John Edmunds revealed what he knew about Richard Colins, Alice, his wife, and their daughter, Joan.

> This Richard Colins, as he was a great doer among these good men, so was he much complained upon by divers . . . for bringing with him a book called *The King of Beeme* [Bohemia] into their company, and did read thereof a great part unto them in this Edmunds' house of Burford.
>
> This Alice likewise was a famous woman among them, and had a good memory, and could recite much of the scriptures, and other good books. And therefore when any conventicle of these men did meet at Burford, commonly she was sent for to recite unto them the declaration of the Ten Commandments, and the epistles of Peter and James.
>
> This Joan also, following her father's and mother's steps, was noted for that she had learned with her father and mother, the Ten Commandments, the Seven Deadly Sins, the Seven Works of Mercy, the Five Wits Bodily and Ghostly, the Eight Blessings, and five chapters of St James's epistle.[1]

Here we can glimpse fleetingly a lollard cell in an Oxfordshire town at which members heard readings and recitations of certain parts of the New Testament and more explicitly lollard books like *The King of Beeme*. Parents initiated children into the sect and women enjoyed an

---

[1] [J. Foxe,] *Acts and Monuments*, 2 vols (London 1684) II, pp 24, 36–7. In all quotations the spelling has been modernised, and some punctuation added.

almost equal footing with men. Yet this reconstruction of a lollard conventicle in Burford has its peculiar problems. In the first place we can
see it not at one remove but at two. We have to consider the extent to
which Foxe may have edited his material. Although modern historians
would scarcely go so far as to suggest that Foxe actually manufactured
his evidence, nevertheless his account of the persecutions in the diocese
of Lincoln cannot be substantiated fully since the episcopal court
records he saw have subsequently disappeared. If we concede that Foxe's
description is based on fact a further problem follows. How far did the
episcopal officials distort or influence the confessions made to them?
This is indeed looking through a glass darkly. Nevertheless, however
imperfect the surviving records, I believe we can know something
about the piety of the later lollards, and of the separatists in the reigns of
the Tudors and early Stuarts until with the lifting of censorship at the
time of the civil war virtually all aspects of popular piety gain free
expression.

The records for unorthodox popular piety fall into two distinct
classes: the records of the persecuting body, first the Roman, then the
English church, and the indigenous records of the separating bodies.
Information brought into a court of law by the prosecution by its very
nature is likely to highlight the differences between the orthodox and
the unorthodox and might attribute to defendants opinions they did
not actually hold, or held in a much more attenuated form. Consequently it may well be that because of the inquisitorial procedure of
heresy trials when suspects were required to answer a series of specific
articles prepared in advance by the bishop's official the negative,
destructive side of lollardy has come to be emphasised at the expense of
its devotional side.[2] Yet it is scarcely plausible that groups of 'known
men' could have survived for generations as they did in certain areas of
south-east and central England solely to attack the sacraments and
undermine the powers of the priesthood. Similarly elizabethan separatists sought first to establish pure religion and had not consciously come
together in a sinister conspiracy to subvert the state as the high commission records might suggest. The bias of the records which the
nonconformist churches themselves kept lies in the opposite direction.
Here chroniclers felt tempted to justify actions after the event and write
history as it should have been, rather than as it actually happened. In
addition, when a separatist church is free from persecution its records,

[2] For the most recent discussion of lollard trial records see A. Hudson, 'The
Examination of Lollards', *BIHR*, 46 (1973) pp 145–59.

like those of an established church, normally give details of aberrant incidents in the life of a community deserving discipline, not of the regular religious life. The sources for the history of nonconformity are imperfect, in some cases highly imperfect but, as is so often the case in historical research, half a loaf is better than no bread.

There can be little doubt that those lollard groups about which detailed information survives owed their very existence to the availability of books of the bible, particularly of the new testament, in the vernacular and to self-appointed evangelists who could expound them. It may well be that lollardy persisted largely because of the rising level of literacy and accessibility of schools in fifteenth-century English society. The lollards in the Chilterns possessed altogether a very considerable collection of books. In the abjurations of 1521 defendants mention by name translations into English of Matthew, Mark, Luke and John together with an exposition of these gospels fair written in English. They had the Acts of the Apostles and the Apocalypse and some of the epistles, certainly those of Paul, Peter and the epistle of James which was by far their favourite reading: many members of the group knew the epistle by heart. Some had read the book of Solomon and perhaps the psalms in the old testament. Outside the canonical scriptures they knew the gospel of Nicodemus and had at different times owned lollard books such as *Wyclif's Wicket*, *The Book named William Thorpe*, a *Book of the Commandments*, a *Book treating of the Seven Sacraments*, *The King of Beeme*, a *Dialogue between a Christian and a Jew*, *The Shepherd's Calendar*. Some of their books may have been entirely orthodox like *Our Lady's Mattins* and *The Prick of Conscience*, though it is difficult to tell from the title alone. A neighbour valued at a hundred marks the books which John Phips burnt in an attempt to avoid detection.[3]

Similar books circulated among Coventry lollards. Richard Cook, a mercer and twice mayor of the city, left two English bibles in his will dated 1507 and another civic official, Thomas Forde, had a book on the old testament.[4] Besides the various books of the new testament, London lollards connected with John Hacker had various lollard works, *The Bayly*, a *Disputation between the Clerk and the Friar*, and a *Treatise of William Thorpe and Sir John Oldcastle*. The Essex lollards uncovered in 1528 had nearly as extensive a range of books as those in the Chilterns: the four gospels and epistles in English and separate copies of the

---

[3] *Acts and Monuments*, II, pp 24–41.
[4] I. Luxton, 'The Lichfield Court Book: a Postscript', *BIHR*, 44 (1971) pp 120–5.

evangelists and particularly the epistles of James, John and Paul, and the apocalypse. Their other 'good books' included a treatise beginning 'The most excellent and glorious Lord', a *Dispute between a Clerk and a Friar*, *The Seven Wise Masters of Rome*, *The Prick of Conscience* and *Wyclif's Wicket*. They were so enthusiastic about having the new version of the bible in the vernacular that they sent some of their members to London to buy copies of Tyndale's translation within a few months of its publication on the continent.[5] Some lollards claimed to have been converted by the reading of these books. Through the influence of *The Shepherd's Calendar* John Edmunds of Burford came to believe that the sacrament of the altar was made in the remembrance of Christ.[6] John Tyball confessed in 1528 that about eight years previously he had had in his possession the four evangelists in English, [the revelation of] John, and certain epistles of Peter and Paul 'and so in continuance of time, by reading of the said books, and specially by a chapter of Paul which he wrote to the Corinthians, . . . fell into those errors and heresies'.[7] Whether they could read for themselves or whether they depended upon others for their readings, these late lollards clearly drew their inspiration from the bible, often from the bible interpreted literally. If any one part of the new testament meant more to them than another it was the epistle of James. 'Blessed is the man that endureth temptation: for when he is tried, he shall receive the crown of life, which the Lord hath promised to them that love him.' 'Every good gift and every perfect gift is from above, and cometh down from the Father of lights, with whom is no variableness, neither shadow of turning.' 'Ye see then how that by works a man is justified, and not by faith only.' 'Confess your faults one to another, and pray one for another, that ye may be healed . . .'[8]

John Pykas, a baker of St Nicholas's parish in Colchester, admitted to the bishop of London's vicar general in 1528 that he had separately discussed the epistle of James with at least two fellow townsmen. With John Girling he had spoken of that chapter of James 'where it appeared that God is father of light, and overshadowed all sin. And therefore we should pray only to him. For we be the beginning of his creatures, and he begat us willingly, by the words of truth.' John Tyball about the same time told the bishop of London that he believed 'that it was as

[5] [J. Strype,] *Ecclesiastical Memorials*, 2 vols (London 1721) I, pp 74–81.
[6] *Acts and Monuments*, II, p 36.
[7] *Ecclesiastical Memorials*, I, appendix p 35.
[8] *Authorised Version*, James, 1: 12, 17; 2: 24; 5: 16.

good for a man to confess himself alone to God, or else to any other layman, as to a priest, upon the saying of St James, where he saith "Show your sins one to another" '. From this he had deduced that the priesthood was not necessary, 'for he thought that every layman might minister the sacraments of the church, as well as any priest'.[9]

Veneration for the literal inspiration of the bible seems to have led automatically to a questioning of the value of the sacraments. John Pykas's mother, who lived in Bury St Edmunds had sent for him 'and moved him that he should not believe in the sacraments of the church, for that was not the right way'. And she gave him a book of Paul's epistles in English, and bade 'him live after the manner and way of the said epistles and gospels, and not after the way that the church doth teach'. He then went on to undermine the faith of his Colchester neighbours. He taught them that the sacrament of the altar after the words of consecration did not become the very body of Christ, but remained bread and wine. Even more interestingly, because here he was expounding a biblical text, he counselled them against baptism as ministered by the church, saying 'that there should be no such things: for there is no baptism, but of the holy ghost, and that he learned in the new testament in English: whereas John saith, "I baptize you but in water, in token of repentance; but he that shall come after me, is stronger than I, he shall baptize you in the Holy Ghost" '.[10] Other Essex lollards, like William Raylond, glossed this text further, and explained that baptism by water was only a token of repentance: when a man came to years of discretion, and kept himself clean after the promise made by his godfathers, that then he should receive the baptism of the holy ghost.[11]

A recollection of the first chapter of the gospel of John seems to lie behind Mrs Girling's pronouncement upon the sacrament of the altar. About 1523 William Raylond asked her, when she was sitting at the table in her own house in the company of Raylond's wife, ' "What is the sacrament of the altar?" To whom she answered and said that the sacrament of the altar was but an host; and that the body of Almighty God was joined in the word: and the word of God was all one, and might not be departed'. John Tyball took at its face value 'the chapter of Paul where he saith these words, "Every bishop ought to be husband of one wife, and to bring forth children" ', and concluded that every priest and every bishop should marry.[12]

[9] *Ecclesiastical Memorials*, I, p 83 and appendix p 35.
[10] *Ibid* I, pp 79–80.   [11] *Ibid* I, p 84.
[12] *Ibid* I, pp 85–6, and appendix p 35.

As might be predicted for a sect under persecution, those parts of the new testament which foretold the ultimate triumph of the righteous had a special attraction. John Pykas and John Girling communed together in Girling's house upon 24 Matthew 'where Christ spake of Jerusalem, and said to it, "If thou knowest, thou wouldest weep: for there shall not a stone of thee be left upon a stone; for thou shalt be destroyed". Meaning thereby, that priests and men of the church which have strong hearts (because they do punish heretics, and be stubborn of heart) should reign a while, and in conclusion, God would strike them, and they should be destroyed for the punishment of heretics'. William Raylond had often heard Mrs Girling 'open' the apocalypse in her house, though he did not elaborate her opinions any further.[13] Both the Essex lollards and the lollards in the Chilterns were periodically visited by father Hacker from London: Matilda Symonds and her husband, John, detected him to the bishop of Lincoln for prophesying 'that there should be a battle of priests, and all the priests should be slain: and that the priests should a while rule, but they should all be destroyed, because they hold against the law of the holy church, and for making of false gods . . .'.[14]

The incidental descriptions of the exposition of biblical texts by lollards appear only rarely in the records of lollard trials and are only frequent in the abjurations made before the bishop of London and his vicar general in 1528. Presumably the ecclesiastical officials on most occasions felt it sufficient merely to note down the names of other suspects but did not record, or did not obtain, circumstantial evidence of their missionary activities. Nevertheless, the familiarity of Essex lollards with the books of the new testament, together with the relative abundance of biblical translations in English among lollards in the Chilterns, in Coventry and in London suggests that in these lollard colonies, too, late lollardy derived its inspiration from the new testament and only secondarily was an anti-sacramental, anti-clerical movement. It is quite clear that the reading of the bible and other works was a corporate activity among these lollards and it seems that their conventicles existed mainly for these readings and expositions. Very occasionally lollards mention special gatherings at weddings or on holy days. John Scrivener detected among many others Nicholas Durdant who lived near Staines, Old Durdant, Isabel, wife of Thomas Harding, Hartop of Windsor, Joan Barret, wife of John Barret of London, Henry

[13] *Ibid* I, pp 83–5.
[14] *Acts and Monuments*, II, p 33.

Miller, Stilman and Taylor because at the marriage of Durdant's daughter 'they assembled together in a barn, and heard a certain epistle of St Paul read, which reading they well liked, but especially Durdant and commended the same'. At another time Thomas Baker of Wheatley, Robert Livord, John Simpson of Steventon, Thomas Reiley of Burford, John Clemson, servant of the prior of Burford, James Edmunds of Burford, William Gunne of Witney and perhaps others met in John Harris's house at Upton at the marriage of Joan, the wife of Robert Burgess and read in a book called Nicodemus gospel which includes the story of the destruction of Jerusalem. On Holy Rood day five or six lollards had come together to read the bible in Robert Burgess's house in Burford.[15]

Besides these ties of blood and marriage which linked the lollards of Essex and the Chilterns, itinerant evangelists brought a tenuous form of organisation to the scattered groups.[16] From the surviving records of the early sixteenth century Thomas Man, who had abjured before the bishop of Lincoln and been imprisoned in St Frideswide's monastery in Oxford in 1512, is known to have returned to his heresies after his release and to have been burnt as a relapsed heretic in 1518. He claimed that he and his wife together had won over six or seven hundred people to their opinions; he had taught in Newbury for fifteen years, and in Amersham for twenty-three as well as in London, Billericay, Chelmsford, Uxbridge, Burnham, Henley-on-Thames, and in Norfolk and Suffolk at the time of the heresy prosecutions in the Chilterns about 1511. In 1521 John Butler of Amersham admitted that he had heard Thomas Man read ten years previously how Adam and Eve were expelled out of paradise.[17] John Hacker, the water carrier of Coleman Street, London, until his capture in 1528 kept in equally close touch with lollards in the Chilterns and in Essex: it was through Hacker's confession in 1528 that the extent of heresy in Essex was uncovered.[18] Apart from his following in London, Hacker seems to have directed most of his attention to Essex but he had contacts with lollardy in the Chilterns: he visited Burford and brought a book of the *Ten Plagues of Pharoh*, and, at another time, a book on *The Seven Sacraments*, and also gave a book of the *Ten Commandments* to Richard Collins of Ging.[19]

Occasionally in their confessions lollards from Essex and from the

[15] *Ibid* II, pp 29, 35.
[16] *Ibid* II, pp 27–30, 35–8.
[17] *Ibid* II, pp 18–20, 30.
[18] *Ecclesiastical Memorials*, I, pp 74–7.
[19] *Acts and Monuments*, II, pp 35, 38.

Chilterns mention Kentish lollards. In all probability the lollards in Kent shared the same zeal for scriptural readings and evangelism with those in Essex and the Chilterns but the accident of the type of evidence which has survived against them makes their activities appear altogether more negative. Ecclesiastical officials put a standard set of nine articles to all the forty or so Kentish lollards who came before archbishop Warham in 1511. These implied that all the accused believed that the sacrament of the altar remained bread after consecration, that auricular confession need not be made to a priest, that priests had no more power than a layman to say divine service, that marriage was no sacrament and that extreme unction was not necessary, that images should not be worshipped, that pilgrimages were not meritorious, that prayer should be made to God alone and that holy bread and holy water had no particular virtue. The lollards who abjured confessed to holding all or a combination of these opinions but the effect of this standardisation of articles by the ecclesiastical authorities has been to remove all individuality from the trial records in the archbishop's register.[20] Certainly a strain of anti-sacramentalism, anti-clericalism and outright scurrility ran through lollard communities in the early tudor period (and John Foxe, to his credit, does not conceal it) but it seems that the churchmen overemphasised it as against lollard piety. Repeatedly the Buckinghamshire lollards said that the sacrament of the altar was a 'holy thing', though they denied it was the body of Christ. Hacker taught that it 'was not the very body of God, but a remembrance of God that was in heaven'. Similarly John Tyball of Steeple Bumpstead seems to have spoken for most Essex lollards when he said he thought the blessed sacrament of the altar was not 'the very body of Christ but bread and wine, and done for a remembrance of Christ's passion'. These would have been offensive sentiments for orthodox catholic ecclesiastics to have heard but they do not seem to have been made by men whose prime intention was to scandalise.[21]

Most of these lollards did not oppose all clerics as a caste, merely bad priests. Thomas Geoffrey, then of Uxbridge and later of Ipswich, and John Butler, both lollards, went up to London several Sundays to hear

[20] These are printed in the *British Magazine*, 23 (1843) pp 394–402, 631–6; 24, pp 133–8, 256–9, 638–43. And see also *Acts and Monuments*, II, pp 531–3; J. F. Davis, 'Lollards, Reformers and St Thomas of Canterbury', *University of Birmingham Historical Journal*, 9 (1963) p 7.

[21] *Acts and Monuments*, II, pp 32–3; *Ecclesiastical Memorials*, I, pp 74–5 and appendix pp 35–6.

Dr Colet preach.[22] John Pykas thought well of more than one cleric and especially approved of Mr Bilney whom he had encountered at Ipswich. He had heard Bilney condemn pilgrimages and considered that this sermon 'was most ghostly, and made best for his purpose and opinions, as any that ever he heard in his life'.[23] Certain lollards, like Thomas Hemsted, were confirmed in their heresy when they found their parish priest also held it.[24] John Tyball, in fact, had worked very hard to influence the priests in his area. His attempt to convert Sir William Stringer and Sir Arthur, parish priests of Bumpstead, failed, but he had better success with the curate there, Richard Fox. After he had shown Fox all the books he had, he gradually won him over to lollard opinions and Fox then proceeded to teach lollard views of the sacrament to some of his parishioners. When Tyball visited Robert Barnes in London to buy copies of Tyndale's new testament he requested him, though a complete stranger, to write to Fox to strengthen him in his faith.[25] Indeed more tudor priests may have been lollards, or at least sympathised with lollardy, than has been supposed. William Sweeting, servant to the prior of St Osyth's, had infected him with his opinions, and he had to recant in 1505.[26] Recently Miss Luxton has revealed that James Preston, doctor of theology of Oxford and vicar of St Michael's, Coventry, who died in 1507, held lollard beliefs, and another priest, Richard Shore, kept heretical books. This group of lollards in Coventry had connections with other priests, Dr Alcock of Ibstock and master Kent of Stanton, both in Leicestershire and both reputed to be lollards.[27]

In Coventry in the reign of Henry VII lollardy counted among its adherents a parish priest of education and standing, a man who had twice been mayor, and other leaders of the community and a physician. The extremely wealthy Wigston family of Leicester may have been implicated. By the 1490s, also, lollardy may have been penetrating the ruling class of London. Lady Young, widow of a former lord mayor, was accounted a lollard martyr, and increasingly substantial merchants

---

[22] *Acts and Monuments*, II, p 30.
[23] *Ecclesiastical Memorials* I, p 80.
[24] *Ibid* I, appendix p 43.
[25] *Ibid* I, appendix pp 36, 42, 43.
[26] *Acts and Monuments*, II, pp 7, 21–2; *The Reign of Henry VII from Contemporary Sources*, ed A. F. Pollard, 3 vols (London 1914) III, p 240.
[27] I. Luxton, 'The Lichfield Court Book: a Postscript', *BIHR*, 44 (1971) pp 120–5; J. Fines, 'Heresy Trials in the Diocese of Coventry and Lichfield, 1511–12', *JEH*, 14 (1963) pp 160–74.

and their wives showed an interest in possessing lollard books.[28] In Buckinghamshire in 1511 Thomas Grove gave Dr Wilcocks £20 to avoid having to do open penance at the time of the great abjuration and one Sanders of Amersham also bought out his penance.[29] These are but straws in the wind and much more research is needed before any positive statements can be made, but a reassessment of the evidence at present available suggests that lollardy in the early sixteenth century was not only less anti-sacramentarian and less anti-clerical and more positively devotional but also less confined to the artisan sector of society than some previous historians have thought.

The Essex lollards had come to Robert Barnes to buy a modern, printed translation of the bible. Some of the doctrines taught by the first generation of protestants in England, the denial of the sacrificial element in the mass, the abandonment of the veneration of saints and relics, the lutheran emphasis on the priesthood of all believers, proved congenial to that strand of popular piety represented by late lollardy. Other key concepts of magisterial protestantism were far less acceptable to certain of the 'forward' among the laity and, as professor Dickens has stressed, it would be erroneous to believe that English lollards without a struggle accepted the new protestant orthodoxy, still essentially clerically dominated, of the reign of Edward VI. With the enforcement of protestantism by the edwardian government lollardy, never a precise creed, became lost to sight, but it must surely be something more than a geographical coincidence that in 1550 heretical protestant conventicles were discovered in Kent and Essex. One Cole of Faversham, a schoolmaster, had asserted within the group that 'the doctrine of predestination was meter for devils than for Christian men'. Elaborating this pronouncement, Henry Hart, who seems to have been the intellectual leader of the meeting, had affirmed 'that there was no man so chosen, but that he might damn himself. Neither yet any man so reprobate but that he might keep God's commandments. He said that St Paul might have damned himself if he listed, and . . . that learned men were the cause of great errors.' Another who was at Cole's house at Faversham on lammas day had said that 'Adam was elected to be saved, and that all men being then in Adam's loins were predestinate to be saved, and that there were no reprobates'.[30] Perhaps to avoid detec-

[28] J. A. F. Thomson, *The Later Lollards* (Oxford 1965) pp 139–71.
[29] *Acts and Monuments*, II, p 28.
[30] BM Harleian MS 421 fols 133–4, printed in [C.] Burrage, [*The*] *Early English Dissenters*, 2 vols (Cambridge 1912) II, pp 1–4.

tion some of these Kentishmen late in 1550 went to Bocking in Essex and held an assembly there at christmas at which about sixty people gathered and fell into an argument of scriptural matters, especially whether it was necessary to stand or kneel, covered or barehead, at prayer. On examination before the privy council some of the dissenters revealed that they had not received communion for more than two years. The privy council bound them over to be of good behaviour, instructing them to take advice of their ordinary if in future they had any doubts in religion.[31]

Pelagianism, however, could not be so easily extirpated from amongst the laity and orthodox marian protestants found to their consternation free-willers sharing in their imprisonment and martyrdom. Strype preserved a letter written by a free-willer from his London prison to encourage his brethren to 'watch, and search diligently the scriptures, and walk while ye have the light of God's word, that the darkness fall not upon you'. 'And say no more,' he continued, 'We be not able to keep his commandments, as many hath said, and doth say. But Christ saith, "He that loveth me, keepeth my commandments." And Christ came not to break the law, but to fulfil it.' Turning to James, whose epistles the lollards had so much cherished, he used a text to confirm his argument:

> Whosoever shall keep the whole law, and yet fail in one point, he is guilty in all. . . . And yet we will say, we have no free will: we can do nothing of ourselves. Truth it is, if God had left us uncreated, and had given us neither understanding nor reason, then might we say that we could do nothing of ourselves. But God hath made us better than unreasonable beasts, and yet they have power to use themselves according to their nature, and yet they are creatures without reason. Are we not better than they? . . .[32]

Marian calvinists won over at least one free-willer in prison, and taught him to read James in the light of the text from Paul, 'Faith only justifieth, and not the deeds of the law'. He then tried to convert his

---

[31] *Acts of the Privy Council*, ed J. R. Dasent (London 1891) III, pp 198–9, 206–7. Strype in *Ecclesiastical Memorials* II, pp 236–7 implies rather misleadingly that this was a group of anabaptists. Neither in the examinations before the privy council nor in Henry Hart's little book, *A Godly, Newe, Short Treatyse . . .*, 1548, is there any criticism of infant baptism, though the doctrine of predestination is openly attacked.

[32] *Ecclesiastical Memorials*, III, appendix pp 113–16.

erstwhile brethren who were still at liberty.[33] Yet it seems that some time elapsed before this type of pelagianism was driven underground. Returning marian exiles on their tours round England in their capacity as royal commissioners at the beginning of Elizabeth's reign thought they recognised signs of anabaptism, arianism and other heresies, while professor Collinson has found traces of pelagian ideas in elizabethan Essex.[34] The sort of layman who had been attracted to lollardy at least partly because he wished to interpret the scriptures for himself was hardly likely to accept an authoritative interpretation from the hands of the protestant clergy. This is the attitude, something more than a mere blind anti-intellectualism, which lies behind the cry 'that learned men were the cause of great errors'.[35]

Although calvinist theology soon triumphed over the protestant populace as it did amongst the protestant clergy as Elizabeth's reign progressed, the calvinism which the people seem to have adopted had a subtle difference. At least in certain areas protestantism was popular, apparently, in almost direct relation to the strength of its reaction against Rome. When the moment of decision came even the clerical radicals like Sampson and Humphrey agreed with the elizabethan bishops that vestments were a matter indifferent, they did not constitute a sufficiently major issue to justify a division in the church. In London and elsewhere in England, some of the laity refused to accept this distinction: they would not attend their parish churches so long as their ministers conformed to the archbishop's directive and wore the surplice, the livery of Rome, and so of the anti-christian church. In 1567, if not earlier, a group of Londoners withdrew from their parish churches, and, so the high commissioners later alleged, held their own assemblies in which they prayed, heard sermons and received the sacraments among themselves.[36]

This Plumbers' Hall congregation in many respects forshadowed the many other separatist or semi-separatist assemblies in England before the civil war which came into being at least partly in reaction to the policy of the crown and the bishops. A new confidence can be recognised in the dissenters' use of publicity: the report of the examination of the

[33] *Ibid* III, appendix pp 116–23.
[34] *Zurich Letters*, [ed H. Robinson], Parker Society, 2 vols (Cambridge 1842) I, p 92. P. Collinson, 'The Godly: Aspects of Popular Protestantism in Elizabethan England', *Past and Present* Conference Papers (7 July 1966) typescript.
[35] Burrage, *Early English Dissenters*, II, p 1.
[36] *Grindal's Remains*, [ed W. Nicholson], Parker Society (Cambridge 1843) pp 199–216.

Plumbers' Hall congregation does not come from the official ecclesiastical sources, though Grindal referred to their activities in one of his letters, but from a collection of puritan propaganda perhaps master minded by John Field and published in 1593 as *A Parte of a Register*.[37] Unlike the lollards of little more than a generation earlier who seem always to have sought anonymity, these separatists obviously considered that an appeal to the public at large would advance their cause. They saw themselves in the main stream of historical progress, as the true successors of the marian protestant martyrs. Already in 1567 they could appeal to Foxe's *Book of Martyrs* as a final authority for their actions: 'It may be shewed in the book of the monuments of the church, that many which were burnt in queen Mary's time, died for standing against popery, as we now do.'[38]

The examination of the members of the Plumbers' Hall congregation by the high commission did not end separatism in London. Early in 1568 an assembly of seventy-seven people, thirty-five men and forty-two women, from parishes all over London was discovered meeting in the house of James Tynne, a goldsmith, in St Martin's in the Fields. The high commissioners bound over some, imprisoned others but still some persisted in their separation and went on to join the privy church of Richard Fitz.[39] This church in its turn marks a new departure not only in the history of English popular religion but also in the record keeping of these unestablished churches. It made use of the printing press to disseminate the reasons why its members abstained from attending their parish churches. In a black letter sheet Richard Fitz set out the protestation the members made before being accepted into the church.[40] Recognising that in this church the word of God and the sacraments were given purely without any traditions of men and that they had escaped the 'filthy canon law' and received in its place discipline altogether agreeable to Christ, a new member made the following declaration:

> Being thoroughly persuaded in my conscience, by the working and by the word of the Almighty, that these relics of anti-christ be abominable before the Lord our God. And also for that by

[37] *Zurich Letters*, I, pp 201–2.
[38] *Grindal's Remains*, p 211.
[39] Burrage, *Early English Dissenters*, II, pp 9–11.
[40] PRO S[tate] P[apers] 15. 20. 107 ii, and see Burrage, *Early English Dissenters*, II, pp 13–15 and *The Seconde Parte of a Register*, ed A. Peel, 2 vols (Cambridge 1915) I, pp 56–7.

the power and mercy, strength and goodness of the Lord my God only, I am escaped from the filthiness and polution of these detestable traditions, through the knowledge of our Lord and Saviour Jesus Christ . . .

I have now joined myself to the church of Christ wherein I have yielded myself subject to the discipline of God's word as I promised at my baptism, which if I should now again forsake and join myself with their traditions, I should then forsake the union wherein I am knit to the body of Christ and join myself to the discipline of anti-christ. For in the church of the traditioners there is no other discipline than that which hath been maintained by the anti-christian popes of Rome, whereby the church of God hath always been afflicted, and is until this day, for which I refuse them.

An elizabethan reporter upon these events added, 'To this protestation the congregation singularly did swear, and after that took the communion for ratification of their assent.'[41]

Burrage took this protestation put out by Fitz's church to be an early form of church covenant. If it was so regarded at the time, those who made it do not seem to have recognised the full implications of their position. The theoretical justification for separatism came in the 1580s with Robert Browne. A great many of the early separatists seem to have left their parish churches conditionally until the English church should be thoroughly reformed: Browne thought of the church rather differently, as churches gathered from the reprobate, or companies of saints living in harmony but without any precise organisation. When persecution threatened, Browne's own congregation in Norwich made a covenant with God and with one another. 'There was a day appointed . . . for cleaving to the Lord in greater obedience. So a covenant was made and their mutual consent was given to hold together. There were certain chief points proved unto them by the scriptures, all which being particularly rehearsed unto them, with exhortation, they agreed upon them, and pronounced their agreement to each thing particularly, saying, "To this we give our consent".'[42] In his chronicle of the dissensions which beset this church when it emigrated apparently early in 1582 to the Netherlands, Browne described in detail the sort of disputes which could arise among men and women who had gone into exile for the

---

[41] Inner Temple, Petyt MS 538. 47 fol 511. This is in manuscript; only the first part of this declaration appears in the printed version, PRO SP 15. 20. 107 ii.

[42] 'A True and Short Declaration' in *The Writings of Robert Harrison and Robert Browne*, ed A. Peel and L. H. Carlson (London 1953) p 422.

sake of religion. The same sort of quarrels had arisen in Frankfort in Mary's reign and an account of them had been published by Thomas Wood in 1574 in his *Brief Discourse of the Troubles at Frankfort*;[43] similar quarrels afflicted Johnson's English congregation in the Netherlands early in the seventeenth century. Browne wrote the account of divisions in his church mainly to justify his decision to abandon the church. These unestablished congregations as yet did not keep a record of their activities for their own sake, even apparently in exile. In England, under persecution any keeping of administrative records would have been dangerous. Most of the information of the religious activities of those protestants who refused to conform to the established church still largely came from the fragmentary records of the high commission: a material difference, however, now regularly appeared. Whereas the records of the late lollard trials invariably came from official ecclesiastical sources, the elizabethan separatists, having learnt from Foxe the value of propaganda, themselves set down the details of their own sufferings before the high commission.

The followers of Barrow and Greenwood in particular seem to have felt the need both for public justification and for hagiography. Even after their imprisonment in 1587 Barrow and Greenwood continued to write and publish separatist exhortations. As Henry Barrow wrote *A Brief Discovery of the False Church* the manuscript was passed out of prison to another member of the sect, James Forester, a physician and Cambridge MA who toned down some of the more abusive parts, and added material of his own. Robert Stokes, as he confessed before the high commissioners early in 1593, had been largely responsible for the printing: Barrow and Greenwood had given him the manuscript of both *A Collection of Certain Slanderous Articles*, and *An Answer to George Gifford's Pretended Defence of Read Prayers*. He had arranged for the manuscripts to be taken to Dort, he had himself paid for the printing of five hundred copies of each, and brought some of the pamphlets back to England for sale and distribution.[44]

Although most separatists in 1593 were very circumspect in what they revealed to the high commissioners, from the sheer number of their examinations, fifty-two in all, a considerable amount of detail emerges on the management of their church. Some time after the

[43] P. Collinson, 'The Authorship of "A Brieff Discours off the Troubles Begonne at Franckford"', *JEH*, 9 (1958) pp 188–208. *A Brief Discourse of the Troubles at Frankfort*, ed E. Arber (London 1908).
[44] *The Writings of John Greenwood and Henry Barrow, 1593*, [ed L. H. Carlson] (London 1970) pp 308–12.

imprisonment of Barrow and Greenwood the church was formally constituted, or reconstituted, in September 1592. In the presence of some fifty or more separatists in Fox's house in St Nicholas Lane Francis Johnson was chosen as pastor, Mr Greenwood as doctor, Bowman and Lee deacons and Studley and Knifton elders. At this same meeting Johnson had baptised several children, some as old as six or seven years, who had been kept from baptism in the parish churches: he had used no other ceremony but the washing of their faces and the words, 'I do baptise thee in the name of the Father, of the Son and of the Holy Ghost'. Johnson had at other times administered holy communion to them. They had had five or more white loaves set on the table which the pastor had broken and given to some of them, and the deacons to the remainder, who were sitting or standing round the table. The pastor had next given the cup to one, and he had passed it to the next, and so on till all had drunk, using the words at the delivery as in 1 Corinthians, 11: 24. At their meetings, some times attended by sixty, some times by as many as a hundred, they had a collection, and the deacons at their discretion used it to maintain the pastor and relieve their poor.[45] Besides in this way preaching sincerely and ministering the sacraments purely the church also instituted discipline. Robert Abraham remembered the time when Robert Stokes, who had paid for the printing of some of Barrow's works, George Collier and another were excommunicated for dissenting from them in certain opinions.[46] When he joined the church Abraham Pulberry 'made a promise to the Lord in the presence of his congregation . . . that he would walk with them as they would walk with the Lord',[47] and many other members seem to have made a similar simple undertaking.[48] They did not consider marriage an ecclesiastical ceremony: at a meeting at which Penry had been present and Thomas Settle had prayed, Christopher Bowman had declared his marriage before friends. Many had an almost irrational dread of formal set prayers, and some prisoners carried this so far as to refuse to recite the Lord's Prayer.[49]

Something can be deduced about the social composition of the church: it seems to have been pretty varied, and certainly not exclusively confined to the poor as the ecclesiastical authorities often implied.

[45] *The Writings of John Greenwood and Henry Barrow, 1593*, pp 306-8.
[46] *Ibid* pp 323-6.
[47] *Ibid* pp 300-3.
[48] *Ibid* pp 365-8.
[49] *Ibid* pp 335-8.

It included other university educated men besides Barrow, Greenwood and Penry: Forester, the physician, had been trained at Cambridge, as had Francis Johnson and his brother, George, a schoolmaster. It had attracted two clerics who had been ordained in the established church, Thomas Settle and William Smith, while Arthur Bellot from Cornwall was described as a scholar and gentleman. There were other school-masters as well as apparently fairly prosperous London citizens, gold-smiths, haberdashers, scriveners, apothecaries. Edward Boys who died in prison in 1593 or 1594 left a legacy of £300 to his wife. Of course, the church also contained its full complement of the poor, cobblers, weavers, coopers, purse makers, tailors, and, interestingly, shipwrights from Deptford. A husbandman had even found his way there from a village near Wisbech.⁵⁰ Approximately half the people examined in April 1593 were able to sign their names.⁵¹

Appearance before the high commission, imprisonment, the execu-tion of Barrow, Greenwood and Penry had the effect of confirming most of these members of Barrow's church in their separatism: few of those examined early in 1593 conformed. The only way in which the civil and ecclesiastical authorities could cope with separatism was by banishment. In 1597 Francis and George Johnson obtained their release from prison on condition that they emigrated to Canada. In fact because of their inhospitable reception there from American Indians and from the French they substituted the Netherlands for their place of exile. A considerable number of the congregation settled with them in the Netherlands and their community was rent with the same sort of quarrels as had troubled Harrison and Browne. A remnant, however, of the church remained underground in London and re-emerged in the seventeenth century with Lee as its pastor, perhaps Nicholas Lee who had been made a deacon 1593.⁵² In 1632 newer separatist bodies referred to this London church as 'the ancient church' of the separa-tion.⁵³

The sporadic attempts by the ecclesiastical authorities in the reigns of James I and Charles I to enforce uniformity caused the emergence of more separatism and semi-separatism, and an increasing stream of emigration to the Netherlands. The church which gathered around the

⁵⁰ *Ibid* pp 329–32.
⁵¹ *Ibid* p 399.
⁵² G. Johnson, *A Discours of some Troubles in the Banished English Church at Amster-dam* (Amsterdam ? 1603) and B. R. White, *The English Separatist Tradition* (Oxford 1971) pp 91–115.
⁵³ Burrage, *Early English Dissenters*, II, p 296.

former Lincoln preacher, John Smith, and Thomas Helwys at Scrooby made a covenant in England before it left for Holland in 1608. Smith's progression from apparently orthodox calvinism through self-baptism and the idea of believer's baptism as the true form of admission to a church to an attempt formally to merge with the Dutch mennonites all happened in Holland. Thomas Helwys refused to follow Smith the whole way towards assimilation with the Dutch anabaptists. He returned to England in 1612 to establish a congregation of English arminian baptists in London, though he knew imprisonment was his almost certain fate. Helwys only lived for a very little while after his return but somehow some baptist groups managed to survive in England. In the records of the Dutch waterlanders there is a letter of 1626 from five English congregations at London, Lincoln, Salisbury, Coventry and Tiverton.[54] With these baptists, the strain of pelagianism was renewed in popular piety which, though hardly significant as yet, was to be of considerable importance in the period of the civil war.

Because of its association with the atrocities in Münster in the 1530s re-baptism remained repellant both to English churchmen and to the populace in general. Most of the lay people who drew apart from the established church to practice their own form of piety as the attempt by the laudians to enforce more rigid uniformity intensified, wished to retain an orthodox form of sixteenth century calvinism. As Laud and his supporters made it increasingly impossible for lecturers to preach legally without conforming fully to all aspects of the ceremonial of the church so they almost certainly increased the phenomenon of separatism and semi-separatism by which forward protestants attempted to replace or supplement what they thought to be the inadequate ministrations of the state church.

The congregation which Henry Jacob instituted in London in 1616 covenanted 'to walk in all God's ways as he had revealed or should make known to them' but did not insist on rigid separation from the established church and its members professed unity with the godly within the church.[55] Many of the members of this congregation who now had John Lathrop as their pastor were captured at a conventicle in 1632 and appeared before the high commission in London. Laud could get little from them, since they all refused the *ex officio* oath and, by implication, the jurisdiction of the ecclesiastical courts.[56] Elizabeth

---

[54] *Ibid* II, p 233.   [55] *Ibid* II, pp 294.

[56] *Ibid* II, pp 311–22; *Reports of Cases in the Courts of Star Chamber and High Commision*, [ed S. R. Gardiner], CS, ns 39 (1886) pp 278, 281, 284, 300, 307, 315.

Melbourn put simply the purpose of their assemblies. 'I do not know any such thing as a conventicle. We did meet to pray and talk of the word of God, which is according to the law of the land.' To this Neile, the new archbishop of York, as succinctly replied, 'God will be served publicly, not in your private house.'[57] It was the independence of the laity which most offended the churchmen. Laud attacked the Londoners for coming out of their parishes to meet to discuss their heretical ideas. These lay people, and the women were as equally assertive as the men, had emancipated themselves from clerical instruction. Hurt pride, incomprehension at this unwillingness to accept guidance, caused George Abbot, the aged archbishop of Canterbury to react in an impassioned, and very revealing, way:

> You do show yourselves the most ungrateful to God and to his majesty the king, and to us the fathers of the church. If you have any knowledge of God, it hath come through and by us, or some of our predecessors. We have taken care under God to give milk to the babes and younglings and strong meat for the men of understanding. You have the word of God to feed you, the sacraments to strengthen you, and we support you by prayer. For all this what despite do you return us? You call us abominable men, to be hated of all, that we carry the mark of the beast, that we are his members. We do bear this patiently, not because we have no law to right us, but because of your obstinacy. But for your dishonouring of God and disobeying the king, it is not to be endured. When you have reading, preaching, singing, teaching, you are your own ministers, the blind lead the blind, whereas his majesty is God's vicegerent in the church: the church is nothing with you, and his ministers not to be regarded, and you run into woods, as if you lived in persecution, such an one you make the king, to whom we are so much bound for his great care for the truth to be preserved among us, and you would have men believe that he is a tyrant – this besides your wickedness, unthankfulness and ungraciousness towards us, the fathers of the church . . .[58]

Wicked, unthankful and ungracious some of the people may have been in persisting in practising their own forms of piety but the churchmen were decades if not centuries too late in their attempt to curb their initiative. With the widespread foundation and re-foundation of schools

[57] *Reports of Cases in Star Chamber and High Commission*, p 295.
[58] *Ibid* pp 309–10.

in the sixteenth century which continued in its momentum in the first half of the seventeenth popular literacy was widespread, the people had the means to read the bible, to judge the established church for themselves. Despite the supervision of the high commission the independent congregations multiplied and subdivided in London in the 1630s and with the lifting of control on the meeting of the long parliament they emerged into the open.[59] Not surprisingly, considering the very different history of the separatist churches, the records of the independent churches founded between 1640 and 1660 reveal very diverse types of popular piety. Most churches could look back to a covenant. As early as 1640 the five founder members of the Bristol Broadmead church under the leadership of Mrs Hazzard 'joined themselves together in the Lord . . . covenanting that they would in the strength and assistance of the Lord, come forth of the world, and worship the Lord more purely, persevering therein to their end'.[60] At this stage, however, they had not determined on absolute separation and still considered it permissible to hear sermons in the established church once the prayer book ceremonies were over. In 1644 the congregational church in Stepney covenanted 'to walk in all the ways of Christ held out unto them in the gospel' but their church was rather a church within the parish church than absolutely separated from it: their pastor, William Greenhill held the post of evening lecturer at Stepney from 1643 and ten years later, while still remaining their minister, became vicar of Stepney.[61] Typical of the independent churches established in the next decade was that of Cockermouth where in 1651 under the influence of Thomas Larkham, pastor of an independent church at Tavistock in Devon, 'seven poor unworthy ones', George Larkham, George Benson, Roger Fieldhouse, Thomas Blethwaite, John Woods, Richard Bowes and Thomas Jackson entered into an agreement 'to walk as a people whom the Lord hath chosen'. They decided that baptism and the Lord's Supper should be the ordinances of the church to be ministered not by private christians but only by lawful officers and that these officers should be no hierarchy but ruling elders and deacons. They owned the practice of baptising the children of constant believers and of singing psalms.[62]

The procedure of the Broadmead church, as it reconstituted itself

[59] Burrage, *Early English Dissenters*, II, pp 298–302.
[60] *Records of a Church of Christ meeting in Broadmead, Bristol*, ed E. B. Underhill, H[anserd] K[nollys] S[ociety] (London 1847) p 18; hereafter *Broadmead Records*.
[61] [A. T. Jones] *Notes of [the Early Days of] Stepney Meeting, 1644–1689* (London 1887) pp 4–16.
[62] *The Christian Reformer*, 10 (1824) pp 1–3.

after its exile in London during the royalist occupation of Bristol, represents the more conservative aspect of separatist popular piety in the commonwealth period. The church called its own ministers, first Dr Angello and then Mr Ewins: it met apart to receive communion from its minister, but did not object to its minister preaching publicly to unseparated congregations in the city. It assembled on the fifth day of the week to discuss a portion of scripture when any brother might speak, though the sisters of the church could only speak through a brother. In 1652 some members of the church began to have doubts about the validity of infant baptism and some were rebaptised, but this did not cause a permanent split in the church as the supporters and opponents of infant baptism continued to worship side by side as the members of the Bedford church also seem to have done.[63] Dr Nuttall has emphasised that those calvinist independents who held believers baptism became a self-conscious community only after the restoration.[64]

The piety of the arminian baptists, whose evolution was quite different, took a considerably more radical form. The records they kept themselves suggest that Thomas Edwards's reporting of their meetings may not have been unduly exaggerated. Edwards, in *Gangraena*, described how in November 1645 about eighty anabaptists met at a great house in Bishopsgate and held a love feast at which five new members were 'dipped'. They began with a prayer, and afterwards every member knelt down and their minister went to each one, and laid his hands upon them, men and women, and prayed that they might receive the Holy Ghost. The intention of the laying on of hands was that those members who received gifts might preach publicly. After this ceremony they had supper, and after that took holy communion. Then a question was propounded, 'Whether Christ died for all men, or no?' and they fell into a dispute and went on discussing this till past eleven at night.[65] The general baptist church of Fenstanton in Huntingdonshire recorded that the laying on of hands on all baptised believers was a commandment of Christ's, and that the breaking of bread after supper was a safe and blameless way to follow. On the fourth day of the tenth month 1653 Henry Denne, their first pastor, felt it would be profitable for the congregation to be instructed on the points which

[63] *Broadmead Records*, pp 32–42; *The Church Book of Bunyan Meeting 1650–1821*, ed G. B. Harrison (London 1928) p 2.
[64] G. F. Nuttall, *Visible Saints* (Oxford 1957) pp 118–20.
[65] T. Edwards, *Gangraena* (London 1646) 'a copy of some letters', p 45.

S.C.H. T

separated the saints from their adversaries – whether Christ died for all men, or only for some particular persons, whether baptism belonged to believers or infants, whether God were the author of sins, whether the ordinances of God, as prayer, exhortation, baptism, the breaking of bread etc. were ceased or continued, and whether there was a possibility for believers to fall away.[66]

The detailed minutes which the Fenstanton church kept of all its meetings incidentally illustrate the volatile aspect of popular piety. Even when laymen had separated from the parish churches they might well not remain constant in their profession. The business of the very first recorded meeting of the Fenstanton church was taken up by Thomas Bagley, John Rich and their wives from Yelling who could not be brought to try the spirit by the scriptures, or agree to the necessity of prayer, preaching or the breaking of bread. At Fenstanton itself John and Elizabeth Offley were excommunicated for holding the same views and for asserting that they were grown to perfection and were gods. John Hatten suffered the same penalty for forsaking the assembly of the saints, marrying a wife who was an 'infidel', for returning to the church of England and for swearing and drunkenness.[67] There can be no doubt that many lay people now, however humble, demanded the right to chose their own theology and worship God as they thought fit. Mistress Mary Brown of Limehouse left the Stepney church 'because the pastor had declared that man hath not power of himself to do anything, and that God had made everything for himself, even the wicked for the day of evil, and that God did upon his will condemn men for sin'. She found a theology which suited her inclination better in John Goodwin's gathered church.[68] At that general baptist church in London where Dr Peter Chamberlen eventually gained dominance, who was physician at the courts of James I, Charles I and (after the restoration) of Charles II, sister Anne Harriman threatened to withdraw because brother Naudin, an elder, had said he would not walk with such as gave liberty to women to speak in church. Here the church after a long discussion between Chamberlen and Naudin on the proper translation from the Greek of 1 Corinthians, 14: 34 ('Let your women keep silence in the churches'), made a concession. They concluded that 'a woman, maid, wife or widow, being a prophetess

[66] *Records of a Church of Christ at Fenstanton, Warboys and Hexham, 1644–1720*, ed E. B. Underhill, HKS (London 1854) pp 68, 82–6; hereafter *Fenstanton Records*.

[67] *Fenstanton Records*, pp 1–11.

[68] *Notes of Stepney Meeting, 1644–1689*, pp 16–18.

(1 Corinthians, 11) may speak, prophesy, pray, with a veil'. In other matters they displayed less generosity: they delivered Eleazar Bar Ishai over to Satan for having long dissembled with the church by going to other assemblies under the pretence of selling books, and for recently having taken his child to be 'sprinkled' by the presbyterians.[69] Most of the gathered churches which have left records seem to have been seriously troubled in the 1650s by 'the wicked whimsies and nonsensical interpretations' of the quakers and to have lost considerable numbers of members to them, while other members seem to have reverted frequently to 'church of England' worship.[70] Among some lay people such a wide degree of tolerance seems to have prevailed that it must have tended to nullify the claims of any exclusive church. As William Marriat protested when the Fenstanton elders tried to persuade him to stay loyal to their gathered church, and to that church alone; 'I do believe that other people which do not observe these ordinances are the people of God, as well as you.'[71] Dr Hill has recently demonstrated the strength of popular hostility to any form of organised religion at this period, although this latitudinarianism, even agnosticism, did not invariably lead to antagonism to all forms of religion.[72]

The elders of the Fenstanton church looked upon the keeping of their church book as a solemn duty, and when they came to the end of the book in December 1658 which they had begun in 1651, they set aside a day for its formal signing by the officers of the church.[73] These commonwealth church books provide a new form of source material for popular piety, a source probably not sufficiently exploited by general ecclesiastical historians, and certainly under-exploited by social historians. After the gathered churches had been constituted, however, their records share some of the same deficiencies with those of the established church in that they, like the ecclesiastical court records, concentrate almost exclusively on the failings of delinquent members and reveal little of the piety of the faithful. Rarely can unorthodox popular piety be studied uncontaminated; it can only be reconstructed from the formal record of episcopal officers, later of the officers of the high commission, from the separatists' own propaganda statements

[69] Oxford Bodleian Rawlinson MS D282 pp 28–32, summarised in some detail in 'A True and Short Declaration', ed C. Burrage, *Transactions of the Baptist Historical Society*, 2 (1910–11) pp 145–7.
[70] *Fenstanton Records*, p 144.
[71] *Ibid* p 40.
[72] C. Hill, *The World Turned Upside Down* (London 1972) especially pp 130–85.
[73] *Fenstanton Records*, p 251.

and finally from the equally, though differently, biased church books. Nevertheless, despite the medium, occasionally the voice of a plain layman, whether lollard, separatist, commonwealth independent, baptist or agnostic, does break through. Had the anglican authorities in 1662 paid more attention to the records of the unestablished churches then perhaps they might have reached rather earlier the conclusion they reluctantly admitted in 1689, that the expression of popular piety was beyond their power to control.

WELSH CHURCH HISTORY:
SOURCES AND PROBLEMS

by NIGEL YATES

WHEN one considers how intimately the ecclesiastical history of Wales has been bound up with that of England from at least the twelfth century until the disestablishment of the Welsh church in 1920, it is perhaps surprising that the subject should present as many problems as it does to those approaching it for the first time, especially to those familiar with the sources of English ecclesiastical history. It will not, of course, be possible in a paper of this length to consider fully all the problems involved, and I wish therefore to confine myself to four which seem to me to be absolutely basic. They are the shortage of primary source material; the lack of competent monographs on many topics; the language barrier which faces those unfamiliar with Welsh; and the dangers inherent in what may be called the 'Welsh Nationalist' approach to Welsh ecclesiastical history.

The dearth of Welsh ecclesiastical records is well known.[1] For the period before the twelfth century there is nothing of substance. The historian of the celtic church in Wales has to rely on the problematic evidence of archaeology and placenames, the lives of the saints (no Welsh source being earlier than the eleventh century and some surviving only as seventeenth-century transcripts or compilations),[2] and texts bristling with difficulties such as the *Liber Landavensis*.[3] Even for the

---

[1] The best guides to what survives are R. I. Jack, *Medieval Wales* (London 1972) pp 127–60, and J. C. Davies, 'The Records of the Church in Wales', *National Library of Wales Journal*, 4 (Aberystwyth 1945–6) pp 1–34; the remainder of the latter volume is devoted to articles on other aspects of Welsh ecclesiastical history and records.

[2] The earliest Welsh text is *Rhigyfarch's Life of St David*, ed J. W. James (Cardiff 1967) composed in the last quarter of the eleventh century. For a general assessment of the value of saints' lives see D. S. Evans's introduction to the new edition of G. H. Doble, *Lives of the Welsh Saints* (Cardiff 1971) pp 1–55.

[3] The standard edition is *The Text of the Book of Llan Dâv*, ed J. G. Evans and J. Rhys (Oxford 1893) replacing the hopelessly inaccurate *Liber Landavensis*, ed W. J. Rees (Llandovery 1840). There has always been a desire in Wales, at present represented by J. W. James and P. C. Bartrum, to believe in the basic genuineness of the text, but most other scholars see its alleged sixth- and

later medieval period the evidence is lamentably thin, and Welsh vernacular poetry becomes a major source of evidence for the ecclesiastical historian.[4] After the reformation, Welsh diocesan, chapter and parish archives are fuller, but they still do not contain either the variety or the quantity of documentation which an English historian has come to expect of his own ecclesiastical repositories. Whereas in England most dioceses contain largely unbroken series of bishops' registers beginning in the thirteenth or fourteenth century, in Wales only the dioceses of St Davids and Bangor have any pre-reformation bishops' registers, and these only cover a total of sixty-five years.[5] Chapter records are just as thin in most cases. Those of St Davids are the fullest, with chapter act books virtually complete from 1560, fabric accounts complete from 1686, sixteenth century transcripts of communars' accounts beginning in 1384, and important collections of material now lost in the manuscripts of archdeacons Edward Yardley (1698–1770) and Thomas Payne (1759–1832).[6] The records of the other Welsh chapters do not survive in any quantity before the second half of the seventeenth century, but Bangor has a volume of pre-1600 documents, mysteriously described as '*Acta* 3', containing both diocesan and chapter records, and St Asaph has a similar *Liber Antiquus*. Even parish records in Wales are thin; only a small minority of parish registers go back as far as the sixteenth century, and seventeenth century churchwardens' accounts are excep-

---

seventh-century charters as fabrications of the twelfth century. In a recent London PhD thesis, Wendy Davies argues that a detailed study of the text suggests that the early 'charters' assembled there may well be summaries of genuine documents now lost; part of her argument is now more widely available in W. E. Davies, 'St Mary's Worcester and the *Liber Landavensis*', *Journal of the Society of Archivists*, 4 (London 1972) pp 459–85.

[4] See, for instance, the list of primary sources cited by Glanmor Williams, *The Welsh Church from Conquest to Reformation* (Cardiff 1962) pp 567–73.

[5] The St Davids' registers run from 1397–1410, 1482–1518, 1636–8, and from 1660. The pre-reformation registers have been misleadingly published as *The Episcopal Registers of St Davids, 1397–1518*, Cymmrodorion Record Series, 6 (London 1917–20). The Bangor registers run from 1408–17, 1508–25, 1542–1636, and from 1682. The earliest register was published by Ivor Pryce in *Archaeologia Cambrensis*, 7 series, 2 (London 1922) pp 80–107. No registers survive for the diocese of Llandaff before 1819.

[6] Yardley's *Menevia Sacra*, which includes precise references to the now lost episcopal registers of Benedict Nicholls and Thomas Rodburn (1417–42), was edited by Francis Green for the Cambrian Archaeological Association in 1927. The two volumes of Payne's *Collectanea Menevensia*, in the National Library of Wales, have yet to find an editor, but their contents were listed by B. G. Owens in *National Library of Wales Journal*, 4 (1945–6) p 211.

tionally rare.[7] In Carmarthenshire, for example, only one parish, St Ishmaels, has registers pre-dating 1600; these registers begin in 1560 but there are no entries at all between 1643 and 1678. Less than a third of the county's medieval churches have pre-1700 registers or pre-1800 vestry books, and in six parishes there are no records at all before 1813 when the keeping of registers was regulated by act of parliament.[8] Only a few Welsh parishes have retained anything apart from their official records; many appear not to have kept service registers until well into the present century, and parish magazines or scrapbooks are only occasionally discovered.[9]

The paucity of record sources for Welsh ecclesiastical history is to some extent compensated for by the fact that they are now easily accessible and kept largely in one repository. Under an agreement made in 1944 between the national library of Wales and the representative body of the church in Wales, all the surviving diocesan and capitular archives were deposited at Aberystwyth, and a large number of Welsh parishes have also deposited their records there. The Welsh county record offices have only managed to acquire a few parish collections, a sore point with some Welsh archivists, and Welsh ecclesiastical records in non-Welsh repositories have, where possible, been photocopied or microfilmed by the national library. Thus, for the Welsh ecclesiastical historian, his basic source material is largely available in Aberystwyth, in a library also containing all the standard printed works that he will require.

It is, therefore, surprising that so little work of importance has been done on most aspects of Welsh ecclesiastical history.[10] There are, of course, exceptions. The late Dr Conway Davies has made available in print, from a variety of sources, most of the documentation relating to

[7] Note, for instance, the importance attached to the surviving accounts for Tenby for the years 1657–73, extracts from which are printed in E. Laws and E. H. Edwards, *Church Book of St Mary the Virgin* (Tenby 1907) pp 239–52.
[8] See T. I. Jeffreys-Jones, 'Carmarthenshire Parish Records', *Carmarthen Antiquary*, 2 (Carmarthen 1945–57) pp 100–7, 141–65. Some parishes were omitted from this survey.
[9] For instance, at Tenby, where a parish magazine was begun by the tractarian rector, George Huntington, in 1869, only the first four volumes survive, and these were chance discoveries by the curator of the local museum. These magazines contain valuable information on the impact of the Oxford movement in south-west Wales.
[10] The basic guide here is *A Bibliography of the History of Wales* (Cardiff 1962); *addenda* are published from time to time in the *Bulletin of the Board of Celtic Studies* (publ Cardiff).

the Welsh church prior to 1272,[11] professor Glanmor Williams has produced an exemplary survey of *The Welsh church from Conquest to Reformation*, and Welsh nonconformity has always attracted a substantial number of historians, writing mostly in Welsh in the periodicals of their respective denominations. But much basic work still needs to be done; important texts, such as the *Llyfr Coch Asaph*, require editors, others, like the *Black Book of St Davids*,[12] need re-editing, and there is an urgent need for good monographs, especially on the celtic church in Wales, and on post-reformation anglicanism and roman catholicism. It was hoped that the foundation of the historical society of the church in Wales in 1946 would provide Welsh ecclesiastical history with the stimulus it needed, but this has not occurred. The society has so far only produced the two volumes of pre-1272 documents edited by Conway Davies, and its journal has not established anything more than a local reputation. But a more vigorous society of this sort is just what Welsh church history needs, though one would prefer to see a journal unrestricted by denominational barriers. Surely the board of celtic studies and the university of Wales press could give the support that is needed here, and at the same time commission a several volume ecclesiastical history of Wales, into which Glanmor Williams's volume on the later middle ages could be incorporated?

One consideration which has without doubt prevented many Welsh historians from taking a specialist interest in ecclesiastical history is that many topics require a good knowledge of Welsh. This is particularly so in the case of the pre-reformation church in Wales, where vernacular poetry and saints' lives are important sources of evidence, and even more so in the case of nonconformity, where both primary and secondary sources are almost exclusively in Welsh. But the language barrier is more widespread than this; the only substantial work on the Oxford movement in Wales, though basically an English import, has been written in Welsh,[13] and the two main anglican periodicals of the nineteenth century, *Y Llan* and *Yr Haul*, were, as their titles

[11] *Episcopal Acts and Cognate Documents relating to the Welsh Dioceses, 1066–1272*, ed J. C. Davies, Historical Society of the Church in Wales (Cardiff 1946–9).

[12] A poor edition with translation, by J. W. Willis-Bund, was published in the Cymmrodorion Record Series, 5 (London, 1902).

[13] Namely a series of thirty articles by H. L. James, 'Yr Hen Lwybrau', contributed to *Yr Haul* during 1932–4, and D. E. Evans, 'Mudiad Rhydychen yng Ngogledd Sir Aberteifi' and subsequent articles contributed to the *Journal of the Historical Society of the Church in Wales* between 1954 and 1960 (publ Cardiff).

suggest, both published in Welsh. These difficulties do not face the many non-Welsh-speaking Welsh historians working in the fields of administrative or political, economic or social history, especially in the post-medieval period, and these topics have consequently attracted more scholars. However, the language barrier can be overcome. Welsh historians with ecclesiastical interests, or ecclesiastical historians with Welsh interests, who are prepared to learn Welsh will find that their efforts are amply repaid by the number of research topics still waiting to be tackled.

The problems of learning Welsh are, in my view, less difficult to overcome than the nationalistic approach to Welsh ecclesiastical history that has been adopted, and which is to some extent still being adopted, by many Welsh historians. The 'Welsh Nationalist' approach to Welsh ecclesiastical history is basically a desire on the part of its protagonists to see the Welsh church as a special, different, independent institution, and therefore to emphasise its peculiarities. In particular, such historians play down English influence in Welsh affairs, or else see it as an unwanted intrusion and imposition which served to destroy the true native qualities of Welsh religion. Because most Welsh writers have a strong national awareness, usually of a cultural rather than a political nature, Welsh historians have been less able to detect the potential presence of nationalism in their work, than they have to understand the problems created by the paucity of records relating to Wales. Thus the problems created by the nationalist approach are perhaps greater, in that they are less obvious, especially to those unfamiliar with the development of Welsh ecclesiastical historiography.

The ecclesiastical historiography of Wales begins with the eighteenth-century antiquary, Browne Willis, whose scholarly approach was repeated by archdeacons Yardley and Payne, mentioned earlier, and by another archdeacon, D. R. Thomas, who published a learned history of the diocese of St Asaph between 1870 and 1874. But, unfortunately, a far greater impact was made in Wales by scholars of lesser stature, who saw the history of their country as a struggle between nationalist aspirations and external domination, and who were not averse to distorting the facts, and sometimes inventing them, to fit their own theories. Many of these eighteenth and nineteenth-century antiquaries were clergy with special interests in Welsh ecclesiastical history and medieval literature, and most of them were prominent in the organisation of *eisteddfodau*. One of the most influential of this group of 'Welsh Nationalist' historians was John Williams 'ab Ithel', who died from overwork in 1862 aged fifty-one,[14] and who published his magnum opus, *The Ecclesiastical Antiquities of the Cymry*, in 1844. This was an important book, and deserves to be better known than it is today, not because of any merits it may have, which are negligible, but because it is the classic statement of 'Welsh Nationalist' ecclesiastical history, and because it puts forward almost every known fiction, invention and superstition relating to the Welsh church before the middle of the twelfth century. Many of his theories were not his own; he was much indebted especially to the earlier work of Iolo Morganwg, the well-known forger of Welsh medieval manuscripts and inventor of the *Gorsedd*,[15] and Rice Rees, who published *An Essay on the Welsh Saints* in 1836.[16] For his account of early British history he, like his colleague, R. W. Morgan, who published *A History of Britain from the Flood to AD 700*,[17] relied on Geoffrey of Monmouth whose *Historia* they both

[14] For the details of his career see *The Dictionary of Welsh Biography* (London 1959) pp 1052–3. 'Ab Ithel' was a clergyman, holding a succession of Welsh livings, a prolific translator of medieval latin hymns into Welsh, and a disciple of the Oxford movement. He collaborated with Henry Longueville Jones to oppose the proposed union of the sees of Bangor and St Asaph, to edit *Archaeologia Cambrensis*, and to found the Cambrian Archaeological Association. Despite the fact that his abilities as an editor and his knowledge of palaeography were negligible, he was chosen to edit the *Annales Cambriae* and *Brut y Tywysogion* for the Rolls Series and four other texts for the Welsh Manuscripts Society, and his name was seriously canvassed for the proposed chair of celtic at Oxford. He was the organiser of the notorious Llangollen eisteddfod of 1858, at which most of the prizes went to his friends and relations, and an important essay by Thomas Stephens, denying that Madoc ap Owen Gwynedd had discovered America in the twelfth century, was denied the prize it should have won because it challenged 'ab Ithel's' own, more romantic, interpretation of Welsh history.

[15] The *Gorsedd* is now an essential part of the Welsh national eisteddfod, its president being the archdruid of Wales. Several of Iolo's 'inventions' were published during his lifetime in the *Myvyrian Archaiology* and many more after his death by his son, Taliesin ab Iolo, apparently quite innocently, in the collection of *Iolo Manuscripts* published by the Welsh Manuscripts Society in 1848 (? Llandovery). These forgeries were accepted as genuine by many Welsh historians until the inter-war period.

[16] Rice Rees (1804–39) was professor of Welsh at St David's college, Lampeter, and fellow of Jesus college, Oxford. He was a far better scholar than 'ab Ithel', and had it not been for his early death he would probably have been able to prevent 'ab Ithel' from acquiring the dominent position in Welsh historical scholarship during the mid-nineteenth century. Rice Rees's uncle, W. J. Rees of Cascob (1772–1855), was a poor editor of the *Liber Landavensis* in 1840 and *The Lives of the Cambro-British Saints* in 1853, having been prevailed upon to complete some of his nephew's projected work.

[17] See P. F. Anson, *Bishops at Large* (London 1964) pp 43–7. Morgan believed that the British were descended from the lost ten tribes of Israel and that saint Paul's

accepted as fact. 'Ab Ithel' believed that Welsh christianity, introduced into Britain by Bran the blessed and his companions,[18] was a logical continuation of the pre-christian bardo-druidic system, which he described in great detail, that the first priests were druids, and that the eucharist was at first celebrated on the druidic altars within their stone circles. He dated the foundation of the diocese of Llandaff to AD 173, accepted the metropolitical status of St Davids and certain other Welsh sees, and described the extent of the celtic 'dioceses' in Wales. He followed Rice Rees in accepting that Welsh churches were dedicated exclusively to local saints until the eighth century, a view still widely held in Wales today. The independent nature of celtic christianity as a sort of 'western orthodox' church was emphasised strongly, and its practices described in considerable detail, mostly from obscure and unreliable sources.

Many of his views are still held, in some form at least, by respected Welsh scholars today. Chancellor J. W. James still believes that the Welsh dioceses existed long before the Norman conquest and were originally coterminous with the ancient principalities of Wales, and professor Emrys Bowen still believes that the patterns of celtic dedications in Wales reveal the missionary journeys of the 'saints' themselves, that the diocese of St Asaph was actually founded by saint Kentigern, and so on.[19] Moreover, the 'Welsh Nationalist' approach has led to new allegations in recent years. 'Ab Ithel' and his colleagues accepted that the cult of *Garmon Sant* in Wales was that of saint Germanus of Auxerre, though they often credited him with Welsh parentage. But recently this view has been dismissed as linguistically unsound.[20] According to the ordinary rules of Welsh word-formation, Latin *Germanus* should make Welsh *Gerfawn*, with a soft mutation, and not *Garmon*, just as

---

missionary journeys included one to Britain. He was both an anglican clergyman and an autocephalous bishop in his own Ancient British Church.

[18] This was another invention by Iolo Morganwg who deliberately substituted the words *llinus Brân vab Llŷr* for *llinus Joseph o Arimathia* in his edition of the Welsh triads; see Rachel Bromwich, *Trioedd Ynys Prydein* (Cardiff 1961) p 203.

[19] For a detailed criticism of James's and Bowen's views, see C. N. L. Brooke, 'St Peter of Gloucester and St Cadoc of Llancarfan', *Celt and Saxon*, ed N. K. Chadwick (Cambridge 1964) pp 315–22; W. O. Chadwick, 'The Evidence of Dedications in the Early History of the Welsh Church', *Studies in Early British History*, ed N. K. Chadwick (Cambridge 1959) pp 173–88; and K. H. Jackson, 'Sources for the Life of St Kentigern', *Studies in the Early British Church*, ed N. K. Chadwick (Cambridge 1958) pp 313–18.

[20] By Sir Ifor Williams, 'Hen Chwedlau', *Transactions of the Honourable Society of Cymmrodorion* (London 1946–7) p 53 and Melville Richards, 'Places and Persons of the Early Welsh Church', *Welsh History Review*, 5 (Cardiff 1970–1) p 335.

Latin *terminus* makes Welsh *terfyn*. But then who was *Garmon Sant*? An obscure member of the royal family of Powys, as professor Melville Richards suggests? If he is right, then the cult of *Garmon Sant* is the only significant and widespread one in Wales to an otherwise unknown celtic saint, and this would have important historical implications which professor Richards seems not to have considered.

Although it is principally in the field of Welsh ecclesiastical history before the twelfth century that the 'Welsh Nationalist' approach is so marked, it is by no means absent in the historiography of later periods. Following Rice Rees, most Welsh historians have emphasised that the cult of Our Lady in Wales was an English import, and basically this is true. But what is important is that the cult was not regarded by the Welsh as an alien one; the Welsh princes themselves founded churches in her honour, the cistercians (who had a special devotion to Our Lady) were the most popular and influential religious order in Wales, and important shrines of Our Lady were established in the later middle ages at Penrys, Cardigan and elsewhere. The real trouble in Welsh ecclesiastical history is that there has been a strong tendency to regard the Welsh relationship with England as an 'us' and 'them' situation. This has meant on the one hand that historians have been at pains to emphasise, and frequently distort in the process, the welshness of the Welsh church, and on the other that they resent all English influences as alien impositions, when often, as in the case of devotion to Our Lady, an English import became in time a Welsh tradition.

I believe that the issues raised in this paper are important ones. My argument is that, partly because of the paucity of records and partly because of the cultural division between Wales and England, Welsh church history has often proceeded along dubious paths. Welsh church historians need to look again at their documents, and also to take greater account of ecclesiastical events outside Wales, before an authoritative ecclesiastical history of the principality can be written. Professor Glanmor Williams has shown us what can be done in one period of Welsh church history, despite the problems surrounding the sources; it is now up to other Welsh historians to provide comparable studies of other periods, particularly in some of the priority areas that I have indicated in this paper.

NINETEENTH-CENTURY PAROCHIAL
SOURCES

by ROBERT DUNNING

ECCLESIASTICAL history of the nineteenth century, and of other periods where records are plentiful, can be written on three main levels. It can and has been studied at national level in broad movements and through the activities of prominent churchmen. It can and has been studied, though less often and less successfully, at diocesan level, in an analysis of visitation returns, in the activities of diocesan bishops and in the work of lesser churchmen. And it can and should more often be written from parochial sources, since it is from them that the effects of national movements can be traced and their success or failure assessed. The task may seem, on the face of it, to be daunting, but the survival of useful material has, in fact, been poor in every diocese, and the total task becomes therefore much more manageable.

The particular parochial sources in question are limited in range. They are, first and foremost, registers of services, whose rate of survival even in the twentieth century is appalling. The earliest in Bath and Wells diocese date from the 1840s. They are supplemented by the strictly ecclesiastical entries in vestry minute books and churchwardens' account books, through which may be traced the liturgical developments in the parish. An active parish priest might well produce other, less formal records, such as a list of his parishioners to guide his visiting. He might himself have been secretary of a Sunday school teachers' association, and have left the minute book in his own parish safe. And he might, and very often did, keep some kind of record either of his own activities or of general parish events in the form of a journal or diary.

One of the early service books in Somerset comes from the parish of Huish Episcopi and begins in 1840.[1] Huish was then an undistinguished parish, though it included the virtually autonomous chapelry of Langport within its boundaries. Services at Huish in 1840, conducted by two curates, were at 11 am on one Sunday and at 2.30 pm on the

[1] S[omerset] R[ecord] O[ffice], D/P/h.ep. 2/5/1.

next, so far as they are regularly recorded, and the 'sacrament' was celebrated about once a quarter. The number of communicants was usually given, together with the amount of alms collected. Once during that year the school children were catechised, and twelve days later the aged bishop Law, accompanied by his eldest son, chancellor J. T. Law, and his secretary, confirmed 'about 345 persons' from Huish, Langport and neighbouring parishes.

The register for the next few years was not properly entered but after a fire in Langport church in 1845 its congregation moved temporarily to Huish. The two communities, like the two churches, were physically very close, but spiritually and socially were not akin; they could not possibly worship together even though they shared the same clergy. On the fourth Sunday in Lent Langport people worshipped at Huish in the morning and Huish people worshipped in the afternoon. Easter was no better: Huish people received the 'sacrament' on Good Friday and Langport on Easter Day. This situation continued at least until Trinity Sunday when twenty-five Langport people communicated and gave £1 10s 6d in alms. The corporation of Langport attended that service in memory of Vincent Stuckey, banker, shipowner, formerly private secretary to Pitt and Huskisson at the treasury, and grandfather of one of the leading figures in the catholic revival, Vincent Stuckey Stratton Coles.[2]

The entries in the service register continued fitfully and included for 1852 the names of sixty-three people confirmed at Langport by bishop George Trevor Spencer, DD, formerly bishop of Madras. The bishop was attended by local clergy and by the archdeacon of Taunton, the venerable G. A. Denison, himself a figure of some importance as the target of attack for his exposition of eucharistic doctrine in 1856. He was a family friend of the Coles, and the attack on him is said to have made an 'ineffaceable mark' on the mind of Stuckey Coles.[3] The Huish register is then silent until 1884. By then services were held at 11 o'clock and 3 o'clock every Sunday with monthly celebrations of the Holy Communion, and the vicar, resident for the first time in years, adds both his text and 'remarks', remarks relating to the size of his congregation – small, fair, fairly good, good and very good, 'very wet afternoon' or 'volunteers attended'.

The Huish register was chosen for its age as much as for its value in assessing the spiritual life of a traditional parish. In a parish only a few

[2] *DNB*, article by S. L. Ollard.
[3] *Ibid.*

miles distant and still in Somerset, that remarkable man Vincent Stuckey Coles lived and worked, a man whose 'spiritual power influenced not Oxford only but penetrated the whole Anglican Communion'.[4] Coles left behind him, and his successors preserved, a remarkably full record of his short term as rector of Shepton Beauchamp (1872–84); his successors there and at neighbouring Barrington continued his tradition of churchmanship and of full and accurate record-keeping so that the progress of the catholic revival in those two country parishes comes fully and accurately alive.

Survival has, inevitably, not been complete but the key, the register of services, is much more than a simple record of the daily worship at the parish church. It is also a record of Stuckey Coles's preaching engagements throughout the country. The services at Shepton from the 1870s are entered in the greatest detail.[5] Churchings include the name of the woman, baptisms the names of the godparents, catechism the topic, sermons the text, celebrations the time of service and the number of communicants. There were normally two celebrations each Sunday with three at Easter, and celebrations on certain weekdays and saints' days. There were sermons at both Sunday services and on most Thursdays. All these services were maintained even when the rector was absent.

Stuckey Coles was away often and the list of his preaching engagements reveals his influence and popularity and also his churchmanship. He frequently returned to Wantage where his ministry began under W. J. Butler in 1869,[6] but he was in demand in many other places: St Barnabas's and St Paul's, Oxford; All Saints', Margaret Street; All Saints', Clifton; St Augustine's, Kilburn; St Luke's, Torquay; St Martin's, Scarborough. His friendship with Liddon and dean Church brought him invitations to St Paul's Cathedral. He was especially requested for missions: in 1874 he was at St Paul's, Knightsbridge, taking part in the second London mission, and later in that year conducted a mission at West Bromwich, though the sermons for this were not entered in detail because they were, so he wrote, 'mostly old'.

This register of services, amplified by the record of Stuckey Coles's many sermons, cannot be supplemented by material in either vestry minute books or churchwardens' account books, since the former concern civil matters alone[7] and the latter have not survived for the period

[4] *Ibid.*
[5] SRO, D/P/she.b. 2/5/1.
[6] *DNB.*
[7] SRO, D/P/she.b. 9/1/1 (1822–1921).

in question.[8] But there has survived the minute book of a parish organisation, the Society of Holy Innocents, beginning in 1873.[9] The object
of this society was to encourage girls to become weekly communicants
and to provide some spiritual guidance. The guidance was given by the
'manager' of the society, the rector's sister, Julia Mary Coles.[10] Monthly
meetings, at which each member was given 'a little talk' by Miss
Coles, involved collections of $\frac{1}{2}$d a member, cups of tea and occasional
outings and dances. These were later augmented if not overtaken by
sewing meetings. The rector's mission to America in 1876 and to
Plymouth a year or two later were occasions for special prayers and for
practical work as the girls, provided with calico by Miss Coles, sewed
garments for distribution not only to the poor in their own village but
also to the needy in the parish of St Peter, Plymouth. The collections at
each meeting mounted slowly but helped towards providing stained
glass windows and a banner for the parish church.

Shepton Beauchamp had more than one association of this kind: the
societies of St Gabriel (united with the Holy Innocents in 1889) and St
Stephen were already in existence in 1872. Miss Coles later established
St Michael's Home 'for the reception of young girls who have fallen',
where training was given in laundry and housework.[11] The influence of
such groups in a parish can hardly be accurately assessed, and most of
the Holy Innocents, at least, were soon scattered throughout the
country in service, possibly on occasion placed through the rector's
connexions. One went to West Bromwich, several to Cardiff and
London, and others to Clewer, Henley in Arden and Canterbury. At
least two emigrated. Equally, the work of the rector and his curates,
based on Shepton clergy house, can hardly be assessed with accuracy
though there are, for example, figures for communicants which might
be induced to produce a trend. Communicants at Christmas and Easter
varied very much from year to year in the period 1872–83, slightly
higher at Easter when they ranged in number between 176 and 216,
and slightly less at Christmas ranging between 98 and 151. Ash Wednes-
day celebrations produced a range between six and sixty-one during the
same period. The parish has been described as 'a model parish of the
Catholic Revival'.[12] Statistics alone do not seem to support an increase
in popular attraction to the eucharist which ought to be its sign.

---

[8] *Ibid* 4/1/1 (1705–1828), 4/1/2 (1894–1954).   [9] *Ibid* 2/5/7.
[10] She also took classes for girls at Barrington and with her mother was actively
interested in the schools of both villages.
[11] *Bath and Wells Diocesan Kalendar*, 1887.   [12] *DNB*.

In the neighbouring parish of Barrington, worked with Shepton, a register of services has been preserved dating from 1878[13] which is very like that of Shepton. From 1879 the parish was under the care of Arthur Lethbridge, formerly curate at Shepton, and from 1884 under Joseph Hamlet, both of whom lived in the clergy house at Shepton and continued the catholic tradition. Stuckey Coles himself conducted missions at Barrington as recorded in the service register. During the second, in 1893–4, '113 persons made resolutions with the clergy, 14 children made total abstinence pledges'. Afterwards 34 people were confirmed and the Easter communicants rose in number from 62 in 1893 to 111 in 1894, 50 of them attending a service at 5.45 am before going to work.

The progress of the catholic revival in Barrington is, however, better charted in the vestry minute book, where gifts to the church and other events are recorded.[14] In 1888 the vestry 'noted the alterations, improvement and decoration of the chancel, and with great thankfulness the Mission preached in Epiphanytide by the Revd. V. S. S. Coles and the Revd. N. E. Campbell'. Gifts to the church in the reverend Mr Lethbridge's time were duly listed for the benefit of the vestry and entered into the churchwardens' book. They included brass vases and candlesticks, an oak altar cross, coloured altar frontals and superfrontals, white, red and green burses, veils and stoles.[15] Later gifts included in 1895 a framed oil painting of the annunciation given by Mrs Coles; in 1896 a 'better white silk vestment', a banner of the Blessed Sacrament, and side curtains for the altar. In 1898 there were new windows by Kempe in the chancel and a statue of the Virgin and Holy Child over the porch.

The parish had come a long way from the alternate morning and evening services of 1815[16] or the two Sunday services of 1851,[17] though it is doubtful whether the congregations could have improved on the 1851 figures of 175 (including 93 children) in the morning and 254 (100 children) in the afternoon in a parish of 511 inhabitants.[18] The communion figures from 1879 onwards certainly show an overall increase at a time when the population was declining; indeed the Easter figure after the 1893–4 mission, 111, represents something over a quarter of the total population.[19] This enthusiasm did not, however,

---

[13] SRO, D/P/barr 2/5/1.
[14] *Ibid* 9/1/1 (1862–1923).
[15] *Ibid* 4/3/2.
[16] SRO, D/D/V returns 1815.
[17] PRO H.O. 129/317/3/11/17.
[18] *Victoria History of Somerset* ii. 348.
[19] The population in 1891 was 416: *Victoria History of Somerset* ii. 348.

last very long, and was never reflected in greatly increased numbers at weekly celebrations.

Statistics, and especially numbers of communicants, seem to have been almost an obsession with the reverend Samuel Ogilvy Baker, perpetual curate of Muchelney from 1872 and a near neighbour of Stuckey Coles. This is not revealed by service registers, for none has survived, but by a kind of parish log book[20] in which are recorded not only natural phenomena in his frequently flooded parish, but also the names of children confirmed, the names of communicants, and the average number of such each year. The nearest approach his parish made to ritual was two brass almsdishes which appeared in 1873, but within a few months of his arrival the chancel was 'fitted with seats for the singers' and the barrel organ (which is still there) was replaced by a hired harmonium. Baker's notes on his communicants are revealing. In 1873 four boys and five girls were confirmed, but only two of the girls became communicants, and the lists for later years include never more than four men though the total was usually about 20 in a parish of some 250 souls.[21]

By 'earnest request of the bishop' baptisms from 1873 onwards were to be administered in time of divine service on the first Sunday in each month and Holy Communion was celebrated on the second Sunday. The curate himself preached for various diocesan societies and in 1877 pledged himself to total abstinence. In the following year he noted with satisfaction that 'the public House closed altogether'. Baker's interests centred on the choir, which he took on annual outings, and on the village school. In 1880 he noted that he was outvoted by the school committee on the use of the schoolroom for parish dances. But there was no indication of further changes in the services and the only additions to the furniture were an incongruous stone pulpit and a brass lectern, both turned out of the lord mayor's chapel in Bristol and the gift of the lord mayor himself.

In contrast to this record from Muchelney, and from a slightly earlier periods is the journal of the reverend J. J. Toogood, vicar of North Petherton from 1835 until 1850.[22] Here is no journal of a Woodforde or a Kilvert, but an example of an extremely valuable source for ecclesiastical historians which is more common than is generally realised.

[20] SRO, D/P/much. 23/4.
[21] 278 in 1871, 256 in 1881, 240 in 1891: *Victoria History of Somerset* ii. 348.
[22] The journal survives as extracts made by Toogood's grandson, the reverend P. L. Snowden, now in the custody of the vicar of North Petherton, the reverend B. A. A. Whiting.

Toogood was a young, wealthy, hunting parson who was a member of the first Oxford boat race crew. He found North Petherton in a bad state: the church in poor repair, no church school, 'the singing in the church was very bad, and the choir weak', the tithes and rates difficult to collect, and large parts of his scattered parish so far from the parish church that the inhabitants thought that the white witch was the ruling power, and only attended the church 'for a funeral or a baptism, when they too often got drunk'. Surviving extracts from this journal, the original of which covered or covers five volumes, show how Toogood fought against the general malaise in the parish, saw through the tithe commutation agreement, restored and re-seated his church, built a daughter church and a school. There is correspondence with his school friend T. D. Acland (later Sir T. D. Acland, 1809–98) on the subject of education, with the National Society and other bodies about finance, with local landowners for land or subscriptions. There is comparatively little about the services of the church though in 1840 he preached a sermon in which he stated his 'intention of having daily service in the church every morning at 8 o'clock', and a little earlier in the year he abolished the custom whereby the Holy Communion was administered quarterly on two following Sundays, 'to the bettermost folks, as it was termed, on the first Sunday, and the poor on the second Sunday'. Thereafter monthly celebrations 'for all' became the rule. There is no register of services for the period to supplement this meagre information.[23]

From an ecclesiastical point of view perhaps the most interesting part of the journal is the correspondence which Toogood as rural dean had to conduct with the diocesan authorities about the behaviour of the reverend Henry Prince, curate of Charlinch, whose views finally forced him to leave the church and later to establish his 'Abode of Love' in the Quantock hills. Prince first attracted attention in 1841: 'Strange things are said to be done in the church . . . On one occasion Mr Prince . . . excused himself from preaching because the Spirit did not move him . . . On another occasion he divided his congregation into the converted, the about to be converted, and the devilish . . .' Chancellor J. T. Law, virtually in charge of the diocese as special commissary for his ailing father, dealt with the matter when it came to a head again in the following year and Toogood was sent to interview the offending curate and his malleable rector. After a long interview in which the rural dean virtually had to threaten to have his licence withdrawn, Prince still

[23] A 'Preachers' Book' survives from 1851.

refused both to discontinue his practices and to resign. But all was polite and friendly. 'We then had some luncheon,' wrote Toogood, 'and talked on other matters, and I wished them good-morning.'

Vestry minutes, churchwardens' accounts, service registers and diaries are usually in manuscript; with the exception of the diaries they are official in character. One final source, though much less common, can be invaluable when damp and disaster have overtaken the parish safe. This is the parish almanac, precursor of the parish magazine, through which the incumbent reached his flock to remind them about the services. The reverend C. P. Berryman, himself an acceptable preacher at Barrington[24] and clearly in the catholic tradition, found Pitney, near Langport, a lifeless parish when he arrived in 1879. He at once introduced more services, especially on weekdays, taught the children with great care, and developed a system of regular visiting. His annual almanac left his people in no doubt as to what was happening at the church, and his rather sad letters to them reveal how small were the results. But if his parish did not fully appreciate their rector, the rector himself appreciated the power of the press, losing no opportunity of contributing items of church news from the parish to the local newspaper. From these cuttings, collected like the almanac into his private scrap-book,[25] can be traced the gradual introduction of coloured altar frontals and pulpit falls, brass candlesticks and a cross. But for all his efforts his letters to his people remained sad, and when he left in 1885 his parishioners remembered him as a splendid fellow at a fête and as an enthusiastic tenor at a musical evening.

Parochial sources such as those described are likely to survive badly and unevenly. These highlights come from six parishes out of nearly thirty studied in some depth but otherwise chosen at random; the others produced virtually nothing. There has been in the past a tendency to respect some of these sources rather more than others; service registers have a curious way of being outside the parish safe and diaries tend to be 'borrowed' because of their 'interest' and not returned. The ecclesiastical historian will find them far more useful than the registers of baptisms, marriages and burials which in all but a few cases are treated with a respect they do not in this context deserve.

[24] SRO, D/P/barr. 2/5/1.
[25] SRO, D/P/pitn. 23/1.

SUPERNATURALISED CULTURE: CATHOLIC ATTITUDES AND LATIN LANDS 1840-60

by SHERIDAN GILLEY

T HERE is still a remarkable book to be written about a phenomenon as yet little recognised or understood: the sudden appearance in England of a serious and scholarly interest in religious experience as a subject worthy of study in itself, at the beginning of the twentieth century. Possibly the two best-known landmarks of the movement were William James's Gifford Lectures[1] and dean Inge's *Christian Mysticism*,[2] which popularised mystical theology beyond the circles to which it had been for the most part confined, within the roman catholic church. Dean Inge had many harsh words for the popish mysticism associated with monasticism,[3] and pervaded by an easy familiarity with the 'supernatural suspensions of physical law' of roman catholic hagiography.[4] He passed these strictures on French and Belgian treatises and seminary textbooks,[5] but he might have found materials as outrageous in English, in the writings of the mid-nineteenth century ultramontanes who had striven to reproduce in native dress the religious forms of Italy, France and Spain, and to recreate in England a foreign and professedly 'supernatural' culture which accepted mystical experience as an ordinary fact of life.

This use of 'culture' in a victorian context will be familiar to readers of Raymond Williams' *Culture and Society*,[6] which demonstrated the value of the idea to an understanding of the nineteenth century in its

---

[1] *The Varieties of Religious Experience, a study in human nature: being the Gifford Lectures on Natural Religion delivered at Edinburgh in 1901–1902* (London 1902).
[2] *Christian Mysticism* (London 1899).
[3] 'the debased supernaturalism which usurps the name of Mysticism in Roman Catholic countries', *ibid*, p viii.
[4] *Ibid* p 3.
[5] He intended to publish as an appendix to *Christian Mysticism* a hostile analysis of J. Ribet's *La Mystique Divine* 3 vols (Paris 1895), which 'would have opened the eyes of some of my readers to the irreconcilable antagonism between the Roman Church and science; but though I translated and summarized my author faithfully, the result had the appearance of a malicious travesty'. *Ibid* p ix.
[6] *Culture and Society 1780–1950* (London 1958).

own terms, as it understood itself.[7] Indeed Williams dealt with the mid-victorian romantic fascination with medieval culture;[8] but he was only incidentally interested in its religious role, and did not treat of its conflict with the rival ultramontane cultural ideal, within roman catholicism. For ultramontanes also employed the conception of culture, if not the word itself, as they believed that only roman catholic countries gave a due prominence and proper encouragement to the calling to the perfection of the saints, by mediating through the most common of social conventions a feeling for the claims of faith. From this arose controversy which roman catholic historians have given detailed treatment in terms of the well-known quarrel between the catholic champions of medieval culture who wanted gothic churches and chasubles, and those papists, mostly converts and foreigners, who preferred the roman baroque. But there has been little detailed systematic analysis of the point that baroque basilicas and vestments were only important to the ultramontanes for the spirituality which they enshrined: an 'integral Catholicism' in Dessain's happy phrase,[9] stemming from a culture in which religious values were honoured if less wholeheartedly obeyed.

There was of course more to roman catholic attitudes to latin societies than deference to mysticism and mystics. For the cultivated nineteenth-century Englishman of means who was out of sympathy with the age of steam, there was always a possible imaginative escape to the alternative culture of the south. Victorian Englishmen loved Italy especially, and for many reasons: from an attachment to Italian nationalism, or high hopes of Italian protestantism, or an enthusiasm for the classical past or for venetian gothic or the renaissance, or out of liking for the colour of Italian street life; or just for a seat under the cypresses and a life-giving sun. But for English roman catholics in the victorian era, Italy and the other latin lands were both a polemic opportunity and an embarrassment. Theirs was the isolation of the modern British communist, who is at odds with his society, and like him, they romanticised foreign countries while taking a jaundiced view of their own. Their highest loyalties were supranational and they were felt to be imperfectly English and incurred the charge of disloyalty because their church was an 'Italian mission' owing its allegiance to

---

[7] *Ibid* p 16, for the nineteenth century history and meaning of 'culture'.
[8] *Ibid* chapter viii especially.
[9] *Letters and Diaries [of John Henry Newman]*, ed C. S. Dessain (London 1962–73) 12, p 386.

Rome. And as a communist might defend the *mores* and institutions of those happier lands in which his philosophy prevails, so many an English roman catholic strove to prove the superior excellence of Italy to England, and to pen apologetics for those allegedly latin vices which his fellow-countrymen despised. Nor was that sort of blinkered but idiosyncratic insight without its value. The nineteenth century catholic revival helped to restore a fuller understanding of the middle ages, just because it inspired much bad romantic history; and as romantics rescued the medieval centuries from the incomprehension of their fathers, so ultramontanes achieved a wider appreciation of the latin nations even in the act of idealising them.

This sort of catholic apologetic was made necessary by considerations which were wholly of the nineteenth century, when the most convincing point of popular protestant polemic was that catholicism was disproved by the moral and material conditions of catholic cultures. This protestant moral superiority had been less obvious in the England of Walpole and Fielding before the impact of the evangelical revival; her material superiority was the outcome of the industrial revolution, for as long as Rome and Paris had remained the capitals of European civilisation there was little point to the thesis that prosperity was the fruit of protestantism. A more popular idea among protestants had been the darkness of the popish middle ages, from which the reformation had come as a deliverance; but that argument was answered for catholics by the early nineteenth-century romantic defence of the ages of faith, at the very moment that the idea of the cultural decadence of catholic Europe was conceived as a weapon against catholicism. There were two possible answers to the charge. The first was to deny the inferiority of catholic culture, and stress the catholic contribution to civilisation. The other sidestepped the question, and sought to demonstrate that whatever the material failings of catholic cultures only they gave the proper social sanctions to the godgiven means for saving souls. In the great mass of literary and journalistic ephemera which survives of this controversy, the first kind of apologetic is epitomised in the reverend J. Balmes' *Protestantism and Catholicity compared in their Effects on the Civilization of Europe*, first published in Spanish in 1840, and appearing in an English translation in 1849.[10] The second controversial position is most brilliantly and sensitively stated by John Henry Newman in two of his lectures on the stock anglican objections to popery, arguing that the 'Political State' and 'Religious Character' of catholic countries were

[10] Translated from the French version by C. J. Hanford and R. Kershaw.

'no Prejudice to the Sanctity of the Church'[11] – for, claimed Newman, whatever their vices, catholic countries encouraged sanctity through those very cultural forms which might seem to be objections to catholicism.

Newman had been strongly touched by affection for Italy even before his conversion; but in his new roman loyalties he had to reason out and refute to his own satisfaction those 'Anglican difficulties' which had once discredited popery for him. In his famous distinction in *Tract 90* between romish corruptions and the tridentine decrees, he had maintained that Rome showed one face in her official teaching, and another as a popular system which was polytheistic and idolatrous.[12] The future cardinal Wiseman wrote to refute the distinction, drawing on his long familiarity with Italian culture, sacred and profane, already declared in essays on tourists in Italy, and about Italian learned institutions and Italian gesticulation, as well as on Italian piety.[13] Wiseman had been imbued with a love of Italy by years of residence, and was a catholic cosmopolitan in the widest sense, by virtue of Irish and Spanish ancestry, and an English education. In his enthusiasm for Rome as the 'panting heart' of the universal church, he encouraged converts to follow Italian models as truly catholic, and this aspiration was embodied in the oratory which Newman founded in England on the pattern of the roman institute created by Philip Neri, who as the 'Apostle of Rome' in the sixteenth century, had done more than any other man to re-convert the city to catholicism.

But even the patronage of a roman saint and an enthusiasm for baroque and a tolerance for fleas in church left in Newman's mind a painful gulf between catholic belief and practice; and as he was never more penetrating than when articulating his doubts and resolving them, so his fastidious and agonised attempt in his lectures on anglican difficulties to state what was distasteful about catholic cultures was a minor masterpiece of tragic-comic description, at once profound and funny.

[11] Chapters viii and ix, 'Political State of Catholic Countries no Prejudice to the Sanctity of the Church', 'The Religious Character of Catholic Countries no Prejudice to the Sanctity of the Church', in [J. H.] Newman, *Lectures [on certain difficulties felt by Anglicans in submitting to the Catholic Church]* (London 1850) pp 191–242.

[12] Especially '*Purgatory, Pardons, Images, Relics, Invocation of Saints*', *Tracts for the Times*, no 90, pp 23–42.

[13] 'Superficial Travelling', 'Italian Guides and Tourists', 'Religion in Italy', 'Italian Gesticulation', 'Early Italian Academies', in N. Wiseman, *Essays on Various Subjects* (London 1853) III, pp 439–582; originally published in the *Dublin Review*, February 1843, January 1836 and July 1837.

Newman saw tragedy in the degeneration of the highest values among the lost and sinning masses of mankind; the comedy arises in the picaresque detail of his sketches of the latin types beloved of protestant polemic: 'highwaymen and brigands devout to the Madonna'; saints depicted above 'the resorts of sin'; relic mongers selling medicinal talismans; a nun who has faked the stigmata; the lady who jumps the queue to the confessional; the thief who believes in the Real Presence but runs off with the ciborium; the 'feeble old woman, who first genuflects before the Blessed Sacrament, and then steals her neighbour's handkerchief'.[14] Newman ranges back in time to the ecclesiastical scandals of other ages; as of those crusaders who 'kept the Friday's abstinence, and planted the tents of their mistresses within the shadow of the pavillion of the glorious St Louis'.[15] But Newman saw no difference between the corruptions of medieval and modern catholicism, and as most of his materials were contemporary, so directly did he face the problem of contemporary catholic corruption that Kingsley could mistake honesty for lipsmacking gusto in the famous quarrel of 1864.[16]

Newman reconciled the difference by arguing that in catholic societies, medieval and modern, unregenerate human nature and the supernatural visibly interact with each other, the supernatural exalting and fulfilling nature, and nature debasing the outward expression of the supernatural by making it her own. For Newman, catholicism assumed the external forms of a catholic culture, which even in its partial corruptions made the supernatural visible to all, through the all-pervading presence of the church, and through the saints with their wonder-working powers. Thus in a wholly self-consistent supernaturalised system, grace produces its physical effects to the eye of man, not least in those ecclesiastical miracles which were probable in being of a kind with those of scripture, by making grace dramatically visible to everyone.[17] Newman's tolerance for the incredible made Kingsley doubt his sincerity, and caused Huxley to call the *Essay on Ecclesiastical Miracles* a 'Primer of Infidelity',[18] and even professor Chadwick

[14] Newman, *Lectures* pp 230, 234–8.
[15] *Ibid* p 231.
[16] 'after using the blasphemy and profanity which he confesses to be so common in Catholic countries, as an argument for, and not against, the "Catholic Faith", he takes a seeming pleasure in detailing instances of dishonesty on the part of Catholics . . .', Charles Kingsley, *What, then, does Dr Newman mean?* (London 1864) p 34 *et seq.*
[17] J. H. Newman, 'An Essay on Miracles', prefixed to Claude Fleury, *Ecclesiastical History* (Oxford 1842).
[18] Cited John Moody, *John Henry Newman* (London 1946) p 231.

described it as showing Newman's mind 'at its most tortuous and uncritical.[19] But as James Anthony Froude was to see, even in his disillusionment with his old master, Newman cared above all for truth, even at the cost of seeming hopelessly credulous,[20] and felt bound to affirm that all edifying and orthodox manifestations of the spirit were *a priori* possible: even such extraordinary visible visitations of grace as Rose's finger-biting self-mortifications at three months,[21] and the liquefaction of the blood of San Gennaro, and the weeping Italian pictures of the Madonna, and Walberga's curative oil.[22] And thus it was characteristic of catholic countries that 'faith impresses the mind with supernatural truths, as if it were sight'.[23] The very corruptions of popular catholicism testified to the catholic's faith in an unseen world as real as this; and even the profanity of miracle play was 'not profane to those who believe wholly, who, one and all, have a vision within, which corresponds with what they see . . .'[24]

Thus God gave his graces through his church in spite of the blasphemies of popular catholicism, and despite that rough and rude and mechanical over-familiarity with spiritual things characteristic of catholic societies, and 'indescribably offensive to any person of ordinary refinement'.[25] The bad catholic cursed the church, and joked about God and the saints just because he believed in them with a conviction that might save him at the hour of death. 'The enemy rushes on him, to overthrow the faith on which he is built; but the whole tenor of his past life, his very jesting, and his very oaths, have been overruled, to create in him a habit of faith, girding round and protecting the supernatural principle.[26] And thus it was in the providence of God that catholicism should be 'a popular religion',[27] offering salvation to the poorest. And thus there was hope for even that living protestant objection to catholicism: 'a mere beggar-woman, lazy, ragged, filthy, and not over scrupulous of truth', who was yet 'chaste, and sober, and cheerful, and goes to her religious duties' which clothed her with a supernatural grace denied to 'the [protestant] state's pattern-man' possessed of 'a mere natural virtue'.[28]

[19] W. O. Chadwick, *The Victorian Church* (London 1970) part I, p 195.
[20] J. A. Froude, *Short Studies in Great Subjects* (London 1907) V, p 325.
[21] Newman to Henry Wilberforce, 1 January 1849, *Letters and Diaries*, 13, pp 3–4.
[22] Appendix, *Apologia pro Vita Sua* (London 1864) p 57.
[23] *Lectures* p 238.　　[24] *Ibid* p 237.　　[25] *Ibid* p 221.　　[26] *Ibid* p 242.
[27] As in the famous London church scene in *Loss and Gain* (London 1848) p 426: 'Reding said to himself, "This *is* a popular religion" '.
[28] *Lectures* p 207.

But Newman was eventually to fall out with the more italianate of his disciples, and especially in matters of spirituality had come by 1860 to prefer an English catholic piety which was appropriate to England, as Italian devotion was to Italy.[29] Indeed Newman's ambivalent relations with ultramontanism had a long history, predating his conversion. At Oxford he lagged behind the young wildmen like Frederick William Faber and W. G. Ward, who were dragging the tractarians Romeward. To give them a safely anglo-catholic occupation in their unsettlement as anglicans, he had edited a series of lives of the English saints, in which some of the contributors had shown an undiscriminating taste for miracles and marvels which was later to distinguish their ultramontanism:[30] most notably Faber, who was to bring to his new position an extraordinary learning and passion for continental hagiography.

Faber conceived the most notorious of the literary monuments to his ultramontane enthusiasm in 1846, in projecting a collection of biographies of saints nearly all native to Italy, France and Spain. These *Lives of the Saints and Servants of God* included a few medieval figures, but most belonged to the counter-reformation and were to be generally described as 'modern saints', to distinguish them from the medieval.[32] The title was appropriate to Faber's defence of the post-tridentine church as the 'modern church', against those romantic souls who preferred the forms of medieval catholicism, and was intended to familiarise roman catholic Englishmen with 'modern' catholic spirituality. This dictated Faber's choice of materials, for despite the superior stylistic possibilities of original composition, the *Lives* were free and fluent translations of biographies deliberately chosen as specimen devotional reading of the latin countries, a majority of them Italian compositions of the seventeenth and eighteenth century.[33] To reproduce the authentic character of catholicism at its capital, Faber expressed a preference for *Lives* compiled from the processes of canonisation, which

---

[29] '. . . my mind in no long time fell back to what seems to me a safer and more practical course'. J. H. Newman, *A letter to the Rev E. B. Pusey on his recent Eirenicon* (London 1866) p 24.

[30] What Mark Pattison called their 'lurking fondness for stories of miracles', *Memoirs* (London 1885) p 212, cited J. Derek Holmes, 'Newman's reputation and The Lives of the English Saints', *Catholic Historical Review*, 51 (London, January 1966) p 538.

[31] 42 vols (London and Derby for all the lives cited below, 1847–56).

[32] F. W. Faber, 'St Philip the Representative Saint of Modern Times', Lecture Second in *The Spirit [and genius] of St Philip Neri [Founder of the Oratory]* (London 1850).

[33] *Prospectus* for the *Lives*, Feast of the Purification, 1847.

he explained and justified to English readers in an essay prefixed to the life of Alphonso de Ligouri,[34] and through a three volume translation of Benedict XIV's study of 'heroic virtue' taken from the pope's *Treatise on Beatification and Canonisation*.[35] This stamp of papal approval, Faber claimed, conferred an implicit authority on the series,[36] and gave a sort of ecclesiastical sanction to the mystical and miraculous anecdotes grouped in many of the *Lives* on the pattern of their originals, under the headings of the theological and cardinal virtues, which stood in the place of an ordered narrative and an overall chronology.[37]

Faber recognized that hagiography held a wealth of psychological and historical interest dependent of the *éclat* of sanctity; but his series was meant to edify rather than inform, and to stir the heart rather than the intelligence.[38] As 'a commonplace contribution to the interior life,'[39] and a '*help to mental prayer*',[40] and a 'devotional exercise' with its appointed hour and duration,[41] each of the *Lives* was a calling to the perfection of those elected souls wise in 'the practice of the Presence of God'.[42] For properly considered hagiography was a practical demonstration and 'sort of summary of spiritual theology';[43] it subordinated the solely natural fascinations of historical and psychological study to the overriding purpose of showing the workings of supernatural grace upon men and women who were holy. One of Faber's hopes for the collection was to 'supernaturalise' the English catholic nunneries

[34] [F. W.] Faber, [*An*] *Essay on* [*Beatification,*] *Canonization* [*and the Processes of the Congregation of Rites*] (London 1848). Also prefixed to *The life of St Alphonso* [*Maria de Ligouri*] 6 vols (1848–9) I.

[35] *Heroic Virtue: a portion of the treatise of Benedict XIV on the beatification of the servants of God*, 3 vols (1850–2).

[36] From the outset the series had the warm support of Wiseman, who promised but never wrote an introduction for it, and gave it an imprimatur also signed by his superior Thomas Walsh, vicar apostolic of the midland district, and dated 29 October 1847. Faber secured the imprimatur to discourage the attacks on the series by other, hostile bishops of the English hierarchy (Faber to an unnamed professor of Ushaw College, Co Durham, 28 December 1847: Faber Letters, Brompton Oratory). As cardinal archbishop of Westminster, Wiseman conferred two further imprimaturs on the series, in 1850 and 1851.

[37] Faber, *Essay on Canonization*, pp 80–3.

[38] 'they would be less spiritual if more interest of a foreign kind, whether historical or psychological, were introduced into them . . .' F. W. Faber, [*On the Interest and*] *Characteristics* [*of the Lives of the Saints*] (London 1853). Also prefixed to *The life of St Francis of Assissi* (1853).

[39] Faber, *Characteristics*, p 6.

[40] *Ibid* p 5: italicised from Faber, *Essay on Canonization*, p 48.

[41] Faber, *Characteristics*, p 21.

[42] *Ibid* p 18.

[43] *Ibid* p 28.

through biographies of those conventuals who exemplified the teachings of mystical theology. Indeed the claims of the contemplative life
were so much to the fore of the *Lives* as to provoke complaint from
subscribers[44] and the series was rich in women mystics, especially those
of the third order of Dominic, modelled on Catherine of Siena.[45]

Faber had planned the *Lives* while still superior of a short-lived order
of his own foundation, the brothers of the Will of God, who had the
English Wilfrid for their patron. But by joining himself and his followers to Newman's oratorians, he gave Newman an ultimate responsibility for the series, and made it the medium for popularising a roman
piety. This ambition was to weight the collection with active as well as
contemplative saints, especially with the founders of the great religious
orders, the earliest and greatest of them Francis.[46] The first volume to
be published about the 'active' saints was one of two on Philip Neri;[47]
and three more followed about the founders and members of oratories
elsewhere in Italy, in Turin, Padua, Forli, Camerino and Naples.[48]
Lesser Italian religious orders were represented by biographies of the
founders of the ministers of the sick, of the piarists, and of the congregation of christian doctrine,[49] while the active devotional interests of
contemporary continental catholic charity were represented by a life of
the eighteenth century beggar saint, Benedict Labre.[50] Of the two great
Italian orders of eighteenth century foundation introduced into England
after 1830, the redemptorists received their due in a six volume biography of Alphonso de Ligouri and his companions,[51] the passionists

---

[44] Preface to *The lives of St Catherine of Ricci, of the Third Order of St Dominick;
St Agnes of Montepulciano; B Benvenuta of Bojan; and St Catherine Raconigi of the
Order of St Dominick* (1852).

[45] As the saints in the preceeding footnote: also Rose of Lima and the blessed
Colomba of Rieti (*Lives* 1847) – esctatics of a type with St Mary Magdalene of
Pazzi, carmelitess (*Life* 1849).

[46] See footnote 38.

[47] 2 vols (1847).

[48] Fabrio dall' Aste, founder of the oratory of Forli, and Mariano Sozzini of the
roman oratory (*Lives* 1848); blessed Sebastian Valfré, of the oratory of Turin,
Antonio de Santi, founder of the oratory of Padua and Angelo Matteucci,
founder of the oratory of Camerino (*Lives* 1849); Antonio Talpa and the
venerable father Eustachio, of the Naples oratory; Giambattista Prever, of the
Turin oratory (*Lives* 1851).

[49] St Camillus of Lellis, founder of the clerks regular ministers of the sick (*Life*
2 vols 1850). St Joseph Calasanctius, founder of the pious schools, and the
blessed Ippolito Galantini, founder of the congregation of christian doctrine
(*Lives* 1850).

[50] (1850).

[51] See footnote 34.

theirs in a three volume life of blessed Paul of the Cross.[52] A short essay
on the introduction of the redemptorists to England was supplied for
the life of Alphonso by the superior of the order in Britain;[53] while a
preface and appendix to the life of blessed Paul sketched the background
to the passionists in England, drawing on the correspondence of the
leader of their first body of missionaries, the now-beatified Dominic
Barberi.[54] These biographies each had a further social significance: the
cultus of Paul symbolised the hope for converting England, while
Alphonso was supremely the doctor of the dominant probabilist
casuistry of the roman church, and as the author of the celebrated
Glories of Mary, the object of much protestant abuse.[55] Again, through
their lives ran the theme of a catholic revivalism based upon popular
preaching of an atonement theology, which Faber systematically discussed in his essay on *Catholic Home Missions* prefixed to the biographies
of the seventeenth century jesuit revival preachers Paul Segneri and
Peter Pinamonti.[56] So too the lives of Ignatius himself[57] and of other
members of his society[58] were not only a politic tribute to the largest
and most controversial and influential of English religious orders,[59] but
advanced the merits of the father-founder and the principal guardians
of the spirituality of the missions and retreats which redemptorists and
passionists performed.

These modern active orders were the natural agents and standard-
bearers of an 'integral catholicism', and were unpopular with those

[52] 3 vols (1853).

[53] *The Life of St Alphonso* IV, pp xi–xx.

[54] 'Introduction, by the late Father Dominic of the Mother of God, Passionist',
The life of the Blessed Paul of the Cross, 3 vols (London 1853) I, pp 1–25; 'Supplement . . .' III, pp 191–366.

[55] There was also a mass of mid-nineteenth century writing in English about St
Alphonso and translations from his works, mostly by members of the redemp-
torist order. A full bibliography would run to many pages.

[56] Also published with a biography of the venerable John de Britto, SJ, and a
brief account of the celebrated Robert de Nobili, SJ, apostle of the brahmins.

[57] 2 vols (1848–9).

[58] There were three more volumes of jesuit biography in the series: of the venerable
Peter Claver, SJ, apostle of the West Indies, and cardinal Odescalchi, SJ (*Lives*
1849); Joseph Anchieta, SJ, and the venerable John Berchmans, SJ (*Lives* 1849);
and the venerable Ludovico de Ponte SJ, and the venerable Luigi La Nuza, SJ
(*Lives* 1851). The briefs for the beatification of Claver and Berchmans appeared
in 1852, and were published in a preface to the lives of blessed Leonard of
Port Maurice and Nicholas Fattore (1852).

[59] 'If we cd get S. Ignazio out early it wd perhaps get ye Jesuits to our side . . .'
Faber, St Wilfrid's, Cheadle, to Michael Watts-Russell (11 December 1847)
Faber Letters, Brompton Oratory. Watts-Russell lived in Florence, and col-
lected many of the Italian biographies from which Faber made his translations.

roman catholics who preferred their native spiritual tradition to a popery which prided itself on seeming foreign. But it was the first contemplative *Life* in the series, of Rose of Lima, which raised a storm of controversy, centering upon her extraordinary austerities. This dispute has already been described by Wilfrid and Bernard Ward,[60] by Cuthbert Butler[61] and Faber's two biographers;[62] and the mistakes of the earlier writers have been recently patiently corrected by Dessain in his edition of Newman's *Letters and Diaries*, which supplies additional matter from Newman's correspondence, and surveys the relevant periodical literature.[63] From these materials the reader can reconstruct his own narrative of the quarrel, and see it entire; and there is no need here to stress those strands of the argument which are irrelevant to this double theme of latin culture, and its relation to the life of the spirit.

But it was Faber's difficulty to be unable to distinguish the husk of popish civilisation from the religion which it enshrined. 'Rome and Rome's ways, these are the attractions,' he wrote; 'God has put a spell into them.'[64] In his view, catholic spirituality might exist in a full-bodied form, or a weaker one; but the weaker one was simply less 'supernatural' and less catholic, a shadow of the complete development which faith had given it in countries where catholicism prevailed. That gave catholic sanctity its 'integral' character. 'As one monkey is like another monkey, so one saint is like another saint';[65] and it was foolish to expect too much individual interest from hagiography, when like the geologist who classifies stones, the hagiographer is simply concerned to catalogue the special types of sanctity. 'The geologist is for stones; we are for Saints,'[66] said Faber, disclaiming for the *Lives* any pretensions to literary style; and thus it was useless, he wrote, to object to 'the more than charnel horrors'[67] of the austerities of Rose, when her aspiration to suffer like Christ was part of the church's definition of

---

[60] Wilfrid Ward, *The Life of John Henry Newman* (London 1912) I, p 206 *et seq.*; Bernard Ward, *The Sequel to Catholic Emancipation* (London 1912) II, p 243 *et seq.*

[61] Cuthbert Butler, *The Life and Times of Bishop Ullathorne* (London 1926) I, pp 154–8.

[62] [J. E.] Bowden, [*The*] *Life* [*and Letters*] *of* [*Frederick William*] *Faber* (London 1869) pp 342–58; Ronald Chapman, *Father Faber* (London 1961) pp 190–9.

[63] Dessain, *Letters and Diaries*, 12, pp 278 *et seq.*

[64] [F. W.] Faber, *Notes on* [*Doctrinal and*] *Spiritual Subjects* (London 1866) II, p 110.

[65] Faber, *Characteristics*, p 67.

[66] *Ibid* p 70.

[67] Reverend Edward Price, review of *The lives of St Rose of Lima, . . .*, *Dolmans Magazine* (September 1848); cited *Letters and Diaries*, 12, p 403.

the sanctity possessed by thousands of other saints before and after her.[68] But if Rose's self-flagellations and iron crown of thorns could be considered a wholly proper if extreme example of the asceticism inspired by catholic mystical theology, so the annals of mysticism also told of every sort of supernatural incredibility as countless servants of God had known of them: celestial marriages to the Christ child;[69] the nun's wedding ring of flesh;[70] the' preternatural discernment' by the senses of both good and evil;[71] revelations from heaven and hell and purgatory of the glory or torment of departed souls;[72] the stigmata and a sanctity marvellously manifested from the cradle by babes who 'refused the breast on Fridays' in obedience to the fasts of holy church.[73] For the church of God was above all declared by the 'supernatural character' of its religion, manifested in 'Extensive Asceticism', 'Ecstatic nuns and supernatural Convents' and 'Rumours of constant miracles';[74] and so Faber delighted in saints who 'live[d] on the Blessed Eucharist alone'[75] and were famous for the 'almost unconscious exercise of miraculous powers, the occurrence of raptures, visions, bodily transformations, power over demons, the intermingling of the visible and invisible worlds, the reading of the secrets of the heart':[76] as also for those gifts of 'levitation', 'bilocation', 'incandescence', 'radiation', and other miraculous tokens of divine favour anathematised by dean Inge.[77]

After such a recitation of the extraordinary, it might seem perverse to point out that despite his fondness for the fantastic, Faber was not wholly lacking in critical spirit.[78] Like Newman he did not scruple to

---

[68] Faber, Preface, *Heroic Virtue* I, p xxii.

[69] Or as Anthony Hutchison noted, 'one of the commonest things possible in the genuine Lives of the Saints' was marriage to the Infant Jesus: as in the lives of Catherine of Siena, Rose, Veronica Giuliani 'and a host of others', Bowden, *Life of Faber* p 353.

[70] The 'visible rings of the two Catherines, Agnes, Rose, and Mary Magdalene of Pazzi', Faber, *Characteristics* pp 80–1.

[71] *Ibid* pp 45 *et seq*: as in the famous passage on the holy Sturmes' 'preternatural discernment' of the evil of some unconverted Germans by their smell, in Newman's biography of Walberga in the *Lives of the English Saints*, quoted and attacked by Kingsley, *What, then, does Dr. Newman mean?* p 27.

[72] Faber, *Characteristics* pp 88–92.

[73] *Ibid* p 97.

[74] Faber, *Notes on Spiritual Subjects* II, p 102.

[75] Faber, *Characteristics* p 45; compare Faber, *The Blessed Sacrament* (London 1855) pp 520–5.

[76] Faber, *Essay on Canonization* p 26.

[77] Inge, *Christian Mysticism* p 264.

[78] As in his discussion of how far the visions of the mystics could be considered a source of dogma: Faber, *Characteristics* pp 15–17.

describe the corruptions of catholicism: these were God's means for putting His saints to the test.[79] Faber also acknowledged the need to discriminate between the 'supernatural and the superstitious',[80] and drew the old prudent English catholic distinction between an ethic which everyone ought to practise, and those special virtues which were to be admired rather than copied by men who were less than holy.[81] But he also insisted that to dissolve the supernatural into the superstitious was to destroy the essence of heroic sanctity which distinguished the saints from merely 'good catholics' through the 'combination of the marvellous and the eccentric'.[82] For the catholic saints had two almost inevitable characteristics, Faber wrote, marks or notes of their sanctity: an ability to work miracles, and an indifference to respectable opinion shown in odd behaviour which was the outcome of 'a special instinct of the Holy Ghost',[83] and which provoked persecution by the catholic authorities for its oddity.[84] These were just the most obvious and unvarying of the fruits of the spirit; and to censor a marvel or an oddity was to tamper with the criteria by which the saint could be seen for what he was.

Faber preached this 'supernaturalism' with the argument that to refuse assent to such phenomena was in principle if not in particular cases to sell the pass to protestantism, by a half-hearted reluctance to confess that catholicism was supremely true.[85] Such worldly counsels were resoundingly repudiated in an antiphon cited on the title page on every volume of the *Lives*: *Gaude Virgo Maria, quia cunctas haereses sola interemisti in universo mundo*. To non-roman catholics that must have seemed a bigoted denial that the spirit blows where it wills, even beyond the boundaries of the roman church. And yet these heresies were anathema to Faber just because they seemed to him to deny souls that passion of their own self-perfection by which they might come to desire the divine love; and in his own eyes, his sectarian extre-

---

[79] Hence his ready answer to the attack on the life of Alphonso for exposing 'with too truthful and unsparing a hand the state of disorder, neglect, and depravity, which prevailed in St Alphonso's diocese and in other parts of the kingdom of Naples at that time'. Faber, *The Life of St Alphonso* II, p xiii.

[80] '. . . a long work and a hard one . . .', Faber, *The Life of St Rose* p x.

[81] Faber, *Characteristics* pp 33, 108 *et seq.*

[82] Faber, *Essay on Canonization* p 37.

[83] *Ibid* p 36.

[84] As with Theresa of Avila, John of the Cross etc: *ibid* pp 41–3.

[85] 'Moving in society for years without being known to be Catholics – horror at this – poor Jesus Christ, as St Alphonso said . . .', Faber, *Notes on Spiritual Subjects* II, p 104.

mism was simply a logical consequence of the call to the highest holiness. *All for Jesus* was the title of one of his most popular books.[86] 'It may be doubted if ever men were more enthusiastic than they are now . . .' he wrote elsewhere. 'Among the countless enthusiasms of the day, why not, then, an enthusiasm of being all for God?' 'The relaxing softness of domestic ease, of fashionable voluptuousness, of sumptuous tables, of costly varieties of dress, of luxurious equipages, of multitudes of servants, of grand furniture, of insidious mental refinement, or inordinate worship of health, and of ambitions, – . . . Do we Catholics stand out from all this corruption . . . ? . . And yet we are the descendants of those for whom Hilton and Baker wrote – and yet we have a nation to convert, who can only be converted by our holiness . . .'[87] Thus the *Lives of the Saints* praised those famous men 'whose every word and work was a condemnation of cowardice, of time serving, of timidity, of pusillanimity, of all unworthy concession, of all trembling in the face of power, of all bartering of principle for peace or gain, of all circuitous roads to a rightful and godly end'.[88] And above all hagiography especially told of those who had trodden the mystics' way and seen their Maker face to face, and reflected something of His glory as a light to others to follow them.

Italy and Spain were the model integral catholic cultures, but the *Lives of the Saints* also gave significant space to France, despite its revolutionary apostasy. This was but one of the many points at which France influenced nineteenth-century English catholicism, and one as yet little described in detail, though archbishop Mathew has indicated the importance for Faber and his circle of the mystical classics of the *Grand Siècle*:[98] in Faber's words 'When God granted to the French Church the wonderful movement of the seventeenth century'.[90] Mathew has also drawn attention to the growth of the English Carmel,[91] which was both French and Spanish in background; and the first English translations of John of the Cross, by Faber's friend David Lewis, appeared

---

[86] (London 1853).
[87] Faber, Preface to *The life of St Francis Xavier*, from the Italian of D. Bartoli and J. P. Maffei (London 1858) pp vi–vii. This biography was not in the series of modern saints' lives.
[88] Sermon on 'St Thomas of Canterbury', preached on St Thomas's Day, 29 December 1848, in reply to the critics of the modern saints' lives: Faber, *Notes on Spiritual Subjects* I, p 359.
[89] [David] Mathew, [Lord] Acton [and his Times] (London 1968) p 215.
[90] Faber, *The Spirit of St Philip Neri* p 98.
[91] Mathew, *Acton* p 215.

in the year after Faber's death.[92] That flowering in England of the contemplative life was the ultimate justification of Faber's delvings in continental hagiography; and that remains to his credit however limiting his assumption that only an integral catholicism gave the Creator his due, teaching His creatures their proper destiny, to seek and adore Him forever.

[92] *The Complete Works of St John of the Cross of the Order of Our Lady of Mount Carmel*, translated from the original Spanish by David Lewis MA, 2 vols (London 1864). Lewis also translated the writings of Theresa of Avila and collected a great library of works on catholic spirituality now housed at the Brompton oratory. He had been Newman's curate at Littlemore. See *DNB*.

VICTORIAN RELIGIOUS PERIODICALS:
FRAGMENTS THAT REMAIN

by PATRICK SCOTT

'VICTORIAN Britain was not only the first urbanising society,' Michael Wolff has recently reminded us, '... it was the first "journalising" society,' also.[1] Recent research, resulting from professor Wolff's victorian periodicals project, shows that there were upwards of eighteen *thousand* periodicals of differing title, published during the victorian period.[2] Of course, these periodicals varied greatly both in duration and in influence, but the average 'run' of a victorian periodical was about twenty-eight years, and most victorians would have agreed with professor Wolff's verdict that the magazines were one of the major new characteristics of their age. 'We look for our monthly and weekly magazines,' wrote one correspondent to the *British Controversialist* in 1862, 'as readily as we look for our daily food.' 'Periodical literature,' agreed another, 'is essentially an outgrowth of modern times.'[3] They were both contributing to a debate, in a monthly periodical, on the question, 'Does the present multiplicity of periodicals retard rather than foster intellectual progress'?

The growth of periodicals, like the growth of book-publishing, is closely connected with developments in victorian religious attitudes.

---

[1] *V[ictorian] P[eriodicals] N[ewsletter]*, 8 (Bloomington 1970) p 5. Compare [Michael] Wolff, 'Charting the golden stream: [thoughts on a directory of Victorian periodicals]', in *Editing Nineteenth Century Texts*, ed John M. Robson (Toronto 1967) pp 37–59.

[2] These titles will be listed alphabetically with publication details in the *Waterloo Directory of Victorian Periodicals*, ed Dorothy Deering and John North (forthcoming). Until then, see the three shorter lists, in *BM Catalogue*, under 'Periodical Publications' (arranged by place of publication), the *Times Tercentenary Handlist* (arranged by date of commencement), and *British Union-Catalogue of Periodicals* (arranged alphabetically, and giving locations for surviving runs). None of these will include more than a fraction of parish magazines. By 1936, there were 11,085 of these, with a total monthly circulation of 2,763,000: J. M. Swift, *The Parish Magazine* (London 1939) p 12.

[3] *[British] Controversialist*, 3 series, 8 (London 1862) pp 205, 276. Compare the famous phrase 'the age of periodicals' in Wilkie Collins, 'The unknown public', *Household Words*, 18 (London 1858) p 222.

One victorian writer noted that 'Creeds of almost every denomination, representing every episode of belief and unbelief, are defended by a phalanx of journals, with the *Record* and the *Tablet* at the extremities, and the *Jewish Chronicle* in the rear'.[4] Another correspondent to that same debate of 1862 estimated that of 516 magazines then in the course of publication, no less than 213 'are of a decidedly religious character'.[5] Similar figures have been gathered in more recent research.[6] This proportion, nearly 40 per cent, is substantially higher than the proportion of religious book titles to general book titles being published in the same period, and R. D. Altick has printed some useful statistics, originally gathered by the *Athenaeum* in 1864, which show that not only did religious periodicals hold their own in numbers of titles, but that they equalled, at that date, the secular press in terms of total circulation.[7]

The sorts of statistics which have been adduced so far, however, conceal very marked variations, both in the character of the periodicals, and also in the functions they served for their readers. In secular periodicals, there is a very broad development across the period, from relatively infrequent quarterlies and monthlies, with heavy-weight, full-length articles, and a limited circulation, towards a mass-circulation press, of weekly papers, with much lighter-weight and more varied material: the twentieth century development which followed was the mass daily newspaper. Table I shows how strongly the 'religious' periodicals of the mid-victorian period were clustered in the magazine sector, although there were also a surprising number of religious weekly papers following the more modern pattern of greater publication frequency. Successive technical innovations – stereotyping (to allow multiple-printing), the steam-press, the cylindrical press, continuous paper webs,

---

[4] Anon., *The Newspaper Press of the Present Day* (London 1860) p 34. For short descriptions of 32 major religious periodicals see [Alvar] Ellegård, [*The Readership of the Periodical Press in Mid-Victorian Britain*], Gotseborgs Hogskolas Årsskrift, 63 (Gotseborg 1957) tables 9, 11, 14: reprinted in *VPN*, 13 (1971) pp 3–22. There are narrative surveys of the victorian religious press in *Fraser's Magazine*, 18 (London 1838) pp 330–8; *Dublin Review*, 89 (London 1881) pp 1–29; L. E. Elliott-Binns, *Religion in the Victorian Era* (2 ed London 1946) pp 331–7; [E. E.] Kellett, 'The Press', in *Early Victorian England*, ed G. M. Young (London 1934) II, pp 1–97; [T. H.] Darlow, [*William Robertson Nicoll, Life and Letters*] (London 1925) pp 57–66; and H. W. Peet, 'The religious press: a wide field', *Times Anniversary Number* (London, 1 January 1935) p xxi.

[5] *Controversialist*, 8 (1862) p 201.

[6] [R. D.] Altick, [*The English Common Reader 1800–1900*] (Chicago 1957) p 361, gives 253 religious periodicals out of 630, in 1870. In *VPN*, 16 (1972) p 1, I found 179 religious periodicals out of 355 in 1860.

[7] Altick, p 151. For book statistics, see *SCH*, 10 (1973) p 224.

and machine-typesetting – combined with the much faster distribution methods available from the 1850s, to mean that speed of production, frequency of issue, and size of circulation, could all increase so much as to change the function, not just the possible influence, of victorian periodicals. The reduction of stamp-duty in 1836, and the successive repeals of advertisement duty in 1853, stamp-duty in 1855, and paper-duty in 1861, only gave the press legal freedom to do what had already become a technical possibility. The effect of this changed market situation for general periodicals elicited two different kinds of response from the publishers of religious periodicals. One response, similar to that seen in victorian religious book-publishing, was to cling to the older-fashioned model, and keep to a monthly format of 'religious' material. The other was to try and replace the 'secular' press for their readers, to imitate the new patterns of periodical journalism, and hope for the necessarily-larger readership needed. Both patterns of response to the periodical situation parallel attitudes widespread in victorian religious response to other modern phenomena – urbanisation, for instance. It is the purpose of this paper to distinguish the effects on victorian religious attitudes of the enforced choice between the two patterns.

In the early years of the century, the religious periodicals were reaching a larger readership, at a probably slightly lower social level, than the high-class reviews on which (literary) historians have concentrated. Nearly all were monthlies, so escaping tax, and the proportion of 'timeless' religious articles to news, even in denominational magazines like the *General Baptist Repository*, was high: the news that was included was for the record, rather than information about events as they were happening. It seems likely that most of their readers took them instead of secular reviews, and the titles favoured in the early years of the century – the *Spiritual Treasury*, *Zion's Casket*, the *Repository*, the *Magazine* (that is, storehouse) – all these suggest a timeless orientation, as does the frequent survival of bound copies. The magazines of the early nineteenth century might many of them just as well be undated. (The exceptions, the fierce broadsheets of particularly 1829 and 1832, were mostly short-lived.) An advertisement for the *Instructor* (founded 1808) stated that it would be 'supplied with pious reflections; suitable comments to improve the dispensations of Providence; and the whole to be conducted with an eye to our temporal, as well as spiritual welfare'.[8] The religious magazines made use of the new cylindrical steam-presses before the heavy secular reviews, not because

[8] *Press of the Present Day*, p 39, quoting advertisement of 1807.

they were dependent on rapid production to include late news, but simply because their circulations were larger. The *Edinburgh* or *Quarterly* in their hey-day only just touched fifteen thousand. The *Evangelical Magazine* and the *Methodist Magazine* were both in the 1840s printing 24,000 copies a month, which on steam-presses could be done in a mere three days of press-work.[9] There was a subsidiary side to religious periodical publishing in the early period, the tract-magazine, usually undated, and often for loan rather than free distribution: this like its parent the tract followed the form of the eighteenth-century popular chap-book, right down to the wood-cut on the front page. The pattern of periodical first established for religious readers was one which gave them a strong sense of commitment to a timeless editorial creed. Articles were anonymous, and advertisements excluded.

This pattern continued to be held to by many periodicals, because it corresponded to a continuing element in victorian belief. As late as 1877, for instance, a new periodical *The Bible Witness and Review, for the Presentation and Defence of Revealed Truth* could be initiated, successfully, in which the four-hundred-odd pages a year covered only ten articles in the first year and eleven in the second, and in which every article was 'religious' in subject-matter, except for the 130 pages in volume two devoted to exposing the illogicality and infidelity of Mill's *System of Logic*. Subscription to a periodical, almost irrespective of its content-matter, served victorians as a kind of religious self-identification. This was particularly so if they were caught up in an ecclesiastical organisation with divergent tendencies. Church of England readers, for instance, found a more stable statement of their beliefs from the *Christian Observer* or the *British and Foreign Evangelical Review*, on one side, or from the *British Critic* or the *Christian Remembrancer* on the other, than they would find in the disputed formularies of their church. Similarly, with the very fluid, and non-denominational, network of strict baptists, it was the periodicals to which they subscribed which distinguished the two groups of calvinists. Of the group led by William Gadsby, and later J. C. Philpot, A. C. Underwood has written: 'The churches of this group are linked together by the *Gospel Standard* and by very little else, thus adhering to the teaching of Gadsby,

---

[9] William Savage, *A Dictionary of the Art of Printing* (London 1841) p 467. On hand-presses, the work on the last sheet of each number had to be started ten days before publication. The *Evangelical Magazine* had already circulated 18,000 to 20,000 copies monthly by 1807 (Altick p 392), but slumped badly in the 1850s: in 1856, it gave its 'present circulation' as 9,500, N[ewspaper] P[ress] D[irectory] (London 1856) p 125.

who always questioned the value of churches associating together.'[10] On the other hand, the other group of particular baptists, though they did belong to a regional association of chapels, were linked through their magazines, the *Gospel Herald, or Poor Christian's Magazine* (founded 1833), and, more belligerently, C. W. Banks's *Earthen Vessel* (founded 1843).[11] Rather similarly, later in the century, subscription to the *Revival*, later the *Christian*, became a non-denominational party-badge for certain kinds of evangelical: Dr Barnardo wrote that, 'to see the *Christian* lying on a drawing-room table is a guarantee that you are among people who sympathise with all good work'.[12] Even for catholic readers, periodicals which were seriously opinion-based, could serve this kind of function. Why else should the *Tablet*, for a standard reference work of 1879, describe its editorial principles as 'To seek Justice and Truth in whatever party they may be found', while the rival, but declining, *Weekly Register* announced itself as being 'Essentially and intensely Catholic, its views being in absolute harmony with the Encyclical *Quanta Cura* and the Syllabus'?[13]

Of course, with the pressures of weekly journalism in the later part of the century, there were very virulent controversies between periodicals, ostensibly in theological terms, all fighting to control the same readership: weekly journalism demanded bigger circulations, while with monthly magazines there was more possibility of peaceful co-existence. A writer in 1862 attributed a 'sectarianising and sectionising effect' to the periodical medium itself. 'All this specialisation, while it commends itself to the several divisions of the public, exerts a prejudicial influence on that very public, and tends to stereotype our manifold parties and sects.'[14] Papers could go under if they had no loyal

[10] [A. C.] Underwood, [*A History of the English Baptists*] (London 1947) pp 245–6. I am indebted to Mr J. H. Y. Briggs for this reference. The *Gospel Standard, or Feeble Christian's Support* was founded in 1835, and edited by Philpot for twenty years from 1849. The circulation touched 17,000 at its peak. Miss Rosemary Taylor, of the Institute of Historical Research, is at present completing a bibliographical survey of baptist periodicals.

[11] Underwood, pp 245–7: the two papers eventually merged. The *Earthen Vessel* claimed in 1849 a circulation of 5,000, and that it was 'read by double that number, and by a class of persons who seldom see any other publication' (Underwood, p 245, n 1).

[12] *VPN*, 16 (1972) p 11. Compare 'The publications of Evangelical papers such as the *Christian* or the *Life of Faith* assisted this healthy sense of unity': B. F. C. Atkinson, *Valiant in Fight* (London 1937) p 187.

[13] *NPD* (1879) pp 36, 37. See also John R. Fletcher, 'Early Catholic Periodicals in England', *Dublin Review*, 4 series, 198 (1936) pp 284–310.

[14] *Controversialist*, 8 (1862) p 203.

constituency to look to: the publisher of the *English Review* (high church, founded 1844) wrote that 'it represented no one in particular, though it had many well-wishers at the start', and it had to be discontinued in 1853.[15] When a denomination was about to divide, as happened so often in the second quarter of the century, it was partly through periodicals that the differing parties acquired a nation-wide identity. One religious publisher wrote, rather cynically, and from the safe distance of the twentieth century, that victorian protestants 'had a magazine or a church paper, with its editor, for every shade of belief. They fought their battles and washed their daily linen in full view of a public which loved a religious fight, if for no other reason than that prize-fighting was strictly *verboten*.'[16] Again, a selection of titles illustrate the attitude: the *British Banner*, the *British Standard*, the *Guardian*, the *Banner of Israel*, the *Banner of Truth*, the *Rock*. The prize-fight, or controversial, element of late-victorian religious journalism is the running-to-seed of the early victorian tradition of heavyweight 'party' reviews. But much more typical of those who maintained the older tradition of religious periodicals were the many small-circulation monthlies, of heavily theological content: they were serving unfashionably small readerships, and the favoured titles towards the end of the century are cryptic, the signals of small freemasonries of the like-minded: the *King's Highway*, *Things New and Old*, *Out and Out*, *Words of Grace*, *A Voice for the Faithful*, *Trusting and Toiling*, the *Girdle of Truth*, and the sixpenny monthly that provides the sub-title for this essay, *Fragments that Remain*. None of these were primarily news magazines; none of them admitted fiction; and none of them were weeklies. The opinion-based, 'religious' pattern for periodicals might seem to develop to a very small-group, other-wordly kind of religious consciousness, but in the number of these late-victorian journals still adhering to the old format can be seen the continuance of early victorian earnestness.

There was, however, a substantial change in the religious consciousness of many victorian church-goers in the second half of the century, and the change was mirrored more quickly in religious periodicals than in ecclesiastical organisation. From the beginning of the century, for evangelistic purposes, religious periodicals were founded in imitation of successful new secular periodicals: in the second half of the century, religious periodicals were adopting the methods of the new

[15] Septimus Rivington, *The Publishing Family of Rivington* (London 1919) p 142.
[16] G. H. Doran, *Chronicles of Barabbas 1884–1934* (London 1935) p 300.

secular large-circulation weekly for readers who already identified themselves as religious. This pattern of imitation, rather than withdrawal, is the second major response by religious periodicals to general periodical developments.

I have already pointed out that the tract-magazine derived its format from the secular chap-book, just as the tract-colporteurs worked in the tradition of the chap-book hawkers. An important feature of periodical publishing in the eighteen-twenties to forties was the illustrated, silk-bound, annual volume, of mixed prose and poetry: the secular annuals *Friendship's Offering* (1824–44), *The Keepsake* (1828–57), and *The Gem* (1829–32) had their religious imitations in such volumes as *The Sacred Offering* (1831–8), *The Christian Keepsake* (1833–40), and *The Amethyst: or Christian's Annual* (1832–4).[17] This was imitation at an upper-middle class level, for the daughters of earnest families. At a lower social level, one of the earliest successes of mass periodical publishing was Charles Knight's *The Penny Magazine* (1832–45): this was immediately followed by the *Christian's Penny Magazine* (1832–7), and *Zion's Trumpet: or the Penny Spiritual Magazine* (1833–68).[18] These were started to make use of a medium of proved secular success for evangelistic purposes, and both kept to traditionally-oriented content-matter.

Rather similar to these imitations, in using a secular format for religious purposes, were the religious reviews of the later part of the century. In the eighteen-sixties and seventies, partly as an élite response to the new mass-circulation weeklies, there was founded a clutch of heavyweight monthlies and quarterlies, which operated with very liberal editorial policies, and allowed the signed articles of contributors to include views not endorsed by the editors. The most famous examples are the *Contemporary Review*, John Morley's *Fortnightly Review*, and J. T. Knowles's *Nineteenth Century*. Various denominations founded, or adapted, journals to this new model, which allowed the expression of divergent views among their leaders, and thus 'contained' potentially schismatic debate, just as the secular reviews 'contained' differences of opinion among secular leaders. The congregationalist *British Quarterly Review*, the wesleyan *London Quarterly Review*, the anglican *Church Quarterly Review*, and in its later stages the *Primitive*

---

[17] This is only a selection of religious imitations: see *New Cambridge Bibliography of English Literature* III (London 1969) cols 1873–8. The whole section on periodicals (cols 1755–1884, by H. and S. Rosenberg) is the best guide to the secondary literature and publication details on individual magazines.

[18] *Times Tercentenary Handlist of English and Welsh Newspapers 1620–1920* (London 1920), under 1832.

Methodist Quarterly all assumed this role. The catholic *Rambler* had a special class of articles 'communicated' to the editors, which did not have editorial endorsement. These reviews were usually of very small circulation, needing denominational or private subsidy. This kind of imitation, like denominational boarding-schools, was a status-symbol, a bid for equality by the clergy with the secular clerisy.[19]

Two big developments in secular periodical publishing were of much longer-term effect than the relatively-minor innovations which gave rise to the imitations so far considered. These were the development of weekly fiction-magazines in the eighteen-forties, and of cheap weekly news magazines in the fifties. The religious weeklies of the later victorian period grew from these two new developments. A typical secular fiction-weekly, *The Family Herald*, was selling 125,000 copies a week by 1849.[20] The popular news medium for mid-victorians was a Sunday paper, like *Lloyd's Weekly* or the *News of the World*, both with circulations of over 100,000. The growing provincial press, from 1855, and the national *Daily Telegraph* increased the daily news readership, but the mass victorian news market was in weeklies, not in dailies.[21] Faced with the twin challenges of fiction and news, some religious publishers set out to keep readers committed to 'religious' rather than 'secular' periodicals. In these fields, 'religious' imitations were the expression of an attempted cultural control, particularly over children and the poor, rather than an imaginative liberalisation. It was, as we shall see, a policy that paid diminishing returns.

The fiction of the *Family Herald* elicited direct responses in the publication of the *Leisure Hour: a family journal* (1852), and the Religious Tract Society's *Sunday at Home* (1854); the society's daring in this venture is illustrated by the fact that they had to answer criticisms two years later (apparently based solely on their title) that the magazine's gripping tales encouraged readers to stay away from church.[22] A similar innovation followed rapidly for a slightly higher social class. Upper-middle class readers in the 1860s switched allegiance from

[19] Thirteen such reviews will be included in the *Wellesley Index to Victorian Periodicals 1824–1900*, 4 vols (Toronto and London 1966–): the first two volumes (1966, 1972) include the *Home and Foreign Review*, the *Dublin Review*, and the *Rambler*. On the secular development see Christopher Kent, 'Higher journalism and the mid-Victorian clerisy', *Victorian Studies*, 13 (Bloomington 1969) pp 181–98.

[20] Kellett, p 69.

[21] [Raymond] Williams, ['The growth of the popular press'], in his *The Long Revolution* (London 1961, 2 ed 1965) part II, cap 3.

[22] *NPD* (1856) advertisement section.

reviews to monthly magazines which included for the first time serial fiction. The most famous example is the *Cornhill Magazine*, started in January 1860 with Thackeray as editor, but *Macmillan's* (November 1859), *Temple Bar* (December 1860), and *Belgravia* (1866) all followed the same pattern. In the very month that the *Cornhill* appeared, Alexander Strahan began the publication of a new religious periodical, *Good Words*, edited by Norman Macleod. In later years, the impression was frequently given that Strahan and Macleod had had an editorial policy clear from the start of the venture. Macleod's son wrote that his father could see no reason 'for leaving the power of wholesome fiction, the discussion of questions on physical and social science, together with all the humour and fun of life, to serials which excluded Christianity from their pages: the success of the magazine was at once assured'.[23] Macleod himself remembered his decision to use signed articles rather than anonymous ones as a decision to make each contributor responsible only for the views of his own work, not for the whole periodical.[24] In fact, *Good Words* did not have an immediately successful start: Strahan recorded that 'it had an uphill battle to fight for some time'.[25] The first number opened with no expression of liberal sympathies, but with a request to the readers for prayer that 'good words only' might be included, and eight of the ten articles in that first number were 'religious' material (the other two articles were informative, one on natural history, the other on astronomy, in the old natural theology tradition). The articles were unsigned, and there was no fiction.[26] Against the slow start of this unexceptionable material, the *Cornhill's* rapid success must have made a tantalising contrast. Serial fiction first appeared in the sixth number of *Good Words*, and the famous policy that it was to be 'a periodical for *all the week*' was not adumbrated until the last page of the first volume, which also announced a new serial 'by the Author of *John Halifax, Gentleman*', for the next volume.[27] Anonymity was broken down, therefore, at least partly to utilise the selling-power of a well-known contributor's name, not from high-minded reasons of authorial independence. Macleod's evolving policy was rewarded by a rapid increase in circulation, to the scale of his secular

[23] *Good Words*, ns I (London, 5 May 1906) p 2.
[24] [Donald] Macleod, [*Memoir of Norman Macleod D.D.*] (London 1876) II, p 136.
[25] Alexander Strahan, *Norman Macleod D.D. A Slight contribution towards his biography* (London 1872) p 10; compare p 19 also, 'the first year or two was not a success'.
[26] *Good Words* I (London, January 1860) p 1.
[27] *Good Words* I (London, December 1860) p 796.

rivals. Sales reached 110,000 monthly by 1863.[28] Such innovations, in a magazine started as orthodox evangelical in backing, did not go un-challenged. An anonymous Scottish pamphleteer claimed:

> Your fair *Good Words* had cleared the way
> To rid us o' the Sabbath day;
> Besides commandments twa or three nae
> I need naw.[29]

The equally anonymous leader-writer of the *Record*, which because of its outdated newspaper format was dropping in circulation from 4,000 to 3,500 per number in the period 1860–65,[30] acknowledged that *Good Words* 'stood, and still stands, in the very forefront of our monthlies, religious and otherwise', but detected in its 'trashy tales, and the weak, watery and sentimental "poetry"', the 'evil leaven' of Kingsley and Stanley. In a revealing reversal of the sugar-and-pill image frequently used about the introduction of religious fiction, the *Record* claimed that the presence of some well-known evangelical con-tributors was only 'the sugar to sweeten the noxious, the deadly draught' of serial fiction.[31] But the path which Strahan and Macleod (author of 'Courage, brother, do not stumble/Though thy path be dark as night'), had arrived on in their editorial trials and errors in the early numbers of *Good Words*, was the path followed by most religious publishers and editors aspiring to large circulations. By the eighteen-seventies, it was common for weekly religious papers to include fiction, with the mild concession that the handsome hero was frequently a nonconformist minister of liberal principles, or if orthodox, was 'of the old school' and had a heart of gold, and un*Record*ite sympathies. The innovations of the 1850s and 1860s led, not to the 'best and healthiest fiction' of their times, but to 'religious fiction'. In the 1860s, *Good Words* included fiction by Kingsley and Trollope. Fifty years later it was relying on Annie S. Swan, and its contemporaries were serialising the Hockings, or S. R. Crockett, or even Mark Guy Pearse. As early as 1876, the young Eugene Stock, by no means a theological

[28] Macleod, p 136. Ellegård estimated circulations of 30,000 (1860), 70,000 (1865), and 80,000 (1870), and cites the *Freeman* (7 January 1863) as giving *Good Words*'s circulation as 70,000 (Ellegård, table 16).

[29] Anon., *Norman's Blast. A Rejected Contribution to 'Good Words'* (Glasgow 1865, 1866; Edinburgh 1866; 2 ed with music, Glasgow 1866; 3 ed 1866).

[30] Ellegård, table 9.

[31] '*Good Words*': *the theology of its Editor, and of some of its contributors, reprinted from the 'Record' newspaper* (London 1863) pp 3, 4, 6.

reactionary, complained, 'How long are we to have those very milk-and-water stories which appear in all kinds and descriptions of our religious periodicals? Are they really essential to the sale?'.[32] The inclusion of fiction in the later victorian religious periodicals, and the consequent unceasing demand for 'suitable' serials of predictable outcome, was a major concession by religious groups to secular attitudes, but should hardly be presented as a great step forward.

The second great challenge of the growth of the secular press was the problem of news coverage. It was the weekly periodicals that confronted this problem best, at a time when few people took in a daily paper. The major religious success in opposition to the secular Sunday newspapers, was the *Christian World*, at least after James Clark took it over in 1860. Clark arranged the use of telegraphed news for his weekly coverage, but relied for continued subscriptions also on the fiction of Emma Jane Worboise. By 1880, the circulation had reached 130,000 weekly.[33] An increasingly similar periodical, which moved across from being a paper concerned with the contemporary fulfilment of prophecy to being a general religious newspaper, was Michael Baxter's *Christian Herald, and Signs of the Times* (founded 1866), which by 1881 was selling 195,000 weekly.[34] Even the *Christian*, which never included fiction, was driven to including a general news column with a prophetic gloss, under the heading 'Signs of the Times', from 1870. These were commercial, non-denominational papers. A speaker at the church congress at Plymouth in 1876 claimed that the church of England should be sponsoring such a venture also, a 'Church newspaper for the million'; 'I want in the first place a good honest *weekly newspaper*, of a high tone and character.'[35] A later speaker in the same debate juxtaposed a reinforcement of that plea with an analysis of the six major secular Sunday newspapers.[36] These anglican plans apparently came to nothing, but for them to be made at all in such terms, suggests that the late-victorian religious weeklies were trying to be much more to their subscribers than 'religious' magazines: they were a takeover bid, in news and fiction as well as beliefs, of all the functions of the then-dominant communications medium. It was rather as if

[32] *Authorised Report [of the Church Congress held at Plymouth, October 3, 4, 5, and 6, 1876]* (London 1877) p 283.
[33] Arthur Porritt, *More and More of Memories* (London 1947) p 76.
[34] Altick, p 395.
[35] Reverend Godfrey Thring, in *Authorised Report* pp 262–8: Thring's detailed plan is a remarkable precursor of the pattern later realised in the *British Weekly*.
[36] *Authorised Report* pp 271–81.

church leaders were seriously proposing to set up a fourth television channel to serve the total viewing needs of church-goers. The enormous political power which is frequently attributed to Robertson Nicoll's *British Weekly, A Journal of Christian and Social Progress* need not have been illusory, for the ambitions of such editors were to challenge the secular press on its own ground, not to fill some special niche as a 'religious' periodical.[37]

But the number of years in which such ambitions were possible was limited, because of further developments in the secular press. The growth of the weekly newspaper was followed by the growth of the daily newspaper. The daily-newspaper-buying public doubled in the period 1896–1906, and doubled again by the first world war. By 1920, five million national newspapers were sold each day, and thirteen million Sunday newspapers each weekend.[38] Just as the victorian news-medium of the weekly survey was overtaken, by the daily newspaper, so the victorian entertainment-medium of serial fiction was in time overtaken by the cinema and television. The imitative innovations which had so much increased the circulation of the religious press were precisely what made it vulnerable to subsequent changes in the secular media.

Professor Wolff has argued that 'the basic unit for the study of Victorian cultural history is the individual issue of a Victorian periodical'.[39] An early number of *Good Words* would contain about ten longish articles or stories, on book-sized pages with no advertisements, and no religious gossip about ecclesiastical personages. A number from fifty years later included no devotional article or sermon, and no prose argument; it was on tabloid-size newsprint, and had a short story, no less than three serials (one by Silas K. Hocking, another entitled 'Queen of the Rushes: A Great Story of the Welsh Revival'), a piece by Annie S. Swan on 'When should a girl say "Yes" ', and an article on 'Why I do not play golf' by the reverend R. J. Campbell. There were eight full pages of advertisements, mostly for bicycles or patent medicines, including a large-type announcement of the miracle cure with Zam-Buk

---

[37] The *British Weekly* made its impact by adopting the broken-up format of the New Journalism of the 1880s: for rather kind estimates of Nicoll, see Darlow, and also G. W. Lawrence, 'William Robertson Nicoll (1851–1923) and Religious Journalism in the Nineteenth Century', unpublished PhD thesis (Edinburgh 1954). For a hostile caricature, see H. G. Wells, *The New Machiavelli* (London 1911) bk I, cap 3.

[38] Williams, p. 227.

[39] Wolff, 'Charting the golden stream', p 43.

of a local preacher's torturing eczema.[40] Faced with a change of this kind in an important religious periodical, the historian may perhaps begin to consider any debate within a denominational organisation of the same reverend R. J. Campbell's *New Theology* as relatively peripheral to religious developments of the period. One is happy to record that *Good Words* closed down four years later, in 1910. The *British Weekly* saved more of its respectability, but that *Journal of Christian and Social Progress* celebrated Christmas 1933 with a supplement consisting of James Hilton's new story *Goodbye, Mr. Chips*, where the hero dies disgruntled and puzzled in a post-war fog. By 1925, the circulation of the once-impregnable *Christian World* had sunk to a still impressive 30,000 weekly – it's a curiously-painful personal decision to give up subscribing to a religious paper: what will the newsagent infer? But the *Christian World* had to close down in 1961. The brave, culturally imperialistic attitudes of the weekly editors of the late-victorian period eventually led to the substantial weakening of editorial content, not in the direction of a newly-liberal theology, but in that of intellectual feebleness. Topicality led to triviality, and in the long run the ephemerality of the imitative periodicals proved as limiting as the timeless orientation of the old-fashioned devotional monthlies.

Both patterns of development are of substantial interest to the ecclesiastical historian. The developments have been shown in this paper as operating in non-denominational periodicals, because publishers without formal institutional ties seem to have been very responsive to changes in reader-attitudes. Similarly divergent patterns of religious response to the victorian periodicals explosion could though be demonstrated for denominational magazines, with the limitation that the 'imitative' fiction-and-news alternative was only available to magazines serving the larger denominations, because the new journalism needed large circulations. Dr Currie has already depicted the steady secularisation of methodist magazines in the 1880s and 1890s.[41] The 'sectarianising' function of periodicals can be seen acting within a denomination with the continuing publication of, say, the *English Churchman*. But although periodical developments interact with denominational ones, periodicals also form quasi-institutional groupings of subscribers which cut across,

---

[40] *Good Words*, ns I (London, 5 May 1906): with the 7 July number was given away a coloured picture of Edward VII at worship in Westminster Abbey. In 1899, the *Gospel Herald*, when soliciting advertisers, stated 'Patent medicine advertisements not admitted' (*NPD*, 1899, p 343).
[41] Robert Currie, *Methodism Divided: a study in the sociology of ecumenicalism* (London 1968) pp 134–8.

as well as sub-dividing, denominational boundaries. Professors Berger and Luckman have suggested that there is a special importance in such quasi-institutional groupings: a sociologist who 'operates exclusively with an ecclesiastically-oriented definition of religion', they write, 'has an altogether too narrow, and, as it were, juridical concept of institution . . . There is a significant sociological problem involved in the loss of monopoly status by the major legitimating systems of Western civilisation. We believe that this process is one of the social causes of the privatization of belief, that is, of the withdrawal of religious commitments from their traditionally designated locations in society'.[42] The enormous quantity, and varying functions, of victorian religious periodicals seem to illustrate Berger and Luckman's proposition: they challenged the monopoly status of church or chapel based religion, just as much as once dissent had challenged church. The periodicals, in their variety, divisiveness, and patterns of development may image victorian religious allegiances in a way at least as significant historically as the development of denominational organisations. Subscription to a religious periodical was a form of religious commitment, alongside commitment to a church or chapel. What the modern sociologists discern was discerned also by a still-unidentified writer in the *Dublin Review* in 1881, who wrote: 'No one, in fact, can make any study of these so-called "religious" papers without arriving at a tolerably definite opinion that the tendency towards unbelief, which is so eminently characteristic of the present day, is due in no small degree to the operations of these prints'.[43] Similarly, one can see an awesome irony in the contemporary claim of the reverend Charles Bullock, editor of *Home Words*, that 'in the printing press of the nineteenth century we seem to have realised the possibility of *a pulpit in every home*'.[44] Religious periodicals do not only provide invaluable information about victorian religious life: in an important sense, the periodical medium itself made possible much of its character.

---

[42] P. Berger and T. Luckman, 'The sociology of religion and the sociology of knowledge', in *Sociology of Religion*, ed Roland Robertson (Hardmondsworth 1969) pp 65, 70–1: reprinted from *Sociology and Social Research*, 47 (London 1963) pp 417–27.

[43] *Dublin Review*, 89 (1881) p 3.

[44] *Authorised Report* p 272. There is striking confirmation, of the two responses sketched here for periodical sources, in a general interpretation of victorian attitudes to secular activities, which became available after this paper was written: Haddon Willmer, '"Holy Worldliness" in nineteenth-century England', *SCH*, 10 (1973) pp 193–211.

TABLE I

Victorian Religious Periodicals and Publication Frequency, 1860–1900

	1860	1880	1900
1. London-based weekly and fortnightly periodicals:			
total	183	454	847
religious	31	71	88
percentage of religious	16·9%	15·6%	10·4%
2. Monthly periodicals:			
total	345	813	1410
religious	174	348	402
percentage of religious	50·4%	42·8%	28·5%
3. Quarterly periodicals:			
total	57	125	282
religious	18	37	61
percentage of religious	31·6%	29·6%	21·7%
TOTAL PERIODICAL TITLES CURRENT	535	1392	2539
TOTAL RELIGIOUS TITLES	223	456	551
percentage of religious	38·1%	32·8%	21·7%

Note: These figures are calculated from the lists in Mitchell's *Newspaper Press Directory and Advertiser's Guide* (London), omitting the daily newspapers and provincial weekly newspapers, but including other periodicals published in the provinces: Mitchell's (1860) pp 19–32, 109–19; (1880) pp 24–41, 137–60; (1900) pp 60–79, 221–64

THE SIGNIFICANCE OF
TERRITORIAL CHURCH HISTORY FOR
CHURCH HISTORY IN GENERAL

by MARTIN BRECHT

WITHIN the general frame-theme of methodological problems in church history I shall be concerned in this paper
with the question of the relation of territorial church history
to church history as a whole. This seems to be a very dry subject of less
general interest today than for example at the beginning of this century, when historical positivism flourished. Of course my concern is
not that of reviving a form of historical thinking which belongs to the
past, nor do I want to fall into a false romanticism, but I want to direct
attention to a permanent task of church history, whose importance is at
present either underestimated or even overlooked altogether. The
beginnings of my own work as a church historian were precisely in the
field of territorial church history. When I was a young student I had
the opportunity of taking a course, which provided an introduction
into the work of archives. Afterwards as a student I undertook the
reorganisation of the archives of several deaneries and parishes. In this
way I became acquainted with a large complex of historical sources,
which often contained very interesting and hitherto unknown material
about important figures or developments. This pointed the direction
for my own historical work. Again and again I learned how
very fruitful it can be in historical research both for the gaining
of new insights and for the criticism of existing opinions to look
for the connexion between territorial or local and universal church
history. With this as my starting point I shall deal with three aspects
of my theme:

1. The relation between territorial and universal church history as
a methodological and scientific problem and task.
2. The significance of regional church history for the historical
consciousness of people, communities and society in the individual
region.

3. To what extent territorial history is a problem confined to German scholarship.

As Droysen did in his famous *Historik* I shall try to illustrate my statements with examples.

I

Whenever church history is not pursued in a totally abstract way, as *Geistesgeschichte* or history of theology, it always includes a regional or local component. For instance it is one of the strengths of the excellent biography of Augustine by Peter Brown, that the author describes so carefully the local background of North Africa. At least since the period of the middle ages the writing of church history has always included a geographical point of view according to the interests and requirements of the readers with a special reference to the events, say in England, France or Germany. I distinguish from this national historiography the territorial as the smaller unit, although the distinction cannot be made too rigidly: in the early middle ages France and Germany belonged together in the carolingian empire. Switzerland, the Netherlands, Austria or Bohemia had a common history with Germany for long periods. They were all territories within the German historical sphere, until they became independent and went separate ways, in their church history as in other respects. As far as Switzerland, Bohemia and the Netherlands are concerned the reformation is a very interesting transition-period in this connexion, and one in which one should avoid holding apart within national divisions matters which belong together. To my mind this has not always been respected in the writing of Swiss history.

There is no doubt that our historical consciousness is dominated by the great movements and developments in history: christianisation, monasticism and its orders, scholasticism, the reformation, the formation of the denominations, puritanism, methodism, the enlightenment, the modern dechristianisation, the revival movement; added to this there are the great figures and the important influences of their thought – Augustine, Anselm, Wyclif, Thomas Aquinas, Luther, Calvin, John Wesley or great leaders like Charlemagne or some of the popes, or Cromwell. I do not want in any way to question the importance of the great developments, institutions, personalities and ideas in church history, but I do want to point out that we must never forget the deep roots which all these have in the local or regional situation. Consider, for instance, in the case of Jan Hus the combination of Wyclif's ideas and his own Czech background. It cannot be overlooked that Luther's roots in the prince's state in Saxony had important consequences for his political thinking, and the same is true, for Zwingli, of his involvement in the city-state of Zürich. Martin Bucer's conception of the church as the kingdom of God grew up in the imperial city of Strasbourg, before he wrote *De regno Dei* for the church of England. Research into the local background of important figures like Thomas Müntzer in recent years has given to us new insights. The as yet unanswered question as to the essence of German idealism will only be solved if the growth of this thinking in the context of Tübingen and Jena is investigated in minute detail. Like a detective we have to find out all the personal and literary contacts and influences of the young Hegel, Hölderlin and Schelling. It is surprising that up to now this has not been done, although it looks a promising undertaking.

We come now to another aspect of the problem: the great ideas of important thinkers often undergo change as they are propagated. A single person cannot carry out this propagation. Other people with different backgrounds and other interests have to participate. Often the original intentions are altered, distorted and developed or combined with other traditions. One should remember what happened to Luther's ideas under the influence of humanism, for example at the hands of Zwingli and Bucer. How many influences came to England in the reformation period: lutheran, upper-German, zwinglian, calvinistic ideas, and what happened to all these, once they reached England? Ideas and programmes cannot be realised unless they are taken up at the local level, unless they are put into effect and made concrete in individual communities. It would clearly be better in reformation history, and not only in reformation history, if more attention were paid to this transformation of ideas instead of another dozen books being written about Luther's theology. Our picture of the historical reality would become richer and more differentiated in this way. Fortunately efforts have recently been made in this direction.

The great devotional movements both in the middle ages and modern times always have been borne by certain groups within the population: from among the nobility, the clergy, the middle classes or the peasantry. It is with good reason that our attention is drawn today to the fact that the contribution of whole groups of classes to certain historical events must not be forgotten in favour of the role of individuals in them. One can only become aware of these groups by the analysis of deeds of gift, of legal records and registers. This must always be done first in a particular region, town or country. Our historical ideas will often be modified by the analysis of such material. For example the activities of sects and groups on the edge of the church from the sixteenth to the eighteenth century can be grasped only in part from the books of their leaders. This must be completed by investigations into their followers in the particular towns and villages. Only then do we receive a correct picture of the importance and effect of those groups. We can study the growth of modern secularisation in the books of the progressive thinkers, but this should be completed by investigation into the change in the political, social and moral behaviour of broader groups. This is one of the points where cooperation between church history and sociology may be useful. We all know that abortive developments or abuses call forth reactions. But often such strivings after reform become independent and develop their own inner laws. The political government was already intensively involved in the church reform of the fifteenth century. The reformed church order including the secularisation of church property was developed from these medieval beginnings in a very different way in each particular territory. We can only discover the relation between popular piety and political interests by investigating the situation in each territory.

We often have the situation in church history that a certain region becomes important and plays a leading rôle in larger and more extensive developments, for instance Calvin's Geneva or Strasbourg in the reformation period, or Halle and Herrnhut in the period of pietism. Walter Köhler has been able to demonstrate the widespread influence of the consistory of Zürich on the church orders of many cities. In the same way he has been able to show the history of the conflict about the Lord's Supper between Luther and Zwingli in the imperial cities. The development of the monastic orders is again and again concentrated in centres, from which new daughter communities go out. Sometimes it is possible to recognise this even in the architecture. The same is true in the history of medieval missions. English methodism sometimes received certain impulses from particular regions like Yorkshire.

In conclusion: the portrayal and demonstration of great historical lines of development must be accompanied by their verification by reference to particular areas, small enough to be clearly grasped. In this way it is often possible to recognise and to redefine a historical process in its individuality on the basis of the registers, and on the basis of the sum of individual phenomena. The interdependence of the historical survey and the intensive research into detail should perhaps be generally even more clearly and consciously acknowledged and practised today than it is already. This presupposes that this detailed research will also be well acquainted with the scientific methods of historical research and the wider historical context. Detailed historical research should not only be a playground for amateurs and dilettantes. The work of detailed historical research done without the necessary overall view often becomes provincial and idyllic, for it loses the wider perspectives. On the other hand universal history or *Geistesgeschichte* without detailed verification loses its foundations.

The critical function of territorial church history can be well demonstrated by reference to J. Wallmann's book: *Philipp Jakob Spener und die Anfänge des Pietismus* (1970). Before Wallmann it had never been possible to clarify the relations of Spener to Labadie. Everybody supposed there must be some relationship, but there was nothing more than hypothesis, which was threatening to become *communis opinio*. Now Wallmann has been able to discover the points of contact between Labadie and the radicals among the Frankfurt pietists in a painstaking investigation of the situation in Frankfurt. The result is the knowledge that Spener's and Labadie's chiliasm originated from English sources (Joseph Mede). This is an example of how detailed historical work can lead to a view of the wider relations. Conversely Carl Hinrichs in his book: *Preussentum und Pietismus* (1971) has been able to derive from the rôle of Francke's pietism in Halle within the Prussian state a new overall understanding of the pietism in Halle which sees the latter as the execution of the universal and utopian reform ideas of the seventeenth century. In this context Francke's work appears to be a very interesting parallel to English puritanism. Both examples show, how creative the synthesis of universal conceptions and detailed work in history can be. An exclusive concentration in a limited field of church history however without reference to the greater context can be dangerous, because the individual phenomena cannot be classified. Such problems can be observed sometimes in American research works, which investigate with great eagerness very special problems for instance in German reformation history, often however the horizon is too narrow, and therefore their results cannot be really satisfying. Here, better cooperation between the specialists could often contribute to a better overall view and a proper formulation of the question.

It may be of interest at the end of this first part of my paper to outline the way in which the work of territorial church history is done in

Germany at the present time. First of all there are individual secular or church-historians who occupy themselves with problems of territorial church history: for instance Hubatsch, Hinrichs, Kupisch in Prussia, Schlesinger in Saxony, Goeters and Mühlhaupt in the Rhineland, Stupperich in Westfalia, Lehmann and I myself in Württemberg. Doctoral theses are also initiated by these scholars. The so-called *Landesgeschichte* (territorial history) in German secular history is acknowledged and well established at the universities as one historical discipline beside those of ancient, medieval or modern history. Territorial church history however has not been able to establish itself in the same way up to the present time. There are only a few chairs, in Mainz and Göttingen, and some invitations to lecture on this subject. The history of important territorial churches (*Landeskirchen*) is scarcely represented at the universities. The institution of chairs for territorial church history of all the larger *Landeskirchen*, which was planned ten years ago, could not be realised because of the lack of money and the diminishing historical interest, although this was something, which was genuinely desired by church historians. This means that it is not very easy to obtain qualified scholars in the field of territorial church history. Territorial church history is carried out above all by a series of territorial church historical societies and similar institutions, which usually have close relations with the archives of the *Landeskirchen*. Most of these societies publish their periodicals and series of historical researches. Some of them are of a very high standard and fill an important place in the work of church history. The structure and formation of these societies varies. Often the majority of the members are older. The strength of their links with church institutions also varies. Some of the societies also deal deliberately with religious customs and questions of religious sociology. I think, the societies are right, when they define the tasks not only from a historical point of view but also try to awaken and preserve the awareness and sense of responsibility for traditions of the individual *Landeskirche*. They also advise the church government, for instance in the development of church orders, liturgies, and catechisms. Obviously this is an important function to which, perhaps, the churches still have too little recourse. Sometimes the church governments decide important problems without knowledge of their own tradition. The societies on the other hand have not always seen that the awareness and discussion of their own tradition must also be critical: that they should demonstrate not only the riches and possibilities of their traditions, but also their limitations and problems. A mere unbroken traditionalism would make the work of the societies sterile. The church history society of Württemberg has deliberately dealt with themes of broad interest and topicality like the *Kirchenkampf*, pietism, which in recent years has grown stronger, and the peasants' war; and I think this decision was sensible. Cooperation among the various societies for territorial church history as is practised in secular history is only just beginning. This is a problem of the growing together of the *Evangelische Kirche* in Germany. Finally there is the important task of awakening and preserving the awareness of their own church history amongst ministers and in the parishes. This is not very easy, because it is often difficult today to interest ministers and laymen in church history. Nevertheless, one must spare no pains and must not be discouraged from doing this. For otherwise church history would become simply the hobby of a few specialists and interested people.

II

The time seems to be past, when the knowledge of history was considered to be one of the most important means of understanding the conditions of our existence. The interest has shifted to other regions of experience such as the natural sciences or at the present time psychology and sociology. If the heritage of history and its effects are still noticed, what is seen is the history of failure, intolerance, repression. In particular the history of the church and christianity is criticised. People are scandalised by the way in which the religion of love and liberty failed to rise to its inner demand, how often it was abused by power and riches. People expect little from the heritage of church history, and refer, at most, to the lesser traditions of minorities and emancipatory movements. There is a certain justification in putting these critical questions to history and church history. Mere lamentation about the lack of interest in history does not help at all. It is rather the task of all who understand and value history to insist that the important share of history in all the conditions of our life must not be forgotten nor overlooked, but is, rather, something we must be aware of. If we were to relinquish history and its experience, we should lose an important part of reality, we should no longer understand the way, in which our life and our world are codetermined by history, whether we realise it or not.

But the question is, how to make people aware of the reality of history. Generally, the forces which guide history are felt to be anonymous, impersonal and remote – ideas, which cannot be grasped, which spring up somehow and somewhere, solitary thinkers and unapproachable rulers, to whom no one has any relation. People are usually unaware that history and its traces surround us everywhere and shape our environment, even in matters like our traffic or housing conditions.

I would like to illustrate this with an example which I sometimes also use for my students – the presence of church history in the town and district where I live, in Tübingen. The earliest traces of christianity are some Lombard crosses, found in princes' graves in a suburb of Tübingen. In the same suburb a *patrocinium* of saint Ottmar shows the link with one of the greatest and most important Alemannian monasteries, namely St Gall in Switzerland. St Gall was founded by Gallus, one of the disciples of Columbanus.

In upper Germany one of the origins of christian mission was the work of the Iro-Scottish monks. The main church of the town is situated in the middle of a former Alemannian cemetery. One of its patron saints is Martin. This is testimony to West Franconian influence in this region. The history of the church and of devotion in the middle ages can be found in several buildings, which are still standing. The only romanesque building in the town is the chapel of an old farm, which the counts palatinate of Tübingen gave to the monastery of Blaubeuren, a daughter of the monastery of Hirsau, which was one of the most important centres of the reform movement of Cluny. The conflict between the pope and emperor was very sharp precisely in the Swabian territory. The counts of Tübingen took the pope's part. They sponsored new monastic movements in the twelfth century. First, they gave a large farm to the premonstratensians, then followed near Tübingen the foundation of the cistercian monastery of Bebenhausen, which soon became the richest monastery in Württemberg. Later on, the counts of Tübingen had to mortgage their own residence city Tübingen to this monastery for a certain time. Among the old buildings of Tübingen you can still find the great and large storehouses of these monasteries, which demonstrate their wealth. In the thirteenth century two monasteries of the mendicant friars settled in the town, the augustinian hermits and the black friars, and there was also a little settlement of the beguines in the so-called *Nonnenhaus* (nuns' house). In the fifteenth century all these monasteries were reformed. Then at the end of the fifteenth century we have once more a new monastic foundation, the house of the brethren of common life, a movement joined with the *devotio moderna*, which came from the Netherlands. One of the priors of the augustinians from 1497–1500 was Johannes Staupitz, before he went to

Wittemberg, where he became Luther's superior. You can still find today the old institutions of the ecclesiastical sanitary and social service. The old hospital of St James and the former hospital for incurables today are both used as homes for the aged. The church of the hospital became the second parish church of the town. Together with the castle the great new building of the church from the fifteenth century dominates the town. Its wonderful stained glass windows show the piety of this time and the grave-stones in the church commemorate the most important persons of the town and the parish. The modern age has scarcely changed the situation. But now the spiritual movements can be demonstrated from the written sources. One of the earliest and best representatives of the baptists, Michael Sattler, was burnt in the neighbouring town of Rottenburg in 1527. Even to today the very simple liturgy tells us that the character of the reformation in Württemberg was a compromise between the lutheran and the Swiss directions. For long years there was a very strong influence from the spiritualist Kaspar Schwenckfeld. In the seventeenth and eighteenth century there arose the conflict between the lutherans and new movements of devotion stemming from Jakob Böhme and Johann Arndt. Spener lived in Tübingen after his studies. Francke and Zinzendorf preached in the churches of the town. The Salzburg emigrants came through Tübingen. The ecclesiastical life of the town was touched by the French revolution. Later on Tübingen became a centre of the revival movement. The methodists acquired a firm footing. The conflict between church and national socialism also took place in the town. In 1938 the synagogue was burnt.

I have tried briefly to demonstrate some of the great connexions, which join the church history of this town with church history in general. Of course these relations were of differing nature and varying intensity. It is my opinion that history can begin to lose its anonymity in this way. But you will perhaps say, that a town like Tübingen is in this respect an exceptional example, although I did not refer to the special rôle of the town as a seat of an old university. But if we look more closely we can find such connexions also in every village, with its successions of ministers, in its legal, institutional, economic or personal circumstances. This is certainly the case, if we go beyond the single parish and take into consideration the region, although there are again differences in the historical significance of the regions. Since the period of the Alemanni southwest Germany has had a very rich church history. The duchy of Swabia soon became one of the most important of the empire. From here the Staufer, Welf, Habsburgs and Hohenzollerns originated. This region is very rich in towns and urban culture (Nürnberg, Augsburg, Strasbourg, Konstanz, Ulm). Every one of these cities for instance gave its own contribution to reformation history. In the southwest three or four medieval universities were founded: Heidelberg, Freiburg, Tübingen and Basel. At the beginning of the modern period Habsburg and Württemberg strove for predominance in this region. This had its consequences for the spreading of the reformation. The Habsburg Austrian territory began three miles outside Tübingen. This area is still predominantly catholic, and till some years ago even political behaviour was shaped by the past just as much as in the protestant territories, although the Swabian possessions of the Habsburgs had belonged to Württemberg since Napoleon's new political order of Germany in 1810. The denominational importance of the lutheran duchy of Württemberg lay in the fact, that it was one of the best organised lutheran churches in Germany, and therefore exercised a strong and widespread influence. At the end of the seventeenth century this church opened itself to the influence of pietism. Since then Württemberg has had a mediating rôle among the German *Landeskirchen*.

In conclusion: we meet always, of course in differing intensity, in the single parish the historical conditions, which to the present day determine positively or negatively ecclesiastical life, and we meet as well religious factors, which influence life in general: the varying decrease of industrialisation in Württemberg results from denominational conditions too. The protestant north is industrialised far more than the catholic south. The puritanical, pietistic tradition still shapes the way of life, as do certain catholic customs (*Carneval*). Even today there is a denominational inequality in the level of education. Very old traditions live on in the ecclesiastical order and constitution. The supremacy of the princes over the church can be found to a certain extent still in the centralised administration of the church, and, in an English context, it is well known how the outdated organisation of parishes could hinder the church in new situations. Certain problems of ecclesiastical life can be understood better, knowing the historical background. Hidden or unknown traditions can perhaps stimulate us in new ways. Because the members of the church and of society are also concerned with church history the knowledge of this history should not be limited to a few specialists. The presence of this history is most real in the single town or in the region, and there, more than anywhere, it is possible to encounter history. A further thought: today we are learning more and more that our world becomes and remains inhabitable when we look after the heritage of the past. The humanity of our world consists also in this, that we are informed how present things came to be as they are, and that we take possession of them reverently and critically at the same time. The science of history, and of church history, have a rôle here of the information and education of the society, and are not only limited to research; we should not withdraw from that task. Here history needs good public relations and needs to make imaginative offers. If these are done I think a positive echo will be forthcoming.

III

From what I have said so far, it might seem that the problem of territorial church history is, more or less, only a German one, and is therefore not important for English church history scholarship. Perhaps you have met in your own historical work at some time the difficult problem, that if you had to deal with German history, you mostly were confronted with one of the German states like Prussia, the Palatinate, Hannover or Hamburg (to mention only the countries, which have had more intensive contacts with England) – but scarcely with the German *Reich* or German church as a whole. If historical events are seen from the outside, it may happen, that some individuals like Niemöller and Bonhoeffer become the only representatives of the church struggle, while a person like bishop Wurm of Württemberg, the exponent of the so-called intact South German Churches and important initiator of the present *Evangelische Kirche* in Germany, is scarcely known.

In this context, I think, two remarks are necessary, one about the real peculiarity of German history and one about territorial history as an overlapping general problem. It is a matter of fact that the political structure of Germany has always been a federal one. Germany has never been a centralised state. The map of southwest Germany in 1800 looks like a very colourful carpet with its numerous medium sized and small dominions of knights and monasteries and cities, all independent, belonging only to the *Reich*. Already in the middle ages there were the tribal duchies of Swabia, Bavaria, Franconia, Saxonia, with the Staufer, Wittelsbacher, Welf, Habsburger, Askanier, and Wettiner as leading principalities. After the decline of the Staufer in the thirteenth century many cities and ecclesiastical and aristocratic dominions became immediate to the *Reich*. Besides these little dominions however there grew up greater states like Bavaria, Hessen, the Palatinate, Brandenburg – Prussia, Habsburg – Austria or Württemberg. They often followed their independent policies, and church policies too. In the fifteenth century the duke of Cleve is described as being the pope within his own lands. German reformation history is shaped very intensively by this political situation. For the reformation could be carried out only in connexion and cooperation with the individual territories – *Cuius regio eius religio*. The emperor's religious policy however was a failure. Therefore the history of German protestantism in many respects is a history of single *Landeskirchen* with their own universities and church history. In Prussia it could develop differently from in Saxony or Würrtemberg. This did not really change even in the nineteenth century, when the number of German territories was drastically diminished by Napoleon; although the influence of Prussia and Berlin then increased because of their size. But the essential independence of the *Landeskirchen* remained. If I am right, from the English point of view German history is often seen as analogous to the French. In France the centralised state succeeded. Therefore, to draw a parallel between Germany and France misunderstands an important peculiarity of German history. We only can speak of a German church history in a very abstract sense, for instance of *Geistesgeschichte*. The rich and manifold shaping of reformation, orthodoxy, pietism, and enlightenment in Germany is to a large extent determined by territorialism. More and more historical and church historical research is respecting this aspect, as far as it is not concerned only with single persons or ideas, and an awareness of it can only assist in the study of German history.

But it would be wrong to think, that territorialism is only a problem of German history. As far as I know, early English church history is very narrowly connected with the particular political circumstances. German territorialism is rooted in the medieval feudal state, in which a central power had not yet developed. There is a very similar situation in Germany and France in the middle ages, and I think, it can hardly have been different in England. The political and even the hierarchical circumstances of the middle ages permitted certain developments and movements. In this context we can ask how far such peculiar developments did exist in the individual dioceses, for how long, and how strong they were. What was the peculiar rôle of the local or regional gentry? Certainly the particular developments did not end once the central state was established. The religious pluralism in seventeenth century England may also doubtless have its local and regional components. It was probably not only the capital that set the fashion. As the development in contemporary French historiography shows, where research is heavily occupied with the history of single departments, it may be fertile even with regard to the central state to respect the regional aspect of history. Only if this aspect is appropriately respected will we encounter the history of men and their circumstances.

I have probably explained from my German point of view many things, which are quite self-evident and already practised outside Germany. Nevertheless I hope that this brief discussion of the rôle and place of territorial church history in Germany is not altogether barren of ideas and stimulus for non-German historians of the church.

INSTITUTIONS AND ILLUSIONS:
THE DILEMMA OF
THE MODERN ECCLESIASTICAL HISTORIAN

by KEITH ROBBINS

THE modern ecclesiastical historian is an uncertain and hesitant creature; an acute case, it may be thought, of status deprivation. He looks with envy at his august and serene colleagues who have the history of the medieval church as their field of study. He knows that they are in process of uncovering the different layers of belief in medieval or early modern society. It is, no doubt, an illusion to suppose that an 'age of faith' ever existed. Nevertheless, at all levels of society, the church seems to be central to the life of the time. If we consider the reformation or counter-reformation periods, church questions seem to be in the forefront. The 'Wars of Religion' may not be at bottom about religion, but we cannot avoid some consideration of religious issues.

The ecclesiastical historian of these centuries can, I imagine, carry out his work in the knowledge that the main political and intellectual developments cannot be understood without reference to the position of the church or the churches. Granted such a presupposition, even undergraduates are prepared to wrestle seriously with theological ideas and ecclesiastical structures. Doubtless, pervaded by the prevailing secular ideas, the churches were not always as coherent and powerful as they seemed. Yet, whatever the precise relations between church and state, ecclesiastical claims could not be ignored. In this situation, presumably, no ecclesiastical historian feels inhibited and apologetic. He is, after all, dealing with a major aspect of the life of a period. A special subject in an undergraduate history course on the elizabethan church or the reformation in Germany and Switzerland seems entirely appropriate and will cause few raised eyebrows in the common room. Since their labour is worthy of their hire, such ecclesiastical historians can even indulge in the luxury of research without feeling they ought to be doing something else.

If we may take the French revolution as the beginning of modern history, then these years also saw the first systematic attempt to replace organised christianity. As we all know, the endeavour failed. Catholic christianity was eventually restored but, in one sense of that much-discussed term, the era of 'secularisation' had set in. Whether we regard subsequent developments in Europe as a blessed release from the trammels of power or as manifest decline, there can be no doubt that the modern ecclesiastical historian has few defined landmarks within which to work. He is a diffident fellow, to be nurtured and treated with care lest his light goes out. For the most part, indeed, we hide our lights under more popular bushels. We define our interests as political, social or diplomatic or whatever, adding quickly, as though in penitent after-thought, 'and ecclesiastical'. Publishers or selection committees nod knowingly. Everybody has to have some eccentricity but luckily, where it really matters, the fellow seems pretty sound. So long, therefore, as we have other strings to our bow, we are safe. Woe betide the modern historian who ventures out with an ecclesiastical ticket alone. The dilemmas of the modern historian of the church are acute for the scope and nature of his subject are uncertain. Accordingly, the 'sources, materials and methods' of modern ecclesiastical history will vary with our conception of its purpose and significance.

The theme of this paper is that there are, broadly speaking, two main approaches to the writing of church history. I use the word 'approaches' rather than 'schools' since I do not wish to suggest tight-knit or antithetical groups of historians. Certain people may feel that they adopt both approaches, or do not recognise themselves in the description of either. Equally, although I think the division applies with most force in the modern period, it is not confined to it.

The distinction can perhaps be most simply conveyed by referring to 'church historians' on the one hand and 'historians of the church' or 'historians of religion and society' on the other. Unfortunately, the former is considerably more concise than the latter! Inevitably at issue is the prefixing of 'church' or (worse) 'ecclesiastical' to 'history'. The point is at once trivial and profound. It will not surprise you to learn that there are those for whom 'ecclesiastical history' is too redolent of the trollopean universe and too defiantly archaic to warrant serious attention. It is not that the idea of a sub-discipline offends such critics, for many of them are busily creating one of their own. It is very largely a reaction triggered off by prejudices and feelings connected with the word 'church'.

To consider the problems of 'church history' first. It is undeniable that the history of the christian churches is a rich field and offers scope for very different types of historical investigation. Many notable ecclesiastical histories have been written; many still will be. We can all think of 'church historians' who excite our admiration and respect, yet there seem to be a number of reasons why they themselves and their genre have contemporary difficulties.

The linked questions of the appropriate stance towards the churches and the commitment to their beliefs immediately spring to mind. Historically, of course, the history of the churches has been primarily a study for churchmen. It has been studied by historians, both clerical and lay, who have been drawn to it by their own christian beliefs. In large measure, they have accepted the christian understanding of the nature and mission of the church. 'Church historians' have accepted the existence of God and have not been inclined to suppose that the worshipping life of the churches is an illusion. It is not surprising, therefore, that 'church history' has been most commonly taught in an ecclesiastical context. Where specific provision for it exists in British universities, the historians concerned have usually had closer connexions with a department of theology than with a department of history. Many students of ecclesiastical history have been ordinands not disposed to challenge a christian understanding of the church.

At a different level, church history has been frequently studied from a denominational standpoint. In the past, history has been the arena for contests between spokesmen of different churches. Each church has found in the past confirmation of its present peculiarities and claims. However diminished at the moment is the fervour of these claims, the imprint of the denominational basis of 'church history' can still clearly be seen. It has meant that histories have been written on a denominational basis. It has been customary for them to be written by historians who are themselves members. The advantages of this situation are obvious. There is perhaps no substitute for personal knowledge when writing the history of any institution and churches are no exception. The disadvantages are equally plain.

It should also be stated that some 'anti-church history' has also been written by agnostics or atheists who have been equally committed in their writing. They have been anxious primarily to expose the fraudulent or inadequate bases of christian belief and to reveal the shortcomings of ecclesiastical practice in their lurid detail.

A commitment of some kind has therefore seemed a prerequisite for a 'church historian'. The rules seem to have been laid down in advance. Even the Ecclesiastical History Society seems a rather tainted organisation! In such a context, the question of whether detached yet sympathetic writing on recent ecclesiastical history is possible is one which remains open and unresolved.

The second aspect of 'church history' is more closely related to methodology. The 'church historian', at whatever point he chooses to make his particular investigations, cannot escape either the past or the ongoing life of the institution. The ubiquity of the church and its activities at very different social levels make it peculiarly difficult to study extensively through history. Put another way, the continuity of the church defeats our contemporary professional historical world. Few of us are capable of mastering church history in its chronological entirety. Even if we do gain a comprehensive knowledge we can probably only do so with a patchy and superficial understanding of the changing intellectual and political situations in which the church has had to exist through the centuries. It is perhaps the feeling that the 'church historian' simply does not know enough general history which causes many to have reservations about the validity of 'church history'.

This dilemma is, of course, an old one, though that does not make it any easier to solve. The modern 'church historian' has very often come to this study from an interest in earlier periods. If not formally trained in theology, he is at least well acquainted with the history of theological ideas. Committed or uncommitted, the focus of his interest lies in the church itself. He understands, for example, the complex historical inheritance of the european churches in 1800. With care and skill he traces the way in which the churches react to the pressures of a revolutionary age. It would be an error to suppose that he sees nothing new under the sun, but he is sceptical of glib generalisations about the decline of the church. He knows well that the churches have endured the heat and burden of the day in past centuries. While acknowledging that all ecclesiastical institutions cannot be isolated from the world, he stresses that they have a self-consciousness and resilience which enable them to withstand fads and fashions.

In such a perspective, the task of the 'church historian' is resolutely, even defiantly, to continue to write the history of the churches as discrete phenomena. He can write a history of the church of England, the methodist church, the church of Scotland, the French reformed church or whatever, within such chronological limits as he sets himself. His sources and materials are largely determined by such an objective. He tries to get inside the life of the institution he is studying. We are shown how it is organised and governed, what its beliefs and practices are, and its success or failure in propagating or maintaining them.

If we take the question of government and ecclesiastical authority it of course figures prominently in accounts of any nineteenth century church, both internally and in its relations with state authority. The story generally is one of separation and schism. English methodism was repeatedly disrupted; baptists and congregationalists found themselves troubled by the tension between independency and the pressures towards centralisation; Scotland provided a classic case of disruption, paralleled in Switzerland; the Oxford movement, in one aspect, was a reassertion of the autonomous life of the church – and so on in a comprehensive list. The material for the study of these questions is abundant. The nineteenth century 'church historian' is troubled by the richness of relevant sources – printed debates, broadsheets, periodical literature, printed books, memoirs and biographies. There is also an abundance of manuscript material which is far from fully exploited.

We can all think of successful history written on such foundations. The sources allow the writer to produce a broad account of developments and at the same time grapple with the details. When one moves into the twentieth century, however, the situation is more disturbing. The private papers of an alarmingly high number of ecclesiastical figures have disappeared, presumed destroyed. In the nineteenth century, it would be virtually possible to write a corporate biography of the Society of Friends. It would be much more difficult in the twentieth. On reflexion, as one currently engaged in a life of John Bright and finding no scarcity of primary sources, perhaps the decline in output is not such a disaster! Lucky the contemporary bishop, however, who can confidently expect a biography by virtue of his office! Rare the publisher who seeks a volume of decanal memoirs! The decline in the number of ecclesiastical periodicals has gone on at a rapid pace. Not, of course, that the paucity of such sources is a problem simply for the 'church historian'. The contemporary historian in general knows that his enemies are telephones and television.

In any case, it might be argued that 'church history' written from the traditional medley of sources is no longer adequate, at least by itself. The view from the metropolitan denominational headquarters looks very different from a west-country chapel pew. The scene surveyed from an episcopal bench looks very different from the church choir. Perhaps too much 'church history' has been from the standpoint of the shepherds and too little from that of the flock. Church historians therefore need to shift their studies from clergy to laity and, at the same

KEITH ROBBINS

time, from the national to the local level.[1] There is, of course, a great
deal of work being done on local ecclesiastical history and even more is
needed. Information is emerging about the levels of church attendance
and membership in different parts of the British Isles. We can begin to
assess the causes of these variations and assess their significance.

In consequence, modern 'church history' which has been written
from a demographic standpoint can look very different from one
which is based on literary or biographical sources. On the one hand, we
are often presented with a forest of maps and statistical tables. They are
highly informative, but also somewhat indigestible. On the other, we
are fortunate in having a number of recent 'church histories' notable
for their literary skill and elegant presentation. The difficulty is to marry
the two approaches in such a way that the virtues and insights of both
are preserved.

It would be presumptuous to suggest how this should be done, but
the challenge it presents cannot be ignored. It is, after all, commonplace that statistical accounts do not tell us many of the things we wish
to know about the significance of church membership and attendance.
Unless we know what importance various churches attach to regularity
of attendance or what they understand by membership, the mere compilation of lists and league tables is pointless. It is also the case that local
studies, by themselves, bewilder as much as they illuminate. It is a
favourite trick for historians to produce an impeccable and meticulous
article on church life in a specific locality and to demonstrate how, in
almost every particular, it contradicts what is widely held to be the
'national picture'. This happens so frequently, and of course not only in
respect of 'church history' that it is often tempting to believe that there
is no national picture at all. Indeed, we are never sure whether the
research in question is meant to lead us to this conclusion or to the view
that it constituted a most exceptional case proving some general rule.
Clearly, a balance between differing approaches has to be struck somewhere, but it is perhaps too early to try to strike it.

A similar kind of problem exists in the world of ideas. It would be a
poor kind of 'church history' which was concerned simply with the
organisation and distribution of churches. The traditional answer has
been to produce histories of theological thought, or to insert chapters
on 'thought' within general histories. These insertions have not infre-

[1] Dr Kitson Clark's interesting *Churchmen and the Condition of England 1832–1885*
(London 1973) for example, largely equates churchmen with the clergy of the
established church.

quently been distillations of these larger works. While again, not mini-mising the difficulties of the enterprise, such treatment is surely inadequate. Karl Barth's *Protestant Theology in the Nineteenth Century* is a very brilliant work. Besides telling us a great deal about Barth him-self, we are given a provocative treatment of those theologians Barth considers we ought to be bothered with. Some years ago the former archbishop of Canterbury gave us *From Gore to Temple* and recently Reardon has taken course *From Coleridge to Gore*. As surveys of certain theological developments they are excellent in themselves, even if the thinkers chosen for discussion are rather predictable. Professor Welch's first volume of his *Protestant Thought in the Nineteenth Century* is more ambitious than the other volumes. He tries to look at protestant thought in the United States, Britain and on the continent and to trace connex-ions and common themes. Once again, however, the gallery is a theo-logian's gallery of theologians.[2]

If we take the history of theology to be a branch of the history of ideas, then perhaps there is little cause for alarm at this state of affairs. If we consider it to be a branch of 'church history' there is cause for con-cern. We need to be sensitive to a whole range of beliefs and not simply consider the writings of those thinkers whom we consider to be the most profound or stimulating. Arguably the 'best' theologians had the least impact on the mass of church goers. A history of thought which contained no reference to Kierkegaard would seem odd; to include him as 'typical' or 'representative' would be even odder. The Scottish theologian James Denney was reading him long before he is generally supposed to have been discovered in Britain, but any impact was obviously on a later age than his own. If we wish to know what the average man in the pulpit was preaching we start with his sermons and we go to the obscure and unknown preachers as much as to the great and famous. In the nineteenth century, being obscure and unknown was, fortunately, not an insuperable obstacle to publication. The themes and arguments to emerge from even the most rudimentary content analysis of the vast volume of published sermons would, in all proba-bility, present a striking contrast to the 'History of Theology' as it is generally conceived. As yet, the use of sermons, tracts, hymns in a systematic way with this end in view has hardly begun. The thought

[2] K. Barth, *Protestant Theology in the Nineteenth Century; its background and history* (London 1972): A. M. Ramsey, *From Gore To Temple* (London 1960); B. M. G. Reardon, *From Coleridge to Gore* (London 1972); C. Welch, *Protestant Thought in the Nineteenth Century I. 1799–1870* (New Haven 1972).

of any age is not monolithic and we have to recognize the different
audiences and constituencies for which writers and preachers prepared.
We must have room for British Israelitism, for millennarianism and for
bishop Gore. The tendency of writers to plump for one kind of belief
rather than the other only produces distortion. Why should not J. H.
Newman and J. N. Darby appear in the same volume?

These methodological differences appear within 'church history'.
They become even greater when we consider the attitudes of the historian of 'religion and society'. There is, of course, a very considerable
overlap in the use of sources and materials between the two sets of
practitioners. In part, too, the distinction is merely verbal. Many of us
have probably had the experience of offering a lecture course which, as
'religion and society' attracted twice the audience drawn by 'church
and state'. 'Religion', it would appear, is popular whereas 'church' is
not. However, a preference for 'religion and society' is not simply a
slavish following of contemporary fashion. It appears to give the
historian a freedom and a scope which 'church history' does not allow.

In the first place, although one might suppose there is something
rather odd about the joining of 'religion and society' as if religion
could exist apart from society, the emphasis is not institutional. Inevitably, a great deal of attention is given to the history of the churches,
but 'religion' may exist outside the forms of the churches. Considerable
impetus to such an approach comes from contemporary sociology of
religion. If we leave aside some of the more wearisome 'Prolegomena
towards a medium-term definition of a Church-Sect typology', which
we have all encountered, it would be idle to deny the enormous benefit
which can be gained from sociology. Our categories are challenged,
our simplicities exposed and our awareness deepened. We may feel
resilient under criticism, lost in some of the higher criticism or indignant
at opaque and pretentious language but, after a prolonged exposure, we
cannot return to our old ways.

A concentration upon the history of religion, however we define it,
paradoxically allows us to be more clear-sighted, perhaps, about the
churches themselves. The circumstances in which 'church history' has
been written have tended to reinforce stereotypes. Denominational
historians, whether consciously or unconsciously have often brought
back their denominations to the intentions of their founders when they
have erred and strayed. In addition, they have exaggerated the differences between denominations, though this is not to say that the student

of religion sees uniformity in either belief or practice. However, particularly if he has an adequate knowledge of different countries and
societies he may be more struck by the similarities of ethos and outlook
between denominations within one society in contrast to another. He
may also be able to deal more adequately with those whose religious
beliefs are firm but whose ecclesiastical allegiance is accidental and unimportant, depending on a host of factors which can include such things
as family and geographical convenience. As far as I know, no systematic
work has been done on the problem, but analyses of the number of
'conversions' or, less dramatically, 'transfers' from one church to
another must have been considerable. Consideration of the traffic-flow
may tell one more about the central religious issues of an age than the
assumption that one or other church adequately catered for the needs
of individuals. Of course, it is possible for such an approach to descend
to a primitive anti-institutionalism – but perhaps there are worse faults.
John Bright, no friend of the clergy or of the established church frequently expressed the opinion that christianity would not come into
its own until 'churchianity' was brought low. He was not alone in this
opinion in his own age and it is not unknown for such sentiments to be
uttered today. Such convictions show how dangerous it is to equate the
'decline of the churches' with the 'decline of religion'.

'Society' receives as much attention as 'religion' in this alternative
approach. It is vital for the historian to know as much, if not more,
about the context in which religion operates than about the 'religion'
itself. He will be conscious of parallels and movements in the wider
society which, perhaps, the church historian is apt to feel are peculiar to
the churches. This is not the place to embark on a detailed consideration
of causation, but it often becomes difficult to determine in any particular
set of circumstances whether 'religious' attitudes determine 'secular'
values, whether 'secular' attitudes determine 'religious' values, or
whether both have their origin in the psychological make-up of individuals or the economic structure. If false consciousness abounds, which
consciousness is false? I wrote a thesis on conscientious objection in the
first world war in Great Britain. One set of objectors were labelled
'religious' and another 'political'. What was apparent was that both
groups, though not without their differences, had more in common
with each other than they did with their confrères in religious or political bodies who were not conscientious objectors. Alternatively, we may
look at the political and religious history of modern Ireland. In
Northern Ireland, is the conflict 'about' religion as one might assume

from the use of the terms 'catholic' and 'protestant' by the BBC, or is it 'political', between 'republican' and 'anti-republican' factions, or is it 'national' between 'Irish' and 'Scots-Irish', or is it a confused mixture of all three? No doubt we all have our own views, but it would seem unduly naive to suppose that we could write just a 'church history' of Ireland. Nothing less than a total history of Ireland can make sense of its ecclesiastical institutions.[3] The sources and materials which are relevant to the task take on a new order of complexity.

It is not my purpose to argue that one approach is wrong and the other right. In any case to attempt to distinguish two such categories may well smack too much of sociological 'ideal types' to be convincing! What matters is not the label but that the interpenetration of the church and the world, of religion and society, should be treated seriously and fully to the benefit of historiography as a whole. At the moment, unfortunately, far too many examples of partial history exist for one to feel at all complacent. 'Church historians' writing modern church history need to be warned against exaggerating the significance of the churches and perhaps underwriting the illusions of churchmen. General historians need to be warned against writing off the churches prematurely and subscribing to facile notions of secularisation too early. The 'church historian' needs to examine sources and materials far beyond those which are narrowly concerned with the life of the institution if he is to gain an adequate perspective. The general historian in turn must take church materials seriously. We must not feel inhibited if a colleague, busy on his social history of the football pools, feels that an interest in modern papal history is very outré. Some brief illustrations, touching on my own personal interests, may serve to make the point more sharply.

Not surprisingly, a good deal of international history concerning Anglo-German relations has been written, yet very little on the close ecclesiastical and theological connexions between England, Scotland and Germany. International history is ceasing to be narrowly diplomatic in emphasis but the study of international christianity is only now getting under way in the modern period. It is obvious that eighteenth century 'pietism', the nineteenth century 'réveil' or roman catholic modernism can only be comprehended in an international context. On the other hand, it is important not to accept the overestimation by contemporary church leaders of their own importance and standing. It

[3] J. H. Whyte, *Church and State in Modern Ireland* (Dublin 1971).

is salutary to read the proceedings of the 1941 Malvern conference, or books like *Towards a Christian Order* or *Christian Counter-Attack*, and set them alongside the section on religious broadcasting during the second world war in professor Briggs' history of broadcasting. In turn, there is little point in supposing that the theological and ecclesiastical wrangles which were a feature of the German church struggle from 1933–45 can be waved away and the contestants cast in convenient political rôles. Yet the theological battles must not be taken too seriously; theologians even more than politicians have their own inimitable controversial manners.

My final example is a case where one-sided use of sources by different groups of historians has produced an inadequate understanding of a complex figure. I refer to the reverend R. J. Campbell, congregationalist minister of the City Temple in London from 1903 to 1915. He was a popular preacher of considerable renown, with many published volumes of sermons, although D. H. Lawrence, after listening to him, modestly thought that he could do as well. He suddenly became a public figure with the publication of his controversial *The New Theology* in 1907. With the perhaps characteristic exception of Dr Vidler, it has since been treated by most historians of theology as a piece of immanentist detritus, hardly worth reading. Yet, while not claiming that the book is 'original' working out the influences and sources upon which Campbell based his writing is a fascinating exercise. His real significance, however, lies as a broker of ideas, and the reverberations of the *New Theology* and the sermons, from West Wales to Durham and Northumberland need to be studied. On the other hand, labour historians have noted his *Christianity and the Social Order* and his sudden and fleeting involvement in the labour movement, but they take little cognisance of his 'religious' activities. By referring only to a narrow range of sources and materials, historians of theology, ecclesiastical historians and labour historians find themselves in some instances making the most jejune comments about the general significance of Campbell's career.[4] In the process of compartmentalisation, the many-sided impact he made on edwardian England is lost. However, I have, no doubt, pontificated long enough on methodological issues, and at least as far as Campbell is concerned, I must practise what I preach before I again detain a captive congregation for so long.

[4] R. J. Campbell, *The New Theology* (London 1907); R. J. Campbell, *Christianity and the Social Order* (London 1907); J. T. Boulton (ed), *Lawrence in Love* (Nottingham 1968) p 140; A. R. Vidler, *Twentieth Century Defenders of the Faith* (London 1965) pp 26–8; P. Thompson, *Socialists, Liberals and Labour* (London 1967) pp 23–4.

ABBREVIATIONS

AASRP	Associated Archaeological Societies Reports and Papers
ACO	Acta Conciliorum Oecumenicorum, ed E. Schwartz (Berlin/Leipzig 1914–40)
ACW	Ancient Christian Writers, ed J. Quasten and J. C. Plumpe (Westminster, Maryland/London 1946–)
AHP	Archivum historiae pontificiae (Rome 1963–)
AKPAW	Abhandlungen der Königlichen Preussischen Akademie der Wissenschaften zu Berlin (Berlin 1815–)
An Bol	Analecta Bollandiana (Brussels 1882–)
Annales	Annales: Economies, Sociétés, Civilisations (Paris 1946–)
ASB	Acta Sanctorum Bollandiana (Brussels etc. 1643–)
ASC	Anglo Saxon Chronicle
ASOC	Analecta Sacri Ordinis Cisterciensis (Analecta Cisterciensia since 1965) (Rome 1945–)
ASOSB	Acta Sanctorum Ordinis Sancti Benedicti, ed L. D'Achery and J. Mabillon (Paris 1668–1701)
ASP	Archivio della Società [Deputazione from 1935] Romana di Storia Patria (Rome 1878–1934, 1935 ff)
BEC	Bibliothèque de l'école des chartes (Paris 1839–)
BIHR	Bulletin of the Institute of Historical Research (London 1923–)
BJRL	Bulletin of the John Rylands Library (Manchester 1903–)
BM	British Museum, London
Byz	Byzantion (Brussels/Boston 1924–)
BZ	Byzantinische Zeitschrift (Leipzig 1892–)
CAH	Cambridge Ancient History
CC	Corpus Christianorum (Turnholt 1952–)
CHB	Cambridge History of the Bible
CHJ	Cambridge Historical Journal (Cambridge 1925–57)
CIG	Corpus Inscriptionum Graecarum, ed A. Boeckh, J. Franz, E. Curtius, A. Kirchhoff, 4 vols (Berlin 1825–77)
CMH	Cambridge Medieval History
CModH	Cambridge Modern History
COCR	Collectanea Ordinis Cisterciensium Reformatorum (Rome and Westmalle 1934–)
COD	Conciliorum oecumenicorum decreta (3 ed Bologna 1973)
CS	Cartularium Saxonicum, ed W. de G. Birch, 3 vols (London 1885–93)
CSCO	Corpus Scriptorum Christianorum Orientalium (Paris 1903–)
CSEL	Corpus Scriptorum Ecclesiasticorum Latinorum (Vienna 1866–)
CSer	Camden Series (London 1838–)
CSHByz	Corpus Scriptorum Historiae Byzantinae (Bonn 1828–78)
CYS	Canterbury and York Society (London 1907–)
DA	Deutsches Archiv für [Geschichte, Weimar 1937–43] die Erforschung des Mittelalters (Cologne, Graz 1950–)
DACL	Dictionnaire d'Archéologie chrétienne et de Liturgie, ed F. Cabrol and H. Leclercq (Paris 1924–)
DDC	Dictionnaire de Droit Canonique, ed R. Naz (Paris 1935–)

DHGE	*Dictionnaire d'Histoire et de Géographie ecclésiastiques*, ed A. Baudrillart and others. (Paris 1912–)
DNB	*Dictionary of National Biography* (London 1885–)
DSAM	*Dictionnaire de Spiritualité, Ascetique et Mystique*, ed M. Viller (Paris 1932–)
DTC	*Dictionnaire de Théologie Catholique*, ed A. Vacant, E. Mangenot, E. Amann, 15 vols (Paris 1903–50)
Ec.HR	*Economic History Review* (London 1927–)
EETS	*Early English Text Society*
EHD	*English Historical Documents* (London 1953–)
EHR	*English Historical Review* (London 1886–)
EYC	*Early Yorkshire Charters*, ed W. Farrer and C. T. Clay, 12 vols (Edinburgh, Wakefield 1914–65)
FGH	*Die Fragmente der griechischen Historiker*, ed F. Jacoby (Berlin 1926–30)
FM	*Histoire de l'église depuis les origines jusqu'à nos jours*, ed A. Fliche and V. Martin (Paris 1935–)
GCS	*Die griechischen christlichen Schriftsteller der erste drei Jahrhunderte* (Leipzig 1897–)
HBS	*Henry Bradshaw Society* (London, Canterbury 1891–)
HE	*Historia Ecclesiastica*
HJ	*Historical Journal* (Cambridge 1958–)
HJch	*Historisches Jahrbuch der Görres Gesellschaft* (Cologne 1880 ff, Munich 1950–)
HL	C. J. Hefele and H. Leclercq, *Histore des Conciles*, 10 vols (Paris 1907–35)
HMC	Historical Manuscripts Commission
Houedene	*Chronica Magistri Rogeri de Houedene*, ed W. Stubbs, 4 vols, *RS* 51 (London 1868–71)
HRH	*The Heads of Religious Houses, England and Wales, 940–1216*, ed D. Knowles, C. N. L. Brooke, V. C. M. London (Cambridge 1972)
HS	*Hispania sacra* (Madrid 1948–)
HZ	*Historische Zeitschrift* (Munich 1859–)
IER	*Irish Ecclesiastical Record* (Dublin 1864–)
Jaffé	*Regesta Pontificum Romanorum ab condita ecclesia ad a. 1198*, 2 ed S. Loewenfeld, F. Kaltenbrunner, P. Ewald, 2 vols (Berlin 1885–8, repr Graz 1958)
JEH	*Journal of Ecclesiastical History* (London 1950–)
JFHS	*Journal of the Friends Historical Society* (London/Philadelphia 1903–)
JMH	*Journal of Modern History* (Chicago 1929–)
JRS	*Journal of Roman Studies* (London 1910–)
JRSAI	*Journal of the Royal Society of Antiquaries of Ireland* (Dublin 1871–)
JTS	*Journal of Theological Studies* (London 1899–)
LRS	*Lincoln Record Society*
LQR	*Law Quarterly Review* (London 1885–)
LThK	*Lexikon für Theologie und Kirche*, ed J. Höfer and K. Rahner (2 ed Freiburg-im-Breisgau 1957–)
MA	*Monasticon Anglicanum*, ed R. Dodsworth and W. Dugdale, 3 vols (London 1655–73); new ed J. Caley, H. Ellis, B. Bandinel, 6 vols in 8 (London 1817–30)
Mansi	J. D. Mansi, *Sacrorum conciliorum nova et amplissima collectio*, 31 vols

	(Florence/Venice 1757–98); new impression and continuation, ed L. Petit and J. B. Martin, 60 vols (Paris 1899–1927)
Med A	*Medium Aevum* (Oxford 1932–)
MGH	*Monumenta Germaniae Historica inde ab a. c.500 usque ad a. 1500*, ed G. H. Pertz etc (Berlin, Hanover, 1826–)
AA	*Auctores Antiquissimi*
Cap.	*Capitularia*
Conc.	*Concilia*
Const.	*Constitutiones*
Dip.	*Diplomata*
Epp.	*Epistolae*
Form.	*Formularia*
Leg.	*Leges*
Lib.	*Libelli de Lite*
SS	*Scriptores*
SRG	*Scriptores rerum Germanicarum in usum scholarum*
SRL	*Scriptores rerum langobardicarum et italicarum*
SRM	*Scriptores rerum merovingicarum*
Moyen Age	*Le moyen âge. Revue d'histoire et de philologie* (Paris 1888–)
MS	Manuscript
NCE	*New Catholic Encyclopedia*, 15 vols (New York 1967)
NCModH	*New Cambridge Modern History*, 14 vols (Cambridge 1957–70)
NH	*Northern History* (Leeds 1966–)
ns	new series
ODCC	*Oxford Dictionary of the Christian Church*, ed F. L. Cross (Oxford 1957)
PBA	*Proceedings of the British Academy*
PG	*Patrologia Graeca*, ed J. P. Migne, 161 vols (Paris 1857–66)
PL	*Patrologia Latina*, ed J. P. Migne, 217+4 index vols (Paris 1841–64)
PO	*Patrologia Orientalis*, ed J. Graffin and F. Nau (Paris 1903–)
Potthast	*Regesta Pontificum Romanorum inde ab a. post Christum natum 1198 ad a. 1304*, ed A. Potthast, 2 vols (1874–5 repr Graz 1957)
PP	*Past and Present* (London 1952–)
PRIA	*Proceedings of the Royal Irish Academy* (Dublin 1836–)
PRO	Public Record Office
PW	*Paulys Realencyklopädie der klassischen Altertumwissenschaft*, new ed G. Wissowa and W. Kroll (Stuttgart 1893–)
QFIAB	*Quellen & Forschungen aus italienischen Archiven und Bibliotheken* (Rome 1897–)
RB	*Revue Bénédictine* (Maredsous 1884–)
RE	*Realencyclopädie für protestantische Theologie*, ed A. Hauck, 24 vols (3 ed Leipzig 1896–1913)
RecS	Record Series
RH	*Revue historique* (Paris 1876–)
RHD	*Revue d'histoire du droit* (Haarlem, Gronigen 1923–)
RHDFE	*Revue historique du droit francais et étranger* (Paris 1922–)
RHE	*Revue d'Histoire Ecclesiastique* (Louvain 1900–)
RHEF	*Revue d'Histoire de l'Eglise de France* (Paris 1910–)
RR	*Regesta Regum Anglo-Normannorum*, ed H. W. C. Davis, H. A. Cronne, Charles Johnson, R. H. C. Davis, 4 vols (Oxford 1913–69)
RS	*Rerum Brittanicarum Medii Aevi Scriptores*, 99 vols (London 1858–1911). *Rolls Series*

Abbreviations

RSR	*Revue des sciences religieuses* (Strasbourg 1921–)
RTAM	*Recherches de théologie ancienne et médiévale* (Louvain 1929–)
RSI	*Rivista di storia della chiesa in Italia* (Rome 1947–)
RStI	*Rivista storica italiana* (Naples 1884–)
SA	*Studia Anselmiana* (Rome 1933–)
SB	*Sitzungsberichte*
SCH	*Studies in Church History* (London 1964–)
SCR	*Sources chrétiennes*, ed H. de Lubac and J. Daniélou (Paris 1941–)
SGra	*Studia Gratiana*, ed J. Forchielli and A. M. Stickler (Bologna 1953–)
SGre	*Studi Gregoriani*, ed G. Borino, 7 vols (Rome 1947–61)
SM	*Studia Monastica* (Montserrat, Barcelona 1959–)
Speculum	*Speculum, A Journal of Medieval Studies* (Cambridge, Mass 1926–)
SS	*Surtees Society* (Durham 1835–)
TRHS	*Transactions of the Royal Historical Society* (London 1871–)
TU	*Texte und Untersuchungen zur Geschichte der altchristlichen Literatur. Archiv für die griechisch-christlichen Schriftstellen der ersten drei Jahrhunderte* (Leipzig/Berlin 1882–)
VCH	*Victoria County History* (London 1900–)
WA	*D. Martin Luthers Werke*, ed J. C. F. Knaake, Weimare Ausgabe (Weimar 1883–)
Wilkins	*Concilia Magnae Britanniae et Hiberniae A.D. 446–1717*, 4 vols, ed D. Wilkins (London 1737)
YAJ	*Yorkshire Archaeological Journal* (London, Leeds 1870–)
ZKG	*Zeitschrift für Kirchengeschichte* (Gotha, Stuttgart 1878–)
ZRG	*Zeitschrift der Savigny-Stiftung für Rechtsgeschichte* (Weimar)
– GA	*Germanistische Abteilung* (1863–)
– KA	*Kanonistische Abteilung* (1911–)
– RA	*Romanistische Abteilung* (1880–)